"Jonathan Menn has provided us with a thorough biblical Christology. Based on the fact that the entire biblical text testifies to Jesus Christ, it is a careful analysis of the major themes that elevate Jesus's person and work. This is by no means an exercise in the heresy of Christomonism, as the careful and detailed exposition of Christ means that we, through his mediation, know God as Trinity. If we know Christ, we have his Spirit and know the Father. The revived concern for biblical theology, once a neglected discipline, is to be welcomed, as is the valuable contribution of this book. The specific focus of this volume makes it especially relevant to the Christological confusion that has troubled modern Christianity. I recommend it to both preachers and laypeople."

—**Graeme Goldsworthy**, Former Lecturer in Biblical Theology and Hermeneutics, Moore Theological College, Sydney, Australia

"The author has made a very valuable contribution to weaving together the canonical and theological connections of the two testaments by tracing the storyline of Scripture, by connecting themes, and by enhancing the trinitarian awareness."

—**Willem VanGemeren**, Professor Emeritus of Old Testament and Semitic Languages, Trinity Evangelical Divinity School

"When I was asked to recommend a book that explains the place of Jesus in the Old Testament, a book for a skillful, teachable lay Bible teacher, I thought immediately of Jonathan Menn's book that you hold in your hands. It came to my mind for good reason. Namely, it supplies a comprehensive yet accessible answer to the question: Where is Jesus in the Bible? The answer: Everywhere. That is because Jesus fulfills the whole range of promises, prefigurements, portrayals, and predictions in the Old Testament. Even those readers who believe wholeheartedly in the hermeneutic of fulfillment but reject the idea of replacement can find value here. Readers may see Jesus where they had not have previously seen him. But Menn does not, like some preachers, shoehorn the Savior into every passage at the expense of the biblical texts themselves; he opens multiple texts and lets the Holy Spirit point to the Lord Jesus, whose presence in the whole canon displays the unity of Scripture. Take up and read."

—**Greg Scharf**, Professor Emeritus of Homiletics and Pastoral Theology, Trinity Evangelical Divinity School

Biblical Theology

Biblical Theology
The Story of the Christ

JONATHAN MENN

RESOURCE *Publications* • Eugene, Oregon

BIBLICAL THEOLOGY
The Story of the Christ

Copyright © 2025 Jonathan Menn. All rights reserved. Except for brief quotations in critical publications or reviews, no part of this book may be reproduced in any manner without prior written permission from the publisher. Write: Permissions, Wipf and Stock Publishers, 199 W. 8th Ave., Suite 3, Eugene, OR 97401.

Resource Publications
An Imprint of Wipf and Stock Publishers
199 W. 8th Ave., Suite 3
Eugene, OR 97401

www.wipfandstock.com

PAPERBACK ISBN: 979-8-3852-6012-6
HARDCOVER ISBN: 979-8-3852-6013-3
EBOOK ISBN: 979-8-3852-6014-0
VERSION NUMBER 11/19/25

Unless otherwise indicated, all Scripture quotations are taken from the New American Standard Bible®, Copyright © 1960, 1962, 1963, 1968, 1971, 1972, 1973, 1975, 1977, 1995 by The Lockman Foundation. Used by permission. (www.Lockman.org)

Scripture quotations marked ESV are from the ESV The Holy Bible, English Standard Version® (ESV®), copyright © 2001 by Crossway, a publishing ministry of Good News Publishers. All rights reserved.

Scripture quotations marked NIV are taken from THE HOLY BIBLE, NEW INTERNATIONAL VERSION®, NIV® Copyright © 1973, 1978, 1984, 2011 by Biblica, Inc.™ Used by permission. All rights reserved worldwide.

To those whom God had in mind from the very beginning—
Christ's body on earth, the church.

Contents

List of Tables | ix
Preface | xi
List of Abbreviations | xiii
Introduction | xv

1   Biblical Theology: Introduction | 1
2   The Basic Biblical Storyline | 8
3   Two Biblical Themes Concerning God's Relationship with Mankind | 36
4   Christ in the Old Testament: Pre-Incarnate Appearances of Christ | 48
5   Christ in the Old Testament: Prophecy | 61
6   Christ and the Church are the Prophesied "Servant of the Lord" | 94
7   Christ in the Old Testament: Typology | 100
8   Christ Fulfills the Promises of the Old Testament | 136
9   Christ and the Church Fulfill the Abrahamic, Davidic, and New Covenants | 138
10 Christ and the Church are the New, True, Spiritual Israel | 151
11 Christ and the Church Fulfill and Replace the Old Testament Tabernacle and Temple | 169
12 Christ Fulfills and Replaces the Old Testament Sacrificial System and Priesthood | 178
13 Christ Fulfills and Replaces the Old Testament Law | 184

14 Christ Fulfills and Replaces the Old Testament Sabbath | 194

15 Christ and the Church Fulfill and Replace
the Old Testament Feasts | 199

Appendix 1: Jesus Is Fully God and Fully Man | 221

Appendix 2: The Trinity | 237

Bibliography | 253

Subject and Name Index | 269

Scripture Index | 283

List of Tables

Prophecies relating to Jesus' identity as Messiah | 62

Prophecies relating to Jesus' death, burial, and resurrection | 64

Parallelism of 1 Pet 3:20–21 | 129

Comparison of Acts 2 and Acts 13 | 137

Comparison of Ezekiel 37 and Ephesians 2 | 166

OT Israel's Calendar | 200

Names/Titles/Attributes applied to God and Jesus | 225

Names/Titles/Attributes applied to God the Father, God the Son, and God the Holy Spirit | 241

Preface

PARTICULARLY SINCE I LEFT the practice of law at the end of 2005, the Bible has been my constant companion, first while I was pursuing an MDiv at Trinity Evangelical Divinity School and, since then, in my writing and teaching biblical subjects in East Africa in my capacity as president of Equipping Church Leaders East Africa, Inc. (www.eclea.net). This is my third book on biblical subjects which has been published by Wipf & Stock Publishers. The first was *Biblical Eschatology*, 2nd ed. (Resource, 2018) and the second *Is Christianity True?* (Resource, 2024). With this book, the three actually constitute a logical trilogy: *Is Christianity True?* is a book of apologetics, so it forms the logical first book in the trilogy; this book, since it deals with the overall biblical storyline, would be the logical second part of the trilogy; and since *Biblical Eschatology*, 2nd ed. is the study of the "last things," it represents the logical completion of the trilogy.

It has been said, "If you want to learn—teach." I have found that to be true, especially with respect to the Bible. What I endeavor to do here is provide the fruit of my research, study, thought, and writing about the Bible, which has been the focus of my teaching and writing for now over 20 years. While there have been many good books written on biblical theology, I think this book presents important biblical material that I have not seen, at least in this way, elsewhere. In particular, this book is unique in its specific and detailed discussions of Christ's pre-incarnate appearances, the prophecies of Christ in the OT, the many specific instances of Christ in typological form, and the comprehensive ways in which Christ fulfills the major covenants and what OT Israel and its major institutions, i.e., the nation itself, the tabernacle and temple, sacrificial system and priesthood, Law, Sabbath, and Feasts, were pointing to.

I am grateful for the encouragement I have received from many others. In particular, I want to acknowledge and thank Dr. Graeme Goldsworthy, formerly lecturer in Biblical Theology and Hermeneutics at Moore

Theological College, Sydney, Australia, Dr. Willem VanGemeren, Professor Emeritus of Old Testament and Semitic Languages, Trinity Evangelical Divinity School, and Dr. Greg Scharf, Professor Emeritus of Homiletics and Pastoral Theology, Trinity Evangelical Divinity School, for their endorsements of this book. Both Dr. VanGemeren and Dr. Scharf were my professors at Trinity. Dr. Goldsworthy and Dr. VanGemeren have written extensively in the field of biblical theology and are both recognized internationally as leading experts in this field of study. Dr. Scharf's primary field of homiletics of necessity implicates, and required me to think deeply about, biblical theology in studying the Bible and crafting sermons faithful to the biblical storyline. In short, having the endorsements of these three leaders of their fields not only is very gratifying but also is humbling.

One other aspect of the endorsements from Drs. Goldsworthy, VanGemeren, and Scharf is worthy of note. That is, each of those men comes from a different tradition or branch of Christianity: Dr. Goldsworthy from the Anglican tradition, Dr. VanGemeren from the Reformed tradition, and Dr. Scharf from the Evangelical tradition. That, I hope, is some indication that this book is not narrow or parochial in its approach but may appeal to Christians of all traditions and also to non-Christians who wish to get a new perspective and learn more about the Bible and Jesus Christ.

In short, I hope that this book will cause the reader to see the amazing depth and subtlety of the Bible. That, in turn, should lead the reader to a greater and deeper understanding, appreciation, and even awe of God, of his Word, the Bible, and of Jesus Christ. As an aid to furthering the reader's study of the Bible and biblical theology, I have included the web addresses for all the sources I have cited that are online.

List of Abbreviations

AnBib	Analecta Biblica
BECNT	Baker Exegetical Commentary on the New Testament
BT	Biblical theology
BTCB	Brazos Theological Commentary on the Bible
ICC	International Critical Commentary
JSNTSup	*Journal for the Study of the New Testament*, Supplement series
NAC	New American Commentary
NICNT	New International Commentary on the New Testament
NIGTC	New International Greek Testament Commentary
NIVAC	NIV Application Commentary
NSBT	New Studies in Biblical Theology
PNTC	Pillar New Testament Commentary
TNTC	Tyndale New Testament Commentary
TOTC	Tyndale Old Testament Commentary
WBC	Word Biblical Commentary
ZECNT	Zondervan Exegetical Commentary on the New Testament

Introduction

THE BIBLE IS GOD's story of the world, of humanity, and of himself and his relation to the world and humanity, from his creation of the world and humanity to what will be the new creation, "the new heaven and the new earth." Jesus Christ is at the heart of that story. He is its main character. He is the one who holds the entire Bible together.

This is a book of biblical theology. Biblical theology is the study of the unfolding storyline of the Bible from beginning (Genesis) to end (Revelation). Chapters 1 and 2 introduce biblical theology and go through the basic biblical storyline. But biblical theology does more. Biblical theology seeks to demonstrate the inner unity and coherence of the Bible. When you think about it, that is an amazing endeavor. The reason is that, although the Bible is usually thought of as one large book, it actually is a small library consisting of 66 "books": 39 in the Old Testament (OT), i.e., the Hebrew Bible, the sacred Scriptures of the Jews; and 27 in the New Testament (NT). Further, the books of the Bible were written by approximately 40 authors over a period of approximately 1500 years (the OT being written from approximately 1450 BC to 430 BC and the NT from approximately AD 50–95). The books which compose the Bible were written in different cultures and circumstances, on three continents (Asia, Africa, and Europe), in three languages (Hebrew, Aramaic, and Greek), and in multiple genres (historical narratives, poetry, proverbs, prophecy and apocalyptic, and others). Given such diversity of time, place, culture, circumstance, authorship, and style, any other book composed in such a manner would be an incoherent mish-mash consisting primarily of ancient superstition that has little or no relevance to us today. However, that is not the case with the Bible.

That biblical storyline is fleshed out in chapter 3, which deals with two biblical themes concerning God's relationship with mankind. These themes use similar imagery and show how God acts consistently with similar patterns. As such, they help us to understand the biblical storyline and reveal something about the nature and purposes of God. The first theme concerns God's dwelling with mankind and employs the imagery of the Garden of Eden; the tabernacle; the temple; and, ultimately, the New Jerusalem. They demonstrate that the Bible describes the unfolding of a unified plan of God to dwell with his holy people (mankind) in a holy place (the earth). The second theme discusses God's relationship with humanity expressed in terms of marriage. God instituted marriage when he created Adam and Eve. Gen 2:24 says that *"a man shall leave his father and his mother, and be joined to his wife; and they shall become one flesh."* That actually is a paradigm which describes the relationship God desires to have with his people. In keeping with this theme, throughout the Bible, sexual immorality and infidelity are equated with spiritual infidelity (forsaking God to pursue other gods and ungodly practices), and *vice versa*. In the OT, God's marital bond with his people is implied, but Israel was unfaithful. In the NT, the marital theme is extended and made explicit in Christ and the church. In Revelation, the Bible's marital imagery for God's relationship with his people is brought to consummation in Christ, his bride (the church), and New Jerusalem. Thus, biblical theology reveals that the Bible is an amazingly interwoven book that is far deeper than may appear on the surface or when one is reading the different biblical accounts and narratives without having the overall picture in mind.

The reason why the Bible is not an incoherent mish-mash, but has an inner unity and coherence and tells one overall story, is because of Jesus Christ. The interesting thing is that Jesus Christ is not even named in the OT, which covers the vast and momentous epochs from the creation of the world, through humanity's fall into sin, Noah and the Flood, the calling of Abraham, the beginning of the nation of Israel, Moses and the exodus out of Egypt, the wandering of the nation in the wilderness, the conquest of the promised land under Joshua, the united kingdom under David and Solomon, the divided kingdom, and the taking over the land of Israel by the Assyrians, the Babylonians, and the Persians.

Despite all of these epochal events over the thousands of years of OT history, Jesus Christ nevertheless is present and active throughout the OT. He appears in three ways: in pre-incarnate appearances, i.e., appearances in human form before he came to earth as Jesus Christ, the son of Mary; in prophecy; and in what the NT calls "types" and "shadows," i.e., OT persons, things, events, and institutions that pointed beyond themselves to something greater. Biblical theology reveals this. Chapters 4–7 cover these issues in some detail.

But biblical theology does more even than this. It shows that the great covenants God enacted with mankind, particularly the covenant with

Abraham (which some have called the "theological backbone" of the entire Bible), the covenant with David, and the New Covenant (first announced by the prophet Jeremiah), all were pointing to and find their fulfillment in Jesus Christ and those connected to Christ by faith. We will see this in chapters 8–9. More than that, biblical theology reveals that OT Israel and its major institutions, i.e., the nation itself, the tabernacle and temple, sacrificial system and priesthood, Law, Sabbath, and Feasts, were themselves "types" and "shadows" pointing to and finding their ultimate fulfillment in Jesus Christ and those connected to Christ by faith. Chapters 10–15 make this clear.

In light of this, I need to say a brief word about "fulfillment" and "replacement" theology, especially since I use the words "fulfill and replace" in the titles of chapters 11–15. In Matt 5:17, Jesus said, *"Do not think that I came to abolish the Law or the Prophets; I did not come to abolish but to fulfill."* The word "fulfill" (Greek = *plēroō*) normally means "to bring to its intended meaning,"[1] or to "bring something to completion."[2] That is what Christ has done. Sam Storms puts it this way, "The butterfly doesn't replace the caterpillar. The butterfly IS the caterpillar in a more developed and consummate form. The butterfly is what God intended the caterpillar to become. Likewise, the church doesn't replace Israel. The church IS Israel as God always intended it to be. . . . Gentiles have now been included in the commonwealth of Israel and are as much 'true Jews' as are believing ethnic Jews. It isn't replacement, but fulfillment."[3] I use the word "replace" only in the theological sense that, while the modern nation of Israel has been reborn, OT Israel and its various institutions no longer exist.[4] They were pointing to and found their fulfillment in Christ and in those connected to him by faith; in that sense they have been fulfilled, superseded, and replaced, or, as Heb 8:13 says, they have become "obsolete." There are those who hold a form of "fulfillment theology" that implies that contemporary Israel is the fulfillment of various prophecies and, for example, that the promise of "land" in the Abrahamic Covenant still applies to contemporary

---

1. Hays, "Applying," 29.
2. Poythress, *Shadow of Christ*, 368.
3. Storms, "Replacement Theology or Inclusion Theology?," n.p.
4. Although contemporary Israel exists, the temple, the priesthood, and the sacrificial system do not. While contemporary Jews may celebrate the various Jewish feasts and festivals, Judaism as a whole and the feasts and festivals (especially Passover, the Feast of Weeks, and the Feast of Tabernacles, which required all Jewish males to go to the temple in Jerusalem, but which is now impossible) cannot be practiced as ordained and required by God in the Hebrew Bible (OT). Modern practices and rituals may have been invented as substitutes, but they are not biblical.

ethnic Israel.[5] Those discussions are beyond the scope of this book, which deals largely with finding Christ in the OT and the effect of his first coming to earth.

Our understanding, appreciation, and even awe of God and his Word, the Bible, cannot help but be raised to an extraordinary degree by the study of biblical theology. That should lead us to a deeper understanding, appreciation, and awe of Jesus Christ. That is because he, himself, is without parallel. As we point out in appendix 1, Jesus Christ is both fully God yet, at the same time, fully man, i.e., he is the almighty God who came to earth as a human being. He is able to be and do this because the nature of God is triune, i.e., there is only one God, but he is in three persons: Father, Son, and Holy Spirit. That is the Christian doctrine of the Trinity. As we will see in appendix 2, the Trinity emerges clearly from the Bible, is not illogical, is reasonably understandable, and conforms to and explains reality as it exists.

In short, biblical theology is a grand and profound study of the most important things in the world. It is exciting. By understanding and appreciating the biblical story, we ourselves can be changed as we see more deeply who God in Christ is, what he has done, and what he has for those who trust him with their lives. There is no greater story than this.

---

5. See FIRM Staff, "Fulfillment Theology"; McDermott, "Gerald McDermott on Why the Land."

1

Biblical Theology: Introduction

THE NATURE OF BIBLICAL THEOLOGY

Description of Biblical Theology

BIBLICAL THEOLOGY (BT) is the study of the unfolding storyline of the Bible from beginning (Genesis) to end (Revelation). It is "the search for the inner unity of the Bible."[1] BT "follows the progress of revelation from the first word of God to man through the unveiling of the full glory of Christ. It examines the several stages of biblical history and their relationship to one another. It thus provides the basis for understanding how texts in one part of the Bible relate to all other texts."[2]

Because BT describes the inner unity of the Bible on its own terms, it is "descriptive and historical in a way that theological interpretation and systematic theology are not."[3] Although BT is a descriptive and historical discipline, the Bible is selective in the historical details it describes. That selectivity is based on the overall *theology* that the Bible unfolds. Thus, the Bible emphasizes the line of Seth, not that of Cain; Abraham, not Lot; David, not Saul; the nation of Israel, not Assyria or Babylon. The most significant emphasis in the Hebrew Bible, i.e., the Old Testament (OT) is on those people, places, and events that prefigure and lead up to Jesus Christ as the Messiah. The New Testament (NT) finds in Jesus the culmination and fulfillment of all that had gone before.

---

1. Bartholomew, "Biblical Theology," 84.
2. Goldsworthy, *According to Plan*, 32.
3. Bartholomew, "Biblical Theology," 86.

Presuppositions of Biblical Theology

The Bible tells a coherent story, and Jesus Christ is at the heart of that story.[4] Each book of the Bible contributes something to that story, and the over-all story offers a framework within which each book may be best interpreted. Although the Bible tells a unified story, God's revelation is *progressive*—it unfolds throughout the Bible. A number of important principles flow from these facts:

1. *Scripture will never contradict Scripture.* Two passages which appear to contradict each other will be found not to do so when they are closely analyzed. One passage may modify or qualify the other but will not contradict it.

2. *Both the stage of redemptive history and "the whole counsel of God" (Acts 20:27) must be taken into account in order to rightly understand any particular passage.* Because the truths of the Bible are not revealed all at once but are progressively revealed, the full meaning of any particular passage or biblical doctrine may not be clear unless the whole Bible is taken into consideration.

3. *The NT interprets the OT.* All biblical texts need to be read within the framework of their grammatical (the language and genre of the text) and historical contexts. The NT is built on the foundation of the OT. Many NT concepts are based on the OT. Our understanding of the NT is greatly enriched by understanding the OT. At the same time, we should not read the OT as if the NT did not exist. There is both continuity and discontinuity between the OT and the NT. The NT builds on OT concepts, often in surprising ways. That is particularly true with how the NT treats OT prophecy.

4. *The centrality of Jesus Christ.* As mentioned above, Jesus Christ is at the heart of the story of the Bible. He is its main character. He is the one who holds the entire Bible together. In fact, Jesus Christ is at the very center of God's plan for all of existence. Eph 1:9–10 states, "*He made known to us the mystery of His will, according to His kind intention which He purposed in Him with a view to an administration suitable to the fullness of the times, that is, the summing up of all things in Christ, things in the heavens and things on the earth.*"[5] In other words,

---

4. See McCartney and Clayton, *Let the Reader,* 47–58.

5. Unless otherwise noted, all biblical quotations are from the 1995 edition of the New American Standard Bible.

the unification of all things in heaven and earth under the sovereignty of Jesus Christ is God's purpose for why reality exists.

Although Jesus is not named in the OT, he is present throughout the OT in pre-incarnate appearances, in prophecy, in what the NT calls "types" and "shadows," and by analogy. Jesus Christ and those connected to him by faith fulfill what the entire OT, and especially OT Israel and all of its institutions, were pointing to. Thus, both Jesus and the NT authors applied the entire OT to Jesus:

- *"And he said to them, 'O foolish men and slow of heart to believe in all that the prophets have spoken! Was it not necessary for the Christ to suffer these things and to enter into his glory? Then beginning with Moses and with all the prophets, he explained to them the things concerning himself in all the Scriptures."* (Luke 24:25–27; see also Luke 24:44–47)
- *"You search the Scriptures because you think that in them you have eternal life; it is these that testify about me; and you are unwilling to come to me so that you may have life. . . . For if you believed Moses, you would have believed me, for he wrote about me."* (John 5:39–40, 46)
- *"Of him [Jesus] all the prophets bear witness that through his name everyone who believes in him receives forgiveness of sins."* (Acts 10:43; see also Acts 3:18, 24; 26:22–23; 1 Pet 1:10–12)

In light of this, when we consider the overall picture of the Bible, we should "read the Old Covenant Scriptures through the lens of the New Covenant Scriptures."[6] As it is said, "The New is in the Old concealed; the Old is in the New revealed."

THE STORYLINE AND THEMES OF BIBLICAL THEOLOGY: OVERVIEW

The Basic Storyline of the Bible

In the most general sense, the Bible is the story of the creation, history, and destiny of the world and of mankind, as told primarily from a theological viewpoint. God created a beautiful world and human beings to live joyful, fulfilled lives in fellowship with him. Through our sin, we lost that fellowship and brought evil and death into the world. However, God did not leave us in our sin and death. By means of a grand plan which involved calling

---

6. Lehrer, *New Covenant Theology*, 177.

Abraham and the nation of Israel, God prepared the way for his own coming to earth, in the person of Jesus Christ, to bring forgiveness of sin and to restore fellowship with him and with each other. To complete the storyline, Jesus will come again to utterly destroy sin and death without destroying us. He will consummate our restoration and our relationship with him and will renew the earth to be even more glorious than when it was first created.

The basic biblical storyline can therefore be conceived as a drama in four acts: (1) *Creation* (Genesis 1–2); (2) *The Fall and its Aftermath* (Genesis 3–11); (3) *Redemption* (Genesis 12–Revelation 20); (4) *Re-Creation* (Revelation 21–22). The Bible is God's revelation of himself and of his plan (the gospel) to mankind. Consequently, the biblical storyline also may be viewed as the unfolding of the gospel: (1) the OT is the preparation of the gospel; (2) the Gospels (Matthew, Mark, Luke, John) are the manifestation of the gospel; (3) the book of Acts is the expansion of the gospel; (4) the Epistles are the explanation of the gospel; (5) the book of Revelation is the consummation of the gospel.

Commentators have described the Bible's story of God's relationship with mankind, from creation to re-creation, in slightly different ways:

- "In Christian narrative, God's world is the *setting*, the *theme* is the rescue of the fallen world and of humankind; the *plots* are the biblical narratives, from creation, election, to incarnation, crucifixion, resurrection and ascension; the *resolution* is the last judgement, heaven and hell."[7]
- "Biblical theology is about God's bringing in his kingdom in which all relationships are restored to perfection."[8]
- God's ultimate purpose is "God's people, in God's place, under God's rule, living God's way, in God's holy and loving presence, as family."[9]

The Themes of BT

Within the Bible, important themes and concepts regularly occur which help to focus and "flesh out" the overall biblical story. Some of the more important themes and concepts are:

---

7. Sykes, *Story*, 14.
8. Goldsworthy, *According to Plan*, 76.
9. Cole, *IG 500*, n.p.

1. *Promise and Fulfillment.* God is faithful to keep his promises; but often his promises are fulfilled in surprising ways. The ultimate fulfillment of God's promises is found in Jesus Christ (see Eph 1:9–10).

2. *The Covenants of God.* God made a number of important covenants (solemn agreements) over the course of biblical history. The major covenants are: Noahic Covenant (Gen 8:20—9:17); Abrahamic Covenant (Gen 12:1–3; 13:14–17; 15:1–21; 17:1–21; 22:15–18); Mosaic Covenant (Exodus 19–24), also known as the Old Covenant (2 Cor 3:14; Heb 8:6, 13); Davidic Covenant (2 Sam 7:8–17; Ps 89:1–4); and New Covenant (Jer 31:31–34; 32:40; Ezek 36:22–28; 37:15–28; Luke 22:20; 1 Cor 11:25; 2 Cor 3:6; Heb 8:6–13; 10:15–17). In many respects, God's entire plan of redemption may be seen as the outworking of the Abrahamic Covenant. As the story of redemption proceeds, the Abrahamic, Mosaic, and Davidic Covenants all find their fulfillment in the New Covenant—and that covenant finds its fulfillment in Christ and his people, the church.

3. *Type-Antitype; Shadow-Substance.* A "type" is "an event which offers likeness to something in the future, but yet does not really fulfill this something";[10] the fulfillment or antitype is always greater than the shadow or type. God first called Abraham, then Isaac, then Jacob, through whom he created the nation of Israel, to be the instruments by which his plan for the redemption of the world became reality. However, in a theological or spiritual sense, all of the OT examples or institutions—such as the tabernacle and temple, the sacrificial system, the law, the feasts and festivals, the Promised Land, the kingdom, Zion, Jerusalem, and Israel itself—represented physical, earthly "types" or "shadows" which pointed to future, New Covenant, spiritual realities.[11] The true realities to which the OT types and shadows pointed are found in Christ, the church, heaven, New Jerusalem, and the new heaven and the new earth.

4. *The "pattern of reversal" (i.e., God's choosing the younger, the weaker, the outsider in order to accomplish his purposes).* God's grace is demonstrated by his sovereign choices of Seth over Cain (Gen 4:25); Isaac over Ishmael (Gen 17:18–19); Jacob over Esau (Gen 25:23; see Rom 9:10–13); Ephraim over Manasseh (Gen 48:8–21); and Judah over his older brothers (Gen 49:1–12). This shows that God does not value the power, prestige, and wealth that the world values but by his grace chooses "the

---

10. Danielou, *From Shadows to Reality,* 125.
11. See chapters 7–15, below.

least of these" (see Matt 25:40, 45). God demonstrates this same pattern again and again, e.g., Moses over Pharaoh (Exod 2:1—14:31; Heb 11:25–29); Israel over the other nations (Deut 7:7–8); David over his older brothers (1 Sam 16:1–13); Solomon over his older brothers (1 Kgs 1:5–40; 1 Chron 3:1–5); the Gentile widow of Zarephath over Israelite widows (1 Kgs 17:9; see Luke 4:25–26); Naaman the Syrian over Israelite lepers (2 Kgs 5:1–14; see Luke 4:27). Jesus himself was a poor man and a servant of all (Matt 20:25–28; Phil 2:5–8). Thus, he tells us, *"The one who is greatest among you must become like the youngest, and the leader like the servant"* (Luke 22:26) and *"If anyone wants to be first, he shall be last of all and servant of all"* (Mark 9:35). He adds, *"the one who is least among all of you, this is the one who is great"* (Luke 9:48). He concludes, *"Whoever then humbles himself as this child, he is the greatest in the kingdom of heaven"* (Matt 18:4).

5 *Exile and return.* The theme of exile and return is not limited to geographical exile but ultimately is related to the greatest exile—separation from God. We see both aspects of this theme beginning with Adam and Eve, who are exiled from the garden as a result of their sin (Gen 3:23–24). Cain is sentenced to be *"a vagrant and a wanderer on the earth"* because of his sin of killing Abel (Gen 4:9–15). God tells Abram to leave his own land and family to go to a land God will show him (Gen 12:1). Jacob takes Esau's birthright, deceives his father, and must flee into exile for years before he finally can return to his homeland (Gen 27:1–45). David flees from Saul and then from Absalom before returning to his rightful place (1 Sam 27:1–3; 2 Sam 2:1–4; 15:13–16; 19:8–15). Israel, as a whole, repeats the pattern. First, it is enslaved in Egypt. When it finally enters the land, it falls away from God, is oppressed, cries out for deliverance, and finds temporary deliverance with judges. The nation goes after other gods and later is taken into exile in Babylon. Even after it returns to the land, the prophets speak of a new exodus, a new land, and a new rule of God. Thus, geographic exile was a sign of the more fundamental estrangement from God. Christ is the one who brings the true and lasting return to God, and that is consummated geographically in the new heaven and new earth which will be permanent and in which God and Christ will dwell among their people.

6 *God's pattern for relationship.* God has always sought a people for himself. The recurrent pattern throughout the Bible, in order for people to be in right relationship with God, is that God initiates, and his people respond by faith, which essentially means "trust and obedience, from the heart." Consequently, recurrent statements throughout the Bible

Biblical Theology: Introduction

(with some variations) are, *"I will be their God, and they will be my people"*[12] and *"the just shall live by faith."*[13]

God acts with grace toward people. God began the process by creating Adam and Eve and communed with them in the Garden of Eden (Gen 2:7, 15–25; 3:8). After Adam and Eve fell into sin, by grace God initiated his plan of redemption by promising a savior (Gen 3:15) and sacrificing animals to clothe them (Gen 3:21). By grace, God chose to save Noah and his family when he destroyed the rest of the world in the Flood, and Noah responded in faith (Gen 6:5–22). By grace, God chose Abraham, who responded in faith (Gen 12:1–5; 15:5–6). By grace, God sent the prophets to warn Israel of the consequences of their sins and call them back to faithfulness. Finally, by grace, God himself became a man in the person of Jesus Christ to save people from their sin and restore right relationship between God and mankind.

Because people are inherently sinful, they cannot "earn" or "work" their way into a right relationship with God (Acts 13:39; Gal 2:16; 3:11; Eph 2:1–3, 8–9). The only way people can be in right relationship with God is if they respond in faith to what God, by his grace, has done for them. Unfortunately, the pattern consistently has been that most people do not put their faith in God, although there has always been a "faithful remnant" who have done so.[14]

---

12. Gen 17:8; Exod 6:7; 29:45; Lev 26:12; Jer 7:23; 11:4; 24:7; 30:22; 31:1, 33; 32:38; Ezek 11:19–20; 14:10–11; 36:28; 37:23, 27; Hos 2:23; Zech 8:8; 13:9; 2 Cor 6:16; Heb 8:10; Rev 21:3.

13. Hab 2:4; Rom 1:17; Gal 3:11; Heb 10:38; see also John 6:27–29; 20:26–29; 1 John 3:23.

14. See 1 Kgs 19:11–18; Rom 11:1–5; see also Luke 18:8.

2

The Basic Biblical Storyline

CREATION (GENESIS 1-2)

"Creation is not only a question of beginnings, but of purpose and relationships."[1] In creation we see God as the source of everything. As originally created, we see everything as *"very good"* (Gen 1:31)—God, mankind, the animals, plants, and physical creation are all fulfilling their created purpose and in right relationship with each other.

The biblical storyline begins with God (Gen 1:1)[2]

God alone is eternal and self-existing. God is not a part of the universe or *vice versa*. Everything that exists besides God (matter; angels; human beings, etc.) was created by God and is dependent on God for its very existence.[3] This fact shows that the true, biblical God is unlike the "gods" of other religions. God is unlike the Eastern (e.g., Hindu; Buddhist) idea that God and physical reality are all "one" (the concept of monism). God is also unlike the religions of cultures (including those in the Ancient Near East at the time when the Bible was written), which believe that inanimate objects have "spirits."

God alone is self-sufficient. There is only one God, and he is unlike anything else. Although there is only one God, he exists in three persons

---

1. Goldsworthy, *According to Plan*, 92.
2. For a succinct recounting of the storyline of the Bible, see Bartholomew and Goheen, "Storyline."
3. Acts 17:28; Col 1:17; Heb 1:3.

(Trinity): Father; Son; and Holy Spirit.[4] That is important. If God were a simple unity (like the Islamic conception of Allah), and not a Trinity, God would not be self-sufficient, i.e., he would have *needed* to create other beings in order to have relationship. God did not need to create anything (see Acts 17:24–26)—he already had a perfect love relationship among the three persons of the Trinity before he created the world.

God created everything out of nothing

The world does not consist of pre-existing matter which God then shaped into stars or plants or animals. Rather, God simply spoke or decreed, and the world came into existence out of nothing.[5] Mankind was the crowning event of God's creation. Only human beings are said to have been created *"in the image of God"* (Gen 1:26–27). God blessed the man and woman, spoke to them, and had fellowship with them (Gen 1:28–30; 2:16–17, 19; 3:8–9). Further, whereas each day after he created inanimate objects, plants, or animals, God called his creation *"good"* (Gen 1:4, 10, 12, 18, 21, 25), after he created human beings, God saw that creation was *"very good"* (Gen 1:31).[6]

The creation account of Gen 2:4–25 is a parallel or supplementary account of the account of creation contained in Gen 1:1—2:3. The account of Gen 2:4–25 goes back to fill in the details found in Gen 1:26–27 concerning how God created human beings. Both male and female were part of God's intention from the beginning (see Gen 1:27), although God created

---

4. For an in-depth discussion of the Trinity, see Appendix 2: The Trinity.

5. Gen 1:1, 3, 6–7, 9, 11, 14–16, 20–21, 24, 26–27; see also Exod 20:11; 31:17; Ps 8:3–5; 33:6; Matt 19:4; John 1:3; Acts 14:15; Rom 11:36; 1 Cor 8:6; Col 1:16; Heb 11:3; Rev 4:11. Whether the six days of creation referred to in Genesis 1 are literal or metaphorical is a matter of some debate. See David G. Hagopian, ed., *The Genesis Debate: Three Views on the Days of Creation* (Mission Viejo, CA: Crux, 2001; see also John Walton, *The Lost World of Genesis One* (Downers Grove, IL: IVP Academic, 2009) for the view that Genesis 1 does not deal with the material creation of the world but its functional origin.

6. The depth of the fact that Jesus Christ is at the heart of the biblical story is seen even in the parallels between creation and the death and resurrection of Christ: "On the Friday, the sixth day of the week, Jesus stands before Pilate, who declares 'behold, the man!' [John 19:5], echoing the creation of humankind on the sixth day of creation. On the cross Jesus finishes the work the father has given him to do [John 17:4], ending with the shout of triumph (*tetelestai*, 'it is accomplished' [John 19:30]), corresponding to the completion of creation itself. There follows, as in Genesis, a day of rest, a sabbath day [John 19:31]; and then, while it is yet dark, Mary Magdalene comes to the tomb 'on the first day of the week'. . . . Jesus' public career is to be understood as the completion of the original creation, with the resurrection as the start of the new." Wright, *Resurrection*, 440.

Adam first and then created Eve to be his helper and companion (see Gen 2:18–25). This suggests that male and female natures and roles are to a certain extent complementary and not completely interchangeable, although the extent to which that may be so is debatable.

Both males and females equally bear the image of God. The basic meaning for "man" (Hebrew = *adam*) is the collective "mankind, people," which includes both male and female. That is made clear in Gen 1:26, which says, *"Let Us make man in Our image . . . and let them rule."* Gen 1:27 makes explicit that both male and female are included equally, since it says, *"And God created man [adam] in His own image, in the image of God He created him; male and female He created them."* Further, in Gen 1:28 God blessed "them" (the man and the woman) equally and spoke to "them." In Gen 1:29, when God says *"I have given you every plant yielding seed,"* the "you" is plural, not singular.

God created mankind to have dominion over all of creation (Gen 1:26–28)

Adam and Eve's living with God in the Garden of Eden provides us with the pattern of the kingdom of God. Adam and Eve were commanded to *"be fruitful and multiply, and fill the earth, and subdue it"* (Gen 1:28). Since human beings are uniquely created "in the image of God," by spreading over the earth in obedience to God's command, people would be magnifying God's glory by spreading his image over the entire earth. That "dominion mandate" further indicates they were to extend the geographical boundaries of Eden until it covered the whole earth. By extending Eden to cover the earth, Adam and Eve and their descendants would be turning the earth into a mirror of heaven, i.e., making the whole earth a paradise fit for God and man, filled with holy people.[7] Adam's naming the animals began the process of observation, description, and classification that is at the heart of scientific and other forms of knowledge. However, for both Adam and all of his progeny, observation, description, and classification alone are insufficient to tell us how to relate to God, to other people, and to the world. To do that properly, we need to rely on God and his word.

---

7. Rom 8:29, 2 Cor 3:18, Eph 4:22–24, and Col 3:9–10 all indicate that, in some sense, the "image of God" was tarnished through sin but is being restored in God's people as they come into a saving relationship with the Father through Jesus Christ and progressively become more and more like Jesus. Jesus' "Great Commission" to his followers (Matt 28:18–20; see also Acts 1:8) fulfills in a deeper, spiritual way the "dominion mandate."

MANKIND'S FALL INTO SIN AND ITS AFTERMATH (GENESIS 3-11)

Adam and Eve sin and are excluded from the garden (Genesis 3)

The Bible clearly implies that Satan "fell" before the sin of Adam and Eve, since Satan is the one who tempted Adam and Eve and lied to them about the nature and consequences of eating the fruit of the knowledge of good and evil.[8] Thus, Jesus called Satan both a *"murderer from the beginning"* and *"a liar and the father of lies"* (John 8:44–45).

"*Knowledge of good and evil*" (Gen 2:17) represents moral independence or autonomy. In some OT passages (2 Sam 4:17; 1 Kgs 3:9) the phrase "good and evil" refers essentially to the ability to make a judicial decision. The "tree of the knowledge of good and evil" was not a magical tree that produced knowledge of good and evil in anyone who ate from it. Instead, it is more likely that the choice Adam and Eve faced in deciding whether to eat from the tree was remaining good or becoming evil themselves.[9] What was forbidden was the power to decide on their own what was in their best interests and what was not. Only God is all-knowing, all-wise, and all-loving. Therefore, only God can make the correct and loving decision that is truly in mankind's best interest all the time. When people act autonomously, they make themselves the center of reference for their moral guidelines and decide for themselves what is good and evil. People thereby attempt to be *"like God"* (see Gen 3:5, 22). However, because people are not all-knowing, all-wise, and all-loving, their attempts to be God-like necessarily will fail. Instead, they will end up acting more like *"the god of this world"* (2 Cor 4:4), with similar results. If Adam and Eve passed the test, their trust in and obedience to God would confirm their goodness, and they would know it. If they failed the test (as they did), their distrust of and disobedience to God would turn them into people who have evil at the core of their being, and they would know that, too.

Satan entered the serpent and deceived Eve.[10] Although Eve was deceived, "it was Adam's task to guard the Garden and all within it [Gen 2:15], [therefore] he should have guarded her. . . . He failed to guard the Garden, and admitted the enemy."[11] Adam was present with Eve, did nothing to try to stop her and, not being deceived, willingly chose to follow his wife into

---

8. Compare Gen 2:16–17 and Gen 3:1–4.
9. See Goldsworthy, *According to Plan*, 98.
10. John 8:44; 2 Cor 11:3; Rev 12:9.
11. Jordan, *Through New Eyes*, 137.

sin.[12] As James Boice puts it, "If Adam was not deceived, as 1 Timothy 2:14 clearly states, then he must have sinned in full knowledge of what he was doing. That is, he chose to eat in deliberate disobedience to God."[13] That may be why Adam's sin is greater, and why the consequences to the rest of mankind are said to flow from Adam's sin and not from Eve's.

Satan's strategy was a paradigm for the temptations we face:

- *He approached Eve first* (Gen 3:1). That was a subtle attempt to deceive the person who had not received the command directly from God and to play one person against the other.

- *He focused on the only prohibition God had decreed* (Gen 3:1). Despite God's giving abundant provision, by focusing on the only thing they were not to do, Satan in effect implanted a false or distorted view of reality in their minds.

- *He sought to cast doubt on the truth of God's Word* (Gen 3:1). By asking "has God [really] said, 'you shall not eat from any tree of the garden?'" Satan sought to cast doubt and sow confusion concerning what God really required.

- *He lied and contradicted God's Word* (Gen 3:4). Interestingly, the one truth Satan attacked concerned the wrath of God and the consequences of sin. As was true with Adam and Eve, we also face the choice: whom will we believe? Under Satan's (and the world's) strategy, God's Word is no longer accepted as self-evident truth. Instead, God's Word—and thereby God himself—is to be judged by the creature.

- *He attacked the character of God himself* (Gen 3:5). In effect, Satan was saying that God was unloving to restrict Adam and Eve in what they could eat, and was unloving in wanting his creatures to depend on him for the knowledge of good and evil, rather than making that determination themselves.

- *He appealed to human pride* (Gen 3:4–5). Satan promised Eve that by disobeying God she would have life (*"you surely will not die"*), knowledge (*"your eyes will be opened"*), the happiness of an exalted state (*"you will be like God"*), and the superiority of moral autonomy (*"knowing good and evil"*). Paradoxically, however, for Adam and Eve to make the decision on their own (i.e., moral autonomy) is the *essence of death*, because it is *separation from God*. Thus, at the heart of their sin lay unbelief, i.e., lack of faith and trust in God, manifested by obedience to

---

12. Gen 3:6; 1 Tim 2:14.
13. Boice, *Foundations*, 196.

God. Even from the beginning, God's plan was that people would look to him and trust him for the truth of what is good and evil, and for how we should live our lives, i.e., *"the just shall live by faith."*[14]

Just as Satan's temptation of Eve was paradigmatic for the temptations we face, so Adam and Eve's choice to sin was paradigmatic for our choosing to sin and the consequences such sin brings. Instead of bringing happiness and fulfillment, Adam and Eve's sin brought guilt, shame, fear, estrangement from God, from each other, from the rest of creation, and ultimately death (Gen 3:7-19). Adam and Eve wanted autonomy (independence; separation from God), and they received it. God is the source of life, and life is first of all spiritual life and communion with God. Separation from God is the essence of death and hell. Vern Poythress observes, "On the day when Adam and Eve ate the forbidden fruit, they died in a real and spiritual sense. But physical death is a fitting concomitant to this deeper spiritual death. Because human beings have renounced and destroyed their true life with God, their own physical life is in turn destroyed. Physical death is thus simultaneously a punishment and a symbol of deeper spiritual loss."[15]

Because of what they did, Adam and Eve first experienced shame in connection with their nakedness (Gen 3:7-10). Their very sexuality should have reminded them that they were *not* like God, they were *not* autonomous, they could *not* create out of nothing like God did, but could only procreate.[16] The punishments that God decreed (Gen 3:16-19) on the man (work becomes difficult) and woman (childbearing becomes painful) each relate to essential life functions of men and women. Further, Gen 3:16b reflects the beginning of marital discord and/or sexual power struggle—from now on the relationship between husbands and wives will be tainted by sin.[17]

---

14. Hab 2:4; Rom 1:17; Gal 3:11; Heb 10:38.

15. Poythress, *Shadow of Christ*, 83-84.

16. After Eve *"took and ate"* (Gen 3:6), Jesus Christ had to taste poverty and death before the words *"take, eat"* (Matt 26:26) became words of salvation instead of death.

17. See, e.g., the following different ideas concerning the nature of the interaction between "desire" and "rule" in 3:16: Busenitz, "Woman's Desire," 203-12 (woman will still desire her husband as before the Fall and he will still rule as before the Fall, but both the desire and the rule are now tainted with sin); Cassuto, *Genesis*, 165-66 (as woman caused her husband to do what she wished, although she will continue to yearn for him, now he will rule and cause her to do what he wishes); Walton, *Genesis*, 227-28 (the basic desire of woman to have children puts the man in a position to dominate); Stitzinger, "Genesis 1-3," 41-42 ("desire" is the pre-existing subordinate relationship of the woman, but "rule" means that the man will now dominate harshly); Foh, "What is," 376-83 (woman's desire is to master her husband, and his God-ordained rule will now require effort).

The Bible views all people as having been one with Adam ("in Adam"), with Adam acting as our head or representative.[18] Consequently, Adam and Eve's sin affected not only themselves but everyone else throughout history. As a result of Adam's sin, the entire human race receives universal moral corruption, which leads to universal "legal" guilt,[19] which leads to universal individual sin,[20] which leads to universal individual guilt. The exact mechanism of how and why Adam's posterity has been found guilty and radically corrupted as a result of Adam's sin is a matter of debate. The following are some considerations:

- *The Bible often views groups of people as one "corporate person."*[21] This is similar to viewing Adam like the seed or root of a tree, and his progeny as the branches and leaves: it is all one tree; the branches and leaves receive both their life and nature from the seed and root. Adam, as the head of the race, reproduces fallen, rebellious creatures just as he was after he sinned.[22]

- *Since Adam was created without sin and had every personal and circumstantial advantage, there was no better person to represent humanity as a whole. As our representative, Adam's sin, and thus his guilt, was imputed to us.*[23] The situation is something like "when a head of state declares war on another nation, all children born during the war are at war with the other nation."[24]

- *It was not necessary for God to do anything for all people to become corrupt as a result of Adam's sin.* "Only God's *withdrawing*, as it was highly proper and necessary that he should, from rebel-man, and his *natural* principles being *left to themselves*, is sufficient to account for his becoming entirely corrupt and bent on sinning against God."[25]

- *The result of the Fall, and of our being "in Adam," is that on our own, without Christ, we are "dead in our trespasses and sins"* (Eph 2:1). This means that there is a radical depravity or corruption about every person (also called the power of indwelling sin) which affects everything

---

18. See Rom 5:12–19; 1 Cor 15:21–22; see also Heb 7:9–10.
19. Ps 51:5; Jer 17:9; Rom 3:9; 7:14–25.
20. Rom 3:10–18, 23.
21. See Josh 7:10–26; Rom 5:12–19; 1 Cor 15:21–22.
22. Thus, Gen 5:3 says, *"When Adam had lived one hundred and thirty years, he became the father of a son in his own likeness,"* i.e., in his likeness as a sinful, fallen creature.
23. See Johnson, "Romans 5:12," 298–316.
24. Blocher, *Original Sin*, 129.
25. Edwards, *Original Sin*, 219.

about us, including how we think, reason, speak, act, feel, and relate to people and to God. The result of this corruption is that, apart from Christ's intervention, we are totally unable to come to Christ and believe in him (John 6:44, 65; Rom 3:11; Eph 2:8–9); totally unable even to see the kingdom of God (John 3:3, 5); totally unable to submit to God's law and obey him (Rom 8:6–8); totally unable to understand spiritual truth about God (Rom 3:11; 1 Cor 2:14); totally unable to please God (Rom 3:10–18; Heb 11:6); enslaved by sin, the world, the flesh, and the devil, totally devoid of any spiritual life at all, and are subject to God's wrath and judgment (Rom 6:16–17; Eph 2:1–3).[26]

Because humanity is the representative of the whole creation, Adam's sin affects all of creation.[27] Further, Adam receives some of his own medicine. The curse on the ground was a curse on Adam: just as he rebelled against God's rule, now the rest of creation, over which he is to rule, will rebel against him and, in the end, he will nourish the earth by returning to the dust from which he came. The cosmic effect of the Fall is reflected in Rom 8:18–25 (*"the creation was subjected to futility,"* it is in a state of *"slavery and corruption,"* and *"the whole creation groans and suffers the pains of childbirth together until now"*).

However, even in his judgment on Adam and Eve, God demonstrated his grace. He made adequate garments of animal skin to clothe Adam and Eve (Gen 3:21). Although God expelled Adam and Eve from the garden (Gen 3:22–24), he did not revoke their stewardship over all the earth (compare Gen 2:15 and 3:23). Indeed, the expulsion from the garden helped to effectuate God's plan that mankind fill and subdue the earth (Gen 1:28).

The results of the Fall: from Cain through the Tower of Babel (Genesis 4–11)

After Adam and Eve sinned, their descendants continued to rule the earth. The problem is not humanity's refusal to take dominion over the earth, but that mankind now rules the earth in an ungodly manner: "Adamic man rules to make a name for himself, not to glorify the name of the Lord. . . . God created Adam and Eve to construct a replica of His city on earth. Their descendants constructed the perverted city of Man."[28] This section of the book can be divided into the following seven subsections:

26. See also Edwards, *Original Sin*, 143–233; Owen, *Indwelling Sin*, passim.
27. See Goldsworthy, *According to Plan*, 96.
28. Leithart, "Kingdom," n.p.

1. *Cain and his offspring* (Gen 4:1-24). With Cain we see an intensification of sin: impiety (4:3);[29] anger (4:5); jealousy, deception, and murder (4:7-8); lying (4:9); self-seeking and self-pity (4:13-14); and alienation from God (4:14, 16). The intensification of sin is also apparent in that Cain did not just murder anybody but murdered his own brother who was a "righteous" man (Matt 23:35; Heb 11:4). Again, however, notice God's grace to Cain in protecting him from being murdered by his other brothers and sisters (Gen 4:15).

Cain's later descendant, Lamech (Gen 4:18-19, 23-24), takes moral decline to the bottom. He has turned his back on God's divine intention of monogamy (Gen 2:23-24; Matt 19:3-6). Polygamy is not God's ideal. In the Bible, polygamy is always shown to be negative and leads to bad consequences.[30] Therefore, it is not surprising that Lamech is a proud, arrogant, violent man who has proclaimed his complete independence from God by killing people over minor matters, even boasting about it and claiming God's right to vengeance (see Deut 32:35). His vicious claim to revenge against others *"seventy-sevenfold"* (Gen 4:24) finds its counterpart in Christ's statement that we should forgive others *"seventy times seven"* (Matt 18:21-22).

2. *From Seth to Noah* (Gen 4:25—6:8). Beginning in Gen 4:25 the plot of the book turns to the line of Seth. Thus, the *Toledot* of Adam, beginning in Gen 5:1, focuses on Seth and then of particular descendants of Seth.[31] The Bible does this intentionally because the people it focuses on are central to the unfolding story.[32]

---

29. Abel's offering was by faith (Heb 11:4); Cain's was not. Necessarily, therefore, Cain's offering was by "works," i.e., an attempt to exalt himself and manipulate God. Further, Abel's offering was first-fruits, a recognition that the productivity of the flock is from the Lord and that all of it belongs to the Lord. Abel's offering also was of the best portions of the flock (i.e., "their fat portions"). Implicitly, therefore, Cain's was not of his first-fruits, but was simply some of "the fruit of the ground"—evidently, in contrast to Abel's offering, a thoughtless offering, done without faith, and for improper motives. Hence, 1 John 3:12 calls Cain's deeds (in context referring to the offerings) "evil" and Abel's "righteous." John Cross argues that the crucial difference was that Abel's offering was a blood sacrifice for sin and Cain's was not. Cross, "Where in the Scriptures," n.p.

30. See Köstenberger and Jones, *God, Marriage, and Family*, 32–33.

31. One of the most distinctive features of Genesis is the use of similar headings to introduce the narratives and genealogies which alternate throughout the book. These headings occur at Gen 2:4; 5:1; 6:9; 10:1; 11:10, 27; 25:12, 19; 36:1, 9; and 37:2. The common feature of these headings is the Hebrew word *Toledot*, usually translated as "descendant(s); generations; account; list; record." The *Toledot* headings introduce major narrative sections and focus attention on particular individuals.

32. There is controversy over who were the *"sons of God"* and the *"daughters of men"* in Gen 6:2. The four main theories are: 1. "Sons of God" = fallen angels; "daughters of

The *Toledot* of Adam is also important for another reason: after mentioning each man's age and significant offspring, it repeatedly concludes, *"and he died."*[33] That emphasizes the effect of the "curse" which resulted from Adam's sin (see Gen 2:17; 3:19). Although the people before the Flood lived far longer than people do today, they all were subject to death because each was in the image and likeness *of Adam* (Gen 5:3), i.e., they all had within themselves indwelling sin. The one exception was Enoch (Gen 5:21-24). It was not that Enoch did not have indwelling sin (like all other people, he did). Rather, God's "taking" Enoch was another manifestation of God's grace, because Enoch had "walked with God" as a godly man.

The *Toledot* of Adam also demonstrates the decline of mankind through sin. It begins with Adam in a state of God's blessing (Gen 5:1) and ends with God's sorrow that he made mankind and his determination to cleanse the earth of humanity's presence, because *"every intent of the thoughts of [man's] heart was only evil continually"* (Gen 6:5-7). However, one man, Noah, found grace in God's eyes and thereby provided hope for mankind (Gen 6:8).

3 *Noah and the Flood* (Gen 6:9—9:29). This section is one of contrasts. It begins with God's judgment on the world (Gen 6:11-13) but ends with his entering into a covenant with all living creatures to never again destroy the earth by a flood (Gen 8:21—9:17). On the other hand, this section begins with Noah being described as *"a righteous man, blameless in his time, [who] walked with God"* (Gen 6:9). It ends with Noah drunk and cursing Canaan (Gen 9:20-27).[34] One mark of the Bible's truthfulness is that it does not shy away from describing the sins of even the most important characters.

---

men" = mortals; their sin = marriage between supernatural and mortal beings (but see Matt 22:20). 2. SOG = the Godly line of Seth; DOM = ungodly line of Cain; sin = marriage of holy to unholy. 3. SOG = dynastic rulers; DOM = commoners; sin = polygamy. 4. SOG = demon-possessed dynastic rulers; DOM = commoners; sin = ungodly unions. Note that in theories 1 and 4 the SOG are evil; in theory 2 the SOG are good. See VanGemeren, "Sons of God" for a discussion of the context and language of the passage, the major views, and problems associated with each view.

33. Gen 5:5, 8, 11, 14, 17, 20, 27, 31.

34. There is controversy over what Ham did when he *"saw his father's nakedness,"* and why Noah cursed Canaan (Ham's son), not Ham himself (Gen 9:21-27). Because Genesis is a part of "Torah" (instruction), it is linked to the Ten Commandments, including the commandment to *"honor your father and your mother"* (Exod 20:12; Deut 5:16). Therefore, the most likely explanation is that Ham saw his father's nakedness, and through joking about it dishonored his father. Noah cursed Canaan so that he would then have contempt for his own father.

The flood narrative parallels the original creation narratives and amounts to a "re-creation" of the earth:

> The earth is made inhabitable by the separation of the land from the water (Gen. 8:1–3; cf. Gen. 1:9–10). Living creatures are brought out to repopulate the earth (Gen. 8:17–19; cf. Gen. 1:20–22, 24–25). Days and seasons are re-established (Gen. 8:22; cf. Gen. 1:14–18). Humans are blessed by God (Gen. 9:1; cf. Gen. 1:28a), commanded to "Be fruitful and multiply, and fill the earth" (Gen. 9:1b, 7; cf. Gen. 1:28b), and given dominion over the animal kingdom (Gen 9:2; cf. Gen. 1:28c). God provides humanity—made in his image (Gen. 9:6; cf. Gen. 1:26–27)—with food (Gen. 9:3; cf. Gen. 1:29–30).[35]

Even the immediate post-flood activities of Noah are parallel to the accounts in Genesis 1–3: just as Eden was an elevated location, possibly a mountain (see Ezek 28:14, 16), since from it flowed a river (Gen 2:10), so the ark rested on the mountains of Ararat (Gen 8:4). Just as there was a garden in Eden (Gen 2:15), so Noah planted a vineyard (Gen 9:20). Just as Adam sinned in the garden (Gen 3:6) and his son then sinned (Gen 4:8), so Noah sinned in the vineyard (Gen 9:21) and his son then sinned (Gen 9:22).

4 *The Noahic Covenant* (Gen 8:20—9:17). The covenant that God made with Noah is the first covenant explicitly mentioned in the Bible.[36] In Gen 8:21 God cites humanity's depravity as the reason for his mercy, just as he earlier had cited it as the reason for his judgment (Gen 6:5–7). Were it not for God's mercy and grace in establishing his covenant with Noah, mankind inevitably would be heading for extinction again, just as happened at the time of the Flood. The key provision of the covenant with Noah is, "*While the earth remains, seedtime and harvest, and cold and heat, and summer and winter, and day and night shall not cease*" (Gen 8:22). The covenant is something like the stage and props for a play. The covenant assures us that the earth will continue to exist, so that the biblical drama may be played out to God's ordained end.[37]

---

35. Williamson, *Sealed*, 61.

36. A divine-human covenant may be defined as "the solemn ratification of an existing elective relationship involving promises or obligations that are sealed with an oath." Williamson, *Sealed*, 43; see also Klooster, "Biblical," 149; Beckwith, "Unity," 96). The major covenants in the Bible are the Noahic, Abrahamic, Mosaic, Davidic, and New Covenants.

37. See Williamson, *Sealed*, 67–68.

5   *The Table of Nations* (Gen 10:1–32). The Table of Nations (Gen 10:1–32) probably followed the Tower of Babel (Gen 11:1–9) in history, since the account of Babel talks about the separating and spreading of different nations according to their languages. The author of Genesis probably placed the Table of Nations account first for literary reasons: it follows-up on the histories of Shem, Ham, and Japheth from the end of Genesis 9; it demonstrates that, since all peoples of the world are descended from Noah through Shem, Ham, and Japheth, all peoples are of the same "blood" and ultimately are of the same family; and it functions as the fulfillment of the divine command in Gen 9:1.

6   *The Tower of Babel* (Gen 11:1–9). The Tower of Babel demonstrates mankind's continued rebellion against God. God's initial mandate to human beings was to *"fill the earth"* (Gen 1:28). He repeated the same command to Noah and his sons in Gen 9:1. Nevertheless, despite God's judgment of the Flood, humanity again chooses not to fill the earth but to stay in one place. Further, it wants to build a tower to heaven to exalt its own name and again become like God. In fact, the incident at Babel was even more radical than humanity's actions which occasioned the Flood, because Babel was both universal and organized. Babel was also "the first instance of an organized religion recorded in the Bible. . . . The people, in trying to build a tower to the heavens, were devising their own way of reaching God."[38] Consequently, God *"confused their language"* and *"scattered them abroad from there over the face of the whole earth"* (Gen 11:7–8).[39] From a literary standpoint,

---

38. Cross, *Stranger*, 95.

39. Babel and the scattering of humanity highlight that, although there are many different religions, there are only two *kinds* of religion in the world: Christianity and everything else. All other religions are man's efforts to reach up to God by means of works, sacrifices, rituals, and other efforts. Christianity is God's reaching down to us and, in the person of Jesus Christ, doing for us what we could not do for ourselves. On the day of Pentecost (Acts 2:1–11), God in effect reverses Babel: "God causes representatives from the same scattered nations to unite in Jerusalem in order that they might receive the blessing of understanding different languages as if all these languages were one. . . . The purpose of having a unified understanding is to demonstrate the power of the eschatological Spirit in attesting to Jesus' death, resurrection and ascension to the heavenly throne to reign as cosmic king. Under the kingship of Jesus and through the power of his Spirit the representatives of these nations were to 'scatter' again and subdue the powers of evil by filling the earth with God's presence. . . . The precise manner in which they were to do this was by 'witnessing' through the power of the Spirit in word and deed on behalf of Jesus Christ (see Acts 1:8)." Beale, *Temple*, 202–3. Thus, "Pentecost is the redemptive counterpart to Babel; there, . . . a new unity through the Holy Spirit on the basis of the finished work of Jesus Christ unites believers from all nations of the earth." Klooster, "Biblical," 147.

this account leaves the reader looking for an answer to mankind's continual sinfulness and rebellion against God.

7   *The Toledot of Shem* (Gen 11:10–32). After Babel, the Bible focuses on the line of Shem, which both Noah and God have blessed. This *Toledot* takes us to Abraham, whom God will call and through whom God will enact his plan to redeem and bless the world.

THE DRAMA OF REDEMPTION—GOD'S CALLING A PEOPLE FOR HIMSELF (GEN 12–REVELATION 20)

God's new beginning: from Abraham through Joseph (Gen 12:1—50:26)

In this crucial section of the biblical story, God now chooses one man (Abraham) to begin his specific plan for the redemption of the world. God enters into a covenant with Abraham, the "Abrahamic Covenant,"[40] which is confirmed to Abraham's son Isaac[41] and to Isaac's younger son Jacob.[42] The Abrahamic Covenant, as it is initially formulated and then developed in Genesis, has three basic "core promissory threads": phenomenal posterity (promises relating to "seed"); national territory (promises relating to "land"); and global blessing (promises relating to the blessing of other peoples through Abraham's seed).[43] Whereas the people in Babel wanted to make their own name great (Gen 11:4), by his grace God will make Abraham's name great and bless the world through him (Gen 12:2–3). This covenant unfolds throughout the OT. In many respects, therefore, the Abrahamic Covenant is the theological backbone and blueprint of the rest of the Bible. The true and ultimate fulfillment of the covenant occurs in Christ.[44]

Even though Abraham and his wife Sarah were old and unable to have children of their own, God miraculously caused them to conceive and have a son, Isaac (Gen 18:1–15; 21:1–8). That demonstrated that God was driving matters, to make sure that his plan and the covenant he had made with Abraham would be fulfilled. When Isaac's wife Rebekah was pregnant with

---

40. Gen 12:1–3; 13:14–17; 15:1–21; 17:1–21; 22:15–18.
41. Gen 26:1–5, 24.
42. Gen 28:3–4, 13–15; 35:11–12.
43. Williamson, "Abraham, Israel," 100–101; see also Kaiser, *Toward and Old*, 86; Essex, "Abrahamic," 208; Reisinger, *Abraham's Four*, 6.
44. See chapter 9—Christ and the Church Fulfill the Abrahamic, Davidic, and New Covenants.

twins, the Lord told her that, in reality, two nations were in her and that the older (Esau) would serve the younger (Jacob) (Gen 25:21–26). God later changed Jacob's name to Israel (Gen 32:24–32; 35:9–12).[45] From Jacob (Israel) came the twelve tribes of Israel.[46]

Jacob's children began living immorally like the Canaanites among whom they were dwelling.[47] If that continued, there would be no more Israel. Therefore, God preserved his chosen people by moving them from Canaan to Egypt by means of Joseph's brothers' sin and Joseph's righteousness. God also used Judah's sin with his daughter-in-law Tamar as part of his overall plan of redemption.[48] These accounts highlight that God is sovereign over history and is the one "behind the scenes" who is orchestrating history to fulfill what he has promised. The story about Joseph (Gen 37; 39–50) primarily shows how Israel got to Egypt and how God was working out his plan which he had decreed hundreds of years beforehand to Abraham (Gen 15:13–14). The presence of Israel in Egypt set the stage for the next act of God's dramatic program, the exodus.

The beginning of the nation of Israel: from Egypt to the promised land (Exodus–Deuteronomy)[49]

Four hundred years elapse before the story resumes. During that period, the family of Jacob becomes a great multitude in Egypt. The pharaoh fears the growing size of the Israelites and enslaves them. Nevertheless, in this next great act of God's drama of redemption, God's faithfulness to the covenant he made with Abraham, Isaac, and Jacob results in Israel's becoming a nation and gaining its independence from slavery in Egypt.

The interaction between God and Moses drives this section of the Scriptures. God's action on behalf of Israel was based on the Abrahamic Covenant (see Exod 2:24).[50] In God's self-revelation to Moses—*"I AM WHO I AM"* (Exod 3:14)—God essentially was telling Moses that "I am unique,

---

45. Jacob's struggling with God (Gen 32:24–32) when God changed Jacob's name to Israel is a suggestive foreshadowing of the nation of Israel's own continual struggles against God throughout its history (see Hos 12:1–6).

46. Gen 30:1–24; 35:16–18, 22–27; 41:50–52; 49:1–28.

47. Gen 34:1–31; 35:22; 38:1–26.

48. See Gen 38:12–19; Ruth 4:18; Matt 1:3.

49. Summaries of Israel's history are recounted at Josh 24:1–13; Neh 9:5–37; Ps 105:1–45; 106:6–46, and Acts 7:2–53.

50. When God was making the covenant with Abraham, he even told Abraham that Abraham's descendants would be enslaved and oppressed in a foreign land for 400 years but would come out with many possessions (Gen 15:13–14).

and who I am will be understood by what I do" (see Exod 3:13–22).[51] God's character and nature are more specifically described in Exod 34:6–7. Moses himself dominates the OT. There are 770 references to him in the OT, about one-third of them in Exodus. Despite the close, personal, and miraculous interaction Moses had with God over a period of 40 years, it was Moses's not properly representing God's character (when Moses struck the rock at Meribah, instead of speaking to the rock), that prevented Moses from actually taking the Israelites into the promised land (Num 20:8–13).

The exodus was the decisive event for OT Israel. The exodus was an historical, physical event that dramatized spiritual truth applicable to all of God's people throughout history. It was the preliminary stage necessary to fulfill the promise of nationhood contained in the Abrahamic Covenant. Significantly, in the Ten Commandments, the first word God speaks to Israel is about his *grace* in redeeming them from bondage. Only after that comes the Law.[52] The exodus was the basis for the feast of Passover (Exod 12:1–27). It was frequently recalled in the Psalter.[53] It was used by the prophets to call Israel to return to covenantal faithfulness to God, or as a warning from God.[54]

God's covenant with Moses,[55] and the Mosaic Law,[56] with its sacrificial system, tabernacle, Sabbath, feasts, priesthood, and religious ceremonies, which were intrinsic parts of the covenant,[57] defined the nation of Israel until Christ came and fulfilled them. By means of the Mosaic Covenant, God set Israel apart from other nations. The Mosaic Covenant advanced the Abrahamic Covenant by guaranteeing the preservation of Israel, Abraham's national posterity, in the land. It also regulated how the physical nation-state of Israel was to live when it entered the land (see Lev 26:42).[58] Because

---

51. Interestingly, the worship of God in heaven focuses on *who God is* (his glory; his awesome nature), *and what God has done, is doing, and will do* (creation; salvation; his rule; his coming judgment). See Isa 6:1–8; Rev 4–5; 7:9–17; 11:15–19; 15; 19:1–6. God's nature and His acts are also the focus of worship in the great psalms of worship. See Psalms 8; 19; 24; 29; 33; 46–48; 63; 65–68; 76; 84; 87; 92; 93; 96–100; 103; 104; 111; 113; 115; 117; 135; 145–50.

52. Exod 19:4–6; 20:2; Deut 5:6, 15.

53. See Psalms 66; 77; 80; 81; 105; 106; 114; 135; 136.

54. See Isa 11:16; Jer 2:6; 7:22, 25; 11:4, 7; 16:14; 23:7; 32:21; 34:13; Hos 2:15; 11:1; 12:9, 13; 13:4; Amos 2:10; 3:1; 9:7; Micah 6:4; 7:15.

55. Exodus 19–24; see 2 Cor 3:14; Hebrews 8.

56. Exodus 20–23; Leviticus 11–15; 18–20; 25:23–55; 27; Numbers 5; 27:1–14; 36; Deuteronomy 5; 12–13; 20–22; 24–25.

57. Exodus 23; 25–31; 35–40; Leviticus 1–9; 16–17; 21–25:22; Numbers 3–4; 6–10; 15; 18–19; 28–30; 34–35; Deuteronomy 14–19; 23; 26.

58. When Moses was receiving the Ten Commandments from God the first time, the people fell into sin *based on the very things prohibited by the Ten Commandments*

it served that function, the Mosaic Covenant was significantly different from the Abrahamic Covenant and later biblical covenants in that it was conditional and emphasized the responsibilities of the human party to the covenant (Israel) in ways that the other covenants do not. This is reflected in the foundational "if . . . then" conditional framework which God gave to Moses on Mount Sinai in Exod 19:5–6.

God's blessings and curses were tied in a physical way directly to Israel's obedience or disobedience to Mosaic Law.[59] Through those physical means, God was endeavoring to teach Israel the spiritual principle that, *"you shall be holy, for I the Lord your God am holy."*[60] Further, the covenant and the institutions created as a part of it established the principle that sinful people could only approach God through a mediator. Moses acted as the mediator between God and Israel in the wilderness. At Sinai a priesthood was established. The layout and form of the tabernacle also graphically indicated the separation between sinful people and holy God, which could only be reconciled through sacrifice and the mediatorial office of the priest.

Israel in the land (Joshua–1 Samuel 7)

The book of Joshua recounts how God faithfully kept his promise to give Israel the land, by judging and driving out the ungodly nations who then lived there. However, Israel did not remain faithful to God. The book of Judges details how Israel continually turned to pagan idols. As a result, God allowed pagan nations to subdue and oppress Israel. When Israel repented, God mercifully raised up military leaders (known as judges) to throw off the oppressors. This pattern repeated itself time and again. The last of the judges was Samuel, who also was a priest and a prophet. First Samuel 1–7 describes the last period of Israel's history under the rule of the judges, before the beginning of kingship. It begins with the fall of Eli and his family and the rise of Samuel, and ends with the capture of the ark of the covenant by the Philistines, the return of the ark to Israel, and Israel's deliverance from the Philistines.

---

themselves (Exod 32:1–6). Moses' appeal to God to spare the people was based on the Abrahamic Covenant (Exod 32:11–14). As a result, God did not destroy the people but gave Moses a second set of the Ten Commandments (Exodus 34).

59. See Leviticus 26; Deuteronomy 4; 6–9; 11; 27–29.
60. Lev 19:2; "holy" occurs 152 times in Leviticus.

Israel as a United Kingdom (1 Samuel 8–2 Samuel; 1 Kings 11; 1 Chronicles 1–2 Chronicles 9; Psalms–Song of Solomon)

There were both pro-king (Gen 49:8–10; Deut 17:14–20) and anti-king (Judg 8:22–23; 1 Sam 8:1–18) strands in Israel's history before they got their first king. However, the people wanted a king in order *"that we also may be like all the nations"* (1 Sam 8:20). As God told Samuel, this was not a rejection of Samuel, but a rejection of God (1 Sam 8:7). Nevertheless, God granted their request. God used Samuel to appoint Saul (1050–1010 BC), and then David (1010–970 BC), as the first kings over Israel.

David is the central figure of the United Kingdom. His reign prefigures the Messianic Kingdom itself. God entered into a covenant with David (the "Davidic Covenant").[61] The Davidic Covenant becomes a specific way the Abrahamic Covenant comes to fulfillment. Even its terms allude to the promises God made to Abraham. In this covenant (2 Samuel 7) God promises David: a great name (v. 9; compare Gen 12:2); a place (v. 10; compare Gen 12:7; 13:14–17; 15:7, 18; 17:8); rest from enemies (v. 11; compare Gen 22:17); a "seed" (v. 12; compare Gen 22:18); and an everlasting kingdom and throne (vv. 12–16; compare Gen 12:3; 13:15; 17:5–7).

This covenant found initial fulfillment in David's son Solomon (970–930 BC), who built the temple in Jerusalem. However, despite being given great wisdom from God, Solomon married hundreds of foreign women, which led him to worship other gods. The high taxes he imposed for his many building projects sowed the seeds for the eventual division of the kingdom. The Davidic-Solomonic era foreshadowed the "blessing of the nations" which God had promised in the Abrahamic Covenant. This promise was not fulfilled. The reason is that, although there were a few reforming kings, none of the Davidic dynasty—including David himself—fully complied with the crucial criterion for divine-human relationship: an irreproachable, godly life (see 1 Kgs 2:4; 6:12–13; 8:25; 9:4–9).[62]

With the exception of Job, the Wisdom Literature (Job, Psalms, Proverbs, Ecclesiastes, Song of Solomon) was written during this period. The Wisdom Literature deals with the quest for knowledge, understanding, and relationship with God and others in a world where all relationships have been distorted by sin. "[David's] hymns of praise, contrition, and instruction (the psalms, not all attributable to David) are timely yet timeless models of spiritual insight and thus central to the focus of biblical theology. Likewise the wisdom (given explicitly by God: 1 Kings 3:12) of his

---

61. 2 Sam 7:8–17; 1 Chron 17:3–15; see 2 Sam 23:5; 2 Chron 6:16; Ps 89:1–4, 28–29.
62. See Williamson, *Sealed*, 145.

son Solomon stands at the center of an equally weighty literary corpus for biblical-theological work."[63] Godly wisdom is *not* God's making our decisions for us or simply giving us the correct thoughts to think. Instead, the Wisdom Literature points us to trust in God for our intellectual endeavors, not merely relying on our own worldly wisdom and abilities. Job profoundly uses the universal theme of pain and unjust suffering as the setting for dealing with God's sovereignty over suffering and man's faith in God while in the crucible of suffering.

Israel as a divided Kingdom (1 Kings 12–2 Kings 17; 2 Chronicles 10–31; Isaiah and Micah [prophesied to Israel and Judah]; Joel [prophesied to Judah]; Hosea and Amos [prophesied to Israel]; Obadiah [prophesied to Edom]; Jonah [prophesied to Nineveh])

Rehoboam, Solomon's son, ascended the throne when his father died. The people requested that Rehoboam lighten the oppressive yoke under which Solomon had held them. Rehoboam refused. As a result, the kingdom split: ten tribes formed the northern kingdom of Israel; the two southern tribes (Judah and Benjamin, along with most of the Levites and some people from the northern tribes) formed the southern kingdom of Judah. Each kingdom had its own king, and the two kingdoms never reconciled or merged. The books of 1 and 2 Kings and 1 and 2 Chronicles tell their respective stories. Both kingdoms tended to slide downhill, disobeying God. Although there were a few good kings in Judah, the northern kings invariably acted contrary to God's ways.

Throughout Israel's history, but particularly during the period of the divided kingdom and then extending into the period of the restoration of the southern kingdom, God continually sent prophets to warn the people and bring them back to faithfulness toward God. God's prophets applied God's word during crises in the covenant relation between God and his people. The main activity of OT prophets was *not* predicting the future. Rather, the prophets spoke during times of crisis and all had essentially a twofold message and ministry: (1) They warn God's people of the consequences of disobedience to the Lord's ways by *oracles of judgment;* and (2) They call God's people back to faithfulness by *oracles of hope and salvation.* All OT prophets were concerned with changing people's behavior. Their message essentially was, "if you do this, judgment will come; if you follow the Lord,

---

63. Yarbrough, "Biblical Theology," 64.

blessings will come." Their messages of judgment and salvation are therefore relevant for many generations. By and large, the people of both Israel and Judah did not listen.

The existence, decline, and fall, of the southern kingdom (2 Kings 18–25; 2 Chron 3—36:21; Isaiah–Daniel; Nahum–Zephaniah)

Because the people of both Israel and Judah did not listen to the prophets, repent, and return to the Lord and his ways, in 722 BC the northern kingdom was destroyed and taken into captivity by Assyria. Judah did not change her ways as a result of what happened to Israel. Consequently, in 586 BC the temple in Jerusalem was destroyed by the Babylonians, and southern kingdom of Judah was taken into exile in Babylon.

Historically one can see a shift in prophetic emphasis after Israel's exile in Babylon. Before the exile, the prophets tended to stress Israel's rebelliousness. After the exile, the emphasis shifted toward the responsibility of God's people to prepare for the full establishing of God's kingdom.[64] Particularly after the exile, the prophets talk about a number of themes, including:

- *A new exodus.* God's people will be rescued from their false shepherds (Ezekiel 34). They will be rescued from captivity.[65]

- *A new people.* Sometimes this is depicted as God's faithful remnant.[66] God's failed, captive, and divided people will be remade, reanimated, and reunited (Ezekiel 37). God will bless the nations.[67] Isaiah appears to redefine the "people of God" contrary to the limitations of the Mosaic Covenant (compare Deut 23:1–8 and Isa 56:3–8).

- *A new agent to fulfill God's purposes.* God's agent is his anointed servant (Isa 42:1–9; 61:1–3). God's agent appears as a suffering servant.[68] He appears as a mysterious "son of man" (Dan 7:13–14). He is a new David.[69] Elijah will appear (Mal 4:5–6).

---

64. VanGemeren, *Interpreting*, 213.
65. Isa 40:1–5; 43:1–7, 15–21; 48:20–21; 49:24–26; 51:9–11; Jer 23:7–8.
66. Isa 10:20–23; 11:11–12; 14:1–4; 40:1–2; 46:3–4; 51:11; 61:4–7; Jer 23:1–8; 29:10–14; 30:10–11; 31:7–9; Ezek 34:1–6; 36:22–24; 37:15–22; Micah 2:12.
67. Isa 2:2–4; 19:18–25; 49:5–6; 56:1–8; Micah 4:1–4; Zeph 3:9; Zech 8:20–23.
68. Isa 42:1–9; 49:1–6; 50:4–9; 52:13—53:12.
69. Isa 9:2–7; 11:1–5; 16:5; Jer 23:1–6; Ezek 34:23–24; 37:24–25; Amos 9:11.

- *A new land.* There will be a new Zion.[70] It will be a land of peace, plenty, and prosperity.[71] There will even be a new heaven and earth (Isaiah 42:14–17; 65–66).

- *A New Covenant.*[72] The promise of a "New Covenant" is explicitly mentioned in the OT only in Jer 31:31 but is implicit elsewhere in Jeremiah and Ezekiel. The New Covenant would not be like the Old, Mosaic Covenant which Israel broke. The New Covenant "internalizes" and "personalizes" the relationship between God and his people in ways that none of the other covenants ever attempted. The "newness" of the New Covenant is important; it "incorporates novel dimensions that reflect a radical discontinuity with the past (cf. Jer. 31:32): a complete removal of sin (Jer. 31:34; Ezek. 36:29, 33); an inner transformation of heart (Jer. 31:33; Ezek. 36:26); an intimate relationship with God (Jer. 31:34a; Ezek. 36:27)."[73] There is no hint of the "conditionality" expressed in the Mosaic Covenant. Indeed, sin can no longer imperil the divine-human relationship because, under the New Covenant, God makes the astounding announcement, *"I will forgive their iniquity, and their sin I will remember no more"* (Jer 31:34). This new heart, internalization of God's law, personal relationship with God, and complete forgiveness of sin will result in a new depth of obedience to and faith in God. The New Covenant is the fulfillment of the covenants God made with Abraham, Moses, and David.

- *A new rule of God.* There will be a new presence of God and a new temple.[74] God will pour out his Spirit on his people.[75] Sometimes God himself is described as returning to Zion.[76] His relationship with his people will be restored and renewed.[77]

- *The Day of the Lord.* The concept of the "Day of the Lord" emerges out of the above prophecies. Sometimes it is described as a day coming in the near future;[78] in such cases it often appears to be talking about God's

---

70. Isaiah 2; 11:6–9; 35:1–10; 54; 61:3—62:12; Ezek 34:11–16, 25–31; 36:35–38.
71. Hos 2:14–18; Joel 3:18; Amos 9:13–15; Micah 4:3–4.
72. Jer 31:31–34; 32:38–40; 50:4–5; Ezek 11:16–20; 36:24–32; 37:15–28.
73. Williamson, *Sealed*, 180.
74. Isa 12:6; Ezek 37:27–28; 40–48; Joel 3:16–17; Zeph 3:14–17.
75. Joel 2:28–32; Isa 32:9–20; Ezek 36:25–28.
76. Isa 12:6; Ezek 37:27–28; 40–48; Joel 3:16–17; Zeph 3:14–17.
77. Hos 2:16, 19–20; 3:5.
78. Isa 13:6; Ezek 30:1–3; Joel 1:15; 2:1; 3:14; Obad 15; Zeph 1:7, 14.

destroying OT Israel's enemies.[79] Sometimes the time is not specified. The Day of the Lord is frequently described as a fearsome day of wrath and judgment.[80] These latter senses depict the Day of the Lord as a final, eschatological day of God's visitation in grace and judgment.

These prophetic themes were not systematized into a coherent whole. However, they created hope and expectation that God would visit his people in grace and his enemies in judgment. They "point to a time in history when the Lord will bring to fruition and realize in perfection all of his gracious purposes and covenantal ways with his people."[81] The synthesis is found in Christ, of whom Paul says, *"For as many as are the promises of God, in Him they are yes"* (2 Cor 1:20). The OT prophets mingled items connected with the first coming of Christ and items connected with his second coming. "Not until the New Testament times would it be revealed that what was thought of in Old Testament days as one coming of the Messiah would be fulfilled in two stages: a first and second coming."[82]

The restoration of the southern kingdom (2 Chron 36:22—Esther; Haggai–Malachi)

After over half a century in exile, King Cyrus of Persia (which had taken over the Babylonian Empire) issued a decree permitting the Jews to return to Judah and rebuild the temple. Although some of the Jews did return, most did not. For awhile after the return of exiles from Babylon, leadership was held by a descendant of David, a man named Zerubbabel.[83] Under the leadership of Zerubbabel, Ezra, and Nehemiah, Jerusalem and the temple were rebuilt (536–516 BC). However, both the nation and the new temple were shadows of their former selves.

The narratives of Ezra and Nehemiah make it clear that the restored nation was not the kingdom of God. The post-exilic prophets all point to glory yet to come.[84] The OT ends as a "book without an ending." The He-

---

79. Joel 3:4; Obad 18–21; Zeph 1:7–11; 2:4–15.

80. Isa 2:12–21; 10:3 (*"day of punishment"*); 13:6–13; 26:21; 34:8; 63:1–4a; Jer 46:10 (*"day of vengeance"*); Ezek 7:19; 13:1–5; 30:1–3; Hos 1:11 (*"day of Jezreel"*); Joel 1:15; 2:1, 11; 3:14; Amos 5:18–20; Obad 15–16; Zeph 1:7—2:3; Zech 14:1–7; Mal 4:5. Other passages speak of salvation for the Lord's people on that day. See Isa 35:4; 40:9–11; 63:4b–5; Joel 2:30–32; Obad 17; Zech 2:10–13.

81. Venema, *Promise*, 23.

82. Hoekema, *Bible and the Future*, 12.

83. Ezra 2–5; Haggai 1–2; Matt 1:13; Luke 3:27.

84. Hag 2:6–9; Zech 8:20–23; 14:1–21; Mal 4:1–6.

brew Bible ends with 2 Chronicles, which concludes with the hope of a new temple and a return from exile. The Christian arrangement of the OT ends with Malachi, which concludes with the promise of the sending of Elijah and the coming day of the Lord.

Between the end of the OT and the beginning of the NT there is an interlude of four hundred years. During that time, Israel was under the oppression of the Persians, Greeks, Syrians, and Romans. The Maccabean Revolt (167–160 BC) triumphed over the Seleucid (Syrian) King Antiochus Epiphanes and resulted in Israel's temporarily gaining independence. The Hasmonean Dynasty, which had consolidated power, lasted until 37 BC, when Herod the Great, with heavy Roman support, defeated the last Hasmonean ruler to become a Roman client king. Israel then became the province Judea of the Roman Empire.

> During this time, Israel continues to believe that they are God's chosen people and that God will act in the very near future to bring His kingdom. . . . How God's kingdom will come, who will bring it in, and what way to live until it comes—on these things there is much difference among the Pharisees, Sadducees, Zealots, and Essenes. But all of Israel agrees: their story is waiting for an ending. The kingdom will come soon. And so they wait in hope.[85]

The fulfillment of God's plan of redemption in Jesus Christ (Matthew–Revelation 20)

The NT picks up the story after a gap of about 400 years. John the Baptist arrives on the scene, calling the people back to God in repentance and heralding the arrival of the Messiah. The Gospels describe that what the OT anticipated is fulfilled by Jesus. Matthew's genealogy of Jesus links him with Abraham and David (Matt 1:1). In his life, Jesus brings deliverance and fulfillment. Masses of people flock to him, but most of the religious leaders reject Jesus as the Messiah, because he is not the "warrior-king" Messiah, prepared to throw off the Roman Empire, that they had expected. They did not see that he was, indeed, a warrior-king; he fought and defeated the three greatest enemies all of us face: Satan, sin, and death itself. The four Gospels conclude by presenting the climax of Jesus' ministry as his atoning death and his resurrection from the dead, which validated who he is (God come to earth as a man) and everything he said, did, and believed.

85. Bartholomew and Goheen, "Storyline," 4–5.

Acts and the Epistles document and explain the spread of the church and the Gospel. The book of Acts begins with Jesus commissioning his disciples and promising to send the Holy Spirit (Acts 1:4–8); he then ascends back to the Father (Acts 1:9–11). The coming of the Holy Spirit in Acts 2 ushers in a new boldness in the disciples and results in the conversion of thousands of people to faith in Jesus. Persecution is also unleashed against the disciples and the new Christian movement. The first martyrdom occurs (Acts 7:54–60), but the chief persecutor, Saul of Tarsus (who is renamed Paul), becomes the primary apostle. Beginning with the Roman centurion Cornelius, Gentiles are brought to faith in Christ, and the church begins to spread from Jerusalem, to Judea, Samaria, and to the uttermost parts of the earth.

Epistles are written by Peter, John, James, Paul and others to local churches and individuals to explain and flesh-out the Gospel message. These epistles instruct people in the faith and show Christians how to live faithfully in an often-hostile world. The Gospel story ends with the promise of the return of Christ to the earth, which will entail resurrection of all, judgment of all, and the renewal of the earth.

Jesus' revelation of the true nature of the Messiah, the Kingdom of God, and the church

Although Jesus is God's final and fullest revelation who fulfills the OT prophecies and expectations, he fulfilled them in unanticipated ways. The Gospels, Acts, and the Epistles reveal Jesus' unique revelation of the true nature of the Messiah, the Kingdom of God, and the church.

1 *Jesus the Messiah*. Most Jews expected Messiah to be more of a political figure who would drive out the Romans and re-establish Jerusalem and the temple in splendor as the center of the new earth. Jesus did not meet those expectations. Instead, he synthesized different strands of the OT in ways not systematized before. He revealed that he was fully God incarnate,[86] and yet was also truly a man—the last Adam, the seed of Abraham, the son of David, the true prophet.[87]

Jesus' claims to be God, and his taking the role of the temple onto himself,[88] drove the Jewish leaders into a frenzy of hatred. The reason is that Judaism had an extremely "transcendent" view of God: God was the creator, separate and distinct from his creation. For a human

---

86. John 1:1–14; 10:30; 14:6–11; Phil 2:5–7; Col 1:16–17; 2:9; Titus 2:13; Heb 1:8.
87. Matt 21:9; Luke 14:16–24; Rom 1:3; 5:19; 1 Cor 15:22, 45; Gal 3:16; Col 1:15.
88. See John 2:13–22; 7:37.

being to claim to be God in that context was both inconceivable and blasphemous. Indeed, on more than one occasion, the Jewish leaders sought to stone Jesus to death for blasphemy.[89]

2. *The spiritual nature of the kingdom of God.* The very nature of the kingdom is different from the expectations of the Jews and even of Jesus' own disciples (at first). They had been expecting a renewal of Israel's earthly status and power (see Acts 1:6). Instead, Jesus ordained his church as the visible representation of the kingdom on earth (Matt 16:18–19). He told Pilate, *"My kingdom is not of this world"* (John 18:36). Earlier he had told the Pharisees, *"The kingdom of God is not coming with signs to be observed; nor will they say, 'Look, here it is!' or, 'There it is!' For behold, the kingdom of God is in your midst"* (Luke 17:20–21). Further, the kingdom is not limited either to Jews or to the land of Palestine. Instead, it is radically inclusive. It includes Jews and Gentiles on an equal basis (Acts 10–11; Eph 2:11–22) and includes the entire earth.[90] Acts 1:8 is a template for the spread of the church.

3. *The "already/not yet" aspect of the Kingdom of God.* "Not clearly foreseen, apparently, by either Old Testament prophets or the earliest New Testament disciples, was the already-not yet complexion of the messianic age."[91] When Jesus cast out demons he told the Pharisees, *"The kingdom of God has come upon you"* (Luke 11:20). Jesus has been given all authority in heaven and on earth and even now is reigning from the "throne of David" in heaven.[92] Nevertheless, we still experience sin and evil, and much of the world is opposed to Christ and his rule. This seeming paradox is explained by the "already/not yet" nature of the kingdom of God, i.e., although the kingdom of God and reign of Christ have been inaugurated and realized in principle (the "already" of the kingdom), they have not yet been fully manifested but await a future consummation in all their glory (the "not yet" of the kingdom).[93]

---

89. See Lev 24:10–16; Matt 9:2–3; 26:63–66; Mark 2:5–7; 14:61–64; Luke 22:70–71; John 5:17–18; 8:58–59; 10:30–33; 19:7.

90. Matt 28:18–20; Acts 1:8; Rev 5:9; 7:9.

91. Yarbrough, "Biblical Theology," 65.

92. Matt 28:18; Acts 2:29–36; Eph 1:18–23.

93. The "already/not yet" schema has been discussed by many commentators. See, e.g., Hoekema, *Bible*, 13–22; Venema, *Promise*, 12–32; Vos, *Pauline*, 38 (helpful diagram). It is reflected in the Beatitudes of Matt 5:2–10: vv. 2, 10 are in the present; all other rewards are future. "This distinction is significant, for it underscores that although the kingdom of God (the reign of Christ) is a present reality, the consummated kingdom awaits his return in glory." Alexander, *From Eden*, 95.

This is seen in the following ways:

- Throughout the NT, the writers speak of the "two ages": "this age," and the "age to come." "This age" is characterized by marriage and things temporal,[94] evil (Gal 1:4; Eph 2:2), worldly wisdom (1 Cor 1:20; 2:6–8), and death. On the other hand, "the age to come" is characterized by resurrection life and immortality,[95] the lack of marriage (Luke 20:35), and absence of evil.[96] The first coming of Christ brought with it the inauguration of the kingdom and, hence, an overlapping of the two ages. As a result of Christ's first coming, this age is in its "last days."[97] "This age" will end and the "age to come" will be fully consummated in all its glory at the Second Coming of Christ (see Matt 24:3; Titus 2:12–13).[98]

- The overlapping of the two ages, and the "breaking in" of the age to come into this age, explains why the Bible constantly assumes a "two-stage" character of salvation. "Justification (Romans 5:1; Matthew 12:37), adoption (Romans 8:14–16 with v. 23 of the same chapter and also Galatians 4:4–6 with Eph. 4:30), and redemption (Ephesians 1:7 with 4:30) with many other of the biblical realities associated with salvation can be spoken of both as past realities and future blessings. This is so because *the age to come* which brings salvation unfolds itself in two stages."[99] Some of Jesus' parables, such as the parable of the wheat and the tares (Matt 13:24–30, 36–43) and the parable of the dragnet (Matt 13:47–50), speak of the dual nature of the kingdom. First Cor 15:20–28 indicates the same thing: the resurrection of Christ as firstfruits and then the resurrection of those who are Christ's at his coming mark the inauguration and consummation of the kingdom.

The Kingdom of God comes through the preaching and living out the Gospel under the influence of the Holy Spirit. Just as Jesus presented an unexpected fulfillment of what Messiah and the kingdom truly were, so he introduced a new dimension to OT expectations concerning God's Spirit and the new rule of God: he would be absent in the body but present inside of his followers in the Spirit (John 14–16; Acts 1–2). Jesus began his public

---

94. E.g., Mark 10:30; Luke 20:34; Rom 12:2.

95. E.g., Mark 10:30; 1 Cor 15:50.

96. 1 Cor 6:9–10; Gal 5:21; Eph 5:5. See Riddlebarger, *Case*, 82–83.

97. See Acts 2:17; Heb 1:2; Jas 5:3; 1 Pet 1:20; 1 John 2:18; Jude 18.

98. The "two ages" are discussed in detail in Menn, *Biblical Eschatology*, 2nd ed., 36–61.

99. Waldron, "Structural Considerations," n.p.

ministry by linking the kingdom and the gospel: *"The time is fulfilled, and the kingdom of God is at hand; repent and believe in the gospel"* (Mark 1:15). With the death, resurrection, and ascension of Jesus, the power of the gospel is now available. Acts 2:38 describes what happens when anyone hears the gospel and believes it: his sins are forgiven and he receives the gift of the Holy Spirit. By our faith in Christ, God has *"rescued us from the domain of darkness, and transferred us to the kingdom of His beloved Son"* (Col 1:13).

The church is now a preview of the coming kingdom. Christ ordained his church as the visible manifestation of his body on the earth after he ascended back to the Father (Matt 16:18; see 1 Cor 12:12–28). Christ commissioned the church, *"as the Father has sent me, I also send you"* (John 20:21), and *"Go therefore and make disciples of all the nations, baptizing them in the name of the Father and the Son and the Holy Spirit, teaching them to observe all that I commanded you; and lo, I am with you always, even to the end of the age"* (Matt 28:19–20). The NT epistles instruct the church that the Gospel applies to all aspects of our lives, even those with whom we eat (see Gal 2:11–14). The goal of the Gospel is that we would become just like Jesus: his thoughts become our thoughts; his love and compassion become our love and compassion; his values become our values; and his priorities become our priorities (see Rom 8:29; Eph 4:11–16). The mission of the church "is to make known the good news of the kingdom. This is what gives the contemporary time period its meaning. And since the rule of Jesus covers the whole earth, the mission of God's people is as broad as creation. In effect, God's people are to live lives that say, 'This is how the whole world will be some day when Jesus returns!'"[100]

THE NEW HEAVENS AND THE NEW EARTH (REVELATION 21–22)

The last book of the Bible is Revelation. The first twenty chapters speak of and to the church, largely in symbolic form, of God's plan for the church and the problems it will encounter until Christ's glorious return to the earth. The last two chapters introduce us, again, largely in symbolic form, to the "new heavens and the new earth" that Christ will usher in when he returns. At that time, the curse, which God had pronounced when Adam and Eve sinned, will be reversed. There will be no more sickness, pain, sorrow, or death. God and Christ will dwell among their people, and we will be like him and see him as he is. This glorious new world will last forever, a time of perfect fulfillment for all.

100. Bartholomew and Goheen, "Storyline," 6–7.

The new creation of Revelation links with the original creation of Genesis

The last two chapters of Revelation clearly are linked, often by contrast, with the first three chapters of Genesis as follows:

Genesis	Revelation
"In the beginning God created the heavens and the earth" (Gen 1:1)	"I saw a new heaven and a new earth" (Rev 21:1)
"The darkness He called night" (Gen 1:5)	"There will be no night there" (Rev 21:25; 22:5)
"The gathering of the waters He called seas" (Gen 1:10)	"There is no longer any sea" (Rev 21:1)
"Let there be lights in the expanse of the heavens . . . to give light on the earth" (Gen 1:14–15)	"The city has no need of the sun or of the moon to shine on it" (Rev 21:23; 22:5)
"In the day that you eat from it you will surely die" (Gen 2:17)	"There will no longer be any death" (Rev 21:4)
"The man and his wife hid themselves from the presence of the Lord God" (Gen 3:8)	"God Himself will be among them . . . they will see His face" (Rev 21:3; 22:4)
"I will greatly multiply your pain in childbirth" (Gen 3:16)	"There will no longer be any . . . pain" (Rev 21:4)
"Cursed is the ground because of you" (Gen 3:17)	"There will no longer be any curse" (Rev 22:3)

Sam Hamstra comments, "This obvious correlation between the first and last books of the Bible illustrates the fulfillment of the first messianic prophecy (Gen. 3:15) and God's faithfulness to the covenant (Rev. 21:3)."[101]

The new creation of Revelation surpasses the original creation of Genesis

That there is no more sea or night in the new heavens and new earth (Rev 21:1, 25) alludes to the original creation, which included both seas and night. Douglas Moo concludes by discussing the potentialities of the pre-consummate creation, how those potentialities played out in history, and how God brings the cosmos to an even greater glory than the original creation.

---

101. Hamstra, "Idealist View," 123. T. Desmond Alexander adds, "The very strong links between Genesis 1–3 and Revelation 20–22 suggests that these passages frame the entire biblical meta-story." Alexander, *From Eden*, 10.

The first creation, while good in itself, had had the potential to develop in two directions: if humankind fulfilled its role and lived in harmony with God and the rest of creation, the latent powers of chaos represented especially by the sea and darkness would be forever within the scope of human dominion and would become perhaps sources of creative energy and delight.... But if the covenant between God and his creatures was broken and human beings allied themselves with the serpent and its realm, the forces of chaos would be let loose and the sea become a thing of terror, an abode of evil and an instrument of judgement.[102]

Although humanity has largely chosen the second path, the book of Revelation is assuring us that we have not been abandoned by God to an eternity of sorrow, pain, and death. Instead, through Christ, the entire cosmos will be renewed. There will be no more sorrow, pain, or death. The original plan—that of extending the Garden of Eden throughout the entire world—not only will be realized but will be surpassed. The serpent and the "seed of the serpent" will be gone forever. We will be forever with the Lord; we *"will see His face"* (Rev 22:4); and *"we will be like Him, because we will see Him just as He is"* (1 John 3:2).

---

102. Moo, "Sea," 166–67.

3

Two Biblical Themes Concerning God's Relationship with Mankind

As we have seen so far, the Bible tells a coherent story, progressively revealed, of the relationship of God and humanity, with Jesus Christ at the heart of that story. The entire Bible is tied together, via important covenants and themes, from Genesis to Revelation. In addition to what we have discussed, two other overarching themes, that use similar imagery, link the Bible together from beginning to end. Those themes involve God's dwelling place with mankind and God's relationship with mankind expressed in terms of marriage. These themes show how God acts consistently with similar patterns. As such, they help us to understand the biblical storyline and reveal something about the nature and purposes of God.

GOD'S DWELLING PLACE WITH MANKIND

The biblical story of God's relationship with mankind begins with God's creating man and placing him in a garden (Genesis 1–3). It ends with a vision of *"a new heaven and a new earth"* (Rev 21:1), which Rev 21:2–3, 10 then immediately describe as "a city that is garden-like, in the shape of a temple."[1] As we will see, particularly with respect to our discussion of typology in chapter 7, God tends to follow certain patterns of action. This is reflected in the similar imagery we find concerning God's dwelling with mankind in the Garden of Eden, the tabernacle, the temple, and, ultimately,

---

1. Beale, *Temple*, 23.

the New Jerusalem. This imagery helps knit the biblical story together.[2] It demonstrates that the Bible describes the unfolding of a unified plan of God to dwell with his holy people (mankind) in a holy place (the earth).

The Garden of Eden[3]

The Garden of Eden had a number of features that are characteristic of sacred places, particularly of God's holy temples or dwelling places.

- The Garden was the unique place of God's presence (Gen 3:8).
- The Garden was an elevated location, possibly a mountain (see Ezek 28:14, 16), since from it flowed a river (Gen 2:10).
- The Garden was noted for its gold and precious stones, in addition to its abundant vegetation (Gen 2:11–17; 3:22; see Ezek 28:13).
- As originally created, Adam and Eve were holy (i.e., without sin).
- In Gen 2:15, God placed Adam in the Garden *"to cultivate it and keep it."* The Hebrew word for "cultivate" is *abad* (which also means "work" and "serve"). The Hebrew word for "keep" is *shamar* (which also means "guard" and "protect"). Those words "are found in combination elsewhere in the Pentateuch only in passages that describe the duties of the Levites in the sanctuary (cf. Num. 3:7–8; 8:26; 18:5–6)."[4]
- Eden was entered from the east and was guarded by cherubim (Gen 3:24). "Guard" in 3:24 is the same word (*shamar*) as "keep" in 2:15. The guarding function of the cherubim probably involved "keeping out the sinful and unclean, which suggests that Adam's original role stated in Genesis 2:15 likely entailed much more than cultivating the soil, but also 'guarding' the sacred space."[5]

One other aspect of Adam and Eve's role in the Garden is not directly stated but may be inferred: they were to extend the geographical boundaries of Eden until it covered the whole earth. That follows from God's blessing and command to Adam and Eve to *"be fruitful and multiply, and fill the earth, and subdue it"* (Gen 1:26–28). Human beings are uniquely created *"in the image of God"* (Gen 1:26–27). By spreading over the earth in obedience to

---

2. These themes are discussed in detail by G. K. Beale in *Temple* and T. D. Alexander in *From Eden*.

3. Genesis 2–3; see also Ezek 28:13–16.

4. Alexander, *From Eden*, 22–23.

5. Beale, *Temple*, 70.

God's command, people would be magnifying God's glory, by spreading his image, over the entire earth. "While Genesis 2 merely introduces the start of this process, the long-term outcome is the establishment of an arboreal temple-city where God and humanity coexist in perfect harmony . . . for God is interested in making the whole earth his residence by filling it with holy people."[6]

The Tabernacle[7]

The tabernacle was a special tent used by the Israelites as a special place for worship during their early history. When Israel wandered in the wilderness the tabernacle was moved with them from place to place (Exod 40:36–38). When the Israelites pitched camp in the wilderness, the tabernacle was to be in the center, with the tribes arrayed in a specific order on the four sides of the tabernacle (Numbers 2). The Levites were in charge of the tabernacle and all of its furnishings and camped around the tabernacle (Num 1:47–54). After the conquest of Canaan, the tabernacle was moved to Shiloh where it remained during the period of the judges (Josh 5:10–11; 18:1). Later the tabernacle was located at Nob (1 Sam 21:1–6) and Gibeon (1 Kgs 3:4). When the temple was completed, Solomon had the tabernacle moved to Jerusalem (1 Kgs 8:4), where it apparently had no further use.

The design of the tabernacle was given by God to Moses on Mount Sinai when God also gave Moses the Ten Commandments and the other laws (Exod 25–30).

- *The Outer Courtyard.* The tabernacle had an outer courtyard with a fence around it approximately 150 feet long by 75 feet wide (Exod 27:9–19). The outer courtyard contained a bronze altar for animal sacrifices (Exod 27:1–8) and a laver where the priests washed before entering the tent itself (Exod 30:17–21).

- *The Tabernacle itself.* The tabernacle itself was a tent approximately 45 feet long by 15 feet wide; it had two main sections: the outer room, known as the Holy Place, and the inner room, known as the Holy of Holies (Exod 26:33). The Holy Place contained an altar where incense was burned (Exod 30:1–10); a seven-branched gold candlestick (Exod 25:31–40); and a table for showbread, signifying the presence of God (Exod 25:23–30). The Holy of Holies was a cube measuring 10x10x10

---

6. Alexander, *From Eden*, 25–26, 29.
7. Exodus 25–31, 35–40.

cubits (about 15x15x15 feet) in size.⁸ It was separated from the Holy Place by a veil or curtain (Exod 26:31-37). The Holy of Holies contained the *"ark of the covenant"* (Exod 25:10-15), which was also called the *"ark of the testimony,"* because in it was placed the stone tablets with the Ten Commandments written on them (i.e., "the testimony").⁹ On top of the ark of the covenant was a lid called the *"mercy seat"* made of gold with two gold cherubim which faced each other (Exod 25:17-22). Placed in front of the ark were a pot of manna (Exod 16:31-36), a portion of Moses' incense (Exod 30:36), Aaron's rod that budded (Num 17:8-11), and a copy of the book of the law written by Moses when he commissioned Joshua to bring the sons of Israel into the promised land (Deut 31:24-26; see also Heb 9:3-4).

Like the Garden of Eden, the tabernacle had several features that denoted its special and holy status as God's dwelling place:

- The tabernacle was God's special dwelling place on the earth. "Tabernacle" itself means "dwelling" or "dwelling place." The cloud of God's glory (the "Shekinah") filled the tabernacle and remained with it (Exod 40:34-38; Num 9:15-23). Moses met regularly with God at the tabernacle, which was called the "tent of meeting."[10]

- The ark of the covenant in the Holy of Holies (Exod 25:33) represents the unseen, heavenly reality. The ark of the covenant was called God's "footstool" (1 Chron 28:2; see also Pss 99:5; 132:7). That indicates that God's real throne is in heaven and is not confined to the tabernacle, but it also links heaven and earth or extends the heavenly throne to earth.

- The Cherubim on the mercy seat (Exod 25:18-22) represent the heavenly creatures that guard God's true, heavenly throne.[11] The cherubim recall the cherubim which God placed to *"guard the way to the tree of life"* (Gen 3:24).

The tabernacle had several other features which recalled the Garden of Eden:

- The instructions for the design of the tabernacle and the priests' garments were given to Moses on a mountain (Exod 24:18—25:1, 40).

---

8. Josephus, *Antiquities*, 3.122.
9. Exod 25:16, 22; 40:20; Deut 10:1-5; 1 Kgs 8:9; 2 Chron 5:10.
10. Exod 25:22; 27:21; 28:43; 29:4; 40:2; Lev 1:1; 3:2; Num 1:1; 2:2.
11. See Isa 6:1-6; Ezek 10:1-22; Rev 4:5-9.

- The tabernacle and its furnishings included large amounts of gold and silver (the mercy seat and the lampstand were each made of pure gold).[12]
- The seven-branched lampstand was designed to resemble a tree, possibly the tree of life (Exod 25:31–37).
- Only consecrated priests from the tribe of Levi were permitted to "serve and guard" in the tabernacle itself.[13] The high priest's garments included gold and precious stones (Exod 28:6–30). Later, only the high priest was permitted to enter the Holy of Holies, once per year on the Day of Atonement, following a specified ritual, to make atonement for the sins of the nation before God (Leviticus 16).
- The entrance to the tabernacle was on the east (Exod 38:13–19).
- The tabernacle (and later the temple) was an earthly "shadow" or "copy" of heaven itself.[14] First century Jewish historian Josephus writes that every aspect of the tabernacle was made to imitate and represent the universe,[15] which "conveys the idea that the whole earth is to become God's dwelling place."[16] The layout of the tabernacle was "an imitation of the system of the world," with one veil "embroidered with all sorts of flowers which the earth produces," and other curtains "seemed not at all to differ from the color of the sky."[17] Josephus adds that the colors of the veils signified the "four elements" (air, earth, fire, water), as did the colors and composition of the priests' garments.[18]

The Temple[19]

John Walton notes that "temples in the ancient world were considered symbols of the cosmos."[20] The cosmos itself can be viewed as something like a

---

12. Exod 25:17–18, 31; 38:24–28.
13. Exodus 29; Num 3:5–10; 8:1–26; 18:5–6.
14. Heb 8:1–5; 9:23–24; Rev 15:5.
15. Josephus, *Antiquities*, 3:180; see also Alexander, *From Eden*, 37–40 regarding the tabernacle as a microcosm or model of the cosmos.
16. Alexander, *From Eden*, 42.
17. Josephus, *Antiquities*, 3.123, 126, 132.
18. Josephus, *Antiquities*, 3.179–87.
19. 2 Sam 7:1–17; 1 Kings 6; 8:1–11; 1 Chron 17:1–15; 22:1–16; 28:1—29:9; 2 Chronicles 3–5.
20. Walton, *Lost World*, 78.

temple.[21] The temple was designed to be a permanent dwelling place for God on the earth and in many respects paralleled the Garden of Eden and the tabernacle. The temple became the center of ancient Judaism, was one of the most magnificent buildings in the ancient world, and was the sole place of sacrifice.[22] The interior of the temple followed the pattern of the tabernacle, with a Holy Place and a Holy of Holies.[23] The Holy of Holies was a perfect cube: 20x20x20 cubits (about 30x30x30 feet) in size.[24] The Holy Place and the Holy of Holies were separated by a great veil (2 Chron 3:14).

There are several commonalities between the temple, the Garden of Eden, and the tabernacle:

- The cloud of God's presence filled the temple just as it had filled the tabernacle.[25] The ark of the covenant was placed in the Holy of Holies (1 Kgs 8:1–9; 2 Chron 5:1–10). In the Holy of Holies were two cherubim overlaid with gold whose wings touched the walls and met in the middle (1 Kgs 6:23–28; 2 Chron 3:10–13).

- The temple was built on the top of Mount Moriah ("Zion") where God had told Abraham to sacrifice Isaac (Gen 22:2; 2 Chron 3:1). Thus, in

---

21. See Walton, *Lost World*, 71–91.

22. 1 Kgs 3:2; 1 Chron 28:1—29:22. The temple was destroyed by the Babylonians in 586 BC (2 Kgs 25:1–21; 2 Chron 36:11–21; Psalm 79; Jer 32:28–44; Lamentations). Before the Babylonians destroyed the temple, the cloud of God's glory and presence left it (Ezek 9:3; 10:1–19; 11:22–23). After the exile in Babylon, a temple was rebuilt by Zerubbabel in 515 BC (Ezra 3–6; Haggai 1–2; Zechariah 2–4); that temple was reconstructed under Herod the Great beginning in 20 BC. The interior dimensions and design of the temple (i.e., the Holy Place and the Holy of Holies), as well as the veils, followed the pattern of Solomon's temple. However, Herod greatly expanded the overall size of the temple. It was 100 cubits (about 150 feet) high. Herod also massively expanded the size of the temple courts, which were outside of the building itself. "Temple, the Second," *Jewish Encyclopedia*, n.p. The temple as reconstructed by Herod is the temple that was in existence when Jesus was on the earth. Although the temple itself had been rebuilt, it lacked its most important ingredient: the presence of God. The Bible never says that the glory of the Lord filled the rebuilt temple as he had filled the tabernacle and Solomon's temple. "According to the Babylonian Talmud (Yoma 22b), the Second Temple lacked five things which had been in Solomon's Temple, namely, the Ark, the sacred fire, the Shekinah, the Holy Spirit, and the Urim and Thummim." "Temple of Herod," *Jewish Encyclopedia*, n.p. As a result, the Holy of Holies was empty. Herod's temple was completely destroyed by the Romans in AD 70, just as Jesus said would happen.

23. 1 Kgs 6:16–20; 2 Chron 3:3–8.

24. 1 Kgs 6:20; 2 Chron 3:8.

25. 1 Kgs 8:10–11; 2 Chron 5:11–14; 7:1–2.

a special way the temple and, more generally, Jerusalem and Mount Zion, were said to be God's dwelling place.[26]

- The entire building was overlaid with gold and adorned with precious stones.[27] The Holy of Holies was overlaid with pure gold (1 Kgs 6:20; 2 Chron 3:8). Some associated the splendor of the gold in the temple with God's presence.[28]

- Throughout the temple and its furnishings were garden-like carvings of cherubim, palm trees, and flowers.[29] Lilies and pomegranates decorated the tops of the pillars.[30]

- The main entrance to the temple was the eastern gate, called the "Beautiful Gate."[31]

- First century Jewish historian Josephus saw mystical significance in the veil of the temple (he was writing about the temple that existed in Jesus' time, but that was based on the plan of the temple given to Solomon). The large veil "was a kind of image of the universe. . . . This curtain had also embroidered upon it all that was mystical in the heavens, excepting that of the [twelve] signs, representing living creatures."[32] That suggests that the OT temple was a small model of the entire heaven and earth. Heb 8:1—10:1 similarly suggests that the tabernacle and temple were *"shadows"* or *"copies"* of the real heavenly things.

- The presence of the temple in Jerusalem may be related to the land of Israel being compared to the Garden of Eden.[33]

---

26. Pss 48:1–3, 12–14; 78:68; 84:1–7; 87:1–7; 132:13–14.

27. 1 Kgs 6:20–35; 1 Chron 29:1–8; 2 Chron 3:4–10.

28. See Josephus, *Antiquities*, 3.187.

29. 1 Kgs 6:18, 29, 32, 35; 7:24–26, 49–50.

30. 1 Kgs 7:15–22, 42; 2 Chron 3:15–16.

31. Edersheim, *Temple*, 47; see Acts 3:2, 10.

32. Josephus, *Wars*, 5.212–14; see Exod 26:31; 2 Chron 3:14. Levenson discusses other aspects of the temple that had cosmic symbolism and holds that "the Temple in Jerusalem was indeed conceived as a microcosm" of heaven and earth. Levenson, *Creation and the Persistence*, 78–99; see especially 90–99. See also Alexander, *From Eden*, 40–42 regarding the temple as a model or microcosm of the cosmos.

33. See Gen 13:10; Isa 51:3; Ezek 36:35; Joel 2:3.

The New Heavens and the New Earth, i.e., New Jerusalem (Revelation 21–22)

The New Jerusalem is the consummation of God's eternal plan to dwell in a holy place with his holy people that had been foreshadowed by the Garden, the tabernacle, and the temple:[34]

- The entirety of New Jerusalem is a Holy of Holies. Just like the Holy of Holies (1 Kgs 6:16–20; 2 Chron 3:8), the city is a perfect cube (Rev 21:16). Just as the Holy of Holies was overlaid with pure gold (1 Kgs 6:16–20; 2 Chron 3:8), *"the city was pure gold, like clear glass"* (Rev 21:18). Just as the Holy of Holies was the special place of God's presence and glory, the city is now the place of God's presence and glory (Rev 21:22–23; 22:1, 3–5). Only the Holy of Holies, not the other sections of Israel's temple, is found in Revelation 21. The reason is that God's special presence, which formerly was limited to the Holy of Holies, now encompasses all of his new creation.

- New Jerusalem consummates and surpasses the Holy of Holies with respect to our access to God. Only holy Adam and Eve could be in Eden, and only the high priest could enter the Holy of Holies. In New Jerusalem, all of God's people are without sin, are present, and will serve and reign with the Lord forever (Rev 21:7–8, 27; 22:3–5). On the Day of Atonement—the only day when the high priest could enter the Holy of Holies—the high priest had to offer incense which formed a thick cloud that covered the mercy seat so that he could not see God's glorious appearance or he would die (Lev 16:13; see Exod 33:20). In New Jerusalem, all of God's people will *"see his face"* (Rev 22:4). In the church as it now exists, we have unlimited access to God our Father, through Jesus Christ (Matt 27:51; Heb 10:19–22). In New Jerusalem, we not only will have direct access to God, but we will always be in his immediate presence (Rev 21:3–4, 22–23; 22:3–5). In Rev 3:12, Jesus

---

34. Revelation 21 suggests that *"New Jerusalem"* IS the *"new earth,"* not just a portion of it. John begins by describing *"a new heaven and a new earth"* (Rev 21:1) but then immediately describes *"the holy city, new Jerusalem"* (Rev 21:2–3; 10—22:5). John's focus from Rev 21:2 on is on the city, not anything outside of it or in addition to it. Throughout the Bible, God's "throne" is said to be in heaven (see 1 Kgs 22:19; 2 Chron 18:18; Ps 103:19; Isa 6:1; 66:1; Matt 5:34; 23:22; Acts 7:49; Heb 8:1; Rev 4:2–10; 5:1–13; 6:16; 7:9–15; 8:3; 12:5; 14:3–5; 16:17; 19:4–5; 20:11). In Rev 22:1–3 God's throne is said to be in the New Jerusalem. Thus, New Jerusalem appears to be equivalent to heaven which has now come to earth. The equivalence of the "new heaven and new earth" with the "New Jerusalem" in Revelation 21 also is indicated by the parallel use of those terms in Isaiah 65–66.

promised, *"He who overcomes, I will make him a pillar in the temple of My God."* This means that "the saints are honored within that heavenly temple, which in fact is nothing less than the very presence of God. . . . In short, the expression 'temple' must be interpreted figuratively. God intends to honor his people in his sacred presence."[35]

Other features of New Jerusalem show that it consummates the concepts which the Garden, the tabernacle, and the temple foreshadowed:

- Just as God *"walked in the garden"* (Gen 3:8) and filled the Holy of Holies in the tabernacle and the temple with his presence, so in New Jerusalem *"the tabernacle of God is among men, and he will dwell among them, and they shall be his people, and God Himself will be among them"* (Rev 21:3).

- Just as God himself had *"planted a garden"* in Eden (Gen 2:8) and gave the plans for the tabernacle and temple which corresponded to heavenly realities, so New Jerusalem *"comes down [to the renewed and restored earth] out of heaven from God"* (Rev 21:10; see also Rom 8:18–21).

- Just as Eden, the tabernacle, and the temple were characterized by their gold and precious stones, so New Jerusalem is characterized by its gold and precious stones (Rev 21:18–22).

- Just as Eden, the tabernacle, and the temple were characterized by their vegetation (or garden-like images of vegetation), so New Jerusalem is characterized by its fruit trees (Rev 22:2).

- Just as Eden had the tree of life, so New Jerusalem has the tree of life (Rev 22:2).

- Just as Eden was the source of a river, so New Jerusalem has *"a river of the water of life, clear as crystal, coming from the throne of God and of the Lamb"* (Rev 21:6; 22:1).

- Just as the high priest in the tabernacle and temple wore an engraving *"Holy to the Lord"* on his forehead (Exod 28:36–38), so in New Jerusalem all of God's people will have *"His name on their foreheads"* (Rev 22:4).

- Just as in Eden before the Fall into sin there was no death, sorrow, or pain, so in New Jerusalem there is no more curse, death, sorrow, or pain (Rev 21:4; 22:3).

---

35. Kistemaker, "Temple," 434.

GOD'S RELATIONSHIP WITH HIS PEOPLE IN TERMS OF MARRIAGE

Throughout the Bible, sexual immorality and infidelity are equated with spiritual infidelity (forsaking God to pursue other gods and ungodly practices) and *vice versa*.[36]

Gen 2:24 is a paradigm which describes the relationship God desires to have with his people

Man was to *"leave his father and his mother, and be joined to his wife; and they shall become one flesh"* in marriage (Gen 2:24). Adam and Eve originally walked in unity and harmony with each other and with God in the Garden of Eden. Sin severed the harmonious union between people and God. God's plan of redemption, as it is unfolded throughout the rest of the Bible, is designed to restore a perfect, harmonious marital union between God and his people. Thus, Jesus "left his father" (see Phil 2:6–8) in order to restore the perfect union between God and his people in the relationship between Christ and his bride, the church.

In the OT, God's marital bond with his people is implied, but Israel was unfaithful

Throughout the OT, Israel essentially was unfaithful to God, both before and after it entered the promised land, before and after it had a king, and both when the kingdom was united and divided. Israel's relationship with God is characterized essentially as "playing the harlot with other gods."[37] To "play the harlot" with other gods is to "cultivate a relationship with them, to render them one's obedience and devotion, to walk in their ways and pursue their ideals . . . the imagery is sexual . . . because the larger controlling motif is marital."[38] The specific forms of Israel's harlotry included the shedding of innocent blood, following Canaanite religious practices, economic self-sufficiency, lack of concern for the poor, and the search for political security in the policies of realpolitik (alliances with Egypt and Assyria) instead of

---

36. See, e.g., Jer 3:6–10; Ezek 16:15–22; Hos 2:2; 4:12; Mal 2:13–16; 1 Cor 6:15–18; Jas 4:4; Rev 2:18–22; 14:8; 17:1–5; 18:1–3; 19:1–2.

37. See, e.g., Exod 32:1–6; 34:11–16; Lev 17:3–7; 20:4–6; Num 15:38–40; Deut 31:14–21; Judg 2:16–17; 8:22–35; Ps 50:18; Prov 6:26–32; 7:1–27; 30:20; Isa 1:21–23; 57:1–13; Jeremiah 2–3; Ezekiel 16, 23; Hos 1–2; 11:1–11; 14:1–9; Mic 1:1–7.

38. Ortland, *God's Unfaithful Wife*, 32.

obedience to God (Hos 4:1—10:15). Despite Israel's adulteries against God and the punishment he would bring, he nevertheless recounted his great faithfulness and love to her, yearned for her repentance, and held open the hope of future restoration (Hos 2:1-3, 14-23; 11:1-11; 14:1-9).

In the NT, the marital theme is extended and made specific in Christ and the church

Both John the Baptist and Christ himself specifically identify Jesus as *"the bridegroom."*[39] The OT image of Yahweh's being married to his people is applied in the NT to Jesus himself.

The NT epistles make the "marriage" theme explicit, specifically apply it to the church, and reinforce the connection with Gen 2:24.[40] The bridegroom has sanctified his bride and *"cleansed her by the washing of water with the word, so that he might present to himself the church in all her glory, having no spot or wrinkle or any such thing; but that she would be holy and blameless"* (Eph 5:26-27). Paul concludes by quoting Gen 2:24 and then states, *"This mystery is great; but I am speaking with reference to Christ and the church"* (Eph 5:32).

Jesus and the NT writers compare rejection of Jesus to "adultery."[41] In this regard, 1 Cor 6:15-20 describes the deep spiritual significance of actual physical, sexual immorality. A person who *"joins himself to a prostitute is one body"* with the prostitute (v. 16), but a person who *"joins himself to the Lord is one spirit"* with the Lord (v. 17). By using the same wording in both verses, Paul is telling us what a great *spiritual abomination* sexual sin is. Christians have been united with Christ in the ultimate (*"one spirit"*) union, i.e., Christ, through the Holy Spirit, actually dwells in our bodies (v. 19), and *"we are members of his body"* (Eph 5:30). By sinning sexually, a believer forms a monstrous union between Christ and a prostitute. Instead, we are to *"glorify God in your body"* (1 Cor 6:20) by *"presenting your bodies a living and holy sacrifice, acceptable to God, which is your spiritual service of worship"* (Rom 12:1). In short, what we do with our bodies shows what we really think of Christ.

---

39. Matt 9:14-15; Mark 2:18-20; Luke 5:33-35; John 3:28-30.
40. See, e.g., 2 Cor 11:1-3; Eph 5:29-32.
41. Matt 12:38-39; 16:1-4; Mark 8:38; Jas 4:4; Rev 17:5.

In Revelation, the Bible's marital imagery for God's relationship with his people is brought to consummation in Christ, his bride (the church), and New Jerusalem

Revelation contrasts the bride of Christ and the harlot of the world. The bride is clothed *"in fine linen, bright and clean; for the fine linen is the righteous acts of the saints"* (Rev 19:8); the "Mother of Harlots" is dressed as a harlot (Rev 17:4; 18:16). The harlot is judged and destroyed (Rev 17:1), but the bride of the Lamb is exalted (Rev 21:9).

In Rev 19:5–9 the *"marriage supper of the Lamb"* occurs. In Rev 19:7–8 the bride is the saints, i.e., the church. New Jerusalem is compared with *"a bride adorned for her husband"* (Rev 21:2). The identification of the bride with New Jerusalem is made virtually explicit in Rev 21:9 where the angel says, *"Come here, I will show you the bride, the wife of the Lamb,"* and then in v. 10 immediately it says, *"And he carried me away in the Spirit to a great and high mountain, and showed me the holy city, Jerusalem, coming down out of heaven from God."* New Jerusalem is so closely identified with the people of God that it may be a metaphor for God's people and his relationship with them. Consequently, just as Jesus and the church *are* the new, true temple, so the descriptions of the New Jerusalem are more "personal than topographical," describing God's people and his relationship with them, as opposed to being a description of the new geography that will exist after Christ comes again.[42] "The dwelling of God with man *in the form of a city* may . . . suggest the perfect social union of the redeemed with one another as God's final and eternal answer to the successive societal failures littering the course of human history."[43] Revelation 21–22 thus concludes the biblical storyline by describing the everlasting and perfect marital relationship between Christ and his bride, the church.

---

42. Gundry, "New Jerusalem," 256.
43. Ortland, *God's Unfaithful Wife*, 166n.73.

4

Christ in the Old Testament: Pre-Incarnate Appearances of Christ

THERE IS ONLY ONE God, but God is Trinity—God the Father, God the Son, God the Holy Spirit—one God in three persons.[1] Although the identity of God the Son—Jesus Christ—is only made explicit in the NT as a result of his incarnation, he is present in pre-incarnate form even in the OT.

THE LORD

Most of the references to God in the OT do not distinguish the persons of the Trinity. However, in several OT passages where God is referred to as the "Lord," NT writers and Jesus himself clarify that the "Lord" actually referred to Jesus Christ.

In Gen 18:1–33, "the Lord" appeared to Abraham to announce that he was planning on destroying the city of Sodom. This could not have been God the Father, since no one has seen the Father (John 1:18; 6:46; 1 Tim 6:10). Further, and no one can see him and live (Exod 33:20; 1 Tim 6:16). However, Abraham *did* see "the Lord" and live. Consequently, "the Lord" undoubtedly was God the Son in pre-incarnate form.[2]

---

1. The concept of the Trinity is fleshed out in Appendix 2: The Trinity.

2. Since God is Trinity, one might ask whether or not "the Lord" or "the Angel of the Lord" (see the discussion below concerning "the Angel of the Lord") could be the Holy Spirit. There are five reasons why the answer to that is "no." First, although the Spirit has a number of roles, one of his primary roles is that *"He will glorify Me [Jesus], for He will take of Mine and will disclose it to you"* (John 16:14). He began doing this when he took the form of a dove when Jesus was baptized (Matt 3:16; Mark 1:10; Luke 3:22; John

"Lord" or "the Lord" are referred to repeatedly throughout Exodus 13-14, and 34. Exod 13:21 (*"The Lord was going before them in a pillar of cloud by day to lead them on the way, and in a pillar of fire by night to give them light"*) is identified with "the Angel of the Lord," since Exod 14:19 tells us it was "the Angel of Lord" who *"had been going before the camp of Israel, moved and went behind them; and the pillar of cloud moved from before them and stood behind them."* As discussed below, "the Angel of the Lord" undoubtedly is a pre-incarnate appearance of Christ. Similarly, "the Lord," who appears on Mount Sinai with Moses in Exodus 34, is another pre-incarnate appearance of Christ. This is so because Exod 34:5 repeats the same identification of "the Lord" found in Exodus 14 and tells us, *"The Lord descended in the cloud."* That verse goes on to say that he *"stood there with him as he called upon the name of the Lord."*

Paul discusses the events of Exodus 34 in 2 Cor 3:7-18, particularly how Moses's face shone when he came down from Mount Sinai such that he had to cover it with a veil (see Exod 34:29-35). Paul contrasts the "glory" of the Old, Mosaic Covenant with the infinitely greater glory of the New Covenant in Christ (2 Cor 2:7-9, 12-13, 18). The "glory" upon Moses's face was the result of his seeing and being in the presence of the Lord, i.e., Jesus Christ. In 2 Cor 4:6, Paul makes explicit that *"the glory of the Lord"* refers to Christ: *"For God, who said, 'Light shall shine out of darkness,' is the One who has shone in our hearts to give the Light of the knowledge of the glory of God in the face of Christ."* That is reiterating what had previously been said in John 1:14, *"And the Word became flesh, and dwelt among us, and we saw His glory, glory as of the only begotten from the Father, full of grace and truth."*

1:32-33). The Holy Spirit is not said to have taken corporeal form on any other occasion and never is said to have assumed the form of a man, as did the Son. It is Jesus who is described as *"the image of the invisible God"* (Col 1:15), *"the exact representation of His nature"* (Heb 1:3), and who has explained or revealed the Father (John 1:18). Thus, it is Jesus' role, not that of the Father or the Holy Spirit, to appear in corporeal form to people, especially in corporeal form as a human being. Second, the Holy Spirit never speaks of the particular reason why he is sent, but "the Lord," "the Angel of the Lord," and Jesus do reveal the nature of their mission (see, e.g., Gen 18:10-21; Exod 3:8; John 6:38). Third, Mal 3:1, which prophesies the coming of Jesus, calls him *"the messenger* [i.e., "angel"; Hebrew = *mal'āk*; Greek = *angelos*] *of the covenant."* Fourth, both "the Angel of the Lord" and Jesus share a descriptive name in common, i.e., "wonderful" (Judg 13:18; Isa 9:6). Fifth, after Jesus became incarnate in the NT, he calls himself, and is called by others, "Lord"; "the Angel of the Lord" never appears or is referred to again. In other words, once God the Son appeared as flesh, there was no longer a need for him to appear in any other form except as himself. Hence, it is fair to say that "the Lord" and "the Angel of the Lord" refer to the pre-incarnate Christ who appeared on several occasions for different reasons in the OT.

In Num 12:1–14, Miriam and Aaron spoke against Moses for having married an Ethiopian woman. Then, as in Exod 13:21; 14:19; and 34:5, *"the Lord came down in a pillar of cloud"* and, as in Exod 34:5, he *"stood at the doorway of the tent."* He then rebuked Miriam and Aaron and said that he would speak to Moses *"mouth to mouth"* so that *"he beholds the form of the Lord"* (Num 12:8). The Septuagint of Num 12:8 says *"he has seen the glory of the Lord."*[3] That same wording, *"he saw His glory,"* is used in John 12:41 to refer to Isaiah's vision of "the Lord" in Isaiah 6, whom John identifies as Christ. That "the Lord" in Numbers 12 is Christ is clear not only from the same identification markers as found in Exodus 13, 14, and 34 and John's allusion to Num 12:8, but also from the fact that Moses was able to *"behold the form of the Lord,"* yet did not die (Exod 33:20; John 1:18; 6:46; 1 Tim 6:16).

Second Chron 36:15–16 says, *"The Lord, the God of their fathers, sent word to them again and again by His messengers,"* but the people continually mocked the prophets and despised God's words. Jesus alludes to this and says, *"I am sending you prophets and wise men and scribes,"* but you scourge and persecute and kill them (Matt 23:34).

Ps 45:6–7 says, *"Your throne, O God, is forever and ever; a scepter of righteousness is the scepter of your kingdom. You have loved righteousness and hated wickedness; therefore God, Your God, has anointed you."*[4] Heb 1:8–9 quotes that and applies it to Jesus.

Ps 101:26–27 (LXX) says, *"In the beginning thou, O Lord, didst lay the foundation of the earth; and the heavens are the works of thine hands. They shall perish, but thou remainest: and [they all] shall wax old as a garment."* Heb 1:10–11 quotes that and applies it to Jesus.

Ps 110:1 says, *"The Lord says to my Lord: 'Sit at My right hand Until I make Your enemies a footstool for Your feet.'"* Ps 110:1 is quoted in Matt 22:44; Mark 12:36; Luke 20:42–43; and Acts 2:34–35 and applied to Jesus. Ps 110:1b is quoted in Heb 1:13 and applied to Jesus.

Isa 6:1–13 is a vision of God's glory. Isa 6:1 talks about the "Lord" sitting on a throne in the temple of heaven. In Isa 6:8 the "Lord" says, *"Who will go for us?"* In Isa 6:9–10, Isaiah is commissioned to go to the people but to render them insensitive so that they will not understand and be healed. John 12:39–41 quotes Isa 6:10 and comments, *"These things Isaiah said because he saw His [Jesus'] glory, and he spoke of Him [Jesus]."*

---

3. The Septuagint, also known as the LXX, is the Greek translation of the Hebrew Bible (the OT), which was completed approximately 132 BC. It was often used by the early church.

4. The typical Hebrew word for "Lord" is *adonai*. In Ps 45:6–7, the typical word for "God," *elohim*, is used.

Isa 8:12–13 (LXX) talks about not fearing people, but *"sanctify ye the Lord himself; and he shall be thy fear."* 1 Pet 3:14–15 quotes this passage but says *"sanctify Christ as Lord in your hearts."*

Isa 28:16 (LXX), says, *"Whoever believes in him will not be disappointed."* Rom 10:11 quotes that and applies it to Jesus.

Joel 2:32 (Joel 3:5 LXX) says, *"Whoever calls on the name of the Lord will be saved."* Rom 10:13 quotes that and applies it to faith in Christ.

THE ANGEL OF THE LORD OR THE ANGEL OF GOD[5]

Apart from referring to angels in general, the OT speaks of "the Angel of the Lord." The title is definite—it is *"the* Angel of the Lord," not *"an* Angel of the Lord." This indicates something particular and special about this being. That is corroborated by the fact that, although the Bible speaks of angels, it never uses the plural "Angels of the Lord."

On some occasions "the Angel of the Lord" is identified as God or receives worship as God;[6] on other occasions, "the Angel of the Lord" appears to be distinguished from God.[7] These passages, therefore, "warrant saying that while there is only one God, in some sense there is plurality in the Godhead."[8] This "plurality in the Godhead" refers to the Trinity: there is only one God, but he is in three persons, Father, Son, and Holy Spirit. The phrase "the Angel of the Lord" does not express a relationship of *possession*, i.e., "the Angel is the Lord's." Rather, the two nouns ("Angel" and "Lord") being brought together in this way express a relationship of *identification*, i.e., "the Angel which is the Lord" or "the Angel which is to be identified as the Lord." It is like saying "the city of Jerusalem," which does not mean that the city belongs to Jerusalem but "the city which is Jerusalem."[9] The Hebrew word "angel" (*mal'āk*) essentially means "messenger."[10] Thus, the term "Angel" is used of him because of his role or function.[11] In the OT, "the Angel of the Lord" appeared in different forms:

---

5. The designation is abbreviated to "the Angel" in Gen 48:15–16 and Hos 12:3–4, "My Angel" in Exod 23:20, and "his Angel" in Dan 3:28.

6. Gen 16:7–13; 22:11–16; 31:11–13; Exod 3:2–6; Judg 13:6–22; Isa 63:9 (*"the angel of His presence"*).

7. Num 22:22–35; Judg 13:8–9.

8. Feinberg, *No One*, 453; see also Clowney, *Preaching Christ*, 12–13.

9. See Lunn, *Jesus in the Jewish*, 169–70.

10. Koehler and Baumgartner, *Hebrew and Aramaic Lexicon*, "*mal'āk*," 585–86.

11. See Lunn, *Jesus in the Jewish*, 170.

In Gen 16:7–13, "the Angel of the Lord" appeared to Hagar in the wilderness after Hagar had fled from Sarai. This incident indicates the identification of "the Angel of the Lord" with the Lord God himself in the person of Jesus Christ. The Angel told Hagar to return to Sarai and said *"I will greatly multiply your descendants so that they will be too many to count."* That echoes what God had told Abram in Gen 15:5. The Angel also told Sarai what would become of her son Ishmael, thus indicating that he had the Godlike ability to know the future. The episode concludes by saying, *"Then she called the name of the Lord who spoke to her, 'You are a God who sees'; for she said, 'Have I even remained alive here after seeing Him?'"* (Gen 16:13) Hagar recognized that it was God who had been speaking to her: the Hebrew says that she called the name YHWH who was speaking to her (the Hebrew word translated "spoke" is a participle).

After Sarah gave birth to Isaac, Gen 21:9–19 repeats the events that had taken place in Gen 16:7–13. In Gen 21:17–18, "the Angel of God" called to Hagar, and told her not to fear, *"for God has heard the voice of the lad . . . [and] I will make a great nation of him."* Thus, as had been the case with "the Angel of the Lord" in Genesis 16, "the Angel of God" is here identified with God.

In Gen 22:9–18, "the Angel of the Lord" twice speaks to Abraham, first when he is about to sacrifice his son Isaac and again after Abraham names the place "The Lord will provide." The Angel clearly is identified with God, since in v. 12 he says *"you have not withheld your son . . . from Me,"* obviously referring to God, and in vv. 15–16, the Angel says, *"By Myself I have sworn, declares the Lord."*

In Gen 31:11, "the Angel of God" appeared to Jacob when he was fleeing from Laban. In Gen 31:13, the Angel identifies himself as *"the God of Bethel, where you anointed a pillar, where you made a vow to me."*

In Gen 32:24–32, the night before Jacob was to be reunited with his brother Esau, Jacob wrestled with a man until daybreak. The man touched the socket of Jacob's thigh, crippling him. Jacob asked that the man bless him, so he blessed him and also changed Jacob's name to Israel (which means "he who strives with God, or God strives"), telling Jacob, *"Your name shall no longer be Jacob, but Israel; for you have striven with God and with men and have prevailed"* (Gen 32:28). Hos 12:3–4 says that the man was *"the angel"* and that Jacob had *"contended with God."* Jacob concluded, *"I have seen the face of God, yet my life has been preserved"* (Gen 32:30). Thus, "the Angel" is equated with God come to earth as a man.

In Gen 48:15–16, when Jacob is blessing Joseph's sons, he said, *"The God before whom my fathers Abraham and Isaac walked, the God who has been my shepherd all my life to this day, the angel who has redeemed me from all evil, bless the lads."* Here, he is equating God and "the angel," and attributing to "the angel" the ability to redeem, which is the prerogative of God. As Nick Lunn points out, he is without question only calling upon a single divine person, "for the main verb (*yebārēk*, 'may *he* bless') that applies to both titles is singular in form."[12]

In Exod 3:2, "the Angel of the Lord" appeared to Moses as *"a blazing fire from the midst of a bush."* The Angel told Moses, *"Do not come near here; remove your sandals from your feet, for the place on which you are standing is holy ground"* (Exod 3:5). Only God's presence could make the ground "holy." The Angel also is called "the Lord," "God," and "I AM" in Exod 3:4, 6–7, 11, 13–15, and he always speaks in the first person, *"I am the God of your father, the God of Abraham, the God of Isaac, and the God of Jacob."*

In Exod 14:19, "the Angel of God," who *"had been going before the camp of Israel, moved and went behind them; and the pillar of cloud moved from before them and stood behind them."* Exod 13:21 identifies "the Angel of God" as the Lord, by saying, *"The Lord was going before them in a pillar of cloud by day to lead them on the way, and in a pillar of fire by night to give them light."*

In Exod 23:20, God promised to send *"My angel"* who bears *"My name"* to go before Israel *"to guard you along the way and to bring you into the place which I have prepared."* Moses is also told, *"Do not be rebellious toward him, for he will not pardon your transgression"* (v. 21). That also identifies the Angel as divine, since only God can forgive sins.

In Num 22:22–35, "the Angel of the Lord" appeared to the prophet Balaam, who had been hired by King Balak to curse the Israelites. When Balaam saw the Angel of the Lord, he *"bowed all the way to the ground,"* an evident sign of worship (Num 22:31). The Angel then told Balaam that he could continue his journey to Balak, but *"you shall speak only the word which I tell you"* (Num 22:35). Balaam then told Balak, *"The word that God puts in my mouth, that I shall speak"* (Num 22:38; see also Num 23:5, 12, 16, 26; 24:12–13).

In Judg 2:1–4 "the Angel of the Lord" appeared and rebuked Israel for having made a covenant with the people of the Promised Land instead of driving them out and tearing down their pagan altars. The Angel identifies himself as God by saying *"I brought you up out of Egypt"* (see Exod 20:2), by referring to *"My Covenant with you"* (see Gen 17:7–10; Lev 26:42–44; Deut 7:9), and telling them that they had not *"obeyed Me."*

In Judg 6:11–23 "the Angel of the Lord" appeared to Gideon and commissioned Gideon to lead Israel against Midian. In Judg 6:11, 12, 21 he is

---

12. Lunn, *Jesus in the Jewish*, 167.

identified as "the Angel of the Lord"; in Judg 6:20 he is identified as "the Angel of God." The Angel is identified as "the Lord" in Judg 6:14-15, 23. Thus, they are all one and the same. When the Angel disappeared out of Gideon's sight, Gideon said, *"Alas, O Lord God! For now I have seen the angel of the Lord face to face"* (Judg 6:22). In reply, *"The Lord said to him, 'Peace to you, do not fear; you shall not die'"* (Judg 6:23). That is alluding to Exod 33:20. As discussed above regarding "the Lord," the Angel of the Lord is thus identified as the Lord in the person of Jesus Christ.

In Judg 13:2-23, "the Angel of the Lord" appeared to Manoah and his wife to announce the birth of Samson and instruct Samson's parents on how to care for the boy. After the Angel of the Lord stopped appearing to Manoah and his wife, Manoah said, *"We will surely die, for we have seen God"* (Judg 13:22). He is called "the Angel of the Lord" in Judg 13:3, 13, 15, 16, 17, 18, 20; he is called *"a man of God . . . [whose] appearance was like the appearance of the angel of God"* in Judg 13:6; and is called "the Angel of God" in Judg 13:9. Thus, the "angel of the Lord" and "the angel of God" are the same, and his appearance as "a man of God" indicates that he was Jesus Christ in pre-incarnate form.[13]

In 1 Kgs 19:7; 2 Kgs 1:3, 15, "the Angel of the Lord" met and spoke with the prophet Elijah. Elijah, of course, did not die, which indicates that the "Angel" was actually a pre-incarnate appearance of Jesus Christ.

In 1 Chron 21:9-30, David is offered a choice of punishments for having wrongfully taken a census, one of which being *"the Angel of the Lord destroying throughout all the territory of Israel"* (1 Chron 21:12). David identifies "the Angel of the Lord" as "the Lord" (1 Chron 21:13), and the text does likewise (1 Chron 21:14).[14]

Ps 34:7 says, *"The angel of the Lord encamps around those who fear Him, and rescues them."* This indicates that "the Angel of the Lord" must be omnipresent and, therefore, divine.

---

13. In 2 Sam 14:17, 20 and 19:27, King David's wisdom and his person as king are compared by people to "the Angel of God." Those comparisons evidently would be to God himself. They are the last references to "the Angel of God" in the Bible.

14. As noted in the introduction to this section, sometimes there appears to be a distinction between the Lord and "the Angel of the Lord." This episode is one of those occasions. Although 1 Chron 21:12-14 identifies the Angel of the Lord with the Lord, 1 Chron 21:18 has the Angel of the Lord commanding that David should build an altar *"to the Lord,"* and 1 Chron 21:27 says, *"The Lord commanded the angel, and he put his sword back in its sheath."* This same event is also recounted at 2 Sam 24:11-25. On the other hand, 1 Chron 21:15 says that *"the Angel of the Lord was standing on the threshing floor of Ornan the Jebusite."* 2 Chron 3:1 tells us that it was the Lord who had appeared to David on the threshing floor of Ornan the Jebusite. That confirms the identity of the Angel and the Lord.

Christ in the Old Testament: Pre-Incarnate Appearances of Christ

In Isa 63:7–14, the many mercies of the Lord to Israel are recounted. Isa 63:9 says that *"the Angel of His presence saved them."* It goes on to say that *"in His love and in His mercy he redeemed them."* These are all attributes of the Lord in the person of Jesus Christ.

In Daniel 3, King Nebuchadnezzar cast Shadrach, Meshach, and Abed-nego into the fiery furnace. However, in Dan 3:25, the king said, *"Look! I see four men loosed and walking about in the midst of the fire without harm, and the appearance of the fourth is like a son of the gods!"* Job 1:6; 2:1; 38:7 indicate that "sons of God" are angels. Although it is possible that the fourth man was an angel, it is more likely that the fourth man in the furnace was actually a pre-incarnate appearance of Jesus Christ. The phrase *"his angel"* is not simply "an angel," but is equivalent to "the Angel of the Lord," which refers to Christ.[15] James Montgomery observes that "the term 'angel' was appropriate to common [West Semitic] diction as expressing an appearance-form of Deity."[16] Stephen Miller similarly notes that "the expression 'a son of the gods' ascribes deity to the being, since an offspring of the gods partakes of his divine nature."[17] Further, *"a son of the gods"* grammatically can be rendered *"son of God,"* singular, since the Aramaic *elahin* is equivalent to the Hebrew *elohim*, which is the typical word for "God."[18] Even before Jesus became incarnate, "the Qumran community used this expression ("the Son of God") to refer to the coming Messiah."[19]

Although one might think that Nebuchadnezzar, as a pagan polytheist, would have intended the plural "gods," after Shadrach, Meshach, and Abed-nego were released unharmed from the furnace, he uses the singular when praising *"the God of Shadrach, Meshach and Abed-nego, who has sent His angel"* (Dan 3:28). In Dan 3:29 he further decreed that no one could speak against the God of Shadrach, Meshach, and Abed-nego, and said *"there is no other god who is able to deliver in this way."* In Dan 4:2–3 he called God *"the Most High God."* Thus, Nebuchadnezzar may have intended the singular use of "God" in Dan 3:25. If so, that identifies the fourth man in the furnace as Jesus Christ, since the only specific person referred to in the Bible as the "Son of God" is Jesus.[20] Since the fourth person in the furnace did take the

---

15. *"His angel"* is used again in Dan 6:22 as the evident agent who shut the lions' mouths when Daniel was in the lions' den, but nothing further is said of him.

16. Montgomery, *Critical*, 214.

17. Miller, *Daniel*, 123.

18. This was true in the Babylonian, Aramaic, and Hebrew use of the plural for the singular as referring to God. Montgomery, *Critical*, 214; see also Miller, *Daniel*, 123.

19. "(Dan 3:25) Who is," Response.

20. The one exception to this is in Jesus' genealogy in Luke, which goes back to the creation of Adam and concludes by stating that Jesus is *"the son of Seth, the son of Adam,*

form of a man, it seems likely that this was another pre-incarnate appearance of Christ.

In Zech 1:7–17, Zechariah had a vision and spoke with "the Angel of the Lord." "The Angel of the Lord" spoke with "the Lord of hosts," addressed him as such, and the Lord answered the Angel (Zech 1:12–13). This is akin to Zech 2:8–11 where "the Lord of hosts" says *"He has sent me against the nations"* and *"the Lord of hosts has sent me."* There, one named "Lord of hosts" sends another one named "Lord of hosts." Since there is only one God, this indicates plurality in the Godhead.[21]

In Zech 3:1–7, Joshua was the high priest when the temple in Jerusalem was being rebuilt after the Babylonian captivity. Zechariah was given a vision of Joshua standing before "the Angel of the Lord," with Satan standing at his right to accuse him. Verse 2 then says, *"The Lord said to Satan, 'The Lord rebuke you, Satan!'"* That identifies the Angel of the Lord with the Lord himself. Interestingly, the Lord uses the same words of rebuke that Michael the archangel used when rebuking the devil in Jude 9, when they were disputing over the body of Moses. It could therefore be argued that the Angel of the Lord in this instance was simply an angel, akin to Michael. On the other hand, the words, *"the Lord rebuke you"* could be taken as the intercession of God the Son with God the Father to rebuke Satan and protect Joshua. Zech 3:4 attributes the divine ability to forgive sins to the Angel of the Lord. In Zech 3:6–7 the Angel of the Lord admonishes Joshua, *"Thus says the Lord of hosts, 'If you will walk in My ways and if you will perform My service, then you will also govern My house and also have charge of My courts, and I will grant you free access among these who are standing here.'"*

Zechariah 12 contains a prophecy that Jerusalem will be attacked. Zech 12:8 refers to the Angel of the Lord and equates him with God: *"In that day the Lord will defend the inhabitants of Jerusalem, and the one who is feeble among them in that day will be like David, and the house of David will be like God, like the angel of the Lord before them."*

In all the above cases, for the reasons stated, "the Angel of the Lord" could not have been God the Father or God the Holy Spirit. Consequently, the Angel of the Lord had to have been God the Son in pre-incarnate form.[22]

---

the son of God" (Luke 3:38).

21. See Appendix 2: The Trinity.

22. Christ's pre-incarnate appearances as "the Angel of the Lord" were different from his incarnation. In the incarnation, Christ assumed a human nature while, at the same time, retaining his divine nature. He did this by being supernaturally conceived in the virgin Mary and being born in the normal human manner. This also entailed his ability to suffer and die as a human being. His incarnation was, in one sense, permanent; when he ascended to heaven, he "took his humanity with him," so to say, whereas

MELCHIZEDEK

Several scholars consider Melchizedek to be a "type" of Christ, as opposed to being a pre-incarnate appearance of Christ.[23] However, for the following reasons, I think it is better to view Melchizedek as a pre-incarnate appearance of Christ, rather than simply being a type of Christ. Melchizedek makes his one appearance, in Genesis 14, after Abram defeated four kings in battle. Hebrews describes him in extremely elevated terms, as the *"king of Salem, priest of the Most High God, who met Abraham as he was returning from the slaughter of the kings and blessed him, to whom also Abraham apportioned a tenth part of all the spoils, was first of all, by the translation of his name, king of righteousness, and then also king of Salem, which is king of peace. Without father, without mother, without genealogy, having neither beginning of days nor end of life, but made like the Son of God, he remains a priest perpetually."* (Heb 7:1–3)

The writer of Hebrews does not call Melchizedek a "type" of Christ or Christ an "antitype" of Melchizedek, although he did use the Greek word *tupon* ("type") in Heb 8:5, where it is translated as "pattern," regarding the archetypal tabernacle. He also used the word *antitupa* ("antitypes") in Heb 9:24, where it is translated as "copy," regarding the holy place in the temple.[24] He also called the gifts offered according to the Law by the priests *"a copy and shadow of heavenly things"* (Heb 8:5; *hupodeigma* for *"copy"* and *skia* for "shadow") and called the law itself *"a shadow of the good things to come"* (Heb 10:1, *skia* for "shadow"). In Heb 9:23 he refers to *"copies [hupodeigmata] of the things in the heavens"* as opposed to *"the heavenly things themselves."* He used the Greek word *parabolē* (a figure, type, or similitude) in Heb 9:9 for the tabernacle or temple as a "symbol" for the present time and in Heb 11:19 for Isaac, whom Abraham received back as a "type" of the

---

in his OT, pre-incarnate appearances he merely adopted a human form temporarily. In his pre-incarnate appearances, "he was not the 'God-Man' we read of in the Gospels, but was God, in human form, on an angelic mission. So when he ascended once again into the heavens, he resumed his spiritual existence as pure deity." Lunn, *Jesus in the Jewish*, 177.

Ps 35:5–6; Isa 37:36; and Matt 1:24 also have brief references to "the Angel of the Lord." These are rather non-specific references that do not appear to provide elaboration concerning the Angel's identity.

23. See e.g., Duncan, "Jesus and Melchizedek"; Jackson, "Was Melchizedek"; "Was Melchizedek," *Never Thirsty*; "Jesus Is Better," *Israel My Glory*; Hanson, *Jesus Christ*, 66–68; Carson, "Getting Excited," 162–72. See chapter 7, below, for a discussion and examples of biblical "types."

24. Note that the writer of Hebrews is using the words "type" and "antitype" oppositely to the way we and most contemporary writers use them, i.e., he is using "type" as the higher reality and "antitype" as physical pointer to the higher reality.

resurrection. Since Hebrews uses the words and concept of type and antitype on a several occasions, his not doing so with respect to Melchizedek is significant and indicates that he did not view Melchizedek merely as a type, but as the true reality, which could only have been Jesus Christ himself in a pre-incarnate appearance.

Second, according to Gen 14:18, Melchizedek *"brought out bread and wine."* That clearly points to Christ who instituted the ceremony of the bread and wine (the Lord's Supper) at the "Last Supper."[25] The other descriptions of Melchizedek in Heb 7:1–3 likewise correspond to Christ. For example, Melchizedek is the *"king of Salem"* (Heb 7:2). "Salem" means "peace." Jesus is the *"Prince of Peace"* (Heb 9:6), who gives *"My peace . . . not as the world gives"* (John 14:27). Salem often is considered to be Jerusalem (see Ps 76:2). Jesus was, in fact, "the king of the Jews" (e.g., Matt 2:2; 27:11, 29, 37), whose capital was Jerusalem. Further, Jesus was the prophesied Messiah,[26] one role of which was to be king—the final king of the world—and to rule from Zion (Ps 110:1–2; Jer 23:5–6). Melchizedek is also described as the *"king of righteousness."* Jesus is the ultimate righteous one (Rom 3:25; 10:4; Phil 3:9; 1 John 2:1).

Heb 7:3 describes Melchizedek as being *"without father, without mother."* D. A. Carson observes, "While Jesus is the son of Mary, his ultimate ancestry is grounded in the God of eternity: without father, without mother."[27] Since Heb 7:3 also describes Melchizedek as having *"neither beginning of days nor end of life,"* he "can hardly be reckoned as less ancient than Christ."[28] Having neither a beginning or an end of life means that Melchizedek is uncreated, immortal, and eternal. That rules out any created being, even an angel. Consequently, Melchizedek must be a pre-incarnate manifestation of Jesus Christ, who alone, as God the Son, is uncreated, immortal, and eternal. Heb 7:3 says he was *"made like the Son of God."* Although that wording does not explicitly say that he *was* the Son of God, it does not preclude identifying Melchizedek with Christ, since in Dan 3:25 the fourth figure in the fiery furnace is described as *"like a son of the gods."* The fourth figure in the furnace clearly is intended by Daniel to not merely be "like" a son of the gods, but to actually be a son of the gods, i.e., an angel, as he is described in Dan 3:28, or a pre-incarnate appearance of Jesus Christ.[29] In the same way,

---

25. Matt 26:26–28; Mark 14:22–24; Luke 22:14–20; 1 Cor 11:23–26.
26. See the discussion of the Messiah in chapter 5.
27. Carson, "Getting Excited," 170.
28. Hanson, *Jesus Christ*, 66.
29. See discussion of the Daniel 3 passage in the section on "The Angel of the Lord," above.

Phil 2:6–8, says that Jesus *"existed in the form of God . . . but emptied Himself, taking the form of a bond-servant, and being made in the likeness of men. Being found in appearance as a man. . ."* Jesus really was God and did not just "appear" to be a man but was, in fact, fully man.

In Heb 7:3, the description of Melchizedek concludes by saying that *"he remains a priest perpetually."* As is discussed in chapter 5, Jesus is the Messiah. One role of the Messiah was to be a priest (Ps 110:4; Zech 6:12–13). This fact clearly identifies Melchizedek as Jesus, since Ps 110:4 says about Jesus, *"The Lord has sworn and will not change His mind, 'You are a priest forever according to the order of Melchizedek'"* (see also Heb 5:6, 10; 6:20; 7:11, 15, 17). Christ appeared to Abraham in the person of Melchizedek "thereby indicating the superiority of the coming messianic priesthood to the coming Levitical priesthood."[30] That is cemented in Heb 7:8, which, referring to the tithe Abraham gave to Melchizedek, says, *"In this case mortal men receive tithes, but in that case one receives them, of whom it is witnessed that he lives on."* This is saying that Melchizedek is superior to Levi, because Levi's line of priests is mortal, but Melchizedek lives forever. Anthony Hanson comments that "we only know that Melchisedech lives for ever because of Psalm 110.4, where God promises Christ an eternal priesthood. Therefore Melchisedech is identical with Christ."[31] This is confirmed in Heb 7:25, which identifies one of the qualities of a perfect priesthood as the priest's ability to perpetually intercede on behalf of his subjects. "Melchizedek is said to abide a priest continually so his priesthood definitely has this quality of perfection; yet, only God inherently possesses the power of an endless life therefore only God can truly meet this criteria."[32] Similarly, Heb 7:27–28 points out that the Levitical high priests first offer sacrifices for their own sins; however, because Jesus was and is without sin, he did not have to offer sacrifices for his own sin but is *"perfect forever."* Since Jesus is a priest forever *"according to the order of Melchizedek,"* Melchizedek himself must have been without sin. Therefore, Christ and Melchizedek must be one and the same.

Additionally, he blessed Abraham, which showed his superiority to Abraham, because *"the lesser is blessed by the greater"* (Heb 7:7). Other than the blessing given by Melchizedek, the only person in the Bible to bless Abraham was God, which indicates the correspondence of Melchizedek and God. Abraham tithed to Melchizedek. That not only showed Melchizedek's superiority but also indicated Melchizedek's identity, since *"all the tithe of*

---

30. Hanson, *Jesus Christ*, 72.
31. Hanson, *Jesus Christ*, 70.
32. "13 Reasons," 7, Melchizedek's priesthood.

the land, of the seed of the land or of the fruit of the tree, is the Lord's; it is holy to the Lord" (Lev 27:30).

Finally, "one of the Dead Sea Scrolls (11QMelch) portrays Melchizedek as a heavenly being who will bring salvation (in fulfillment of Isa. 52.7-10 and 61.1-3) and judgment (in fulfillment of Pss. 7.7-8; 82.1-2) at the conclusion of the final Jubilee (Lev. 25)."[33] Salvation and judgment preeminently are the roles of Christ. Jesus even quoted Isa 61:1-2 as applying to himself (Luke 4:18-19). All of this strongly indicates that Melchizedek was a pre-incarnate appearance of Jesus Christ.

THE CAPTAIN OF THE LORD'S HOST

Just before Israel entered the promised land and conquered Jericho, a man with a sword in his hand appeared to Joshua. Joshua asked him, *"Are you for us or for our adversaries?"* (Josh 5:13). The man replied, *"'No; rather I indeed come now as captain of the host of the Lord.' And Joshua fell on his face to the earth, and bowed down, and said to him, 'What has my lord to say to his servant?' The captain of the Lord's host said to Joshua, 'Remove your sandals from your feet, for the place where you are standing is holy.' And Joshua did so."* (Josh 5:14-15) In this encounter, Joshua is told to remove his sandals, because the place he is standing is holy, exactly as God, in the person of "the Angel of the Lord," told Moses to do when Moses encountered God at the burning bush (Exod 3:5). Further, Joshua bows down in worship to the man without being rebuked. The Bible makes it absolutely clear that only God is to be worshipped; when people bowed down to worship ordinary angels or people, they were rebuked.[34] Consequently, it is likely that this captain of the Lord's host was a pre-incarnate appearance of Jesus Christ.[35]

---

33. Nelson, "Melchizedek," 511.

34. Exod 20:3-5; 34:14; Deut 4:19; 5:7-9; 8:19; 1 Kgs 9:6-7; Isa 42:8; Matt 4:10; Luke 4:8; Acts 10:25-26; 14:11-18; Col 2:18; Rev 19:10; 22:8-9.

35. Although some think that the captain of the Lord's host was an angel, he is never called an angel. If he were an angel, he would have been "the Angel of the Lord," i.e., Jesus Christ in pre-incarnate form. Josh 5:13 depicts the man *"with his sword drawn in his hand."* The Angel of the Lord is depicted with a drawn sword in his hand in Num 22:23 and 1 Chron 21:16, 30.

5

Christ in the Old Testament: Prophecy

ALTHOUGH THE BIBLE CONTAINS prophecies relating to many nations, people, and events, here I will focus on prophecies that relate to the Messiah, i.e., Jesus Christ, since he is the central figure of the entire Bible. With respect to the OT prophecies of Jesus Christ, recall that somewhat over 400 years existed between the last books of the OT and the advent of Jesus. Thus, there exists a period of several hundred years, up to a maximum of about 1400 years, between any prophecies relating to the Messiah and their fulfillment.[1]

The importance of prophecy is that prophecies make the claims that Jesus is the Messiah verifiable or, on the other hand, falsifiable.[2] Although it is possible that a few of the prophecies might be said to have been fulfilled by others, Jesus is the only one who could and did fulfill all of them. Jesus had no control over many of the prophecies (e.g., his manner and place of birth, his lineage, his betrayal, the actions of his disciples, accusers, and executioners, the manner of his death, his burial). Consequently, he could not have manipulated events to contrive to fulfill the prophecies.[3] The number and specificity of the prophecies relating to Jesus reveal that there is divine intellect and foreknowledge behind the Bible; it is not credible to contend

---

1. See Geisler, *Christian Apologetics*, 341. J. Barton Payne lists 112 OT prophecies relating to Christ (not including prophecies in later books that incorporate earlier ones) and 79 NT prophecies relating to Christ (not including prophecies quoted from the OT or repeating prophecies that appear in several of the Gospels). Payne, *Encyclopedia*, 665–70.

2. See Deut 18:20–22; 1 Kgs 22:28; Isa 48:5; Jer 28:9; Ezek 33:33; Zech 2:9, 11; 4:9; 6:15.

3. See Geisler, *Christian Apologetics*, 342–43.

that the prophecies just happened to be fulfilled by "chance" (as will be discussed below). The prophecies relate to all areas of Jesus' life.[4] Prophecies relating to Jesus' identity as Messiah include:

Prophecy	OT Source	NT Fulfillment
1. Born of a virgin	Isa 7:14	Matt 1:23; Luke 1:26–35
2. Son of God	Ps 2:7; 2 Sam 7:12–16; 1 Chron 17:11–14	Matt 3:17; Matt 16:16; Mark 9:7; Luke 9:35; 22:70; John 1:34, 49; Acts 13:30–33
3. Seed of Abraham	Gen 13:15; 22:17–18	Gal 3:16
4. Son of Isaac	Gen 21:12	Matt 1:2; Luke 3:23, 34
5. Son of Jacob	Num 24:17	Matt 1:2; Luke 1:33; 3:23, 34
6. Tribe of Judah	Gen 49:10; Micah 5:2	Matt 1:2; Luke 3:23, 33; Heb 7:14
7. Line of Jesse	Isa 11:1, 10	Matt 1:6, Luke 3:23, 32
8. House of David	2 Sam 7:12–16; Ps 132:11; Jer 23:5	Matt 1:1; 9:27; 15:22; 20:30–31; 21:9, 15; 22:41–46; Mark 9:10; 10:47–48; Luke 3:23, 31; 18:38–39; Acts 13:22–23; Rev 22:16
9. Born at Bethlehem	Micah 5:2	Matt 2:1, 4–8; Luke 2:4–7; John 7:42
10. Pre-existent	Micah 5:2	John 1:1–2, 30; 8:58; 17:5, 24; Col 1:17; Rev 1:17; 2:8; 22:13
11. Will be called Immanuel	Isa 7:14	Matt 1:23
12. Will be called the Lord	Ps 110:1; Jer 23:6	Matt 22:43–45; Luke 2:11
13. Will be a prophet	Deut 18:15, 18	Matt 21:11; Luke 7:16; John 4:19; 6:14; 7:40; Acts 3:22; 7:37, 51–52
14. Will be a priest	Ps 110:4	Heb 3:1; 5:5–6
15. Will be a judge	Isa 11:4; 33:22	John 5:30; 2 Tim 4:1; Jas 4:12
16. Will be a king	Ps 2:6; Jer 23:5; Zech 9:9	Matt 21:5; 27:37; John 18:33–38; Rev 19:16
17. The Spirit of God would be upon him	Isa 11:2; 42:1; 61:1–2	Matt 3:16–17; 12:17–21; Mark 1:10–11; Luke 4:18, 21; John 1:32
18. Preceded by a messenger	Isa 40:3; Mal 3:1	Matt 3:1–3; 11:10; Luke 1:17; John 1:23

---

4. Because of the number of prophecies in the Bible, space precludes our discussing anything other than a select few of the more important ones.

Prophecy	OT Source	NT Fulfillment
19. Zealous for God	Ps 69:9	John 2:15–17
20. Anointed by the Spirit to preach good news	Isa 61:1–2	Luke 4:18–21
21. Ministry to begin in Galilee	Isa 9:1	Matt 4:12–13, 17
22. Character of ministry	Isa 42:1–4	Matt 12:17–21
23. Would perform miracles	Isa 32:3–4; 35:5–6	Matt 8:17; 9:32–35; 11:4–6; Mark 7:33–35; John 5:5–9; 9:6–11; 11:43–47
24. Would teach in parables	Ps 78:2	Matt 13:34
25. Would enter the temple	Mal 3:1	Matt 21:12
26. Zeal for God's house	Ps 69:9	John 2:17
27. Would enter Jerusalem on a donkey	Zech 9:9	Matt 21:6–11; Luke 19:35–37
28. Enters Jerusalem to crowds chanting	Ps 118:26	Matt 21:9; Mark 11:9; Luke 19:38; John 12:13
29. Would be a stumbling stone to Jews	Ps 118:22; Isa 8:14; 28:16	Rom 9:32–33; 1 Pet 2:8
30. The "Stone" rejected which became the chief cornerstone	Ps 118:22	Matt 21:42; Mark 1:10; Luke 20:17; Acts 4:11; 1 Pet 2:7
31. Would be a light to Gentiles	Isa 42:6; 49:6; 60:3	Acts 13:47–48; 26:23; 28:28
32. Rejected by his own people	Ps 69:8; Isa 53:3	Matt 21:42–43; John 1:11; 7:5, 48
33. Conspired against by Gentile rulers	Ps 2:1–2	Acts 4:25–26
34. Hated without a cause	Ps 69:4; Isa 49:7	John 15:25
35. Would establish New Covenant	Jer 31:31–34	Luke 22:20

Prophecies relating to Jesus' death, burial, and resurrection include:

Prophecy	OT Source	NT Fulfillment
1. Conspired against by Gentiles and rulers	Ps 2:1–2	Acts 4:25–28
2. Betrayed by a friend	Ps 41:9; 55:12–14; Zech 13:6	Matt 10:4; 26:47–50; Luke 22:19–23
3. Betrayed for 30 pieces of silver	Zech 11:12	Matt 26:15; 27:3
4. Money thrown in God's house	Zech 11:13	Matt 27:5
5. Money given for potter's field	Zech 11:13	Matt 27:6–10[5]
6. Forsaken by his disciples	Zech 13:7	Matt 26:31, 69–74; Mark 14:27, 50
7. Silent before accusers	Isa 53:7	Matt 27:12; Acts 8:32–35
8. Beaten and spat upon	Isa 50:6; 53:5	Matt 26:67; 27:26; Mark 10:33–34
9. Mocked	Ps 22:7–8	Matt 27:31; Luke 22:63–65
10. Hands and feet pierced	Ps 22:16; Zech 12:10	Luke 23:33; John 20:25–27
11. Suffers for the sins of others	Isa 53:5–6, 8, 10–12	Rom 4:25; 1 Cor 15:3
12. Dies with transgressors	Isa 53:12	Matt 27:38; Mark 15:27–28; Luke 22:37

5. Matt 27:9 states that this fulfilled what was *"spoken through Jeremiah the prophet,"* although the words he quotes are primarily taken from Zech 11:13, not Jeremiah. Matthew's quotation is a composite allusion to the imagery and motifs of Jeremiah 18–19 as well as Zechariah 11. Jeremiah 18–19 are prophesies regarding the potter and his breaking and remaking a clay vessel; the context is God's casting off Judah and Jerusalem because of their having forsaken God, having gone after other gods, and having filled the place with the blood of the innocent. Jeremiah's prophecy was fulfilled in Jerusalem's destruction and the deporting of the people by the Babylonians. Zechariah picks up this imagery "in order to resume the prophecy of Jeremiah, and show that a second fulfillment of it was at hand, because the Divine penal justice which had called forth the threatening and its first fulfillment, had been provoked anew, and that in a more fearful manner." Hengstenberg, *Christology*, 360; see also at 363. Judah and Jerusalem's former apostasy "was but slight in comparison with the present, the wicked ingratitude towards the Lord, who had *Himself* [in the person of Jesus Christ] taken charge of his flock [which rejected him]." Hengstenberg, *Christology*, 361, 363. In short, while the "verbal detail" which is fulfilled is from Zechariah, the "thematic substance" of the fulfillment is from Jeremiah. Matthew names Jeremiah to draw attention to the important allusion to Jeremiah 18–19, which otherwise could have been overlooked. Gundy, *Use of the Old Testament*, 122–27; Knowles, *Jeremiah in Matthew's Gospel*, 76–77; Osborne, *Matthew*, 1013–14; France, *Gospel*, 1042–43.

Prophecy	OT Source	NT Fulfillment
13. Intercedes for persecutors	Isa 53:12	Luke 23:34
14. Lots cast for his clothes	Ps 22:18	John 19:23–24
15. Friends stand far away	Ps 38:11	Matt 27:55–56; Mark 15:40; Luke 23:49
16. People wag their heads	Ps 22:7	Matt 27:39
17. People stare at him	Ps 22:17	Luke 23:35
18. He suffers thirst	Ps 22:15; 69:21	John 19:28
19. Given gall and vinegar to drink	Ps 69:21	Matt 27:34; John 19:28–29
20. Cries out when forsaken by God	Ps 22:1	Matt 27:46
21. Commits his spirit to God	Ps 31:5	Luke 23:46
22. His bones are not broken	Ps 34:20	John 19:33
23. His side is pierced	Zech 12:10	John 19:34–37
24. Heart broken	Ps 22:14; 69:20	John 19:34
25. Darkness over the land	Gen 15:17; Amos 8:9	Matt 27:45
26. Buried in a rich man's tomb	Isa 53:9	Matt 27:57–60
27. Dead body did not decay	Ps 16:10	Acts 2:31
28. Would rise from the dead	Ps 2:7; 16:10; Hos 6:2	Matt 28:6; Mark 16:6; Luke 24:21, 46; Acts 2:31; 13:33
29. Would ascend to the Father	Ps 68:18	Acts 1:9; Eph 4:8
30. Seated at the right hand of God	Ps 110:1	Mark 16:19; Acts 2:34–35; Heb 1:3

Important prophecies concerning Jesus are found in all the major sections of the OT. We shall consider many of the most important prophecies in roughly canonical order.

THE PROTOEVANGELIUM

In Genesis 3, *"the serpent"* had deceived Eve, which led to Adam and Eve's eating the forbidden fruit, thus bringing sin upon themselves and the world (Gen 3:1–13). At the heart of the deception was the serpent's lie, *"You surely will not die!"* (v. 4). God then speaks his judgment, first to the serpent in vv. 14–15, and then to Eve and Adam in vv. 16–19. In Gen 3:15, God declared, *"And I will put enmity between you and the woman, and between your seed and her seed; he shall bruise you on the head, and you shall bruise him on the heel."* Gen 3:15 has been called "the *protoevangelium* (the 'first gospel') because it was the original proclamation of the promise of God's plan for the whole world. . . . The 'seed/offspring' mentioned in this verse became the root from which the tree of the OT promise of a Messiah grew. This, then, was the 'mother prophecy' to all the rest of the promises."[6]

Although the serpent was the instrument or agent of the deception, the broader context of Scripture makes clear that the principal behind and author of the deception was Satan himself. Thus, Rev 12:9 says, *"And the great dragon was thrown down, the serpent of old who is called the devil and Satan."* Jesus says of the devil, *"He was a murderer from the beginning, and does not stand in the truth because there is no truth in him. Whenever he speaks a lie, he speaks from his own nature, for he is a liar and the father of lies."* (John 8:44) Satan brought sin into the world, because *"the devil has sinned from the beginning"* (1 John 3:8).

In his judgment, God said that he would put "enmity" between Satan and his seed and the woman and her seed. "Enmity" can only be experienced by rational creatures, which is an indication that in v. 15 God is speaking to Satan, not simply to an irrational reptile. Similarly, while Eve is in view in the passage, the "woman" God refers to extends beyond Eve. In short, the "woman" represents the mother of the righteous or those faithful to God.[7] As a spiritual being, Satan does not bear biological children, but the Bible on several occasions indicates that he does, indeed, have seed or offspring: John the Baptist and Jesus called certain people a *"brood of vipers"* (Matt 3:7; 12:34; 22:33; Luke 3:7); Paul called a certain man a *"son of the devil"* (Acts 13:10); and John speaks of *"children of the devil"* (1 John 3:10). In 1 John 3:8, 10, John defined, in substance, who the "seed of the serpent" and, implicitly by contrast, the "seed of the woman" are, *"The one who practices sin is of the devil. . . . By this the children of God and the children of the devil are obvious: anyone who does not practice righteousness is not of God, nor the*

---

6. Kaiser, *Messiah*, 37–38; see also Briggs, *Messianic Prophecy*, 478.
7. See, e.g., Isa 37:22; 62:5; Eph 5:31–32; Rev 12:1–6; 21:9.

one who does not love his brother." This unremitting enmity is seen at the end of the Bible, where the "serpent" continues to persecute the "woman" (Rev 12:15–16).

Although the prophecy in v. 15 contrasted *"your seed and her seed,"* the next line has a direct confrontation between one member of the *"seed of the woman"* and "you," i.e., Satan himself.[8] According to this prophecy, a male individual from among the woman's seed will deal a death blow to Satan—"To crush the head of a snake is a completely decisive stroke, which will terminate its life"[9]—while Satan will bruise man's heel, or cause him to suffer and possibly die.

In the Bible, all people are seen as related to Adam (Rom 5:12–19; 1 Cor 15:22), and the "seed" or descendants are always traced through the male line.[10] Gen 3:15 is the only place in the Bible where someone is identified as "the seed of the woman." That points to Jesus, since he and he alone was born of a virgin, with no human father (see Isa 7:14; Matt 1:23; Luke 1:27). Both *Targum Jerusalem* and *Targum Jonathan,* Aramaic translations and interpretations of the Hebrew Scriptures, add the explanation that the fulfillment of Gen 3:15 will be "in the days of the king Meshiha [Messiah]."[11] The NT confirms this by picking up on the language of Gen 3:15 when it describes Jesus as *"born of a woman"* (Gal 4:4). At the wedding in Cana, when Mary told Jesus that the wine had run out, Jesus called his mother, "Woman" (John 2:4). He added, *"My hour has not yet come"* (John 2:4). His "hour" is a reference to when he would be crucified (John 12:23–28; see also Matt 26:45; Mark 14:35, 41). He again called Mary "Woman" while he was on the cross (John 19:26). Thus, Jesus never is recorded as calling Mary his "mother," but both at the beginning of his public ministry and at the end of his earthly life he called her "woman."[12] First John 3:8 tells us, *"The*

---

8. While the prophecy speaks of *"your seed and her seed,"* it then says that "he" (not "it") *"shall bruise you on the head,"* and *"you shall bruise him"* (not "it") *"on the heel."* This is particularly significant in the Septuagint, because, in Greek, "seed" is neuter, but "he" and "him" are masculine. R. A. Martin observes, "In none of the instances where the [Septuagint] translator has translated literally does he do violence to agreement in Greek between the pronoun and its antecedent, except here in Gen 3:15." Martin, "Earliest Messianic," 427. It is "unlikely that this is mere coincidence or oversight [but] the translator has in this way indicated his messianic understanding of this verse." Martin, "Earliest Messianic," 427.

9. Lunn, *Jesus in the Jewish,* 43.

10. See, e.g., Gen 4:16–22; 5:1–32; 10:1–32; 22:18; 25;12–16, 19; 36:9–43.

11. *Targum Jerusalem,* Gen 3:15; *Targum Jonathan,* Gen 3:15.

12. Significantly, the only time Jesus called Mary "mother" was from the cross when he was giving charge of Mary to the disciple John. In John 19:27, Jesus was speaking to John and said, *"Behold,* your *mother."*

Son of God appeared for this purpose, to destroy the works of the devil" (see also Heb 2:14, *"through death He might render powerless him who had the power of death, that is, the devil"*).[13] Jesus' use of "woman" for his mother in those circumstances and contexts clearly relates back and alludes to Gen 3:15. Jesus accomplished the defeat of Satan by dying for our sins on the cross. In doing so, he created a new humanity in which Satan no longer has any power over those who are in Christ (see Jas 4:7). When he comes again, he will finally and utterly destroy Satan forever (Rev 20:10).

This prophecy is more stunning because of a literal component to it. Genesis, including Gen 3:15, was written approximately 1000 years before the Persians invented crucifixion between 300–400 BC. "As Jesus hangs on the cross, the weight of His body pulls down on the diaphragm and the air moves into His lungs and remains there. Jesus must push up on His nailed feet (causing more pain) to exhale."[14] That continuous process of the body sinking down and Jesus having to push himself up in order to breath lasted for hours and would have resulted in deep bruising of the heels or heel (if one foot was nailed on top of the other), thus literally fulfilling the prophecy of Gen 3:15.

RATIFICATION OF THE ABRAHAMIC COVENANT

Perhaps the most fascinating prophecy is found in Gen 15:1–18. There, God was ratifying the covenant he previously had made with Abraham (then known as Abram). Abram asked, *"O Lord God, how will I know that I will possess [the land God had promised him]?"* (Gen 15:8) To assuage Abram's doubt, God told Abram to bring certain animals. Abram knew that God was going to ratify a covenant with him, so he brought the animals and then cut them in two and laid the halves opposite each other. In the Ancient Near East, typically both parties then would walk through the pieces of the dead animals. What they were doing was symbolizing, "If I violate the terms of this agreement, may I become just like these dead animals here."[15] In this

---

13. Rev 12:4 alludes to Gen 3:15 when it says, *"And the dragon stood before the woman who was about to give birth, so that when she gave birth he might devour her child."* Rom 16:20 also alludes to Gen 3:15 when it says, *"The God of peace will soon crush Satan under your feet."* There, Paul regards the church, i.e., the body of Christ, as "Eve's offspring to whom God gives victory over the adversary." Goppelt, *Typos*, 13n.17; see also Hengstenberg, *Christology*, 38n.1.

14. Shrier, "Science," Matthew 27:33–56; see also Myers, "Crucifixion," Crucifixion Methods; Gidley, "facts," What actually kills; Davis, "Physician Analyzes," On the Cross; Kagin, "Crucifixion of Jesus."

15. Alter, *Genesis*, 65n.8; Payne, *Encyclopedia*,162.

case, however, only God (in the symbolic form of a *"smoking oven and flaming torch,"* Gen 15:17) passed through the pieces of the dead animals.¹⁶ By passing through the pieces of animals on his own behalf and also on behalf of Abram, God was saying, "Abram, if I violate the terms of this covenant, may I become like these dead animals." But he was also saying, "Abram, if *you* violate the terms of this covenant, by not believing me, by not following me, may *I*, not you, become like these dead animals."

This covenant which God acted out also was a prophecy (see Gal 3:16). Approximately 2000 years later, on a hill called Calvary or Golgotha, in the person of Jesus Christ, God did it for real. What makes the prophecy of Genesis 15 so amazing is the *detail* of its fulfillment. Just as the animals were killed, so was Jesus. However, the animals were not merely killed, but were cut in two. Matt 27:51 tells us that when Jesus died, *"the veil of the temple was torn in two from top to bottom."* Heb 10:19–20 tells us the meaning of that. It says, *"We have confidence to enter the holy place by the blood of Jesus, by a new and living way which He inaugurated for us through the veil, that is, His flesh."* That veil was showing that, on the cross, Jesus Christ fulfilled the Abrahamic Covenant.¹⁷ Additionally, Gen 15:17 says, *"When the sun had set, it was very dark."* That was when the smoking oven and flaming torch passed through the pieces. Matt 27:45 tells us that when Jesus was on the cross, *"from the sixth hour darkness fell upon all the land until the ninth hour."* The judgment of sin is eternal separation from God, otherwise known as hell. Hell is described in various places in the Bible as *"outer darkness"* (Matt 8:12; 22:13; 25:30). The darkness of the sky when Jesus was on the cross was a sign of God's judgment on the sin that Jesus was bearing. That darkness was symbolizing the outer darkness of hell itself. Since the essence of hell is separation from God, when Jesus cried out from the cross, *"My God, my God, why have you forsaken me?"* (Matt 27:46), he was actually experiencing hell. These events did not happen by coincidence, and they could not have been "faked," since no one could control the weather or cause the veil of the temple to rip in two. The only reasonable explanation is that the God of the Bible exists, he knows *"the end from the beginning"* (Isa 46:10), and he was using prophecy and its fulfillment to demonstrate his reality, to verify who Jesus Christ is, and to confirm the truth of the gospel.

---

16. We know that the smoking oven and flaming torch signified God himself, because later he led Israel out of captivity in Egypt (which was also prophesied in Gen 15:13–14) as a pillar of cloud by day and a pillar of smoke by night (Exod 13:21); when he appeared on Mount Sinai to give the Ten Commandments to Moses, *"Mount Sinai was all in smoke because the Lord descended upon it in fire; and its smoke ascended like the smoke of a furnace"* (Exod 19:18).

17. See Payne, *Encyclopedia*, 162.

THE BLESSING OF JUDAH

In Genesis 49, Jacob blessed his sons. We know that Jacob's words to his sons were prophetic, since in Gen 49:1 he said, *"Assemble yourselves that I may tell you what will befall you in the days to come."* In Gen 49:8–12 he blessed his son Judah, and that blessing was a prophecy of the coming of Messiah. Gen 49:9 says, *"Judah is a lion's whelp; From the prey, my son, you have gone up. He couches, he lies down as a lion, and as a lion, who dares rouse him up?"* That is applied to Jesus in Rev 5:5, which calls him *"the Lion that is from the tribe of Judah."*

Gen 49:10 then goes on to say, *"The scepter shall not depart from Judah, nor the ruler's staff from between his feet, until Shiloh comes, and to him shall be the obedience of the peoples."* Historically, Judah *"prevailed over his brothers, and from him came the leader [i.e., David and his line]"* (1 Chron 5:2). "Shiloh" is used multiple times in the OT for the city of Shiloh in the land of Ephraim; that was where the tabernacle and the ark of the covenant were located for approximately three centuries. However, in this context, it cannot refer to the city, since Shiloh was destroyed and abandoned long before Judah rose to power.[18] This passage is the one reference to Shiloh as a person. Gen 49:10 was interpreted messianically before the Christian era. The Qumran community paraphrased the word "Shiloh" as "the rightful Messiah" or "the Messiah of righteousness."[19] Ancient Jewish, rabbinic writings from the first-seventh centuries AD, *Targum Onkelos, Targum Jerusalem,* and the *Babylonian Talmud,* also took "Shiloh" of Gen 49:10 messianically.[20] This interpretation is corroborated in that Jacob was telling his sons what would happen *"in the days to come."* That phrase typically is translated as *"the last days"* or *"the latter days,"* and literally is *"end of the days."*[21] It specifically is referring to the days of the Messiah, as Heb 1:2 makes clear (see Isa 2:2; Hos 3:5; Mic 4:1).[22]

The word "Shiloh" sometimes is interpreted as "the seed," "the sent," or "the peaceable or prosperous one." All such references pertain to Jesus as Messiah, since he is "the seed" of Gen 15:5 (see Gal 3:16); he is *"Jesus Christ whom You have sent"* (John 17:3); and *"He Himself is our peace"* (Eph 2:14; see also Phil 4:7; Isa 9:6, *"Prince of Peace"*); as Jesus said in John 14:27, "Peace I leave with you; My peace I give to you; not as the world gives do I

---

18. 1 Sam 4: 10–11; Ps 78:54–64; Jer 7:12–14; Payne, *Encyclopedia,* 170.
19. "Shiloh," *Encyclopedia of the Bible,* 3.
20. "Who is Shilo?," *Kol HaTor.*
21. NASB, 49:1n.1.
22. Owen, *Exposition,* 1:188.

give to you."²³ On the other hand, John Sailhamer states that "Shiloh" is "an untranslated form of the Hebrew expression meaning 'one to whom it belongs.'"²⁴ That, again, would point to Jesus as the Messiah, since the angel Gabriel promises that *"the Lord God will give Him the throne of His father David"* (Luke 1:32), i.e., the throne to whom it belongs.

The prophecy of Judah having the "scepter" and "ruler's staff" began with the first king from Judah, namely, David. Many take the prophecy as signifying, "Before Shiloh arrives, the rule belongs to the tribe of Judah, a prophecy fulfilled through the Davidic line of kings. Then, when Shiloh comes, the rule is transferred to Him—the King of Kings—and remains with Him to this day."²⁵ Kevin Smyth summarizes, "There seems to be a fundamental identity between the sceptre of Juda and that of the Messias. There is no opposition in this prophecy between Juda and the Messias; in fact, it is a messianic blessing and promise to Juda. The context seems to indicate that Juda will retain the sceptre and hand it over, as it were, to the Messias when he comes. It is this sceptre of Juda that belongs to the Messias by native right."²⁶ On the other hand, Walter Kaiser notes that the Hebrew word for "until" "often takes an inclusive sense, suggesting that Judah's rule and reign will reach up to the coming of Shiloh and beyond."²⁷ In other words, Shiloh will be part of Judah, and Judah, therefore, will not have to "hand the scepter over" to Shiloh when he comes.

Paul Twiss has a slightly more nuanced reading of the prophecy, although essentially with the same end result. He notes that, when taken in conjunction with Jacob's blessings of his other sons in Genesis 49, Joseph, not Judah, was manifestly chosen as the favored son and head of the family (Gen 49:22–26; see also Gen 48:15–20). However, this would not be permanent. Historically, Psalm 78 records that God abandoned his dwelling place at Shiloh in Ephraim, where the tabernacle had been located (Ps 78:60), rejected the tent of Joseph (Ps 78:67), and chose the tribe of Judah (Ps 78:68). In light of this, the key word "until" in Gen 49:10 (*"until Shiloh comes"*), though often read as a point of cessation, should be taken as a point of culmination. In other words, it references a final state "without giving comment on what comes before," i.e., "The scepter shall not depart from

---

23. See Hengstenberg, *Christology,* 46–47 for reasons why "peacemaker" is the best translation.

24. Sailhamer, "Genesis," 276; see also Briggs, *Messianic Prophecy,* 96n.1; Payne, *Encyclopedia,* 170. Ezek 21:27 indicates this understanding in his use of the longer form of the same word.

25. "Historical and Spiritual," *Sar-El,* Yeshua Called Shiloh.

26. Smyth, "Prophecy Concerning Juda," 296.

27. Kaiser, *Messiah,* 52.

Judah, nor the ruler's staff from between his feet, *until* (at the time when) Shiloh shall come."²⁸ Twiss notes that the collocation of "until" and "comes" with an imperfect verb is exceptional. The pairing "places an accent on the forward-looking nature of Jacob's words. Judah's rule shall be *realized* when Shiloh comes, and not before. He shall hold a scepter then, but not now."²⁹ In short, the "scepter' and "ruler's staff" refer to Messiah, not to David and his line of kings.

That this prophecy is a prophecy of the Messiah is clear from the fact that Judah's holding the scepter is permanent, i.e., *"The scepter shall not depart from Judah, nor the ruler's staff from between his feet"* (Gen 49:10). Although the Davidic line of kings lasted for a few hundred years, it came to an end. On the other hand, even before his birth, it was prophesied by the angel Gabriel that Jesus *"will be great and will be called the Son of the Most High; and the Lord God will give Him the throne of His father David; and He will reign over the house of Jacob forever, and His kingdom will have no end"* (Luke 1:32–33). That points directly to the prophecy of Gen 49:10. Heb 1:8–9 picks up on the "scepter" language by quoting Ps 45:6–7, which parallels Gen 49:10, and applies it to Jesus as the one on the everlasting throne, *"Your throne, O God, is forever and ever, and the righteous scepter is the scepter of His kingdom. You have loved righteousness and hated lawlessness; Therefore God, Your God, has anointed You with the oil of gladness above Your companions."* On the Day of Pentecost, Peter related that Jesus has, through his resurrection and ascension, been seated on the "throne of David," and is reigning forever, *"And so, because he [David] was a prophet and knew that God had sworn to him with an oath to seat one of his descendants on his throne, he looked ahead and spoke of the resurrection of the Christ, that He was neither abandoned to Hades, nor did His flesh suffer decay. This Jesus God raised up again, to which we are all witnesses. . . . Therefore let all the house of Israel know for certain that God has made Him both Lord and Christ—this Jesus whom you crucified."* (Acts 2:32–36)³⁰

---

28. Twill, "Tale of Two," 263–64.

29. Twill, "Tale of Two," 264, emph. added. To a similar effect is Hengstenberg, *Christology*, 48–49, who states that, according to the prophecy, Judah "shall be exalted to higher honour and glory through the great Redeemer who shall spring from it."

30. Peter's discourse in Acts 2 began by his quoting Joel 2:28–32 as having been fulfilled by the outpouring of the Holy Spirit on the Day of Pentecost. He is clearly seeing this as the inauguration, not the consummation, of the fulfillment. His telling the people in Acts 2:38 to repent and be baptized in order to receive the Holy Spirit, and his statement in v. 39 that *"the promise is for you and your children and for all who are far off"* indicates this. Rom 10:12–13 similarly applies Joel 2:32 to the gospel's call to both Jews and Gentiles to come to faith in Christ. The events on the Day of Pentecost and the subsequent coming to faith of Jews and Gentiles are related, since it is the Holy Spirit's

The last sentence of Gen 49:10, *"And to him shall be the obedience of the peoples,"* also indicates that the prophecy is referring to Jesus as Messiah, not to Judah, David, or the Davidic line of kings. The reason is that "peoples" is plural, not singular. It shows that the permanent scepter, ruler's staff, and kingship extends far beyond the nation of Israel, and far beyond the rule of David or any of Israel's kings. Kevin Smyth observes that "peoples" must be understood as "the peoples of the earth. The [term] is also used of the heathen peoples who are to enter into the ... messianic kingdom in Ps. 45:6.18; 47:2.10; Is. 2:3; and in general of heathen peoples in Deut. 28:10; Is. 10:13; 11:10; 14:6; 17:12, etc."[31] This finds its fulfillment only in Jesus *"when He [God] raised Him [Jesus] from the dead and seated Him at His right hand in the heavenly places, far above all rule and authority and power and dominion, and every name that is named, not only in this age but also in the one to come"* (Eph 1:20–21). As a result, Jesus has *"purchased for God with Your blood men from every tribe and tongue and people and nation"* (Rev 5:9).

Finally, the statements in vv. 11–12, *"He washes his garments in wine, and his robes in the blood of grapes. His eyes are dull from wine, and his teeth white from milk"* are pictures of an idyllic, messianic, age of prosperity and blessing, not something realized during the time the Davidic kings ruled Israel. That type of imagery is used elsewhere in the OT for the reign of the messianic king (see Ps 72:16; Isa 25:6; Joel 2:21–27). Isaiah picked up on this imagery in Isaiah 63:1–6, in speaking of God as the conquering king, whose garments are *"like the one who treads in the wine press."* This same imagery is applied to Jesus in his judgment on the unrighteous: *"So the angel swung his sickle to the earth and gathered the clusters from the vine of the earth, and threw them into the great wine press of the wrath of God. And the wine press was trodden outside the city"* (Rev 14:19–20); *"He is clothed with a robe dipped in blood, and His name is called The Word of God ... and He treads the wine press of the fierce wrath of God, the Almighty"* (Rev 19:13, 15). In short, from beginning to end, in all of its particulars, the blessing to Judah ultimately was a prophecy about Jesus Christ as Messiah.

THE SHEPHERD AND THE STONE

In Gen 49:22–26, Jacob blessed Joseph. Among the blessings, he said of Joseph, *"His bow remained firm, and his arms were agile, from the hands of the*

---

outpouring on the Day of Pentecost which, in effect, gave birth to the church, and it is the Holy Spirit's continued activity causes the regeneration of Jews and Gentiles and their incorporation into the church.

31. Smyth, "Prophecy Concerning Juda," 298.

Mighty One of Jacob (from there [or, 'through the name'] is the Shepherd, the Stone of Israel)" (Gen 49:24; see also Ps 80:1, which similarly connects the "Shepherd" and Joseph). These are the first times God is called the "Shepherd" and the "Stone" (sometimes translated "Rock").[32] Both the Shepherd and the Stone prophesy the coming of the Messiah, i.e., Jesus, who embodies both the Shepherd and the Stone.

The Shepherd imagery is prominent in Ezekiel 34, which prophesies against the false shepherds of Israel. In Ezek 34:11–12, God says, *"Behold, I Myself will search for My sheep and seek them out. As a shepherd cares for his herd in the day when he is among his scattered sheep, so I will care for My sheep and will deliver them from all the places to which they were scattered on a cloudy and gloomy day."* The passage goes on to say, *"Behold, I will judge between one sheep and another, between the rams and the male goats. . . . Then I will set over them one shepherd, My servant David, and he will feed them; he will feed them himself and be their shepherd."* (Ezek 34:17, 23) These passages find their fulfillment in Jesus. Matt 2:6 quotes Micah 5:4 (he *"will shepherd My people Israel"*) as being fulfilled in Jesus. In John 10:11, Jesus said, *"I am the good shepherd; the good shepherd lays down His life for the sheep,"* as opposed to the false shepherds (see also John 10:14; Heb 13:20). He described the judgment he will carry out with respect to *"all the nations . . . as the shepherd separates the sheep from the goats"* (Matt 25:32).

With respect to the Stone, the same word for "stone" is found in Isaiah 8:14 and 28:16, which are quoted in Matt 21:42, 1 Pet 2:7, Rom 9:32–33, and 1 Pet 2:8 as applying to Jesus. In his parable of the landowner and the vine-growers, Jesus quotes Isa 28:16 as referring to himself, *"The stone which the builders rejected, this became the chief corner stone; this came about from the Lord, and it is marvelous in our eyes?"* The stone imagery was central to Nebuchadnezzar's dream in Daniel 2. Dan 2:34–35 says, *"You continued looking until a stone was cut out without hands, and it struck the statue on its feet of iron and clay and crushed them. . . . But the stone that struck the statue became a great mountain and filled the whole earth."* Daniel interpreted *"the stone that struck the statue became a great mountain and filled the whole earth"* to mean *"the God of heaven will set up a kingdom which will never be destroyed"* (Dan 2:44). This is the kingdom of the Messiah, Jesus Christ.[33]

Zech 3:9 says, *"For behold, the stone that I have set before Joshua; on one stone are seven eyes. Behold, I will engrave an inscription on it,' declares the Lord of hosts, 'and I will remove the iniquity of that land in one day.'"* The

---

32. Some translations of Gen 48:15 say *"God who has been my shepherd all my life to this day,"* which speaks of God's *role* as a shepherd, rather than *naming* him "the Shepherd."

33. See Briggs, *Messianic Prophecy*, 420.

"seven eyes" connote fullness of vision, i.e., omniscience. Jesus is represented as having *"seven eyes"* in Rev 5:6. As Charles Briggs puts it, "The eyes represent the sacred activity of the divine . . . it is the Messiah himself."[34]

A PROPHET LIKE MOSES

In Deut 18:15–19, Moses prophesied, *"¹⁵ The Lord your God will raise up for you a prophet like me from among you, from your countrymen [lit. 'brothers'], you shall listen to him. . . . ¹⁷ The Lord said to me, 'They have spoken well. ¹⁸ I will raise up a prophet from among their countrymen [lit. 'brothers'] like you, and I will put My words in his mouth, and he shall speak to them all that I command him. ¹⁹ It shall come about that whoever will not listen to My words which he shall speak in My name, I Myself will require it of him.'"* On multiple occasions, the NT identifies Christ as the predicted prophet. In John 1:45, after meeting Jesus, Philip found Nathanael and said to him, *"We have found Him of whom Moses in the Law and also the Prophets wrote—Jesus of Nazareth, the son of Joseph."* In John 6:14, after Jesus performed a miraculous sign, the people who witnessed the miracle said, *"This is truly the Prophet who is to come into the world."* The only "Prophet" that can be referring to is the prophet predicted in Deut 18:15–19. Acts 3:22 and Acts 7:37 both quote the prophecy as having been fulfilled by Jesus. On the Mount of Transfiguration, God's voice from the cloud identified Jesus as the prophesied "prophet" by repeating the last part of Deut 18:15 and saying, *"This is My beloved Son, with whom I am well-pleased; listen to Him!"* (Matt 17:5; Mark 9:7; Luke 9:35). Jesus called himself a "prophet" (Luke 13:33) and was considered to be a prophet by others (Matt 21:11; Luke 7:16; 24:19; John 4:19; 6:14; 7:40; 9:17). But the only person who could be a *"prophet like me"* is Jesus, because not only does his life parallel the life of Moses, but he far surpasses Moses.[35]

Further, Deut 18:19 says, *"It shall come about that whoever will not listen to My words which he shall speak in My name, I Myself will require it of him.'"* That is a warning of judgment against and destruction of those who do not listen to the "prophet like Moses." In Acts 3, Peter applies the prophecy to Jesus and then, alluding to Deut 18:19, concludes, *"And it will be that every soul that does not heed that prophet shall be utterly destroyed from among the people"* (Acts 3:23). As John Owen points out, that judgment

---

34. Briggs, *Messianic Prophecy*, 442n.3.

35. See the multiple, important parallels between Moses and Jesus discussed in chapter 7.

"never befell them [Israel] until they had rejected the Lord Jesus, the true and only Messiah," exactly as Jesus said would occur.³⁶

PSALM 2

A number of the psalms are clearly messianic and prophetic of Christ. Psalm 2 is an inauguration psalm for Israelite kings; it is the public declaration of kingship. It is also messianic. E. W. Hengstenberg observes that Psalm 2 "was universally regarded by the ancient Jews as foretelling the Messiah."³⁷ At his trial before the Sanhedrin, the high priest used two of the titles of the expected Messiah found in Psalm 2—"Christ" (i.e., "Anointed") and "Son of God" (Ps 2:2, 7)—in questioning Jesus concerning his identity (see Matt 26:63). The Psalm begins, "'*Why did the Gentiles rage, and the peoples devise futile things? The kings of the earth took their stand, and the rulers were gathered together against the Lord and against His Christ.*" (Ps 2:1–2, as quoted in Acts 4:25–26) The believers in Acts saw this as being fulfilled by the persecution meted out against Christ and the early Christians.

Ps 2:6–8 states, "*⁶ But as for Me, I have installed My King Upon Zion, My holy mountain. ⁷ I will surely tell of the decree of the Lord: He said to Me, 'You are My Son, today I have begotten You. ⁸ Ask of Me, and I will surely give the nations as Your inheritance, and the very ends of the earth as Your possession.'*" The ascription of a Son to Yahweh in Ps 2:7 suggests plurality within the one God. Ps 2:7 is quoted or alluded to at Jesus' baptism (Matt 3:17; Mark 1:11; Luke 3:22), his transfiguration (Matt 17:5; Mark 9:7; Luke 9:35), and in connection with his resurrection and exaltation (Acts 13:33; Heb 1:5; 5:5), thus identifying Jesus as the true "Son of God."

Additionally, Heb 1:5 and 5:5 both quote Ps 2:7 ("*You are my Son; today I have begotten you*") and apply it to Jesus. Acts 13:32–33 quotes Ps 2:7 as having been fulfilled in Jesus' resurrection. Jochen Katz states that, in their respective contexts,

> All of these passages speak about the **resurrection and exaltation** of Christ. It refers to his taking office as king and priest. . . . The expression "the begotten son" of God is never

---

36. Owen, *Exposition*, 1:192; see Matt 21:42–43; 23:34–38; 24:1–2; and the discussion of "The Abomination of Desolation" in chapter 7 and the section "Jesus rejected the nation of Israel as the vehicle for building God's kingdom and gave that role to his own followers, the church" in chapter 10. The judgment on Israel because of its rejection of Jesus is discussed in detail in Menn, *Biblical Eschatology*, 2nd ed., 112–13, 116–17, 125–27.

37. Hengstenberg, *Christology*, 59.

mentioned in respect to his miraculous conception by the Holy Spirit or his birth by the Virgin Mary.... What then is the Biblical meaning? I think Romans 1:4 says it most clearly that Jesus "was declared with power to be the Son of God by his resurrection from the dead: Jesus Christ our Lord." The resurrection was the time of public declaration of what he has been all along.... [T]he resurrection is the public announcement by God about the true identity and authority of Jesus, Messiah, true king of Israel, representative of God among mankind.[38]

In OT prophecy, God was pictured as dwelling with his people on Mount Zion.[39] Ps 2:6–8 had prophesied a restored Israel, with the Messianic King enthroned on Mount Zion, God's *"holy mountain,"* as God's "Son," with the nations and the *"ends of the earth"* given to him as his possession (see also Ps 48:1–2; Isa 2:2–3; Ezek 17:22–23). The nations would have to *come to* Zion in order to experience God's presence and blessings.[40] Jesus reoriented Ps 2:6–8 and similar OT prophecies to himself, his people (the church), and the spread of the gospel. Jesus the "Son" has *"all authority in heaven and on earth"* as Messianic King (Ps 2:6; Matt 28:18). Jesus the Lord gives a decree to his disciples (Ps 2:7; Matt 28:18–20), which applies to *"all the nations"* (Ps 2:8; Matt 28:19). However, instead of people *coming to* God's "holy mountain," Jesus tells his people to *go out* to all people and places to teach the word of the Lord (Matt 28:18–20; Acts 1:6–8). The conclusion of Jesus' charge to his disciples to go *"to the ends of the earth"* (Acts 1:8, NIV) echoes Ps 2:8, which says that the very *"ends of the earth"* have been given to the Messianic King as his possession. "In Jesus' charge to the disciples to go to all the nations 'until the ends of the earth,' the prophetic vision of the nations coming to Jerusalem (Isa 2:2–5, Mic 4:1–5; Zech 8:20–23) is replaced by the reality of Jewish missionaries going to the nations. The anticipated movement from the periphery to the center is redirected in terms of a mission from the center (Jerusalem, where Jesus had died and was raised from the dead) towards the periphery (the ends of the earth)."[41]

The divine nature of Jesus is indicated in that, in Rev 2:26, Jesus quotes Ps 2:8 (*"To him I will give authority over the nations"*) as something he will give to his followers. In the psalm, it was the divine Son who was the

---

38. Katz, "You are," n.p., bold emph. in orig.; see also Guthrie, "Hebrews," 927–28.

39. Ps 2:6; see Ps 9:11; 43:3; 68:16; 76:1–2; Isa 8:18; Joel 3:17; Zech 8:3. E. W. Hengstenberg points out that "the holy mountain does not here come under consideration *as a mountain*, but rather as the *seat* and *central point of the kingdom of God*, and designates *this kingdom itself*." Hengstenberg, *Christology*, 699, emph. in orig.

40. See Isa 2:2–3; 25:6–7; 56:6–8; Micah 4:1–2; Zech 8:20–23.

41. Schnabel, "Israel, the People," 47.

recipient, from God, of the nations as his inheritance and the ends of the earth as his possession. Now, since he is the inheritor of the nations and the possessor of the ends of the earth, he is in the position to bestow them on his followers. After God's Son is promised the nations and the ends of the earth, Ps 2:9 then says, *"You shall break them with a rod of iron, You shall shatter them like earthenware."* That is applied to Jesus in Rev 12:5 and again to Jesus, in the context of his Second Coming, in Rev 19:15. Then, as in Rev 2:26 with respect to giving his followers authority over the nations, in Rev 2:27, Jesus promises to his followers the authority to rule *"with a rod of iron."*

PSALM 16

Psalm 16 is a psalm of David.[42] In Acts 2:25–28, on the Day of Pentecost, Peter quotes from Ps 16:8–11. Ps 16:10, which says, *"You will not abandon my soul to Hades, nor allow Your Holy One to undergo decay,"* is particularly germane to Peter's argument. After quoting the psalm, he then states that *"because he [David] was a prophet and knew that God had sworn to him with an oath to seat one of his descendants on his throne, he looked ahead and spoke of the resurrection of the Christ, that He was neither abandoned to Hades, nor did His flesh suffer decay"* (Acts 2:30–31). Peter also pointed out that, although David wrote the psalm, it could not have applied to him, but of necessity was a prophecy, since David *"both died and was buried, and his tomb is with us to this day"* (Acts 2:29).

Similarly, during his first missionary journey, Paul addressed the synagogue in Pisidian Antioch concerning Christ. He began by recounting the history of God's dealings with Israel, leading to the life of Christ. In Acts 13:34, Paul quotes the LXX of Isa 55:3 and says that the promise of *"the holy and sure blessings of David"* have been fulfilled in the resurrection of Jesus. Thus, Christ's resurrection from the dead is the way that God fulfilled his promise to establish David's throne forever. In Acts 13:35, he then begins, "Therefore," and quotes from Ps 16:10, *"You will not allow your Holy One to undergo decay."* While David may have written this portion of the psalm in the confident hope that death would not keep him from enjoying fellowship with God after his own death, both Peter and Paul see the psalm as a

---

42. It is designated as a "mikhtam" of David, a word of unknown meaning, possibly an epigrammatic poem or an atonement psalm; some see it as signifying "golden" or a song of great value, others view it as a technical term to guide the singer singing the psalm or the musicians playing it. "What is a *michtam*," *Got Questions*; NASB, Psalm 16:1, note.

prophecy of Jesus' own resurrection. As the "greater David,"[43] Jesus' resurrection guarantees not only David's resurrection but also the resurrection of all those who place their faith in Christ (see 1 Cor 15:20–23).

PSALM 22

Psalm 22 was prophetic, especially of the details of Jesus' crucifixion, both physiologically and otherwise. Thus, Ps 22:14, 16b, 17a state, *"I am poured out like water, and all my bones are out of joint; my heart is like wax; it is melted within me. . . . They pierced my hands and my feet. I can count all my bones."* That is exactly what happens as part of a crucifixion and what happened to Jesus. His hands and his feet were pierced.[44] Dr. C. Truman Davis points out, "Within a few minutes of being placed on the Cross, Jesus' shoulders were dislocated. Minutes later Jesus' elbows and wrists became dislocated. . . . After Jesus' wrists, elbows, and shoulders were dislocated, the weight of His body on his upper limbs caused traction forces on the Pectoralis Major muscles of His chest wall. These traction forces caused His rib cage to be pulled upwards and outwards, in a most unnatural state."[45] Additionally, plasma and blood gathered in the space around his heart, preventing it from beating properly.[46] Ps 22:15 adds, *"My strength is dried up like a potsherd, and my tongue cleaves to my jaws."* That accurately describes the extreme muscle fatigue, exhaustion, and dehydration caused by crucifixion.[47] Jesus' statement in John 19:28 (*"I am thirsty"*) alludes to Ps 22:15 (*"my tongue cleaves to my jaws"*). The prophecies of Psalm 22 are remarkable, particularly since the psalm was written approximately 500–600 years before the Persians invented crucifixion.

Psalm 22 accurately prophesied other aspects of Christ's crucifixion. Ps 22:18 states, *"They divide my garments among them, and for my clothing they cast lots."* The Roman soldiers did that with respect to Christ's clothing, and John notes that *"this was to fulfill the Scripture"* (John 19:24–25; see also Mark 15:24; Luke 23:34). From the cross, Jesus quoted Ps 22:1, *"My God, my God, why have You forsaken me?"* (Matt 27:46; Mark 15:34) in fulfillment of what Ps 22:1 was prophesying. The reference in Ps 22:7 to the people's

---

43. See the discussion of David and Solomon in chapter 7.

44. Davis, "Physician Analyzes," Golgotha; John 20:25, 27; see also Luke 24:39. Zech 12:10 also prophesies that *"they will look on Me whom they have pierced."* That is applied to Jesus in John 19:37; Rev 1:7.

45. Davis, "Anatomical," 7, 10, 11.

46. Davis, "Anatomical," 45–48.

47. Davis, "Anatomical," 14, 17, 33, 35, 42.

"wagging their heads" was fulfilled while Jesus was on the cross (Matt 27:39; Mark 15:29). Matt 27:43 reports that some of the bystanders to the crucifixion repeated the words of Ps 22:8, *"He trusts in God; let God rescue Him now, if He delights in Him; for He said, 'I am the Son of God.'"* As he died, Jesus quoted the words of Ps 31:5, *"Into Your hands I commit my spirit."* Heb 2:11–12 concludes the use of Psalm 22 by quoting Ps 22:22, *"I will proclaim Your name to My brethren, In the midst of the congregation I will sing Your praise."* This "utterance of the risen Christ in the midst of the congregation of God's people . . . serves to confirm the solidarity of Christ with his people, and this solidarity emerges not only from the fact that the Christ of Psalm 22 . . . calls them his brothers but also from the fact that he is united with them in suffering, as the rest of the psalm demonstrates."[48] Hengstenberg points out that, while some of the specifics of the psalm might be replicated in individuals other than Jesus, it is beyond statistical probability to suppose that "*all the circumstances* [of Psalm 22] which have so literally concurred in the history of Jesus, can be met with, *in the same combination,* in the life of any other person."[49]

PSALM 69

Psalm 69 is also prophetic of Jesus' actions and people's response to him. In John 2:13–15, Jesus cleansed the temple by driving out the moneychangers. John 2:17 then recounts, *"His disciples remembered that it was written, 'Zeal for Your house will consume me,'"* quoting Ps 69:9. The "me" in Ps 69:9 can only be referring to Jesus. In Rom 15:3, Paul quotes the second half of Ps 69:9 as having been fulfilled in Christ, *"For even Christ did not please Himself; but as it is written, 'The reproaches of those who reproached You fell on Me.'"* In John 15:18–25, Jesus told his disciples that the world will hate them, because it first has hated him; he then quotes Ps 69:4 (and Ps 35:19), saying, *"But they have done this to fulfill the word that is written in their Law, 'They hated Me without a cause'"* (John 15:25). Paul also states that the bulk of Israel rejected Jesus *"just as it is written"* in Ps 69:22–23, which he quotes in Rom 11:8–10. When Jesus was on the cross, Matt 27:34 reports that *"they gave Him wine to drink mixed with gall; and after tasting it, He was unwilling to drink"* (see also Matt 27:48; Mark 15:23, 36; Luke 23:36; John 19:28–30). That was in fulfillment of Ps 69:21, which says, *"They also gave me gall for my food and for my thirst they gave me vinegar to drink."* Ps 69:25 (*"Let his homestead be made desolate, and let no one dwell in it"*) is quoted by Peter in

---

48. Hays, "Christ Prays the Psalms," 126–27.
49. Hengstenberg, *Christology,* 97, emph. in orig.

Acts 1:20 as being predictive of Judas. Peter follows that by quoting Ps 109:8, *"Let another man take his office,"* as being predictive of replacing Judas with Matthias, to fill out the now-missing member of The Twelve.

PSALM 110

Psalm 110 became a key text in the NT (there are 21 quotations or allusions to Ps 110:1 the NT). Ps 110:1 says, *"The Lord says to my Lord: 'Sit at My right hand Until I make Your enemies a footstool for Your feet.'"* After the triumphal entry into Jerusalem, when Jesus was debating with the Pharisees, he asked the Pharisees what they thought about the Christ: *"Whose son is he?"* They responded that he is *"the son of David."* Christ asked, *"Then how does David in the Spirit call him 'Lord'?* and quoted Ps 110:1 which says, *"The Lord said to my Lord. . ."* He then asked, *"If David* [who wrote the psalm] *then calls him 'Lord,' how is He his son?"* (Matt 22:41–46; Mark 12:35–37; Luke 20:41–44) Both Jesus and the Pharisees interpreted Psalm 110 as pertaining to the Messiah.[50] Jesus was pointing to himself as the Messiah, David's "greater son," and was asserting that he was divine. The Pharisees did not question this interpretation, even though it would have been in their interest to do so, if they could have.[51] Ps 110:1 is quoted in Matt 22:44; Mark 12:36; Luke 20:42–43; 22:69; and Acts 2:34–35 and applied to Jesus. Ps 110:1b is quoted in Heb 1:13; 10:12 and applied to Jesus. Ps 110:1 also is alluded to in Matt 26:64; Mark 14:62; 16:19; Acts 2:33; 5:31; 7:55–56; Rom 8:34; 1 Cor 15:25; Eph 1:20–22; Col 3:1; Heb 1:3; 8:1; 12:2; and 1 Pet 3:22, all of which speak of Christ reigning at the right hand of the Father. Ps 80:17 similarly connects the *"man of Your right hand"* (Ps 110:1) with the *"Son of Man"*[52] by saying *"Let Your hand be upon the man of Your right hand, upon the son of man whom You made strong for Yourself."*

PSALM 118

Ps 118:22 states, *"The stone which the builders rejected has become the chief corner stone. This is the Lord's doing; it is marvelous in our eyes."* Jesus applies this to himself in Matt 21:42; Luke 20:17. Peter applies it to Jesus in Acts 4:11, and Paul applies it to Jesus in Eph 2:20. Ps 118:26 (*"Blessed is he*

---

50. For reasons why Psalm 110 cannot be interpreted as pertaining to anyone other than the Messiah, see Hengstenberg, *Christology*, 79–85.

51. See Goppelt, *Typos*, 83 ("The term 'Lord' (*kurios*) makes him equal with God").

52. See discussion below regarding Jesus as the *"Son of Man."*

who comes in the name of the Lord") is quoted by the people as applying to Jesus' triumphal entry into Jerusalem (Matt 21:9; Mark 11:9; Luke 19:38; John 12:13) and by Jesus, in Matt 23:39; Luke 13:35, as applying to his Second Coming. Those two events are related typologically: the first (triumphal entry) is a type of the second (the Second Coming).

ISAIAH

There are multiple prophecies concerning Jesus in the writings of the prophets, primarily Isaiah. In Isaiah 6, God commissioned Isaiah to go to the people and proclaim God's word, but in so commissioning him, God said he was to tell the people, *"Keep on listening, but do not perceive; keep on looking, but do not understand. . . . Otherwise they might see with their eyes, hear with their ears, understand with their hearts, and return and be healed."* (Isa 6:9–10) As originally given, Isa 6:9–10 was carried out in Isaiah's lifetime, but Jesus calls it a *"prophecy"* which *"is being fulfilled"* (Matt 13:14). In Isa 6:9–10, Israel was being judged for worshipping idols. In Jesus' day, Israel was still guilty of idol worship, except that its idols were different: it had substituted man-made tradition in place of the love of God (see Isa 29:9–13; Ezek 14:4, 7; Matt 15:7–9; 23:29–33; Mark 7:6–13) and sought to establish its own righteousness in place of God's righteousness (Rom 10:3). Israel's sin was even worse than in former generations, since they rejected God himself who had come to earth in the person of Jesus. Because the people did not believe in Jesus, he quoted Isa 6:9–10 as the reason why he spoke to them in parables, *"because while seeing they do not see, and while hearing they do not hear, nor do they understand"* (Matt 13:13–15; Mark 4:12; Luke 8:10). In John 12:37–38, the apostle John points out that, despite Jesus' miracles, the people's unbelief in him was *"to fulfill the word of Isaiah the prophet"* in Isa 53:1. He then quotes Isa 6:10 and says, *"These things Isaiah said because he saw His glory, and he spoke of Him [Jesus]"* (John 12:40–41). Similarly, in Acts 28:23–27 Paul quotes Isa 6:9–10, concerning Israel's blindness and deafness, as applying to Israel's rejection of Jesus. In Isa 6:11, Isaiah asked *"how long"* Isarael's spiritual blindness would last. God answered that it would continue even after the remnant returned following their exile in Babylon. G. K. Beale comments, "It is understandable that Jesus saw the majority of unbelieving Israel in his own day as the continuation of that unbelieving and blinded remnant. In this respect, it is also understandable why Jesus saw that Isaiah 6:9–10 was a prophecy of the spiritual condition of Jews in Isaiah's day and also of his own day."[53]

53. Beale, *We Become*, 165.

Other prophecies in Isaiah find their fulfillment in Jesus: *"Therefore the Lord Himself will give you a sign: Behold, a virgin will be with child and bear a son, and she will call His name Immanuel"* (Isa 7:14; applied to Jesus in Matt 1:22–23, which specifies that "Immanuel" means *"God with us"*). Matthew states that Jesus' beginning his ministry in the Capernaum, which is in the region of Zebulon and Naphtali, *"fulfills what was spoken through Isaiah the prophet"* (Matt 4:12–16, quoting Isa 9:1–2). The Gentiles' hoping in, praising, and coming to faith in Christ were prophesied in Deut 32:43; 2 Sam 22:50; Ps 18:49; 117:1; and Isa 11:10, all of which are quoted in Rom 15:8–12 as having been fulfilled. Jesus stated in Matt 15:7–9 and Mark 7:6–7 that the people's hypocritically worshiping him in vain fulfilled the prophecy of Isa 29:13. In Matt 8:16–17, Jesus' miraculous healing of people was explicitly said to *"fulfill what was spoken through Isaiah the prophet"* in Isa 53:4. *"My house will be called a house of prayer"* (Isa 56:7) was applied by Jesus to himself in Matt 21:13. In Luke 4:17–21 Jesus quotes from Isa 61:1–2, which begins, *"The Spirit of the Lord is upon Me. . ."* Jesus concludes, *"Today this Scripture has been fulfilled in your hearing."*

A prophecy does not always have to be stated as having been "fulfilled" to be recognized as having been fulfilled. We see this in a number of prophecies of Isaiah. For example, in Matt 11:5, Jesus quotes Isa 35:5–6 and alludes to Isa 61:1 regarding the blind receiving sight, the lame walking, the deaf hearing, and the gospel being preached; although he does not explicitly use the language of "fulfillment," his point is that he is the fulfillment of those prophecies.

Isa 9:6–7 states, *"For a child will be born to us, a son will be given to us; and the government will rest on His shoulders; and His name will be called Wonderful Counselor, Mighty God, Eternal Father, Prince of Peace. There will be no end to the increase of His government or of peace, on the throne of David and over his kingdom, to establish it and to uphold it with justice and righteousness from then on and forevermore. The zeal of the Lord of hosts will accomplish this."* Although this passage is not specifically quoted in the NT, Jesus' birth, life, resurrection, ascension, and the nature of his kingdom all align with Isaiah's description. Matt 2:6 quotes Micah 5:2–4 as applying to Jesus; Micah 5:5a, which concludes the thought of Micah 5:4, states *"This One will be our peace."* That is in accord with Isaiah's reference to the *"Prince of Peace."* Additionally, the angel Gabriel alluded to Isa 9:7 when he told Mary that *"the Lord God will give Him [Jesus] the throne of His father David"* (Luke 1:32); Peter announced that Jesus is now seated on the "throne of David," and is reigning forever (Acts 2:32–36). Isaiah's descriptions of Christ as divine—*"Mighty God, Eternal Father, Prince of Peace. There will be no end to the increase of His government or of peace . . . from then on and forevermore"*—cannot refer to any earthly ruler, particularly given the Hebrew view of the transcendence of God and their abhorrence of attributing divine attributes to mere men.[54] Finally, in Isa 45:23, God says that *"to Me every knee will bow."* Phil 2:10 quotes this, but changes the wording to say that *"at the name of Jesus every knee will bow."* Although that aspect of the prophecy has not yet been fulfilled, Paul is clearly identifying Jesus as God.

THE SHOOT AND THE BRANCH

Isaiah and Jeremiah prophesied the coming "Shoot" or "Branch." Isa 11:1–2, 10 states, *"Then a shoot will spring from the stem of Jesse, and a branch from his roots will bear fruit. The Spirit of the Lord will rest on Him, the spirit of wisdom and understanding, the spirit of counsel and strength, the spirit of knowledge and the fear of the Lord. . . . Then in that day the nations will resort to the root of Jesse, who will stand as a signal for the peoples; and His resting place will be glorious."* (see also Isa 53:2) Jer 23:5 states, *"Behold, the days are coming, declares the Lord, 'When I will raise up for David a righteous Branch; and He will reign as king and act wisely and do justice and righteousness in the land'"* (see also Isa 4:2; Jer 33:14–16). The "Shoot" or "Branch" refers to his relationship to David: David is the root or main stem of the tree; "growing out of this Davidic kingship is to come another king."[55] This prophecy was pointing to and fulfilled by Jesus. Jesus is from David's line (Matt 1:1–17; Luke 3:23–38) and is the *"son of David."*[56] The prophecy is alluded to in Rev 5:5; 22:16 (*"root of David"*) as applying to Jesus. At Jesus' baptism, Isa 11:2 was fulfilled when John saw *"the Spirit of God descending as a dove and lighting on Him"* (Matt 3:16; see also Mark 1:10; Luke 3:22; John 1:32). Paul quotes Isa 11:10 in Rom 15:12 (*"root of Jesse"*) as applying to Jesus. The angel Gabriel told Mary that Jesus would fulfill Jer 23:5 in that he *"will be great and will be called the Son of the Most High; and the Lord God will give Him the throne of His father David; and He will reign over the house of Jacob forever, and His kingdom will have no end"* (Luke 1:32–33). This has been accomplished (see Matt 28:18–20; Acts 2:24–36; Eph 1:20–22).

Zechariah elaborates the "Branch" prophecy by stating, *"Thus says the Lord of hosts, 'Behold, a man whose name is Branch, for He will branch out from where He is; and He will build the temple of the Lord. Yes, it is He who will build the temple of the Lord, and He who will bear the honor and sit and*

---

54. See Hengstenberg, *Christology*, 195.

55. Mbewe, "Righteous Branch," 94.

56. Matt 9:27; 12:23; 15:22; 20:30–31; 21:9; Mark 10:47–48; 12:35–37; Luke 18:38–39.

rule on His throne. Thus, He will be a priest on His throne, and the counsel of peace will be between the two offices.'" (Zech 6:12–13; see also Zech 3:8) The context of Zechariah's prophecy was the rebuilding of the temple under Joshua and Zerubbabel following the exile in Babylon. In this prophecy, "Branch" has "become a proper name of the Messiah."[57] Charles Briggs concludes, "The Messiah, named Branch, is to be the builder of the temple of Jahveh of which the temple of Zerubbabel was the preparation. He will be crowned, and will be enthroned. He will unite in his crown the royal and the priestly offices. . . . It is in this prediction that Zechariah advances the Messianic idea beyond and of his predecessors. Jesus Christ of Nazareth is the realization of these predictions."[58]

Conrad Mbewe indicates that "branching out" suggests that the "Branch" "will not merely repeat or do his work as the main stem has done, He will do it differently and will bring his people into a new phase of life."[59] This is hinted at in Zech 6:12, which says that Messiah will build *"the temple,"* not *"a temple"* of the Lord. As Hengstenberg says, "The Temple is thus designated as perpetually existing, as constantly the same; it is, however, to be exalted by the Messiah in a glory never anticipated before."[60] That is exactly what Jesus did. Jesus spoke of building the temple when he said, *"Destroy this temple, and in three days I will raise it up"* (John 2:19). However, he was not speaking of raising a physical building, such as David had wanted to construct, Solomon did construct, and Zerubbabel rebuilt. Instead, *"He was speaking of the temple of His body"* (John 2:21). Further, Jesus built a "living temple," the church (Eph 2:19–22), consisting of "living stones" (1 Pet 2:5), which is the true "temple of God" (1 Cor 3:16–17; 2 Cor 6:16). Jesus also unites the offices of king and priest, in fulfillment of Zech 6:13.[61]

A similar thought is indicated in Zech 3:8 which states, *"Now listen, Joshua the high priest, you and your friends who are sitting in front of you—indeed they are men who are a symbol, for behold, I am going to bring in My servant the Branch."* Since Joshua was the high priests, his companions undoubtedly were the priests. They were a "symbol" in the sense that the characteristic of the priestly office consisted in mediating between God and the people, chiefly in procuring the forgiveness of sins through the sacrificial rituals. The Messiah, i.e., the Branch, "can be presented as the antitype of

---

57. Briggs, *Messianic Prophecy*, 442n.2.
58. Briggs, *Messianic Prophecy*, 448; see also Hengstenberg, *Christology*, 309–11.
59. Mbewe, "Righteous Branch," 94.
60. Hengstenberg, *Christology*, 310.
61. He is the king, Matt 21:1–11; Mark 11:1–11; Luke 19:28–40; John 1:49; 12:12–16); he is also the great high priest, Heb 2:17; 4:14—5:15; 7:1—8:6.

the priesthood, only so far as he should *perfectly accomplish* the mediation and deliverance from sin, which was but *imperfectly accomplished* by it."[62]

THE SON OF MAN

Jesus is called the *"Son of Man"* approximately 80 times in the Gospels; it is his most frequent description of himself. The phrase *"Son of Man"* alludes to Dan 7:13–14 (*"I kept looking in the night visions, and behold, with the clouds of heaven One like a Son of Man was coming, and He came up to the Ancient of Days and was presented before Him. And to Him was given dominion, glory and a kingdom, that all the peoples, nations and men of every language might serve Him. His dominion is an everlasting dominion which will not pass away; and His kingdom is one which will not be destroyed."*). Jesus quotes a portion of Dan 7:13 (*"Son of Man was coming"*), with respect to himself, in Matt 16:27–28; 24:27, 30, 37, 39, 44; 25:31; 26:64; Mark 8:38; 13:26; 14:62; Luke 7:34; 9:26; 12:40; 18:8; 21:27. In Rev 1:13–14, John received a revelation from Jesus, who is described as *"one like a son of man . . . [whose] head and His hair were white like wool, like snow."* Those images are taken from Daniel's vision in Dan 7:9, 13. However, in Daniel's vision (Dan 7:9) it was *"the Ancient of Days"* whose *"vesture was like white snow and the hair of His head like pure wool."* Given this context, "John sees 'one like a son of man' who is distinguished from and identified with the Ancient of Days—a mysterious combination but consistent with the fact that he lays claim to the title 'the first and the last' ([Rev] 1:17), by which God proclaimed his divine eternity (Isa. 41:4; 44:6; 48:12). The Son of Man is God, infinite in wisdom and holiness."[63]

Whenever Jesus used the term *"Son of Man"* he was making an assertion that he was, in fact, God come to earth *as a man*. In John 3:13 he explicitly said, *"No one has ascended into heaven, but He who descended from heaven: the Son of Man."* Similarly, in John 6:62 Jesus said, *"What then if you see the Son of Man ascending to where He was before?"* Jesus both came from heaven and returned to heaven, and his reference to *"where He was before"* affirms his pre-existence.[64] In short, he was no mere man.

We see Jesus claiming to be deity in his other references to the *"Son of Man."* For example, Jesus' claim that *"the Son of Man has authority on earth to forgive sins"* (Matt 9:6; Mark 2:10; Luke 5:24) is a claim to be God *come to earth as a man*, because only God has the authority to forgive sins; yet here

---

62. Hengstenberg, *Christology*, 296, emph. in orig.
63. Johnson, *Triumph*, 59.
64. See Carson, *Gospel*, 301.

Jesus is claiming to forgive sins on his own authority. In Matt 12:8; Mark 2:28; Luke 6:5 Jesus said, *"The Son of Man is Lord of the Sabbath."* By saying that, Jesus was claiming to be God himself, since the Sabbath was instituted by God and was the *"Sabbath of the Lord"* (Exod 20:10).[65] In Luke 9:58 Jesus said, *"The Son of Man did not come to destroy men's lives, but to save them"* (see also Luke 19:9–10). The granting of salvation to anyone is something that only God can do. In Matt 13:41–42 Jesus said, *"The Son of Man will send forth His angels, and they will gather out of His kingdom all stumbling blocks, and those who commit lawlessness, and will throw them into the furnace of fire; in that place there will be weeping and gnashing of teeth."* Similarly, in Matt 16:27 Jesus says that *"the Son of Man is going to come in the glory of His Father with His angels, and will then repay every man according to his deeds."* Sending the angels and rendering eternal judgment are the acts of God.

In Matt 24:42–44, the *"Son of Man"* is specifically equated with the "Lord." In Matt 25:31–46, the *"Son of Man"* is equated with the "King" who *"will sit on His glorious throne"* and judge all the people of the earth, sending some to hell and others to eternal life. That, of course, can only refer to God. Thus, again, when Jesus calls himself the *"Son of Man"* he is equating himself with God Almighty. In Matt 19:27–28 Jesus says that *"in the regeneration [or, renewal of all things] when the Son of Man will sit on his glorious throne, you also shall sit upon twelve thrones, judging the twelve tribes of Israel"* (see also Luke 22:29–30). The "throne" can only be the throne of God. In John 6:27 Jesus says that people should work for *"the food which endures to eternal life, which the Son of Man will give to you."* Again, eternal life is something that only God can give, and here Jesus is saying that he will give it (see also John 6:40, 53–54).

Similarly, Jesus equated the *"Son of Man"* with being the divine *"Son of God."* In John 5:19–29, Jesus repeatedly calls himself the *"Son,"* the *"Son of God,"* and the *"Son of Man."* Jesus' references to the *"Son of God"* and the *"Son of Man"* are in the same context of his executing judgment on the day of resurrection and judgment. The two terms therefore are equivalent. The terms are used equivalently by Jesus in Matt 16:13, 16–17 and John 1:49–51.

Finally, at his trial before the high priest in Matt 26:63–65 (Mark 14:61–63; Luke 22:66–71), the following interchange took place: *"The high priest said to Him, 'I adjure You by the living God, that You tell us whether You are the Christ, the Son of God.' Jesus said to him, 'You have said it yourself; nevertheless I tell you, hereafter you will see the Son of Man sitting at the right hand of Power and coming on the clouds of heaven.' Then the high priest tore his robes and said, 'He has blasphemed! What further need do we have of witnesses? Behold, you*

---

65. See also Exod 31:13, 15; 35:2; Lev 19:3; 23:3, 38; 25:2; Deut 5:14; Isa 58:13.

have now heard the blasphemy.'" Craig Blomberg discusses why Jesus' claim to be the "Son of Man" in this context is so significant:

> This "Son of Man" saying, rather than the claim that he was some kind of messiah, is what would have led the high priest to tear his garments and proclaim that Jesus had blasphemed (26:65). Alleging messiahship was no capital offense; otherwise, the Jews could never have received a messiah! But claiming to be the exalted, heavenly Son of Man, one who was Lord and next to the Father himself in heaven, transgressed the boundaries of what most of the Jewish leaders deemed permissible for mere mortals.[66]

Jesus also invested the term *"Son of Man"* with a much richer meaning even than being the divine Son of God. He did this be equating the term *"Son of Man"* with the "Servant of the Lord" of Isa 42:1–9; 49:1–6; 50:4–9; 52:13—53:12.[67] Jesus equated himself with both the "Servant" and the Son of Man by telling his disciples, *"The Son of Man did not come to be served, but to serve, and to give His life a ransom for many"* (Matt 20:28; see also Luke 22:25-27). This humility of the Son of Man was demonstrated throughout Jesus' life. Jesus said, *"The foxes have holes and the birds of the air have nests, but the Son of Man has nowhere to lay His head"* (Luke 9:58). Just as John the Baptist suffered at the hands of the rich and powerful, *"so also the Son of Man is going to suffer at their hands"* (Matt 17:12). Thomas Schreiner summarizes, "According to Daniel 7:9-22 the Son of man was a heavenly figure who would participate in the judgment on the last day; however, Jesus pours new content into the title by claiming that the Son of man must also suffer. Thus, Jesus links together the Son of man and the Suffering Servant (Isa. 52:13—53:12)."[68]

This is important in that it reveals the true nature of God. As Richard Bauckham puts it, "Jesus reveals the divine identity—who God truly is—in humiliation as well as exaltation, and in the connexion of the two. God's own identity is revealed in Jesus, his life and his cross, just as truly as in his exaltation, in a way that is fully continuous and consistent with the Old Testament and Jewish understanding of God, but is also novel and surprising."[69]

---

66. Blomberg, "Matthew," 93.
67. See chapter 6—Christ and the Church are the Prophesied "Servant of the Lord."
68. Schreiner, "Luke," 818.
69. Bauckham, *God Crucified*, viii.

THE MESSIAH[70]

"Messiah" (Hebrew = *mashiach*) itself means "anointed" or "anointed one." The Greek term for "anointed" or "anointed one" is *christos* from which is derived the name "Christ." The term "Messiah" is actually found only two times in the OT, in Dan 9:25-26.[71] "Messiah" denotes "an expected or longed-for savior, especially in the Jewish tradition. . . . In its primary biblical usage, then, 'anointed' is, virtually a synonymous term of 'king,' in particular David and his descendants. . . . Eventually royal language and imagery came to be applied primarily to a hoped-for future king, whose reign would be characterized by everlasting justice, security, and peace."[72]

Although the actual term "Messiah" is only found in Daniel 9, multiple other OT prophecies suggested the Messiah would come in one of three forms: (1) a king (see Jer 23:5-6; Ps 110:1-2); (2) a priest (see 1 Sam 2:35; Ps 110:3-4; Zech 6:12-13); and (3) a prophet (see Deut 18:15-19). Importantly, the Messiah was not merely to be "a king" but was to be "the king"—the *final* king of the world. "In rabbinic thought, the Messiah is the king who will redeem and rule Israel at the climax of human history and the instrument by which the kingdom of God will be established."[73] His priesthood would be "forever" and would not be like the Levitical priests but would be *"according to the order of Melchizedek"* (Ps 110:4). Many OT passages indicated that the Messiah would be a human being;[74] but other passages suggested that the Messiah would be divine.[75] The concept of the Messiah was well-known. In Jesus' encounter with the Samaritan woman at the well of Sychar, the woman said to Jesus, *"I know that Messiah is coming (He who is called Christ); when that One comes, He will declare all things to us"* (John 4:25). Most Jews around the time of Jesus expected Messiah to be

---

70. See also chapter 7 regarding David and Solomon and chapter 9 regarding the Davidic Covenant.

71. The major different interpretations of this passage are discussed in Menn, *Biblical Eschatology*, 2nd ed., 400–439.

72. Sawyer, "Messiah," 513-14.

73. Jacobs, "Messiah," Messiah in Rabbinic Thought.

74. E.g., Gen 3:15; Isa 11:1-5; 42:1-6; 59:20; Jer 30:18-22; 33:14-15.

75. E.g., Ps 2:6-12; 110:1-7; Isa 9:6; Jer 23:5-6; Micah 5:2; Zech 14:9. There are more than 100 direct messianic predictions in the OT as well as numerous "types" that pointed to the Messiah. See Kaiser, *Messiah*, 29, 34; Payne, *Encyclopedia*, 665–72. The messianic prophecies were not disconnected or random. "Instead, it is amazing how the depictions concerning the coming Messiah and his work comprised one continuous plan of God. Each aspect was linked into an ongoing stream of announcements beginning in the prepatriarchal period . . . down to the postexilic times of Israel's last leaders and prophets." Kaiser, *Messiah*, 29.

more of a political figure—a warrior-king like David—who would drive out the Romans and re-establish Jerusalem and the temple in splendor as the center of the new earth.

The NT clearly shows that Jesus Christ fulfills the Israelite expectations of the Messiah. However, he fulfilled the prophecies and role of Messiah in ways that were unexpected; he thereby gave the term a greater and deeper meaning than people had anticipated. He was indeed a triumphant warrior, but his battle was not with the Romans; instead, in his life and on the cross, Jesus defeated the three greatest enemies that every person has to face: sin, Satan, and death itself. Jesus is the king sent by God.[76] He is the perfect high priest *"according to the order of Melchizedek"* in the true temple (Heb 2:17; 4:14—5:10; 7:1—8:6; 10:11-22). Jesus also is the prophet predicted by Moses (John 1:45; 6:14; Acts 3:20-23). Finally, Jesus was both fully man *and* fully God.[77]

The NT repeatedly confirms that Jesus was the "anointed" one of God.[78] Jesus confirmed that he is, in fact, the Messiah. When the woman at the well said, *"I know that Messiah is coming (He who is called Christ); when that One comes, He will declare all things to us,"* Jesus responded, *"I who speak to you am He"* (John 4:25-26). After he stayed in Sychar with the Samaritans for two days, many of them believed that Jesus was the Messiah and told the woman, *"It is no longer because of what you said that we believe, for we have heard for ourselves and know that this One is indeed the Savior of the world"* (John 4:42). Jesus received worship *as the Messiah*.[79] Jesus' crucifixion caused those who believed he was the promised deliverer to lose their hope, because a crucified Messiah seemed to be a contradiction in terms (see Luke 24:19-21). The people did not then understand that the crucifixion was the means by which salvation from sin had to be accomplished. After his resurrection, Jesus explained to his disciples, *"Was it not necessary for the Christ [i.e., the Messiah] to suffer these things and to enter into his glory?"* (Luke 24:26), and *"Thus it is written, that the Christ [i.e., the Messiah] would suffer and rise again from the dead the third day"* (Luke 24:46).

The Messiah was expected to be the "son of David" (Matt 22:41-46; Mark 12:35-37). Jesus was recognized as the greater "son of David."[80]

---

76. See, e.g., Matt 2:4-11; 16:16, 20; 22:42-45; 26:63-64; Mark 8:29; 12:35-37; 14:61-62; Luke 4:41; 20:41-44; 22:67-70; 23:2-3, 39; 24:26, 46; John 4:25-26; 11:25-27; 20:30-31; Acts 2:30-36; 9:22; 17:3; 18:5, 28; 1 John 2:22; 5:1.

77. See Appendix 1: Jesus is Fully God and Fully Man.

78. Luke 4:18; Acts 4:27; 10:38; Heb 1:9.

79. See Matt 9:2-8, 12-13; Mark 2:3-12; Luke 5:17-26, 31-32; 7:47-50; 9:56; 19:10; John 5:33-34; 8:1-11; 10:7-9; 12:47.

80. Matt 1:1; 9:27; 15:22; 20:30-31; 21:9, 15; Mark 10:47-48; Luke 18:38-39.

However, he was more than that. In the covenant God made with David, God said with respect to David's son, *"I will be a father to him and he will be a son to Me"* (2 Sam 7:14). The phrase *"Son of God"* thus became a messianic phrase denoting the promised Davidic king. At Jesus' baptism and transfiguration, God declared of Jesus, *"You are my beloved son, in you I am well-pleased"* (Matt 3:17; Mark 1:11; Luke 3:22). Jesus frequently is called the *"Son of God."*[81] Jesus also referred to himself as the *"Son of God."*[82]

The apostles were able to reason from the OT scriptures that Jesus was the Messiah.[83] Paul even argued that he was arrested and on trial *"for the sake of the hope of Israel"* (Acts 28:20), i.e., "the hope of messianic salvation [that] has been made a present reality by the resurrection of Jesus, who is the one whom God is fulfilling his promises that constituted Israel's hope."[84] Hence, the NT repeatedly proclaims Jesus as the savior—the Messiah, the Christ—who alone can save people from their sins.[85]

THE IMPORTANCE OF MESSIANIC PROPHECIES

There is more to the importance of prophecy even than the above has indicated. Probability analysis demonstrates that it is mathematically impossible for the multiple prophecies concerning Jesus to have been fulfilled by chance in any one person. Several years ago, mathematics and astronomy professor Peter W. Stoner took just eight of the prophecies concerning Jesus (born in Bethlehem, Micah 5:2; had a forerunner to prepare the way, Mal 3:1; entered Jerusalem on a donkey, Zech 9:9; betrayed by a friend causing wounds in his hands, Zech 13:6; betrayed for 30 pieces of silver, Zech 11:12;

---

81. Matt 4:3, 6; 8:29; 26:63; 27:40, 54; Mark 1:1; 3:11; 15:39; Luke 1:35; 3:38; 4:3, 9, 41; John 1:34, 49; 11:27; 20:31; Acts 8:37; 9:20; Rom 1:4; 2 Cor 1:19; Gal 2:20; Eph 4:13; Heb 4:14; 6:6; 7:3; 10:29; 1 John 3:8; 4:15; 5:5, 10, 12, 13, 20.

82. Matt 26:63–64; 27:43; Mark 14:61–62; Luke 22:70; John 3:18; 5:25; 10:36; 11:4; 19:7; Rev 2:18.

83. See Acts 2:29–36; 3:18–20; 4:5–12; 5:29–32; 8:30–37; 9:22; 13:32–39; 17:2–3, 10–12; 18:5, 24–28; 26:22–23; 28:23–24.

84. Schnabel, *Acts*, 1069; see also Marshall, *Acts*, 423 ("What was at issue in his trial, as he had insisted all along, was the true nature of *the hope of Israel* in the coming of the Messiah and the resurrection"); Harrison, *Acts*, 402 ("'the hope of Israel' . . . centered in the person of Jesus of Nazareth as validated by His resurrection from the dead"); Kepple, "Hope," 231–41.

85. Matt 1:21; Luke 2:11; John 1:29; 3:17; 4:42; Acts 3:26; 4:12; 5:31; 13:23, 38–39; 15:11; 16:31; Rom 3:24–26; 4:25; 5:1, 6–11, 15–21; 8:2; 10:9; 1 Cor 1:30; 6:11; 15:17; 2 Cor 5:18–21; Gal 1:3–4; Eph 2:13–16; 4:32; 5:2, 25–26; Phil 3:20; Col 1:12–14; 3:13; 1 Thess 1:10; 5:9–10; 1 Tim 1:15; 2 Tim 2:10; 3:15; Titus 1:4; 2:13–14; Heb 2:17; 5:9; 7:25; 13:20; 1 Pet 1:18–19; 3:18; 2 Pet 1:11; 1 John 3:5; 4:9–10, 14; Rev 5:9; 14:4.

betrayal money cast into house of the Lord to go to a potter, Zech 11:13; oppressed and afflicted but remained silent before his accusers, Isa 53:7; and had his hands and feet pierced, Ps 22:6). A class at Pasadena City College ran a probability analysis, having first come up with reasonable and conservative estimates for the chance of one person fulfilling each of the eight prophecies. The estimates and calculations were as follows: 1 in 2.8 x 10^5 x 10^3 x 10^2 x 10^3 x 10^5 x 10^3 x 10^4 = 1 in 10^{28}.[86] The question is: What is the chance that any person might have lived from the day of those prophecies to the present time and fulfilled all eight prophecies? To answer that, one divides 10^{28} by the total number of people who have lived since the time of the prophecies, then estimated to have been approximately 88 billion. The result is that "the chance that any man might have lived down to the present time and fulfilled all eight prophecies is 1 in 10^{17}."[87]

What does that mean? Stoner wrote that if one took 10^{17} silver dollars and lay them on the face of Texas, they would cover the state two feet deep.[88] He then explained:

> Now mark one of these silver dollars and stir the whole mass thoroughly, all over the state. Blindfold a man and tell him that he can travel as far as he wishes, but he must pick up one silver dollar and say that this is the right one. What chance would he have of getting the right one? Just the same chance that the prophets would have had of writing these eight prophecies and having them all come true in any one man, from their day to the present time, provided they wrote using their own wisdom. . . . This means that the fulfillment of these eight prophecies alone proves that God inspired the writing of those prophecies to a definiteness which lacks only one chance in 10^{17} of being absolute.[89]

Stoner went on to conclude, using the same principles of probability, that the human chance of fulfilling 48 of the prophecies relating to Jesus would be 1 in 10^{157}. That is equivalent to the number of electrons

---

86. Stoner, *Science Speaks*, 59–62. The 2.8 number is derived from the fact that the population of the earth has averaged less than 2 billion people, and the population of Bethlehem has averaged less than 7,150. Hence, one divides 7,150 into 2 billion which results in the chance that one man in 2.8 x 105 was born in Bethlehem. Stoner, *Science Speaks*, 60.

87. Stoner, *Science Speaks*, 63.

88. Texas is 268,597 square miles (695,660 km2) in size. It is between the size of Myanmar (261,228 square miles; 676,578 km2) and Zambia (290,586 square miles; 752,617 km2).

89. Stoner, *Science Speaks*, 63.

comprising 500 solid balls of electrons, each ball having a diameter of 6 billion light-years![90]

The implications of these data are astounding. Stoner explains, "This is not merely evidence. It is proof of the Bible's inspiration by God—proof so definite that the universe is not large enough to hold the evidence."[91] All of this leads to the conclusion that Jesus is exactly who he said he is, God come to earth as a man.

---

90. Stoner, *Science Speaks*, 64–65. In the foreword to Stoner's book, H. Harold Hartzler, Ph.D., professor of mathematics, physics, and astronomy, and secretary-treasurer of the American Scientific Affiliation, stated, "The manuscript for Science Speaks has been carefully reviewed by a committee of the American Scientific Affiliation members and by the Executive Council of the same group and has been found, in general, to be dependable and accurate in regard to the scientific material presented. The mathematical analysis included is based upon principles of probability which are thoroughly sound and Professor Stoner has applied these principles in a proper and convincing way." Hartzler, "Foreword," 4. Stoner added, "If the reader does not agree with the estimates given, he may make his own estimates and then carry them through to their logical conclusions." Stoner, *Science Speaks*, 60.

91. Stoner, *Science Speaks*, 65; see also Kaiser, *Old Testament*, 169; Van de Weghe, *Prepared*, 219–32; Reasons to Believe, *Why the Bible*, 1–4.

6

Christ and the Church are the Prophesied "Servant of the Lord"

JESUS IS THE PROPHESIED "SERVANT OF THE LORD"

IN ISAIAH FOUR PASSAGES are known as "Servant Songs": Isa 42:1–9; 49:1–6 (or, 13); 50:4–9; 52:13—53:12.[1] The specific identity of the "Servant" is ambiguous. Sometimes he is seen as a collective, i.e., all of Israel itself, "ideal" Israel, or the faithful remnant of Israel.[2] However, all of the Servant Songs also describe individualistic characteristics which distinguish the Servant from the nation itself, especially the third and fourth Songs which describe the "Suffering Servant." As described by Isaiah: the Servant has the Spirit of God upon him (42:1); he will bring salvation to Israel and the Gentiles and is a *"light of the nations"* (42:6; 49:6); he is beaten and afflicted (50:6; 52:14, 53:4–5, 7, 10); he is despised and forsaken (53:3); despite persecution he does not open his mouth (42:2; 53:7); and he dies as an offering, bearing the sins of many (53:4–6, 8–12). Jesus both lived like a Servant and described himself as a Servant.[3] The NT writers describe Jesus as the "Servant"[4] and specifically quote and apply the Servant passages to Jesus as the fulfillment of prophecy.

---

1. Although many identify the first Servant Song as Isa 42:1–4, vv. 5–9 appear to unfold the Servant's mission. Similarly, many understand the second Servant Song to be Isa 49:1–6, but vv. 7–13 appear to describe the Servant's mission. See Williamson, *Sealed*, 159n.44.

2. See Isa 41:8–9; 44:1–2; 45:4.

3. Matt 20:28; Mark 10:45; Luke 22:27; John 13:5–16.

4. Acts 3:13, 26; 4:27. 30; Phil 2:7.

First Servant Song: Isa 42:1–9

- Matt 12:17–21 quotes Isa 42:1–4, with slight variations, and applies it to Jesus as the fulfillment of prophecy.
- Isa 42:1 says that God "delights" in his Servant and *"I have put my Spirit upon him."* At his baptism and transfiguration, the Father said that he was *"well-pleased"* with Jesus (baptism—Matt 3:17; Mark 1:11; Luke 3:22; transfiguration—Matt 17:5). At his baptism the Spirit came "upon" him.[5] Jesus himself quoted from Isa 61:1 that *"the Spirit of the Lord is upon me"* in the fulfillment of Scripture (Luke 4:18, 21). Also, at the transfiguration, Jesus is called *"My Chosen One"* (Luke 9:35), which echoes the Servant's title of *"My chosen one"* in Isa 42:1.
- In Mark 14:24, Jesus' statement, *"this is my blood of the covenant, which is poured out for many,"* alludes to Isa 42:6 which says, *"I will appoint You as a covenant to the people."*
- Isa 42:6 describes the Servant as *"a light to the nations."* When Jesus was brought to the temple to be circumcised, the Holy Spirit came upon Simeon who held Jesus in his arms and then quoted or alluded to Isa 9:2; 42:6; 49:6 as referring to Jesus, saying, *"A light of revelation to the Gentiles"* (Luke 2:32; see also John 1:9). Jesus himself alluded to that passage when he said, *"I am the light of the world"* (John 8:12; 9:5; 12:46).

Second Servant Song: Isa 49:1–6 (or, 49:1–13)

- Isa 49:1 says, *"From the body of my mother he [the Lord] named me."* Before Jesus was born the angel Gabriel told Mary that *"you will conceive in your womb and bear a son, and you shall name him Jesus"* (Luke 1:31; see also Matt 1:21–23).
- Isa 49:2 says, *"He has made my mouth like a sharp sword."* Rev 1:16; 2:12; and 19:15 all describe a sharp sword coming from the risen Christ's mouth.
- Isa 49:5–6 appears to give the sequence of restoring Israel first so that salvation may reach to the ends of the earth. In Peter's sermon in Acts 3:11–26, he concludes by saying, *"For you first, God raised up His Servant and sent Him to bless you by turning every one of you from your wicked ways"* (Acts 3:26). "The use of the word *'first'* (*prōton*) implies

---

5. Matt 3:16; Mark 1:10; Luke 3:22; John 1:32.

the sort of sequence portrayed in Isaiah 49:5–6, where the Servant of the Lord is used to 'restore the tribes of Jacob' so that they can be a 'light for the Gentiles' and bring God's salvation 'to the ends of the earth' (cf. Acts 1:6; 13:46–48; 26:16–18). In other words, that significant 'Servant Song', which reveals the way in which God will ultimately fulfill his promise to Abraham, appears to lie behind the final challenge of Peter's sermon."[6]

- Isa 49:6 says, *"I will also make you a light of the nations."* This was quoted or alluded to in Luke 2:32; John 1:9 as referring to Jesus. Jesus himself alluded to this in John 8:12; 9:5; 12:46 as referring to himself.
- In Mark 14:24, Jesus' statement, *"this is my blood of the covenant, which is poured out for many,"* alludes to Isa 49:8 which says, *"I will keep You and give You for a covenant of the people."*

Third Servant Song: Isa 50:4–9

- Isa 50:4 says that the Servant knows how to *"sustain the weary."* Jesus alludes to that in Matt 11:28 when he says, *"Come to Me, all who are weary and heavy-laden, and I will give you rest."*
- Isa 50:6 describes the Servant being beaten, humiliated, and spat upon. In Mark 10:33–34 Jesus alludes to Isa 50:6 to explain what would happen to him when he reached Jerusalem. Before he was crucified, all three of those things happened to Jesus.[7]
- The Servant said *"I have set my face like flint"* to endure such contempt (Isa 50:7), just as Jesus *"set his face to go to Jerusalem,"* knowing what he faced there (Luke 9:51).[8]

---

6. Peterson, *Acts*, 185.

7. Matt 26:67; 27:26–31; Mark 15:15–20; Luke 22:63–65; 23:11; John 18:22; 19:1–3.

8. The NASB translates Luke 9:51 as *"was determined,"* but the Greek literally says *"set his face."*

Fourth Servant Song: Isa 52:13—53:12

- John 12:37-38 and Rom 10:16 quote Isa 53:1 as being fulfilled when people did not believe in Jesus even though he had performed many signs before them.
- In Matt 8:14-17, after Jesus healed the sick and cast out evil spirits from people, Matthew quotes Isa 53:4 as having been fulfilled.
- In Acts 8:32-35, when Philip met the Ethiopian eunuch, the Ethiopian was reading Isa 53:7-8, Philip explained that the passage was about Jesus; thereupon, *"beginning with this Scripture,"* Philip preached Jesus to the man (see also Rev 5:6).
- In 1 Peter 2:21-24 Peter quotes from Isa 53:9, and alludes to Isa 53:4-7, as having been fulfilled by Jesus (see also Rom 4:25).
- In Luke 22:20 Jesus says that the cup of wine symbolizes his blood which is *"poured out"* for his followers, an allusion to Isa 53:12 (*"He poured out Himself to death"*).
- In Luke 22:37 Jesus himself quotes from Isa 53:12 (*"and he was numbered with transgressors"*) as applying to himself in order to fulfill prophecy (see also Mark 15:28).
- In addition to the above explicit quotations and applications, the NT makes many allusions to the Fourth Servant Song as applying to Jesus: Matt 26:38, 56, 69-75; Mark 14:50, 66-72; Luke 22:54-61; John 18:15-18, 25-27 all allude to Isa 53:3, 12. John 1:29; 1 Cor 15:3; 2 Cor 5:21; Heb 9:28 all allude to Isa 53:4-6, 8-12. Matt 26:62-63; 27:12-14; Mark 14:60-61; 15:3-5; Luke 23:9; John 19:9 all allude to Isa 53:7. Matt 27:57-60 alludes to Isa 53:9. Mark 10:45 and Rom 5:18-19 allude to Isa 53:10-12. Phil 2:9 alludes to Isa 52:13.

THE CHURCH IS THE COLLECTIVE "SERVANT OF THE LORD," JUST AS JESUS WAS THE INDIVIDUAL "SERVANT OF THE LORD"

Jesus applied the "Servant" indicators to the church:

Isa 42:1 says, *"I have put My Spirit upon him [i.e., the Servant of the Lord]."* Jesus promised to send the Holy Spirit to his church.[9] In John 20:22 (in what perhaps was an "enacted parable"), *"he breathed on them and said*

---

9. John 14:16-17, 26; 15:26; 16:7-14.

to them, 'Receive the Holy Spirit.'" In Acts 1:8 Jesus promised that *"you will receive power when the Holy Spirit has come upon you."* That occurred on the Day of Pentecost (Acts 2:1–4). Now *"the Spirit of Him who raised Jesus from the dead dwells in you [the church] . . . For all who are being led by the Spirit of God, these are sons of God"* (Rom 8:11, 14). Thus, what was promised of the Servant of the Lord in Isaiah, Jesus was bestowing on the church.

Just as the "Servant of the Lord" was called a "servant,"[10] Jesus told his disciples, *"You know that the rulers of the Gentiles lord it over them, and their great men exercise authority over them. It is not this way among you, but whoever wishes to become great among you shall be your servant, and whoever wishes to be first among you shall be your slave; just as the Son of Man did not come to be served, but to serve, and to give His life a ransom for many."* (Matt 20:25–28)[11] In John 13:5–17 Jesus did the work of a slave when he washed his disciples' feet. He told his disciples, *"I gave you an example that you also should do as I did to you . . . [because] a slave is not greater than his master"* (John 13:15–16).

Isa 42:6; 49:6 say, *"I will make you a light of [or, to] the nations [or, Gentiles]"* In Matt 5:14 Jesus told his disciples, *"You are the light of the world."* In Acts 13:47 Paul quotes Isa 42:6; 49:6, *"I have placed you as a light for the Gentiles, that you may bring salvation to the end of the earth,"* in connection with his own mission to reach the Gentiles with the gospel of Jesus Christ. In Acts 1:7–8 Jesus commissioned his disciples to go *"to the remotest part of the earth."* That also alludes to Isa 49:6, where the Servant likewise is commissioned to bring salvation *"to the end of the earth."* In the Greek, the phrase translated *"to the remotest part of the earth"* is identical to the LXX of Isa 49:6. Further, when speaking to Agrippa in Acts 26:16–18, Paul recounts that he has been commissioned to go to the Gentiles *"to open their eyes so that they may turn from darkness to light and from the dominion of Satan to God."* That alludes to Isa 42:6–7, where the Servant is sent as a light to the nations *"to open blind eyes"* and to bring *"those who dwell in darkness from the prison."* Isa 49:8 says, *"In a favorable time I have answered you, and in a day of salvation I have helped you."* Paul quotes that in 2 Cor 6:2 and applies it to receiving God's grace of salvation in Christ in response to his preaching the gospel. In Rom 15:18–21 Paul quotes from Isa 52:15 as applying to his preaching the gospel of Christ in Jerusalem and many other places, both to Jews and Gentiles. Paul applies the fourth "Servant Song" to the church by quoting Isa 53:1 (*"Lord, who has believed our report?"*) in Rom 10:16, to show that not everyone who heard the gospel believed.

---

10. Isa 42:1; 49:3, 5–6; 52:13.
11. See also Matt 23:11; Mark 9:35; 10:42–45; Luke 22:25–27.

Finally, the Servant of the Lord is rejected, beaten, and afflicted.[12] Jesus told his disciples, *"If they persecuted me, they will also persecute you"* (John 15:20). That has proven to be true throughout the history of the church.[13] Despite opposition and persecution, the book of Acts records how, in winsomeness and resolve, "the apostles carry forward the strongly antithetical approach to pagan religions found in the Isaianic servant songs."[14]

---

12. Isa 50:6; 52:14, 53:1, 4–5, 7, 10.

13. See Acts 4:1–22; 5:17–32; 8:3; 11:19; 12:1–5; 14:19–22; 16:19–24; 21:27–36; 2 Cor 4:8–9; 11:23–33; 2 Tim 3:12.

14. Johnson, "Jesus Against," 352.

7

Christ in the Old Testament: Typology

INTRODUCTION

FIRST PET 1:10–12 SAYS, "*The prophets who prophesied of the grace that would come to you made careful searches and inquiries, seeking to know what person or time the Spirit of Christ within them was indicating as He predicted the sufferings of Christ and the glories to follow. It was revealed to them that they were not serving themselves, but you.*" Jesus said, "*Your father Abraham rejoiced to see My day, and he saw it and was glad*" (John 8:56). From these passages, we should be aware that the OT was not limited to its own redemptive-historical place and time. Instead, as we have discussed previously, the entire Bible, including the OT, concerns and is held together by Jesus Christ. What both Jesus and Peter are saying is that, at least sometimes, the OT writers and characters were aware that they were pointing ahead to something greater and, to them, yet future.[1] Prophecy is one way the OT pointed forward to something greater and future. The other way this is done is by typology.

A "type," sometimes called a "shadow," is an OT person, object, institution, or event that is a model or pattern, designed by God, which corresponds and points to a higher NT reality; that higher NT reality is called

---

1. The extent of the knowledge of the OT writers is unclear and debated. Dr. William Evans raises the question, "When they [the OT writers] wrote passages interpreted by the NT as references to Christ, did they consciously have these Christological meanings in view? The advocates of 'christotelic' interpretation argue that at least some such Christological content was extrapolated by NT writers in light of the Christ event." Evans, "WRF Member Dr. William Evans Asks," n.p. This question applies to the OT prophecies and to the issue of types and shadows.

the "antitype."[2] The term is from the Greek *tupos,* which signifies a mark, form, prototype, archetype, model, pattern, or example.[3] "Fundamental to Christianity is the belief that Christ is the **fulfillment** of the OT. Fulfillment implies anticipation of some sort."[4] That anticipation is the "type." A type is not a formal or explicit prediction or prophecy. "A prediction looks forward to, and demands, an event which is to be its fulfilment; typology, however, consists essentially in looking back and discerning previous examples of a pattern now reaching culmination."[5] God knew from the beginning what his Son would do and experience when he came to earth. Consequently, "the figures of the Hebrew Scriptures are modelled upon matters which from the perspective of simple human chronology are yet future."[6] Typology is based on a consistent pattern of God's action and revelation and therefore indicates unity and coherence between the OT and NT. Typology is "a central way the NT writers use the OT to show the continuity of their message and Christ's person and work with God's previous revelation (i.e., the OT) and His redemptive purposes found therein."[7] While most types foreshadow Christ and the gospel, a few types foreshadow other NT realities.

Because the antitype (the fulfillment) is generally greater than the type (the shadow), there is always an element of contrast between the two. Consequently, when considering types in Scripture, we need to specify how the type is similar to Christ but also how the type is unlike Christ.[8] In this regard, we need to remember that "the leaders of Israel are types only insofar as they enable God to do his redemptive work through them."[9] Thus, Moses

2. Fritsch, "Biblical Typology," 214; see Clowney, "Preaching Christ," 174–75.

3. Danker, *Greek-English Lexicon, tupos,* 1019–20; Zodhiates, *Complete Word Study, tupos,* 1399. Baker, "Typology," 144–46 sets forth a table showing the use of the *tupos* word-group in the LXX (OT) and the NT.

4. Miller, "In Pursuit," My response, bold emph. in orig.

5. France, *Jesus and,* 40. Although typology is not a formal or explicit prophecy or prediction, some scholars call it a form of "indirect prophecy." Thus, Patrick Fairbairn says, "A type ... necessarily possesses something of a prophetical character, and differs in form rather than in nature from what is usually designated prophecy. The one images or prefigures, while the other foretells, coming realities." Fairbairn, *Typology,* 106. See also Beale, *Handbook,* 58 ("indirect typological fulfillment ... fulfills what was implicitly foreshadowed by historical events. ... In this sense, one could identify indirect typological prophecy as 'event prophecy.'"); Fritsch, "Biblical Typology," 215 ("Prophecy predicts mainly by means of the word, whereas typology predicts by institution, act or person.").

6. Lunn, *Jesus in the Jewish,* 115.

7. Miller, "In Pursuit," My response.

8. See Johnson, *Him We Proclaim,* 203.

9. Greidanus, *Preaching Christ,* 260.

is not a type of Christ when he murdered an Egyptian; David is not a type of Christ when he committed adultery, etc.

In considering the issue of types, shadows, analogies, allegories, images, patterns, and prefigures in connection with our exegesis and understanding of the Bible, the question that must be asked is, "Can any criteria be discovered for making a distinction between legitimate and exegetically justifiable typology, on the one hand, and the unwarranted exercise of private and uncontrolled ingenuity on the other?"[10] On this issue, there have been different approaches from apostolic times to today: some schools of thought have found "types" in virtually everything in the OT, while others find biblical typology to be virtually nonexistent.[11]

With respect to determining examples of "legitimate and exegetically justifiable typology," some have taken the position that the only way to distinguish a real from a pretended type is if the OT persons, things, or events "were expressly declared by Christ, or by his Apostles, to have been designed as *pre-figurations* of persons or things relating to the *New* Testament.... But if we assert, that a person, or thing, was designed to pre-figure *another* person or thing, where no such pre-figuration has been declared by *divine authority*, we make an assertion, for which we neither *have*, nor *can* have, the slightest foundation."[12] Those holding this view note that, even when the Bible makes comparisons between OT and NT persons, things, or events, one must distinguish between comparisons made simply for the sake of illustration versus examples where a connection as between type and antitype is declared.[13]

A greater number of scholars have held that legitimate types include not only those explicitly declared as such by the NT, but also those examples that may be inferred as types because they are "conformable to the analogy of faith, and the practice of the inspired writers in regard to similar examples."[14] Where there is no explicit NT designation that an OT person, object, or event is a type, NT allusions to OT texts and the use of similar words, themes, and patterns may establish a type. As McCartney and Clayton state, "Since the NT writers do not cover everything in the OT, we may

---

10. Lampe, "Reasonableness," 21.

11. Fairbairn, *Typology*, 1–41 and Davidson, *Typology in Scripture*, 15–93, among others, provide detailed historical surveys of the different views and schools of typology from the early church fathers to contemporary times.

12. Marsh, *Lectures on the Criticism*, 373.

13. Marsh, *Lectures on the Criticism*, 373.

14. Fairbairn, *Typology*, 11; see also McCartney and Clayton, *Let the Reader*, 160–62.

expect large areas where the typology or *sensus plenior* [fuller or deeper meaning] has not been stated explicitly in the NT."[15]

Those holding this position recognize that there must be various biblical controls to prevent subjective comparisons between alleged types and antitypes that have no just stopping point. Most hold that the correspondence between the type and the antitype must be both historical (i.e., a real person, object, or event of history) and theological (i.e., both the type and antitype deal with events that refer to the relationship between God and people and should embody the same principle of God's working).[16] The grammatical-historical meaning and redemptive-historical function of the type should be known and should show an organic relationship to the antitype; the nature of the type should lie in the main message of the material, not in some incidental detail; the antitype should be greater than the type; and the divinely intended meaning of the typology must be consistent with the total revelation of the Bible and point, in some way, to God's redemption of, and/or dealing with, his people in Christ.[17]

In trying to determine typological relationships, one must be careful to avoid over-allegorizing Scripture, such as was common in medieval Christianity, as exemplified by Origen's view of the parable of the Good Samaritan: The man who was going down is Adam; Jerusalem is paradise; Jericho is the world; the robbers are the hostile powers; the priest is the law; the Levite represents the prophets; the Samaritan is Christ; the wounds represent disobedience; the beast represents the Lord's body; the inn is the church; the two denarii are the Father and the Son; the innkeeper is the chairman of the church; the Samaritan's promise to return points to the second coming of the Savior.[18]

A type is not an allegory or analogy and is more than simply an illustration. An allegory has little concern with the historical character of the OT text. Allegorizing generally takes a text metaphorically and moves away from it and history, with the purpose of finding deeper or hidden meanings in the text.[19] Allegory can often "find 'spiritual' significance in unimportant details or words."[20] G. P. Hugenberger summarizes, "*Allegory* occurs when an exegete or preacher begins with a contemporary application and discerns

---

15. McCartney and Clayton, *Let the Reader*, 157; see also Baker, "Typology," 151.

16. France, *Jesus and*, 41; Goppelt, *Typos*, 146; Baker, "Typology," 152–53; Fritsch, "Biblical Typology," 214–15.

17. McCartney and Clayton, *Let the Reader*, 158, 163–64.

18. Roukema, "Good Samaritan," 62.

19. Goppelt, "Tupos," 251n.23; Goppelt, *Typos*, 7, 9; see also Fritsch, "Biblical Typology," 216–17.

20. Baker, "Typology," 150.

symbolic values within an Old Testament account which an original reader is unlikely to have detected, but which fit the desired application."[21] Similarly, in an analogy one finds certain similarities between the two things being analogized. However, "analogies don't speak to the promise-fulfillment structure that is so foundational to the relationship between the testaments."[22] If there is no NT statement to the effect that "this was to fulfill that which was spoken," or other NT or OT literary, thematic, or contextual features indicating foreshadowing or some kind of fulfillment sense, then the comparison with the OT person, thing, or event is likely an analogy.[23]

The scarlet thread hung by Rahab in the window of her house was the sign that all those in her house would be spared when Israel took Jericho (Josh 2:12–19). The color red and the sparing of the lives of Rahab and her family may suggest the blood of Jesus.[24] However, the situations, events, and pattern or manner of acting between Jericho and Jesus are completely different. The use of scarlet thread was simply incidental; there is no organic connection between the scarlet thread and the blood of Jesus. Thus, the scarlet thread is more properly seen as an allegory or analogy rather than as a type.[25] A similar example is Moses's lifting up his hands when Israel fought against Amalek (Exod 17:11–12), which reminds some of Jesus' lifting up his hands on the cross.[26] However, the events surrounding Moses, his hands, and the outcome of the battle "cannot be conceived of as organically connected with their supposed antitypes, nor do they . . . materially affect

---

21. Hugenberger, "Introductory Notes," 340.

22. Miller, "In Pursuit," My response.

23. See Beale, *Handbook,* 70–71.

24. This was the view of Justin Martyr, *Dialogue with Trypho,* ch. 111, and Clement of Rome, *1 Clement,* ch. 12.

25. The scarlet thread does appear to have an association with the original Passover in Egypt. There, blood was placed on the lintels and door posts of the homes, and all who were inside were protected from the angel of death. Here, the scarlet thread in the window served as the sign that protected all who were inside. The analogy points to the saving of both Jews (the Hebrews in Egypt) and Gentiles (Rahab and her family in Jericho) by the blood of Christ. See Lunn, *Jesus in the Jewish,* 127. Although not a true "type," Rahab herself was a pointer to Christ, the gospel, and the church. She, of course, was a Canaanite prostitute from Jericho (Josh 2:1–2). As such, she is a foreshadow of the church which consists of people "*from every tribe and tongue and people and nation*" (Rev 5:9). Just as Gentiles became part of the church early-on (see Acts 10), so Rahab was a resident of Jericho, the first city taken by the Israelites after they crossed the Jordan River. Her actions in protecting the Israelite spies were done "by faith" (Heb 11:31). Further, Matt 1:4–5 says that she was the mother of Boaz through Salmon and, thus, is part of the line that led to Jesus Christ. Hence, Canaanite blood flowed in the veins of the Son of God.

26. See Danielou, *From Shadows,* 168–69.

the prophetic or exilic periods of Israel's history."[27] The same can be said of Paul's comparison of leaven with boasting, malice, and wickedness in 1 Cor 5:6–8, his comparison of Hagar with the Old Covenant and "the present Jerusalem" and Sarah with the New Covenant and "the Jerusalem above" in Gal 4:21–31,[28] and his comparison of not muzzling oxen (Deut 25:4) with compensating teaching elders in 1 Cor 9:9–10 and 1 Tim 5:17–18.[29] Other cases may be more ambiguous, and it may be difficult to state whether an example is a type or simply an analogy or allegory.

One last caveat should be mentioned. That is, as noted above, types are seen in retrospect. At the time, Israel's covenant leaders probably did not see themselves, and the people did not see them, as types of the Messiah. Nevertheless, despite their sinfulness and incompleteness as "types," to the extent that Israel's covenant leaders acted faithfully, they gave evidence that God was at work. This created hope and engendered the messianic expectations, not explicitly but at least implicitly, that there would come a day when God's promises of a world of righteousness, justice, and peace would be fulfilled by God's sending the true Messiah.

With these cautions and guidelines in mind, it must be remembered that the entire OT is in some way a book about Jesus. Consequently, we can expect typological relationships with Christ throughout the Bible. As Leonhard Goppelt said, "There is no typology that by-passes Christ; he is the antitype of the entire OT."[30] Space does not permit us to include all of the types in the OT, but we will discuss some of the more important persons, things, and events that are typological.[31]

ADAM

In Rom 5:14, Paul explicitly calls Adam a type of Christ. He augments this in 1 Corinthians 15 where he calls Adam the *"first man"* and Christ the *"second man"* and the *"last Adam"* (1 Cor 15:45, 47). All people are either "in Adam" or "in Christ" (1 Cor 15:22). Adam and Christ both act "as a covenantal

---

27. Fritsch, "Biblical Typology," 221–22.

28. In Gal 4:24, Paul explicitly said these comparisons were an allegory; however, he clearly recognizes that the people were real and the events surrounding Sarah and Hagar literally happened.

29. Although some commentators take this as Paul allegorizing, Beale says that "Paul reasons analogically from the lesser (a law about animals) to the greater (applying the principle of this law to humans)." Beale, *Handbook*, 69.

30. Goppelt, *Typos*, 116.

31. J. Barton Payne lists 51 OT types. Payne, *Encyclopedia*, 671–72. Others list far more. See, e.g., Booker, *Miracle*; Habershon, *Study*; Epp, *Portraits of Christ*.

representative whose response to God's authority affects all those whom he represents."[32] The typological relationship between Adam and Christ largely is a study of contrasts: Adam is from the earth; Christ is from heaven (1 Cor 15:47). Adam is natural; Christ is spiritual (1 Cor 15:46). While Eve ate the fruit of the tree of the knowledge of good and evil because she had been deceived (Gen 3:13; 1 Tim 2:14), Adam knew that eating would bring death (Gen 2:17) but consciously and deliberately—without being deceived (1 Tim 2:14)—chose to assume his bride's sin and guilt by taking the fruit from her hand and eating it (Gen 3:6). As the antitype, Christ similarly *"gave himself up"* for his bride, voluntarily taking our sin onto himself (Eph 5:25). M. R. DeHaan concludes, "Adam's transgression was different from any other. We sin because we are sinners. Adam became a sinner because he deliberately chose to share in the sin of Eve. In this he was the *figure (a type)* of Jesus Christ."[33] By following Eve in her sin, Adam brought judgment and death to all people (Rom 5:12–19; 1 Cor 15:21–22). By remaining faithful, Jesus brought justification and life to all who are his (Rom 5:15b–19; 1 Cor 15:21–22). Through Adam, creation *"was subjected to futility,"* but through Christ *"the creation itself also will be set free from its slavery to corruption"* (Rom 8:20–21; see also Gen 3:17–19). Those who follow in Adam's or Christ's footsteps will be like Adam or Christ: *"As is the earthy, so also are those who are earthy; and as is the heavenly, so also are those who are heavenly. Just as we have borne the image of the earthy, we will also bear the image of the heavenly."* (1 Cor 15:48–49; see also Heb 2:14–18) Adam and Christ therefore can be seen as embodying "in themselves and in their acts the old and new aeons, respectively," the old of sin, corruption, and death, the new of regeneration, justification, and life.[34]

The typology of Adam as Christ is extended in Ephesians 5 to include Eve, Adam's bride, as a type of the church. In Eph 5:29–30, Paul says *"No one ever hated his own flesh, but nourishes and cherishes it, just as Christ also does the church, because we are members of His body."* This alludes to Gen 2:23 when Adam said of Eve, *"This is now bone of my bones and flesh of my flesh."* In Eph 5:31–32, Paul quotes Gen 2:24 and makes the typology explicit, *"For this reason a man shall leave his father and mother and shall be joined to his*

---

32. Johnson, *Him We Proclaim*, 202.

33. DeHaan, *Portraits*, 42.

34. Davidson, *Typology in Scripture*, 305. Pages 300–316 of Davidson's book are a detailed exposition of the Adam-Christ typology found in Rom 5:12–21, including a comprehensive syntactical analysis of the comparative conjunctions, the "two age" eschatological structure, the Christological-soteriological structure, and the ecclesiological structure of the passage, all of which show how tightly woven the Adam-Christ typology is.

wife, and the two shall become one flesh. This mystery is great; but I am speaking with reference to Christ and the church." The church also is compared with Eve in 2 Cor 11:3.[35] Ray Ortland concludes, "With Christ, believers stand in a new Eden," and just as "there was no marriage before Adam and Eve, [so] there is none greater after Christ and his church."[36]

There is yet another aspect to the Adam-Christ typology. After Adam and Eve fell into sin, God's replacing the fig leaves which they had sewn to cover their nakedness with animal skins is typological of the salvation we have in Christ. Adam and Eve's sewing fig leaves together (Gen 3:7) typifies salvation by works. God, in his grace, provided adequate clothing for them, particularly since they would be leaving the garden and entering a new, hostile world (Gen 3:17–19, 23–24). The clothing God provided came at a cost—an animal had to die. Heb 9:22 says, *"without shedding of blood there is no forgiveness."* In the same way, by his grace, Christ shed his blood and *"while we were yet sinners, Christ died for us"* (Rom 5:8; see also Luke 22:20; 1 Pet 1:18–19). The animal was an innocent substitute and had no part in Adam and Eve's sin. In the same way, Christ died as an innocent substitute on our behalf (2 Cor 5:21). This pattern is the fundamental lesson that pervades the rest of the Bible and, indeed, all of human history, namely, there are only two kinds of religion in the world: a religion of works and salvation by grace.

ABEL

In the account of Cain and Abel, there are several important commonalities between the Abel and Christ. Abel was a shepherd (Gen 4:2); Jesus is the *"good shepherd"* (John 10:11). Abel brought as an offering to God *"of the firstlings of his flock and of their fat portions"* (Gen 4:4). Jesus is *"the lamb of God who takes away the sin of the world"* (John 1:29); he was *"like a lamb led to slaughter"* (Isa 53:7). *"The Lord had regard for Abel and for his offering"* (Gen 4:4). The Father had regard for Jesus' sacrifice by raising him from the dead, seating him at the right hand of the Father, and making him Lord and Christ (Acts 2:22–36; Heb 10:12). Abel's offering was *"to God,"* and through it he *"obtained the testimony that he was righteous"* (Heb 11:4).

---

35. Goppelt maintains that 2 Cor 11:3 simply "refers in a comparative way to the cunning deception of Satan that now threatens the church through false apostles," and that Eph 5:31–32 applies what is stated about Adam and Eve concerning the relationship of husband and wife allegorically to the perfection of the relationship between Christ and the church. Goppelt, *Typos*, 131n.17.

36. Ortland, *God's Unfaithful Wife*, 152.

Jesus' sacrifice on the cross was *"to God"* (Eph 5:2), and *"when the centurion saw what had happened, he began praising God, saying, 'Certainly this man was innocent [the Greek word literally is "righteous"]'"* (Luke 23:47; see also Rom 5:18; 2 Cor 5:21). Abel was rejected by his brother (Gen 4:8). Jesus *"came to his own, and those who were his own did not receive him"* (John 1:11; see also Isa 53:3; Matt 13:53–58; Mark 6:1–6; John 7:5). Abel was violently killed and shed his blood (Gen 4:8–10). Jesus was violently killed and shed his blood (Matt 27:27–54; Luke 22:20; 1 Pet 1:18–19). God told Cain, "The voice of your brother's blood is crying to Me from the ground" (Gen 4:10). Heb 12:24 alludes to this by speaking of those who come *"to Jesus, the mediator of a new covenant, and to the sprinkled blood, which speaks better than the blood of Abel."* Timothy Keller concludes, "Jesus is the true and better Abel, who, though innocently slain, has blood that cries out for our acquittal, not our condemnation."[37]

ABRAHAM

Abraham is *"the father of all who believe . . . those who are of the faith of Abraham, who is the father of us all"* (Rom 4:11, 16; see Rom 4:1–5, 9–25; Gal 3:1–18, 29). We see that faithfulness in his obedience to the call to leave his home and relatives and go to a land which God would show him (Gen 12:1; Heb 11:8–10) and in his willingness to sacrifice Isaac (Gen 22:1–14; Heb 11:17–19). Abraham's faithfulness typifies the ultimate faithful person, Jesus, who, like Abraham, "answered the call of God to leave the comfortable and familiar and go out into the void 'not knowing whither he went' to create a new people of God,"[38] and who actually sacrificed himself in obedience to God.

ISAAC

Isaac was a son of promise, whose birth was foretold and supernatural (Gen 17:19; 18:10–14; 21:1–2; cp. Matt 1:20–21). When the birth of Isaac was foretold to Sarah, she thought it would be impossible to conceive (Gen 18:11–12). Jesus' birth also was foretold and supernatural; when the birth of Jesus was foretold to Mary, she likewise thought it would be impossible to conceive (Luke 1:26–38). Isaac was the "only" (i.e., unique) and beloved son (Gen 22:2, 12, 16). The references in John 1:14, 18; 3:16, 18; 1 John 4:9

---

37. Keller, *Preaching*, 77.
38. Keller, *Preaching*, 77.

to Jesus as God's *"only begotten Son"* and in Rom 8:32 (he *"did not spare his own Son"*) are clear allusions to Isaac in Genesis 22:2, 12, and 16. Isaac was the physical "seed" promised Abraham. However, the promises made to Abraham actually extended far beyond Isaac and really pertained to Christ, as Paul points out in Gal 3:16, *"Now the promises were spoken to Abraham and to his seed. He does not say, 'And to seeds,' as referring to many, but rather to one, 'And to your seed,' that is, Christ."*

The entire story of Abraham's willingness to sacrifice Isaac prefigured Christ's crucifixion. Abraham was told to sacrifice Isaac in the land of Moriah (Gen 22:2). That is where Jerusalem and the temple were located, and where Jesus was crucified (2 Chron 3:1). Just as Abraham showed his love for God by his willingness to offer his son, so God the Father showed his love for the world by actually offering his Son for our sin. Just as the wood to burn the sacrifice was laid on Isaac (Gen 22:6, 9), so Jesus had to carry the cross to which he was nailed (John 19:17; 20:25–27). Just as Abraham said that *"God will provide for Himself the lamb"* (Gen 22:8) for the sacrifice, so God provided Jesus Christ, *"the lamb of God who takes away the sin of the world"* (John 1:29; see also Rev 5:6). Just as Isaac was obedient to the will of his father, even to the point of death, so Jesus was obedient to the will of his Father, even to death (Matt 26:39; Phil 2:8). In other words, the fulfillment is always greater than the shadow: Isaac was obedient at the *risk* of his life; Christ was obedient at the *cost* of his life. Just as Abraham would have considered Isaac dead for the three days of their journey, since Abraham clearly intended to complete the sacrifice of Isaac's life (Gen 22:4, 9–10), so Jesus was in the grave for three days (Matt 12:40; Luke 24:21; Acts 10:39–40). Finally, just as Abraham believed that God would raise Isaac from the dead, *"he also received him back as a type"* (Heb 11:19), so Jesus literally was resurrected from the dead (Matt 28:1–6; Mark 16:1–13; Luke 24:1–6; John 20:1–28).

Many also have seen the ram as type of Christ.[39] The ram was an innocent substitute, sacrificed so that Isaac could have *physical* life; Christ was an innocent substitute, sacrificed so that his people could have *eternal* life. With types and shadows, the OT person or object may typify more than one NT reality. That is the case with Isaac who, in addition to being a type of Christ, also is a type of the church. Gal 4:28–29 says, *"And you brethren, like Isaac, are*

---

39. See Greidanus, *Preaching Christ*, 310. Augustine states, "Since Isaac was not to be slain . . . who was that ram by the offering of which that sacrifice was completed with typical blood? For when Abraham saw him, he was caught by the horns in a thicket. What, then, did he represent but Jesus, who, before He was offered up, was crowned with thorns by the Jews?" Augustine, *City of God*, XVI, 32.

children of promise. But as at that time he who was born according to the flesh persecuted him who was born according to the Spirit, so it is now also."

JOSEPH

Although the NT recounts Joseph's being sold as a slave into Egypt and the events that followed (Acts 7:9–18), Joseph and Jesus are never directly compared. Nevertheless, Joseph legitimately can be seen as a true type of Christ. The purpose of Joseph's sojourn in Egypt was the saving and preservation of God's people and the fulfillment of the promises God made to Abraham; that is organically related to the salvation Jesus brought as the ultimate fulfillment of the Abrahamic Covenant.[40] In preserving his people (the covenantal line) from starvation, Joseph's "undeserved suffering was integral to his role as savior."[41] Thus, Joseph foreshadows the sufferings of Jesus and the rescue that those sufferings brought. In both cases, the evil done against Joseph and Jesus God had foreordained for good (Gen 45:5–8; 50:20; Acts 2:23; 4:37–38).

Multiple other correspondences between the main events and central details of their lives, in both their quantity and similarity of the language used, corroborate Joseph as a type of Christ.[42] Thus, Joseph was especially loved by his father (Gen 37:3); Jesus was beloved by the Father (Matt 3:17; Mark 1:11; Luke 3:22; John 3:35). It was supernaturally revealed in advance that Joseph would rule and that his family would bow down to him (Gen 37:6–10); it was supernaturally revealed in advance that Jesus will rule (2 Sam 7:12–13; Ps 110:1; Luke 1:32–33) and that *"at the name of Jesus every knee will bow"* (Phil 2:10). Both Joseph and Jesus wore distinctive garments: Joseph's was multicolored (Gen 37:3); Jesus' robe was seamless (John 19:23). In the Greek, the word for each garment is identical, *chitōna*. Both Joseph and Jesus were handed by their kinsmen over to Gentiles to be gotten rid of (Gen 37:27–28; Mark 15:1; John 18:28–31). Joseph's father *"sent him"* to his brothers (Gen 37:14); Jesus said, *"the living Father sent me"* (John 6:57; see also John 3:17). Joseph was hated by his brothers, who were jealous of him (Gen 37:4–5, 11); Jesus was hated by his kinsmen, who wanted him dead out of jealousy (Matt 27:18; Luke 19:14; John 15:24–25). Joseph was rejected by his brothers (Gen 37:18–24); Jesus was rejected by his own (John 1:11).

---

40. McCartney and Clayton, *Let the Reader*, 158; see chapter 9, below, regarding how Christ fulfills the Abrahamic Covenant.

41. Johnson, *Him We Proclaim*, 214.

42. The extent to which some people see parallels between Joseph and Jesus is shown in a lengthy comparative table in Habershon, *Study*, 169–74.

Joseph's brothers *"plotted against him to put him to death"* (Gen 37:18); the chief priests and elders of the people *"plotted together to seize Jesus by stealth and kill him"* (Matt 26:40). Joseph was stripped of his coat (Gen 37:23); Jesus was stripped of everything (John 19:23-24). When Joseph approached his brothers, they said *"come, let us kill him"* (Gen 37:20, LXX); in Jesus' parable of the vine-growers, when the son (representing Jesus) appears, the vine-growers say *"come, let us kill him"* (Matt 21:38). Both accounts continue with the words, *"and they took him and threw him"* (Gen 37:24, LXX; Matt 21:39). The Greek wording of each is identical. Joseph was sold for silver coins (Gen 38:26-28); so was Jesus (Matt 26:14-16).

After Joseph was sold to Potiphar, it repeatedly says that *"the Lord was with him"* (Gen 39:2, 3, 21, 23; Acts 7:9); the same phrase is said of Jesus (John 3:2; Acts 10:38). As a result of the favor in which Joseph was held, *"all that he [Potiphar] owned he put in his charge [lit. 'in his hand']"* (Gen 39:4); likewise, because the Father loves the Son, he *"has given all things into His hand"* (John 3:35). Joseph was innocent and was falsely accused (Gen 39:10-20; 40:15); Jesus likewise was innocent and was falsely accused (Matt 26:60; 27:4; Mark 14:57; Luke 23:2-4). Joseph was imprisoned with two others and foretold the deliverance of one of them (Gen 40:1-13); Jesus was crucified between two others and foretold the salvation of one of them (Luke 23:39-43).

In Joseph's dealings with Pharaoh, *"Joseph was thirty years old when he stood before Pharaoh"* (Gen 41:46); likewise, *"When he began his ministry, Jesus himself was about thirty years of age"* (Luke 3:23). The Pharaoh recognized that the *"divine spirit"* was in Joseph (Gen 41:38); Jesus was *"full of the Holy Spirit"* and was led by the Holy Spirit (Luke 4:1). After his humiliation and imprisonment, Joseph was raised to the right hand of Pharaoh and was set over all the land of Egypt (Gen 41:38-44); after his humiliation and death, Jesus was raised to the right hand of God, where *"all things [are] in subjection under his feet"* (Eph 1:20-22). In Gen 45:9 (LXX), Joseph said, *"God has made [epoiēsen] me lord [kurion] of all Egypt"* in Acts 2:36, Peter said, *"God has made [epoiēsen] Him both Lord [kurion] and Christ."* Pharaoh gave Joseph his wife (Gen 41:45); the Father gives Jesus his wife (John 6:37, 39). Joseph provided bread for the people and saved their earthly lives (Gen 41:55-57; 47:25); Jesus is *"the bread of life"* (John 6:35, 48), and *"if anyone eats of this bread, he will live forever"* (John 6:51).

After Joseph was raised to power, his brothers at first did not recognize him (Gen 42:8); after his resurrection, Jesus' disciples at first did not recognize him (Luke 24:15-16). Later, Joseph made himself known to his brothers, declaring *"I am Joseph"* (Gen 45:1, 3); later, Jesus made himself known to his disciples, declaring *"it is I myself"* (Luke 24:31-35, 39). When Joseph's brothers told their father that Joseph was alive, *"he was stunned, for he did not believe them"* (Gen 45:26); when the women told the disciples after Jesus' burial that Jesus was alive, *"these words appeared to them as nonsense, and they would not believe them"* (Luke 24:11; see also Mark 16:11; Luke 24:41). When Jacob went to Egypt and saw Joseph, he said, *"Now let me die, since I have seen your face, that you are still alive"* (Gen 46:30); when Simeon saw Jesus in the temple, he said, *"Now Lord, You are releasing Your bond-servant to depart in peace, according to Your word; for my eyes have seen Your salvation"* (Luke 2:29–30).

MOSES

There are several parallels between Moses and Jesus.[43] Despite the parallels, Jesus is never directly called a new Moses; instead, as with all types, there is an element of contrast in which Jesus is shown to be incomparably greater than Moses. For example, Moses's first public miracle was turning water into blood, a sign of judgment and death (Exod 7:20–21); Jesus' first public miracle was turning water into wine, a sign of joy and life (John 2:1–11).[44] Moses instituted the first Passover (Exod 12:1–51; Heb 11:28); Jesus instituted the last Passover (Matt 26:20–29; Mark 14:12–25; Luke 2:1–22; John 13:1–3). Thus, the NT shows Jesus as a new and greater Moses who delivers people not just from physical bondage but from spiritual slavery to sin and death (John 1:29; Rom 6:3–23). Hebrews summarizes how Christ is like Moses but greater than Moses (Heb 3:1–6): Christ *"is worthy of more glory than Moses, by just so much as the builder of the house has more honor than the house"* (Heb 3:3); and whereas *"Moses was faithful in all his house as a servant . . . Christ was faithful as a son over his house"* (Heb 3:5–6).

The typological correspondences between Moses and Jesus are seen in that all of the major titles or offices ascribed to Moses are also ascribed to Jesus: God's "servant" (Ps 105:26; Matt 12:18); "prophet" (Deut 18:15, 18; Luke 7:16; John 6:14); "priest" (Ps 99:6; Heb 7:24); "king" (Deut 33:4–5; John 18:33–37; 19:19; Acts 17:7); "judge" (Exod 2:14; 18:13; John 5:22, 27, 30; Acts 7:27, 35; 17:31); "shepherd" (Exod 3:1; John 10:11, 14); "mediator" (Exod 20:18–21; 32:10–14; Deut 5:22–33; 1 Tim 2:5; Heb 9:15); "intercessor"

---

43. The extent to which some people see parallels (and contrasts) between Moses and Jesus is shown in a lengthy comparative table in Habershon, *Study,* 165–68.

44. Wine, of course, is a symbol of Christ's blood, the shedding of which inaugurated the New Covenant, through which people receive the forgiveness of their sins, a new heart, mind, Spirit, and eternal life (Luke 22:20; 1 Cor 11:25).

(Num 21:7; Rom 8:34; Heb 7:25); "deliverer" (Acts 7:35; Rom 11:26); "ruler" (Mic 5:2; Acts 7:27, 35).

Additionally, significant verbal correspondences between Moses and Jesus indicate Moses's typological nature:

- When Moses desired to return to Egypt to rescue his people, the Lord told him, *"Go back to Egypt, for all the men who were seeking your life are dead"* (Exod 4:19); when Joseph was in Egypt with Mary and Jesus, the Lord told him, *"Get up, take the Child and His mother, and go into the land of Israel; for those who sought the Child's life are dead"* (Matt 2:20).

- When Moses brought the plague of gnats, which the Egyptian magicians could not duplicate, they told Pharaoh, *"This is the finger of God"* (Exod 8:19); when Jesus cast out a demon and was accused of acting by the power of Beelzebul, Jesus said, *"If I cast out demons by the finger of God, then the kingdom of God has come upon you"* (Luke 11:20).

- Because God exalted Moses and used him as his instrument to judge Egypt, just before the exodus Moses told Pharaoh, *"All these your servants will come down to me and bow themselves before me"* (Exod 11:8); because God has highly exalted Jesus, *"at the name of Jesus every knee will bow, of those who are in heaven and on earth and under the earth"* (Phil 2:10).

- After receiving the Ten Commandments, *"Moses took the blood and sprinkled it on the people, and said, 'Behold the blood of the covenant, which the Lord has made with you'"* (Exod 24:8; Heb 9:20); at the Last Supper, when Jesus instituted the New Covenant, he said, *"This is My blood of the covenant, which is poured out for many for forgiveness of sins"* (Matt 26:28; Mark 14:24; Luke 22:20; 1 Cor 11:25).

- After receiving the replacements of the tablets of the Ten Commandments on Mount Sinai, *"Moses did not know that the skin of his face shone because of his speaking with Him"* (Exod 34:29); on the Mount of Transfiguration, *"He was transfigured before them; and His face shone like the sun"* (Matt 17:2).

- With respect to Moses's character, *"Now the man Moses was very humble, more than any man who was on the face of the earth"* (Num 12:3); with respect to Jesus' character, *"I am gentle and humble in heart, and you will find rest for your souls"* (Matt 11:29).

We also see correspondences between Moses and Jesus in the significant aspects of their lives from birth to death:

1. *Moses was a precursor of the Messiah.* Moses was unique among the prophets, both for the mighty works he did and for the fact that God did not speak to him in visions and dreams but *"mouth to mouth"* and *"face to face"*[45] as a man speaks to his friend. However, Jesus was far greater than Moses. Jesus *is* the Messiah.[46] Jesus did greater miracles than Moses, including raising the dead and rising from the dead. Jesus surpasses Moses because he is the only one who has seen the Father, since he came from the Father (John 6:46) and is himself *"the exact representation"* of God (Heb 1:3). Jesus did not just speak God's words from time to time; instead, he did nothing on his own initiative, but *everything* he did and said was what the Father had him do.[47] The reason is that Jesus *is* the very Word of God come to earth as a man.[48]

2. *Attempts on their lives as infants.* There are clear parallels between the attempts of Pharaoh and Herod to kill the Hebrew children (Exod 1:16; Matt 2:16). Both Pharaoh and Herod were ungodly rulers who were afraid of the rise of one who might oppose or supplant them (see Exod 1:8–12; Matt 2:1–3).

3. *Return from Egypt.* Both Moses and Jesus escaped to another country (Exod 2:15; Matt 2:13–15). In both cases they were supernaturally told when to return, because those seeking to kill them were dead (Exod 4:19–20; Matt 2:19–21).

4. *Freedom from slavery.* Moses led his people out of slavery in Egypt to a new life of freedom (Exod 12:29–32). Jesus led his people out of the far greater slavery to sin, Satan, death, and bondage to the law, so that *"if you continue in My word, then you are truly disciples of Mine; and you will know the truth, and the truth will make you free"* (John 8:30–31).

5. *Manna.* Just as the Lord provided manna while Moses led Israel in the wilderness (Exod 16:1–21), so Jesus said, *"Truly, truly, I say to you, it is not Moses who has given you the bread out of heaven, but it is my Father who gives you the true bread out of heaven. . . . I am the bread of life."* (John 6:32, 35) The manna was physical and temporary; the bread that Jesus gives (himself) provides eternal life to anyone who eats it (John 6:48–58).

6. *God's law on the mountain.* Just as God gave Moses the Law on the mountain (Exod 19:20), so Jesus gave his law, the "law of Christ," on

---

45. Exod 33:11; Num 12:6–8; Deut 34:10–12.
46. See discussion of "The Messiah" in chapter 5.
47. John 5:19, 30; 6:38; 8:28; 12:49; 14:10.
48. John 1:1, 14; Rev 19:13.

the mountain (Matt 5:1–48; see 1 Cor 9:21; Gal 6:2). However, because Jesus is the far greater antitype, he was able to change the law of God on his own authority (Matt 5:21–22, 27–28, 31–34, 38–44; Mark 7:18–19). Further, the law of Moses and the law of Christ are qualitatively different; the Apostle John says, *"The Law was given through Moses; grace and truth were realized through Jesus Christ"* (John 1:17).

7   *Sacrifice and atonement.* Although Moses offered to make atonement and sacrifice himself for his people's sin (Exod 32:30–32), Jesus actually made atonement and sacrificed himself for his people's sin.[49]

8   *Choosing the 70.* Just as Moses chose 70 elders and gave them authority (Num 11:16–17), so Jesus appointed 70 disciples and sent them out with authority (Luke 10:1–20).

9   *Mediators.* Just as Moses was a mediator between God and Israel (Exod 20:19; Deut 5:5; Gal 3:19), so Jesus is *"the one mediator between God and men"* (1 Tim 2:5).

10 *The covenants.* Moses inaugurated the Old Covenant (Exod 24:8). At the Last Supper Jesus instituted the New Covenant (Luke 22:20; see also Matt 26:28; Mark 14:24). Moses ratified God's Mosaic covenant with the blood of animals, but Jesus surpasses Moses by ratifying the New Covenant in his own blood,[50] which rendered the Mosaic covenant obsolete (Heb 8:13). The Mosaic Covenant did not forgive sins or give eternal life, but the New Covenant does forgive sins and give eternal life.

11 *Salvation from death.* Jesus compared his death to Moses. Jesus said, *"As Moses lifted up the serpent in the wilderness, even so must the Son of Man be lifted up"* (John 3:14; see Num 21:9). To look to the bronze serpent in the wilderness spared a person from physical death; to look to Jesus gives one eternal life and saves a person from the second death.

12 *Dead bodies.* The dead bodies of both Moses and Jesus cannot be found. Deut 34:6 says that Moses was buried in the land of Moab, *"but no man knows his burial place to this day."* Jesus also was buried, but his body also cannot be found because he is risen! (Matt 28:6).

---

49. Rom 3:23–25; 5:6–8; Heb 9:26–28; 10:11–12; 1 John 2:2.
50. Matt 26:28; Mark 14:24; Luke 22:20; see 1 Cor 11:25; Heb 8:7–13; 9:11–14.

JOSHUA

Joshua is another "type" of Christ. In Hebrew, "Joshua" is "Yehoshua" or "Yeshua"; the same name in English is "Jesus." Heb 4:4, 8 use the same Greek word, *Iēsous*, for both Joshua and Jesus. Joshua led the people to victory over their enemies and entered the promised land (Deut 34:9; Josh 1:1—24:31). Nevertheless, Heb 4:8 says he did not give his people true and lasting "rest." As the antitype, on the cross, Jesus defeated the greatest enemies of all—sin, Satan, and death—and led his people to the promised land of salvation and eternal life, our true and permanent "rest." When he comes again, Jesus will bring with him the ultimate promised land of the new heaven and new earth.

ELIJAH AND ELISHA

The Bible specifically compares the prophet Elijah to John the Baptist. It is no coincidence that their physical appearances were similar: Elijah is described as *"a hairy man with a leather girdle bound about his loins"* (2 Kgs 1:8); John the Baptist is described as *"clothed with camel's hair and wore a leather belt around his waist"* (Mark 1:6). They both preached repentance when Israel had turned from God (1 Kgs 18:21; Matt 3:1-2; Luke 3:3). They both were fed from the wildlife of the wilderness near the Jordan River (1 Kgs 17:2-6; Matt 3:4b-6; Luke 3:3). They both, personally and directly, confronted the ungodly and evil behavior of Israel's leaders, including the king (1 Kgs 18:18; 2 Kgs 1:16; Matt 3:7; 14:3-4). Their primary antagonists were wicked queens (Jezebel in the case of Elijah; Herodias in the case of John), who sought to have them killed and succeeded in the case of John the Baptist (1 Kgs 19:2; Matt 14:6-11; Mark 6:17-28). They both suffered from depression and doubt (1 Kgs 19:4; Matt 11:2-3). They both anointed their successors at the Jordan River (2 Kgs 2:9-14; Matt 3:13-17).

In announcing John the Baptist's birth, the angel told Zacharias, *"It is he who will go as a forerunner before Him in the spirit and power of Elijah, to turn the hearts of the fathers back to the children, and the disobedient to the attitude of the righteous, so as to make ready a people prepared for the Lord"* (Luke 1:17). This was based on two prophecies from Malachi: Mal 3:1 says, *"Behold, I am going to send My messenger, and he will clear the way before Me. And the Lord, whom you seek, will suddenly come to His temple."* Mal 4:5-6 adds, *"Behold, I am going to send you Elijah the prophet before the coming of the great and terrible day of the Lord. He will restore the hearts of the fathers to their children and the hearts of the children to their fathers, so that I will not come and smite the land with a curse."* His role also was based on the prophecy of Isa 40:3, *"The voice of one crying in the wilderness, 'Make ready the way of the Lord, make His paths straight!'"* John the Baptist recognized his role as Christ's forerunner, even quoting Isa 40:3 (John 1:23, 26–34; see also Matt 3:11–12).

Matt 3:3; 11:10; Mark 1:2–3; Luke 3:4–6; and John 1:23 quote from Mal 3:1 and Isa 40:3–5 as being fulfilled by John the Baptist.[51] Jesus elaborated on the identification of John the Baptist with Elijah. When John the Baptist was in prison, Jesus said, *"And if you are willing to accept it, John himself is Elijah who was to come"* (Matt 11:14). Later, as Jesus and three of his disciples were coming down from the Mount of Transfiguration, this interchange took place: *"And His disciples asked Him, "Why then do the scribes say that Elijah must come first?" And He answered and said, 'Elijah is coming and will restore all things; but I say to you that Elijah already came, and they did not recognize him, but did to him whatever they wished. So also the Son of Man is going to suffer at their hands.' Then the disciples understood that He had spoken to them about John the Baptist."* (Matt 17:10–13)

In Mark 9:13, Jesus also said of John the Baptist, *"But I say to you that Elijah has indeed come, and they did to him whatever they wished, just as it is written of him."* There was no explicit OT prediction that Elijah or John the Baptist would suffer or be killed. Jesus' statement about the suffering and death of John the Baptist is based on the typological relationship between Elijah and John the Baptist: Elijah suffered and his life was threatened by Queen Jezebel (1 Kgs 19:2–3, 10, 14). As the antitype, John the Baptist's suffering reembodied, to an even greater degree, what Elijah himself had experienced.

Typology is not limited to one OT person or thing standing for only one NT reality. Thus, even though the NT and Jesus himself identified John the Baptist with Elijah, Jesus also identified himself with Elijah and with Elisha. When Jesus preached at the synagogue in his hometown of Nazareth, in Luke 4:23 the people essentially said that he was neglecting his hometown by not doing the kind of miracles he had done at Capernaum. Jesus responded, *"Truly I say to you, no prophet is welcome in his hometown. But I say to you in truth, there were many widows in Israel in the days of Elijah, when the sky was shut up for three years and six months, when a great famine came over all the land; and yet Elijah was sent to none of them, but only to Zarephath, in the land of Sidon, to a woman who was a widow. And there were many lepers in Israel in the time of Elisha the prophet; and none of them was cleansed, but only Naaman the Syrian."* (Luke 4:24–27) Jesus' defense of his

---

51. In John 1:21, John denied being Elijah, i.e., he correctly denied being the actual person of Elijah reincarnated or raised from the dead.

ministry is grounded in "the basic idea behind typology, that the principles of God's working are constant."[52] In other words, just as Elijah and Elisha healed people from Sidon and Syria, when there were many from Israel who were similarly afflicted, so Jesus was working outside of his hometown and his own people.

There are, in fact, a number of parallels between the prophet Elijah and Jesus which indicate that Elijah was a type of Christ. In 1 Kings 17 Elijah multiplied food; Jesus also multiplied food (Mark 6:33–44; 8:1–20). Elijah raised a widow's son from the dead; Jesus raised a widow's son from the dead (Luke 7:11–17). The wording of the conclusion of both of those episodes is virtually identical: Elijah *"gave him to his mother"* (1 Kgs 17:23); Jesus *"gave him back to his mother"* (Luke 7:15). Elijah uttered prophesies that came true (1 Kgs 17:1; 1 Kgs 18:1, 41–45; 2 Kgs 1:1–4, 17); Jesus uttered prophecies that came true (e.g., Matt 12:40; 26:20–21, 31, 34, 47–56). Elijah demonstrated power over nature (1 Kgs 17:1; 18:1, 41–45; 2 Kgs 2:8); Jesus demonstrated power over nature (Matt 8:23–27; 14:22–33). An evil ruler tried, without success, to kill Elijah (1 Kgs 19:2); an evil ruler tried, without success, to kill Jesus (Matt 2:1–23). Elijah fasted for 40 days and 40 nights (1 Kgs 19:8); Jesus fasted for 40 days and 40 nights (Matt 4:2). Elijah fearlessly denounced the sin of an evil leader to his face (1 Kgs 21:17–24); Jesus denounced the sin of evil leaders to their face (Matt 12:34; 23:13–36; John 8:39–44). Most importantly, both Elijah and Jesus are the only two people recorded to have ascended alive to heaven in the presence of witnesses; the same Greek word, translated *"taken up,"* is used for Elijah's ascent in the Septuagint of 2 Kgs 2:11 and for Jesus' ascent in Acts 1:11.

With respect to Elisha, Jesus' miraculously feeding the 5000 (Matt 14:13–21; Mark 6:33–44; Luke 9:12–17) bears a striking resemblance to Elisha's miraculously feeding a hundred men with twenty loaves of barley and ears of grain (2 Kgs 4:42–44). In both cases, there was a large and hungry crowd of people and a small amount of food; Elisha and Jesus each tell their disciples to feed the people, the disciples express doubt that the small amount of available food can feed such a large crowd, the food is multiplied such that everyone ate, and there were leftovers. As R. T. France states, "The presumption is that Jesus was consciously re-enacting on a vastly greater scale the miracle of Elisha. If so, a typological element in Jesus' use of the Old Testament story is probable."[53] Here again, we see the antitype greater than the type: Elisha fed a hundred men with twenty loaves; Jesus fed 5000 men with five loaves.

---

52. France, *Jesus and*, 48.
53. France, *Jesus and*, 48.

The examples of Elijah and Elisha also point to the church. In 2 Kgs 2:1–14 the prophet Elijah was about to be taken from his apprentice Elisha. Elisha asked that *"a double portion of your spirit be upon me"* (2 Kgs 2:9). Elijah said that would happen *"if you see me when I am taken from you"* (2 Kgs 2:10). Elisha did see Elijah taken up to heaven in a chariot of fire and other prophets recognized that *"the spirit of Elijah rests on Elisha"* (2 Kgs 2:15). As a result, Elisha was able to perform great signs, including, among other things, saving a widow and her son by multiplying oil, raising a boy from the dead, and healing a leper (see 2 Kings 4–5).

Shortly before he died, Jesus told his disciples, *"Truly, truly, I say to you, he who believes in Me, the works that I do, he will do also; and greater works than these he will do; because I go to the Father"* (John 14:12). He then promised that he would send the Holy Spirit. After his resurrection, Jesus promised his disciples that they would be *"baptized with the Holy Spirit not many days from now"* and *"you will receive power when the Holy Spirit has come upon you; and you shall be My witnesses both in Jerusalem, and in all Judea and Samaria, and even to the remotest part of the earth"* (Acts 1:5, 8). When Jesus ascended back to the Father, the disciples witnessed it and *"were gazing intently into the sky while He was going"* (Acts 1:10). "The apostles are looking up for the same reason Elisha was looking up: they want to receive the spirit of their master."[54] Shortly thereafter, on the Day of Pentecost, the Holy Spirit was poured out onto the disciples, and they received power and boldness to preach and perform signs, just as Jesus had promised. The rest of the book of Acts recounts their bold preaching, the spread of the gospel, and the signs they performed, including healing the lame and raising the dead.

DAVID AND SOLOMON[55]

When Jesus' disciples picked heads of grain on the Sabbath (Matt 12:1–8; Mark 2:23–28; Luke 6:1–5), they were accused by the Pharisees of breaking the Sabbath. Jesus cites 1 Sam 21:1–6, where David and his followers ate the consecrated "bread of the Presence" from the tabernacle. Jesus noted the illegality of what David did (it *"is not lawful for any to eat except the priests alone"*). Jesus' point is not that David's action justifies what the disciples did. Nor is he simply asserting the priority of human needs over requirements of the law (in this case there is no claim that the disciples were starving or otherwise in need). Nor is he saying that the Scripture allows greater

---

54. Veras, *Jesus of Israel*, 120.

55. See also chapter 5 regarding The Messiah and chapter 9 regarding the Davidic Covenant.

leniency than do the Pharisees. Instead, Jesus is making a Messianic claim: his unexpressed premise is that "a greater than David is here."[56] He does say that *"something greater than the temple is here"* (Matt 12:6) and *"the Son of Man is Lord of the Sabbath"* (Matt 12:8; Mark 2:28; Luke 6:5). Since the temple and the Sabbath were greater than David, *a fortiori*, Jesus is greater than David. R. T. France concludes, "The argument from the authority of David to the greater authority of Jesus is best explained by an underlying typology. If David, the type, had the authority to reinterpret the law, Jesus, the greater antitype, must have that authority in a higher degree."[57]

After David's reign as king, a number of OT statements speak of God's raising David up again as the promised Messiah and king (Jer 30:8-9; Ezek 34:23-24; 37:24; Hos 3:5). Walter Kaiser states, "This does not mean that David will be reincarnated as king once again. Instead, the Messiah will come in David's line and fulfill everything that has been promised to him."[58] The NT clearly shows that Jesus Christ fulfills the Israelite expectations of a king sent by God.[59] This was prophesied by the angel Gabriel to Mary, before Jesus was born, *"He will be great and will be called the Son of the Most High; and the Lord God will give Him the throne of His father David; and He will reign over the house of Jacob forever, and His kingdom will have no end"* (Luke 1:32-33). This was recognized at the beginning of Jesus' ministry (John 1:49, *"Rabbi, you are the Son of God; you are the King of Israel"*). When Jesus entered Jerusalem the final time, all four Gospels interpret that as the coming of the prophesied Davidic king (Zech 9:9; Matt 21:1-11; Mark 11:1-11; Luke 19:28-40; John 12:12-16). His kingship and his sitting on the "throne of David" were proclaimed by Peter on the day of Pentecost as having been fulfilled by Jesus' resurrection and ascension (Acts 2:30-32, 36).

When God told David that he could not build the temple to replace the tabernacle, he said, *"I will raise up your descendant ['seed'] after you, who will come forth from you, and I will establish his kingdom. He shall build a house for My name, and I will establish the throne of his kingdom forever. I will be a father to him and he will be a son to Me."* (2 Sam 7:12-14) The descendant

---

56. See France, *Jesus and*, 46.

57. France, *Jesus and*, 47; see also Moo, "Jesus and the Authority," 8; Beare, "Sabbath," 134.

58. Kaiser, *Messiah*, 189. In Psalm 89, which speaks in considerable detail about the Davidic Covenant and God's raising up a triumphant deliverer or Messiah, David and David's "seed" are conflated (see Ps 89:3-4, 19-37).

59. See, e.g., Matt 2:4-11; 16:16, 20; 22:42-45; 26:63-64; Mark 8:29; 12:35-37; 14:61-62; Luke 4:41; 20:41-44; 22:67-70; 23:2-3, 39; 24:26, 46; John 4:25-26; 11:25-27; 20:30-31; Acts 2:30-36; 9:22; 17:3; 18:5, 28; 1 John 2:22; 5:1.

who would build God's "house" was Solomon. However, neither Solomon nor the entire Davidic line could or did last "forever." Those promises were pointing to Jesus as the ultimate fulfiller, David's "greater son," since he alone is eternal and has an everlasting kingdom. Jesus indicated that *he* was David's "greater son," when he compared himself to Solomon in Matt 12:42, saying, *"The Queen of the South will rise up with this generation at the judgment and will condemn it, because she came from the ends of the earth to hear the wisdom of Solomon; and behold, something greater than Solomon is here"* (see also Luke 11:31). Matthew begins his gospel by describing Jesus as *"the son of David"* (Matt 1:1). The NT writers repeatedly stress that Jesus was *"a descendant ['seed'] of David"*[60] and that he, not Solomon, is the true, ultimate, greater *"son of David."*[61] Jesus applied the term "son of David" to himself when identifying the Messiah (Matt 22:41–46; Mark 12:35–37).

There is one other commonality between David, Solomon, and Jesus. Jesus stated in John 13:18 that his betrayal by one who eats bread with him was the fulfillment of the of Ps 41:9. In context, Ps 41:9 is "a historical reflection by Solomon of his trusted counselor Ahithophel's betraying ('lifting up his heel against') David"; nevertheless, "Jesus sees . . . a pattern foreshadowing Judas's deceptive relationship to Jesus."[62] The typological connection between the two acts of betrayal is deepened in that Ahithophel and Judas are the only two biblical characters who are said to have hanged themselves (2 Sam 17:23; Matt 27:5).

JOB

Job also is a type of Christ. "Jesus is the ultimate Job, the only truly innocent sufferer. . . . As Job was 'naked,' penniless, and in physical pain (Job 1:21), so Jesus was homeless, stripped naked, and tortured on the cross. While Job was relatively innocent, Jesus was absolutely, perfectly innocent, and while Job felt God abandoning him, Jesus actually experienced the real absence of God, as well as the betrayal of his foolish friends and the loss of family."[63] The point of the testing of Job was whether or not he would continue to obey God without knowing whether it would bring him personal benefits; however, as the greater antitype, Jesus knew that to obey his Father would, in fact, result in his death, his becoming sin, and his Father's forsaking him! Likewise, while Job *prayed* for his errant *friends* (Job 42:7–9), Jesus both

---

60. John 7:42; Acts 13:22–23; Rom 1:3; 2 Tim 2:8.
61. Matt 9:27; 12:23; 15:22; 20:30–31; 21:9; Mark 10:47–48; Luke 18:38–39.
62. Beale, *Handbook*, 60.
63. Keller, *Walking*, 293.

prayed and *died* for his *enemies* and now constantly intercedes for us (Luke 23:34; Rom 8:34; Heb 7:25).

JONAH

When the scribes, Pharisees, Sadducees, and crowds asked Jesus for a "sign," Jesus replied that the only sign that would be given was *"the sign of Jonah."* Because this was the only specific "sign" that Jesus promised, and because he specifically compared himself to Jonah, it is important to understand the depth of the "sign of Jonah."

Matt 12:38-41	Matt 16:1-4	Luke 11:29-32
³⁸ Then some of the scribes and Pharisees said to Him, "Teacher, we want to see a sign from You." ³⁹ But He answered and said to them, "An evil and adulterous generation craves for a sign; and *yet* no sign will be given to it but the sign of Jonah the prophet; ⁴⁰ for just as JONAH WAS THREE DAYS AND THREE NIGHTS IN THE BELLY OF THE SEA MONSTER, so will the Son of Man be three days and three nights in the heart of the earth. ⁴¹ The men of Nineveh will stand up with this generation at the judgment, and will condemn it because they repented at the preaching of Jonah; and behold, something greater than Jonah is here.	¹ The Pharisees and Sadducees came up, and testing Jesus, they asked Him to show them a sign from heaven. ² But He replied to them, "When it is evening, you say, '*It will be* fair weather, for the sky is red.' ³ And in the morning, '*There will be* a storm today, for the sky is red and threatening.' Do you know how to discern the appearance of the sky, but cannot *discern* the signs of the times? ⁴ An evil and adulterous generation seeks after a sign; and a sign will not be given it, except the sign of Jonah."	²⁹ As the crowds were increasing, He began to say, "This generation is a wicked generation; it seeks for a sign, and *yet* no sign will be given to it but the sign of Jonah. ³⁰ For just as Jonah became a sign to the Ninevites, so will the Son of Man be to this generation. ³¹ The Queen of the South will rise up with the men of this generation at the judgment and condemn them, because she came from the ends of the earth to hear the wisdom of Solomon; and behold, something greater than Solomon is here. ³² The men of Nineveh will stand up with this generation at the judgment and condemn it, because they repented at the preaching of Jonah; and behold, something greater than Jonah is here.

The "Sign of Jonah"

Luke 11:30 identifies the *person* of Jonah and the Son of Man as the sign; Matt 12:40 identifies the sign of Jonah with the *burial* of Jonah in the belly of the fish and the burial and resurrection of the Son of Man as the sign; both Luke 11:32 and Matt 12:41 identify the *proclamation* of Jonah and the Son of Man with the sign; Matt 16:4 leaves the "sign of Jonah" undefined. The depth of the "sign of Jonah" is seen in the following parallels between Jesus and Jonah.

Identification with Galilee

Jesus was brought up in the town of Nazareth in Galilee.[64] In John 7:52 the chief priests and Pharisees specifically attacked the idea that Jesus was the Messiah, telling Nicodemus *"You are not also from Galilee, are you? Search, and see that no prophet arises out of Galilee."* The Pharisees were wrong. Jonah was from the town of Gath-hepher (2 Kgs 14:25). Gath-hepher is a small village "about three miles northeast of Nazareth" in Galilee.[65]

Identification with the dove

"The name Jonah means 'Dove,' a symbol of peace. Christ is the Prince of Peace and made peace by the death of His cross (Isa. 9:6; Luke 2:14; John 14:27)."[66] Further, at his baptism the Holy Spirit came in the form of a dove and rested on Jesus as a sign that Jesus was the Messiah (Matt 3:16–17; John 1:32–34).

Jonah's being swallowed by the fish and the death and resurrection of Christ

There are several parallels between Jonah and Jesus concerning the fish, death, and resurrection:

1. *The storm at sea* (Jonah 1–2; Matt 8:23–27; Mark 4:35–41; Luke 8:22–25). "Jonah boards a boat headed in the opposite direction of

---

64. Matt 2:22–23; 13:54; 21:11; 26:71; Mark 1:9, 24; 6:1; Luke 1:26; 4:14–16, 34; 18:37; John 1:45–46; Acts 10:38; 26:9.
65. Merrill, "Sign," 25.
66. Stanton, "Prophet," 246.

the nation to which he had been directed to prophesy; Jesus sets off in a boat toward the 'other side,' leaving behind a crowd that presses upon him."[67] The context of both accounts involves the movement from Jewish to Gentile territory. The details of the storm are virtually identical in both cases. Both involved a great storm in which the boats Jonah and Jesus were on were swamped or about to break up (Jonah 1:4; Matt 8:24; Mark 4:37; Luke 8:23). Jonah lay down inside the ship and slept; Jesus slept in the stern of the boat (Jonah 1:5–6; Matt 8:24; Mark 4:38; Luke 8:24). The contrast is that "Jonah was weary *of* God's service. Jesus was weary *in* God's service."[68] In both cases, the sailors cried out in fear of "perishing" (Jonah 1:5–6; Matt 8:25; Mark 4:38; Luke 8:24). Keller observes, "How ironic it is that in Mark 4 the disciples ask, 'Teacher, don't you care if we drown?' (Mark 4:38). They believe he is going to sleep on them in their hour of greatest need. Actually, it is the other way around. In the garden of Gethsemane, *they* will go to sleep on him. They will truly abandon him."[69] When Jonah was cast into the sea, *"the sea stopped its raging"* (Jonah 1:16); when Jesus rebuked the wind and waves, *"they stopped, and it became calm"* (Luke 8:24; see also Matt 8:26; Mark 4:39). After the sea was calmed, Jonah 1:16 (LXX) says, *"and the men feared a great fear"*; the Greek of Mark 4:41 literally says, *"and they feared a great fear."*

2   *Self-sacrifice.* Jonah offered himself sacrificially for the sake of others (Jonah 1:12). The sailors acknowledged that Jonah was *"innocent blood"* (Jonah 1:14). Jesus laid down his life sacrificially for us (John 10:11, 17–18; Rom 5:7–8; 1 John 3:16). Judas admitted that he had betrayed *"innocent blood"* (Matt 27:4), and the centurion who crucified Jesus said, *"Certainly this man was innocent"* (Luke 23:47). "Jonah was thrown overboard for his own sin, but Jesus is thrown into the ultimate storm for *our* sin. Jesus was able to save the disciples from the storm because he was thrown into the ultimate storm."[70] Jonah's sacrifice spared the sailors from physical death; Jesus' greater sacrifice saves humanity from the everlasting "second death."

3   *Descent into Sheol.* In Matt 12:40, Jesus says that, just as Jonah was in the belly of the fish, *"so will the Son of Man be . . . in the heart of the earth."* Although some people believe that Jesus' reference to *"the heart of the earth"* simply refers to the grave, more appears to be involved. In

---

67. Powell, "Echoes," 160.
68. Stanton, "Prophet," 247.
69. Keller, *Preaching*, 79.
70. Keller, *Preaching*, 79–80.

Jonah 2:2, when he was in the belly of the fish, Jonah prayed, *"I cried for help from the depth of Sheol."* Reed Lessing points out, *"Sheol* is the opposite theological extreme of Yahweh's presence and its dominant feature for its inhabitants is their separation from Him. . . . It is exclusively reserved for those under divine judgment. . . . This means that Jonah's use of *Sheol* in 2:3 [2:2 in the Christian Bible] indicates he is under Yahweh's judgment."[71] The term *kardias* ("heart") occurs in Jonah 2:4 (*"You had cast me into the deep, into the heart of the seas"*). In Jonah 2:5 (LXX), Jonah adds, *"I am cast out of thy presence."* According to Matthew 12:40, therefore, the "sign of Jonah" appears to be the correspondence between Jonah's being under divine judgment and being cast out of God's presence *"into the heart of the seas"* and Jesus' bearing God's judgment by being forsaken by the Father on the cross and being *"in the heart of the earth"* (see Matt 27:46).[72]

4. *Resurrection.* Jonah's stay in the belly of the fish "is a prophetic analogue for the death and resurrection of Jesus (explicit in Matt 12:40 and assumed in Matt 16:4). . . . Later in the Gospel (but only in this Gospel), the religious leaders of Israel actually learn of the resurrection of Jesus (Matt 28:11–15). They are thus confronted with the promised sign of Jonah, but they respond not with repentance but with duplicity that only intensifies their opposition to the will and ways of God."[73] In his resurrection, Jesus again is "greater than Jonah": Jonah was not literally raised from the dead (or, if he actually died in the fish, he was only revived and lived to die again); Jesus suffered real, physical death and was truly resurrected to life again, from which he will never die. Further, Jesus is *"the first fruits of those who are asleep"* (1 Cor 15:20) and will bring the resurrection of life to all who are in him (John 5:28–29; 1 Cor 15:12–23, 50–58).

5. *"Three days and three nights."* The fact that Jesus was buried on Friday evening (Matt 27:57–60; Mark 15:42–46; Luke 23:50–56; John 19:31, 38–42) and rose early on the following Sunday morning (Matt 28:1–6; Mark 16:1–6; Luke 24:1–6; John 20:1) does not contradict the reference to *"three days and three nights"* in Matt 12:40. That phrase is an idiom. "The *Babylonian Talmud* (Jewish commentaries) relates that, 'The portion of a day is as the whole of it.' The *Jerusalem Talmud* (so designated because it was written in Jerusalem) says, 'We have a teaching, "A day and a night are an Onah and the portion of an Onah is as

---

71. Lessing, "Dying to Live," 12–13.
72. See Lessing, "Dying to Live," 20–21.
73. Powell, "Echoes," 161–62.

the whole of it."""⁷⁴ Since "Jewish reckoning considered a partial day to be a full day (cf. Gen 42:17–18; 1 Sam 30:12–13; Esth 4:16; 5:1 [see also 1 Kgs 20:29; 2 Chron 10:5, 12]), so Jesus was in the grave Friday, Saturday, and Sunday; and the terminology fits."⁷⁵ Matt 27:63–64 shows the idiomatic usage of "three days" terminology specifically in connection with Jesus' burial. In Matt 27:63 the Pharisees went to Pilate and recalled that Jesus had said, *"After three days I am to rise again."* Therefore, in 27:64 they requested that Pilate *"give orders for the grave to be made secure until the third day."* "If the phrase, 'after three days,' had not been interchangeable with the 'third day,' the Pharisees would have asked for a guard for the fourth day."⁷⁶ That is confirmed in John 2:18–19 where the Jews also asked Jesus for a sign. Jesus replied, *"Destroy this temple, and in three days I will raise it up"* (referring to the temple of His body, John 2:21–22). In commenting on that passage, Martin Luther noted that Jesus' statement is, in substance, what he said in, Matt 12:39–40, i.e., "This shall be your sign: 'Destroy this temple, and in three days I will raise it up.' That is: 'I shall be the Jonah whom you will cast into the ocean and into the jaws of the whale, whom you will crucify and kill; and on the third day I shall rise again.'"⁷⁷

The person

Jonah was a sign *"to the Ninevites"* (Luke 11:30). In that verse "the name Jonah should probably be taken as a genitive of apposition with *sēmeion* ['sign'] so that he himself is the sign."⁷⁸ Although other prophets denounced ungodliness and pronounced judgment on pagan nations in addition to Israel, Jonah "is the only Hebrew prophet who is said to have traveled abroad to denounce in person the wickedness of a foreign nation and to proclaim its overthrow."⁷⁹ The fact that he had been swallowed and regurgitated by a great fish probably was particularly important to the people of Nineveh, since Nineveh was called "Fishtown" and myths described it as having been

---

74. McDowell, *Resurrection*, 122.
75. Osborne, *Matthew*, 486; see also Delling, *"Hēmera,"* 949–50.
76. McDowell, *Resurrection*, 122.
77. Luther, *Luther's Works*, 2:242.
78. Merrill, "Sign," 24n.13; see also Osborne, *Matthew*, 485n.5 (the sign *"of Jonah the prophet"* is "an epexegetical genetive, 'the sign that is Jonah the prophet'").
79. Merrill, "Sign," 20.

founded by a fish-god.[80] Similarly, Jesus left his home in heaven and came to earth. Here again, Jesus shows himself to be "greater than Jonah": *"Jonah didn't so love Nineveh that he gave them God. God so loved Nineveh that he gave them Jonah."*[81] So with Jesus: *"God so loved the world that He gave His only begotten Son, that whoever believes in Him shall not perish, but have eternal life"* (John 3:16).

The proclamation

On its face, Jonah's proclamation to Nineveh (*"Yet forty days and Nineveh will be overthrown,"* Jonah 3:4) was an unqualified message of judgment. Nevertheless, Jonah himself realized that implicit in the message was a call to repentance and mercy (Jonah 4:2). Jesus began his public ministry by explicitly urging repentance and proclaiming God's grace and salvation, *"The time is fulfilled, and the kingdom of God is at hand; repent and believe in the gospel"* (Mark 1:15; see also Matt 4:17). The theme of judgment was implicit. Later in his ministry, Jesus' proclamation of judgment became explicit.[82] Although the pagan Ninevites repented at the preaching of Jonah, Jesus' own people—the nation of Israel—did not repent and believe in Jesus. Jesus therefore argued in Luke 11:32, *"The men of Nineveh will stand up with this generation at the judgment and condemn it, because they repented at the preaching of Jonah; and behold, something greater than Jonah is here."* Mark Powell points out the irony of the situation: Jesus "preaching may represent something greater than that of Jonah, but then the covenant people of God are (or should be) something greater than the people of Nineveh. So there is a double irony: the Son of Man's preaching is turning out to be less effective than that of the reluctant prophet, and the covenant people of God are revealing themselves to be more obstinate than the notorious Ninevites."[83]

THE FLOOD AND THE ARK

The narrative of the Flood (Gen 6:5—8:21), provides us with two "types" of the gospel: the ark as a type of Christ and the water of the flood as a type of baptism.

80. Merrill, "Sign," 26–30.
81. Work, "Converting," 171–72.
82. E.g., Matt 21:33–45; 23:29–39; 24:1–2, 15–19, 32–34; Mark 12:1–12; 13:1–2, 14–19, 28–30; Luke 11:45–51; 13:34–35; 19:41–44; 20:9–19; 21:5–6, 20–24, 29–32; and the "sign of Jonah" passages themselves.
83. Powell, "Echoes," 163–64.

With respect to the ark, the idea and plan for the ark as the way to save Noah and his family was from God, not Noah. Similarly, Jesus as the means for salvation through his crucifixion and resurrection was the predetermined plan of God (Acts 2:22–24; 4:27–28; 1 Pet 1:20). There was only one ark, not a fleet of arks from which Noah could choose. Likewise, there is only one way of salvation; Jesus said, and *"I am the way, and the truth, and the life; no one comes to the Father but through Me"* (John 14:6). The ark had one door (Gen 6:16). Jesus said, *"I am the door; if anyone enters through Me, he will be saved"* (John 10:9). Heb 11:7 says that Noah prepared the ark *"by faith."* Similarly, we are saved only by God's grace *"through faith"* (Eph 2:8). The ark was covered inside and out with pitch, to make it watertight (Gen 6:14); thus, the waters of God's judgment fell onto the ark but could not get into the ark. Likewise, Christ bore the judgment we deserved, so that we who are "in Christ" no longer are condemned. In fact, the Hebrew words translated "cover" or "pitch" as a verb and "pitch" as a noun are not the usual words for pitch or tar. Rather, the basic meaning of pitch as a verb is "atonement," which is how it is almost always translated, and pitch as a noun is usually translated as "ransom" or "redemption."[84] Christ is our propitiation or atoning sacrifice.[85] He gave his life *"a ransom for many"* (Matt 20:28; Mark 10:45); in him we have "redemption."[86] Noah and his family had to be in the ark to escape the waters of the Flood (Gen 7:7); similarly, we are saved only if we are *"in Christ"* (Rom 8:1). God closed the door of the ark after the eight people and the animals had entered (Gen 7:16); thus, all those in the ark were secure. The same is true of all those who are in Christ: we have been *"sealed for the day of redemption"* (Eph 4:30; see also Eph 1:13–14) and *"neither death, nor life, nor angels, nor principalities, nor things present, nor things to come, nor powers, nor height, nor depth, nor any other created thing, will be able to separate us from the love of God, which is in Christ Jesus our Lord"* (Rom 8:38–39). After the Flood, the ark *"rested upon the mountains of Ararat"* (Gen 8:4). This typifies Jesus' resurrection and ascension, since Jesus, after bearing our judgment, *"ascended on high"* (Eph 4:8). Jesus even extends the typology of Noah and the Flood to his second coming: *"For the coming of the Son of Man will be just like the days of Noah. For as in those days before the flood they were eating and drinking, marrying and giving in marriage, until the day that Noah entered the ark, and they did not*

---

84. Koehler and Baumgartner, *Hebrew and Aramaic Lexicon*, "kaphar," "kopher," 493–94.

85. Isa 53:4–12; Matt 26:26–28; Rom 3:25; 5:6–11; 1 Cor 15:3; Heb 9:12–14; 1 John 2:2; Rev 5:9.

86. Luke 1:68; Rom 3:24; 1 Cor 1:30; Eph 1:7; Col 1:14; Heb 9:12, 15.

understand until the flood came and took them all away; so will the coming of the Son of Man be." (Matt 24:37-39; see also Luke 17:26-27)

With respect to baptism, Peter speaks of the ark *"in which a few, that is, eight persons, were brought safely through the water. Corresponding to that, baptism now saves you—not the removal of dirt from the flesh, but an appeal to God for a good conscience—through the resurrection of Jesus Christ"* (1 Pet 3:20-21) The Greek translated *"corresponding to that"* is *antitupon* ("antitype"). Thus, 1 Pet 3:21 could be translated *"which now saves you antitypically, even baptism."*[87] There are three elements of parallelism between Noah's experience and ours: people, salvation, and water. In 1 Peter 3, the parallelism of vv. 20-21 may be seen schematically as follows:[88]

v. 20	v. 21
1. People: eight persons	you
2. Salvation: brought safely through	saves
3. Water: through water	baptism

Peter here is assuming that the mode of baptism is immersion. Wayne Grudem observes, "How incongruous the mention of 'removal of dirt from the body' would be if Peter thought that only a few drops of water were sprinkled on the head."[89] In this passage, the water of the Flood was the means of God's judgment, resulting in destruction and death. Similarly, the water of baptism is symbolic of our death to sin. Rom 6:4 states, *"Therefore we have been buried with Him through baptism into death, so that as Christ was raised from the dead through the glory of the Father, so we too might walk in newness of life."* As the verse states, "Coming up out of the waters of baptism corresponds to being kept safe through the waters of the flood. . . . Baptism thus shows us clearly that in one sense we have 'died' and 'been raised' again, but in another sense we emerge from the waters knowing that we are still alive and have passed through the waters of God's judgment unharmed."[90] In another sense, baptism points us, not to the water *per se*, but to the ark, which was the means by which Noah and his family were brought safely through the water. Baptism is the symbol of "our having been rescued by God through our voluntary entrance into the ark of His salvation."[91] It is not baptism itself that saves us but our being united with

---

87. See Fritsch, "Biblical Typology," 90.
88. See Davidson, *Typology in Scripture*, 321.
89. Grudem, *1 Peter*, 162.
90. Grudem, *1 Peter*, 163.
91. Zodhiates, *Complete Word Study, antitupon*, 196.

Christ, through his death, resurrection, and ascension, to which baptism also points (Rom 6:4–6).[92]

THE EXODUS AND EVENTS CONNECTED WITH THE EXODUS

The exodus of Israel out of Egypt (see Exodus 3–20) is a type of salvation by Christ. Israel was enslaved and under sentence of death in Egypt (Exod 1:8–22); we are enslaved to sin (John 8:34; Rom 6:20) and under sentence of death (Gen 2:17; Ezek 18:20). While Israel faced death, the true Israel, Jesus Christ, endured death. On the night of Passover, God saved the lives of the Israelites by his grace. They killed a lamb and placed its blood on the doorposts and lintels of their houses. When the angel of death saw the blood, all those in the houses were saved, which led to their exodus from Egypt (Exod 12:1–13, 21–34). Jesus is our Passover lamb, who shed his blood for our salvation (Luke 22:20; John 1:29; Eph 2:8–9; Rev 5:6, 8). First Cor 5:7 specifically says, *"Christ our Passover also has been sacrificed."*[93]

Moses was the mediator between God and Pharaoh and between God and the Israelites; Christ is the *"one mediator between God and men"* (1 Tim 2:5). Through Moses, God gave Israel his law and the tabernacle (Exodus 20; 25–27); Christ "tabernacled" among us (John 1:14)[94] and gave us his law (1 Cor 9:21; Gal 6:2). God was present in the midst of Israel throughout their journey to the promised land (Exod 13:17–22; 40:34–38); Jesus is with us and promised, *"I will never desert you, nor will I ever forsake you"* (Heb 13:5). On the Mount of Transfiguration, Jesus explicitly indicates the typological nature of the exodus. Luke 9:31 says that Jesus, Moses, and Elijah *"were speaking of His departure which He was about to accomplish at Jerusalem."* The Greek word translated as "departure" is *"exodus."* Jesus accomplished his "exodus" by his death on the cross and his subsequent resurrection. The

---

92. John Piper describes salvation's relationship to the confession of faith and to baptism in Rom 10:9 and 1 Pet 3:21 this way, "The movement of the lips in the air [Rom 10:9] and the movement of the body in water [1 Pet 3:21] save only in the sense that they give expression to the single justifying act, namely, faith (Rom. 3:28). Baptism is the outward appeal of faith to God in the heart." Piper, *Brothers*, 158.

93. Peter's statement in 1 Pet 1:19 that we have been redeemed *"with precious blood, as of a lamb unblemished and spotless, the blood of Christ,"* alludes to Exod 12:5, which specifies that the Passover lamb was to be *"an unblemished male a year old."*

94. John 1:14 says, *"And the Word became flesh and dwelt among us."* The Greek word for "dwelt" is *eskēnōsen*, past tense of the verb *skēnoō*, which is the verbal form of the noun *skēnos*, which means "tabernacle." Thus, the verse literally is saying that *"the Word became flesh and tabernacled among us."*

exodus led by Moses led people out of physical slavery in Egypt to a new life of freedom in the promised land (Exod 12:29-32). Jesus' "exodus" led his people out of the far greater slavery to sin, Satan, death, and bondage to the law, to the true salvation "rest" that will last forever (Heb 4:1-11; Rev 21:1—22:17.

Following the exodus out of Egypt, several other events that occurred on the way to the promised land acted as types or pointers to Christ. When the Israelites reached the Red Sea, Pharaoh's army was in close pursuit. The Israelites cried out in rebellion against Moses that they wanted to return to Egypt (Exod 14:10-12). God told Moses to stretch out his hand over the sea, and the sea was divided, enabling Israel to cross on dry ground (Exod 14:15-22). When the Egyptian army tried to cross, the waters crashed down upon them, drowning them all (Exod 14:23-31). Heb 11:29 says, *"By faith they [the Israelites] passed through the Red Sea as though they were passing through dry land; and the Egyptians, when they attempted it, were drowned."* Hebrews 11 is all about the importance and nature of faith. The Egyptians did not believe in God and drowned. Timothy Keller adds one other aspect of this: the reason why the waters of God's judgment did not also crash down on the Israelites was because "the Israelites had a mediator. . . . Moses was one man who was so identified with the Israelites that their guilt was upon him, and he was so identified with God that God's power was coming through him. He was a man in the middle."[95] Our mediator, Jesus Christ, is not just a man close to God as was Moses but is fully man and fully God. He so identified with his people that he, who never sinned, became sin for us (2 Cor 5:21). His mediation did not just defeat an army but defeated the greatest foes that all human beings face: sin, Satan, and death itself. Later in their journey, Moses became so frustrated with the Israelite's sin that he said, *"But now, if You will, forgive their sin—and if not, please blot me out from Your book which You have written!"* (Exod 32:32). Keller concludes, "Yet God did not blot him out. But with our Mediator, Jesus, God did. Jesus is the ultimate Mediator, and it's why you and I can cross over."[96]

In 1 Cor 10:1-2, Paul explicitly compares Israel's crossing the Red Sea to baptism: *"For I do not want you to be unaware, brethren, that our fathers were all under the cloud and all passed through the sea; and all were baptized into Moses in the cloud and in the sea."* Baptism symbolizes dying to one's old life of slavery to sin and rising to a new life of freedom in Christ (Rom 6:3-6). That is what happened to the Israelites: their old life of slavery in Egypt was over, and by crossing over the Sea they began a new life of freedom from

---

95. Keller, "Getting Out," 49-50.
96. Keller, "Getting Out," 51.

their former slave-masters. The picture of baptism is heightened when one remembers that two peoples entered the water—Israelites and Egyptians—but only one emerged, the Israelites. The Egyptian army lay dead, which is a graphic picture of the death of our old life of sin.

While Israel was in the wilderness, God provided *"bread from heaven"* (called manna) for them to eat (Exod 16:4). Jesus said, *"I am the living bread that came down out of heaven; if anyone eats of this bread, he will live forever"* (John 6:51). He added, *"I am the bread of life; he who comes to Me will not hunger, and he who believes in Me will never thirst"* (John 6:35; see also v. 48). The manna provided physical food, and since it was graciously provided by God it was called *"spiritual food"* (1 Cor 10:3). As the *"bread of life,"* Jesus gives people not only spiritual nourishment but eternal life. While the people in the wilderness who ate the manna hungered and thirsted, Jesus said in John 6:35, *"he who comes to Me will not hunger, and he who believes in Me will never thirst."* Therefore, he added, *"Do not work for the food which perishes, but for the food which endures to eternal life, which the Son of Man will give to you, for on Him the Father, God, has set His seal"* (John 6:27).

The Israelites also complained of thirst and grumbled against Moses (Exod 17:3). God told Moses, *"Strike the rock, and water will come out of it, that the people may drink"* (Exod 17:6). Because the water was graciously provided by God, it was called *"spiritual drink"* (1 Cor 10:4). First Cor 10:4 specifies the typological nature of the rock by saying that *"all [the Israelites in the wilderness] drank the same spiritual drink, for they were drinking from a spiritual rock which followed them; and the rock was Christ"* (1 Cor 10:4). Although the water that came from the rock Moses struck in the wilderness gave physical life to the people, Jesus, the greater antitype, stated, *"If anyone is thirsty, let him come to Me and drink. He who believes in Me, as the Scripture said, 'From his innermost being will flow rivers of living water.'"* (John 7:37–38). Elsewhere, he added that *"whoever drinks of the water that I will give him shall never thirst; but the water that I will give him will become in him a well of water springing up to eternal life"* (John 4:14)

The fact that the rock which Moses struck was Christ is significant. Later in their journey, the Israelites again complained of having no water, so God told Moses to *"speak to the rock"* in order to obtain water (Num 20:1–8). However, in his anger with the people, Moses did not speak to the rock but *"lifted up his hand and struck the rock twice with his rod; and water came forth abundantly, and the congregation and their beasts drank"* (Num 20:11). As a result, God told Moses, *"Because you have not believed Me, to treat Me as holy in the sight of the sons of Israel, therefore you shall not bring this assembly into the land which I have given them"* (Num 20:12). Moses's sin was so significant precisely because the rock was a type of Christ. Although God was gracious in providing water from the rock the second time, by striking the rock the second time, Moses was misrepresenting the gospel. The reason is that, as the rock, on the cross, Christ was "struck" with the rod of God's justice only once, not twice; he made *"one sacrifice for sins for all time"* (Heb 10:12; see also Heb 10:10, 14). Because of that, we now only have to call out to Jesus (i.e., *"speak to the rock"*), since the sacrifice has already been made.

In Numbers 21, God sent fiery serpents among the people. Many who were bitten died. The people confessed their sin, and Moses interceded. At God's instruction, Moses made a bronze serpent, which he lifted up on a standard (Num 21:8–9). Then, *"if a serpent bit any man, when he looked to the bronze serpent, he lived"* (Num 21:9). In John 3:14 Jesus said, *"As Moses lifted up the serpent in the wilderness, even so must the Son of man be lifted up."* Christ's clear comparison of his own manner of death with the bronze serpent in the wilderness renders the bronze serpent a "type." This is particularly the case since God ordained both the bronze serpent and the crucifixion of Christ as the means of salvation (see Acts 2:23; 4:27–28). From the time of Adam and Eve's temptation and fall, the serpent has been associated with sin.[97] On the cross, Jesus was made *"to be sin on our behalf"* (2 Cor 5:21). Consequently, now all we have to do is "look" to him to be saved from our sin. That the bronze serpent was a type is confirmed by 1 Cor 10:9 which refers to that incident and warns believers, *"Nor let us try the Lord, as some of them did, and were destroyed by the serpents."*

In 1 Cor 10:6–10, Paul also mentions the Israelites' craving of evil things, idolatry, immorality, and grumbling, all of which did not please the Lord and resulted in their being disciplined. In 1 Cor 10:6, Paul tells us why these things have been recorded in Scripture: *"Now these things happened as examples for us, so that we would not crave evil things as they also craved."* First Cor 10:1–11 concludes, *"Now these things happened to them as an example, and they were written for our instruction"* (1 Cor 10:11). Dennis Johnson points out, "God's inscripturation of the books of Moses was not only intended to address Israel's needs but was also directed primarily toward the needs of a future generation, specifically the eschatological generation who has now witnessed the appearance of the Messiah, in whom God's promises are fulfilled."[98] In short, typology exists for hortatory as well as theological reasons.

After they crossed the Jordan River to begin their conquest of the Promised Land, the first thing that the Lord had Israel do was to circumcise the males (Josh 5:2–9). This is also typological. Paul comments in Col

---

97. See Ps 58:4–5; 140:3; Isa 59:5; Jer 51:34; Mic 7:17; Matt 3:7; 12:34; 23:33.
98. Johnson, *Him We Proclaim*, 205.

2:11-12 that *"in Him you were also circumcised with a circumcision made without hands, in the removal of the body of the flesh by the circumcision of Christ; having been buried with Him in baptism, in which you were also raised up with Him through faith in the working of God, who raised Him from the dead."* The circumcision the Israelites performed involved the physical cutting off a piece of flesh. It points to cutting off the fleshly nature when we come to faith in Christ. Recall that, when the fulfillment comes, the "shadow" or type passes away. At the Council of Jerusalem in Acts 15, some Jewish believers did not understand that principle and said that Gentile believers needed to be physically circumcised (Acts 15:1, 5). The Council concluded otherwise (Acts 15:13-19). Since Christians have been *"circumcised with a circumcision made without hands,"* they (whether of Jewish or Gentile ancestry) are considered to be the "true Jews": *"For he is not a Jew who is one outwardly, nor is circumcision that which is outward in the flesh. But he is a Jew who is one inwardly; and circumcision is that which is of the heart, by the Spirit, not by the letter; and his praise is not from men, but from God."* (Rom 2:28-29) Indeed, Paul says that to go back to the types and shadows of the OT essentially means to reject Christ and what he has done: *"if you receive circumcision, Christ will be of no benefit to you"* (Gal 5:2). He goes so far as to call those who were requiring believers to become circumcised the "mutilation" (Gal 5:12).

THE "ABOMINATION OF DESOLATION"

In 167 BC Antiochus Epiphanes, the Seleucid king, sacrificed a swine on the altar of the temple and made the practice of Judaism illegal. That prompted the Maccabean revolt of 167-160 BC.[99] Approximately 360 years before this event, around 530 BC, the prophet Daniel had prophesied this, stating, *"Forces from him will arise, desecrate the sanctuary fortress, and do away with the regular sacrifice. And they will set up the abomination of desolation."* (Dan 11:31; see also Dan 8:13; 9:27; 12:11) In 1 Macc 1:54, the *"abomination of desolation"* was applied to the desecration of the altar by Antiochus, although both in Daniel and 1-2 Maccabees, Israel's own sins were a factor in the desecration caused by Antiochus.[100] Nevertheless, in the first century many in Israel believed that Antiochus had not completely fulfilled Daniel's visions of the *"abomination of desolation."* Desmond Ford relates that Daniel "had promised the advent of the kingdom of God after the profanation of the sanctuary by the willful king. But certainly the kingdom had not come with

---

99. Bartlett, "Maccabees," 476; Metzger, *Introduction*, 132.
100. See Dan 8:12; 9:24; 11:30-35; 12:10; 1 Macc 1:11-15, 43; 2 Macc 7:18, 32.

the rededicated sanctuary in 165 B.C. Therefore, they reasoned, the woes under Antiochus must have been pre-figurative of worse woes to come."[101]

In the Olivet Discourse (Matthew 24-25; Mark 13; Luke 21), Jesus likewise viewed the times of Antiochus as prefigurative of what lay ahead. He takes the same prophetic language—*"when you see the abomination of desolation which was spoken of through Daniel the prophet, standing in the holy place"* (Matt 24:15; Mark 13:14)—and reapplies it, or, rather, says that the true fulfillment will occur when the temple is desecrated and destroyed, primarily as a result of the nation's rejection of him.[102] That desolation and destruction happened in AD 70, when the Romans virtually razed the temple to the ground. That is how first century Jewish historian Josephus took it, "And indeed it so came to pass, that our nation suffered these things under Antiochus Epiphanes, according to Daniel's vision, and that he wrote many years before they came to pass. In the very same manner Daniel also wrote concerning the Roman government, and that our country should be made desolate by them."[103]

In short, we see typology throughout the OT. Both Jesus and the NT writers recognized this. The existence of typology reveals the hand of God behind the events of history and also reveals the depth and subtlety of the Bible.

---

101. Ford, *Abomination*, 157.

102. Compare Dan 7:13 and Mark 13:26; Dan 8:13 and Luke 21:24; Dan 9:27 and Mark 13:14; Dan 11:31 and Mark 13:14; Dan 12:1 and Mark 13:19; and possibly Dan 11:45 and Matt 24:15; see Watts, "Mark," 223-25 ("Israel's rebellious leaders have brought this [the destruction of the temple] on themselves. For Jesus, their defiling abominations are one with the worst in Israel's history: Antiochus' idolatrous pollution of the temple. . . . How else could one describe the outcome of those who kill Dan. 7's Son of Man, in whom Yahweh himself is present?")

103. Josephus, *Antiquities*, 10.11.7. Clement of Alexandria, *Stromata*, 1.21; Tertullian, *Answer*, 8; and early church historian Eusebius, *Ecclesiastical History*, 3.5.4 also took Daniel's vision that way.

8

Christ Fulfills the Promises of the Old Testament

THE FACT THAT JESUS is the ultimate subject of the OT shows that the OT does not stand on its own. We can reach an understanding at the historical level concerning OT events, and can even reach a certain theological understanding from the OT. However, because God's plan finds its culmination in the person and work of Jesus Christ, who both fully reveals and embodies the gospel, to get the full picture of God's acts, plans, and promises, we need the NT, which reveals *"the whole purpose of God"* (Acts 20:27).

JESUS FULFILLS THE OT'S PROMISE OF THE GOSPEL

The Bible can be viewed as the unfolding of the gospel. The gospel of Jesus Christ is founded on and was promised in the OT. The essence of the gospel is that God is holy, just, righteous, and good.[1] However, people are sinful and inclined to evil.[2] Our sin has brought about death and separation from God.[3] We cannot bridge that divide by anything we can do because our problem is within us and we cannot change our own hearts.[4] Consequently, if we are to be accepted by God, God must do for us what we cannot

---

1. Gen 18:25; Exod 34:6–7; Lev 11:44; Job 34:10–12; Ps 5:4; 136:1; 145:17; Hab 1:13; see Rom 1:18; Jas 1:13.

2. Ps 51:1–5; Isa 64:6; see Rom 3:23; 7:8–21.

3. Gen 2:17; Isa 59:1–2; Ezek 18:4; see Rom 5:12–14; 6:23.

4. Eccl 9:3; Isa 1:5–6; Jer 17:9; see Matt 15:18–19; Mark 7:20–23; Rom 1:21; 3:10–18.

do for ourselves by a substitute who will bear our sin and the penalty for that sin so that we may be forgiven.[5] Just as our sins can only be fully paid for by a substitute, so the righteousness we need to stand in God's presence can only be imputed to us by God by his grace through our faith.[6]

Rom 1:1–4 proclaims this by referring to *"the gospel of God, which he promised beforehand through his prophets in the holy Scriptures, concerning his Son, who was born of a descendant of David according to the flesh, who was declared the Son of God with power by the resurrection from the dead."* In other words, the gospel is "God's" gospel, in that it deals with how he, as perfect, righteous, and holy—who cannot dwell with or look at evil (Ps 5:4; Hab 1:13)—can justify and accept sinful people. The gospel primarily concerns Jesus Christ, whose person and work was validated by his resurrection from the dead.

JESUS FULFILLS THE ENTIRE OT

The following chart shows the similarity of Peter's and Paul's initial sermons in Acts. It shows that the entire OT finds its fulfillment Jesus.

Gospel	Peter (Acts 2)	Paul (Acts 13)
1. The OT is fulfilled	2:16–21, 25–31, 34–36	13:16–23, 32–39
2. in the person and work of Jesus	2:22	13:23–26
3. who died	2:23	13:27–29
4. and rose again	2:24, 32	13:30–31, 34–37
5. and is now exalted	2:33, 36	13:34
6. Through Him is forgiveness of sins	2:38	13:38–39
7. Therefore . . .	2:38–40	13:40–41

As we have seen, in the OT, as God progressively revealed his plan, on occasion, Jesus made pre-incarnate appearances before he came to earth as the son of Mary. Primarily, however, God revealed his plan through prophecy and in "types" and "shadows." In particular, God used the nation of Israel and all of its institutions to point to Christ. The following chapters show how Christ and the church are the substance that OT Israel pointed to.

---

5. Gen 15:17–18; 22:1–14; Lev 17:11; Isa 53:4–5; Jer 31:31–34; see 2 Cor 5:21; Heb 10:10; 1 Pet 2:24.

6. Gen 15:6; Ps 32:1–2; Hab 2:4; see Rom 3:21–22, 24; 4:5, 22–25; Eph 2:8–9.

9

Christ and the Church Fulfill the Abrahamic, Davidic, and New Covenants

The covenant God made with Abraham reveals God's plan to save a people and bring them into His land. Under the Old [Mosaic] Covenant, God physically saves the people of Israel (the physical descendants of Abraham) from the Egyptians and brings them into the Promised Land, Palestine. Under the New Covenant, God spiritually saves His people (the spiritual descendants of Abraham) from sin and condemnation and brings them into the spiritual land (salvation rest now and in heaven).[1]

THE ABRAHAMIC COVENANT IS FULFILLED IN CHRIST AND THE CHURCH

"GOD'S COVENANT WITH ABRAHAM lays the foundation for the entire ensuing history of redemption recorded in the Scriptures."[2] It was "the first step to fulfill the prediction made in Genesis 3:15 concerning the Unique Seed coming to die on the cross in fulfillment of the eternal unchanging purpose of grace."[3] In the Abrahamic Covenant there are three basic "core

---

1. Lehrer, *New Covenant Theology*, 29.

2. Holwerda, *Jesus and Israel*, 32. The Abrahamic Covenant is found in Gen 12:1–3; 13:14–17; 15:1–21; 17:1–21; 22:15–18.

3. Reisinger, *Abraham's Four Seeds*, 25.

promissory threads": (A) *phenomenal posterity* (i.e., promises relating to "seed"); (B) *national territory* (i.e., promises relating to "land"); and (C) *global blessing* (promises relating to the blessing of other peoples through Abraham's seed).[4] In one way or another, the other covenants grow out of the Abrahamic Covenant.

God's formulation of the covenant changed over the course of his dealings with Abraham. God initially promised to make Abram *"a great nation"* (Gen 12:2) but later expanded this to make him the father of *"a multitude of nations"* (Gen 17:5). At the same time, God narrowed the "seed" through whom he would establish the covenant: not all of Abraham's biological descendants were included but only the line of Isaac (Gen 17:18–21). Through that seed *"all the nations of the earth shall be blessed"* (Gen 22:18). The "land," initially undefined (Gen 12:1), was first defined as what Abram could see (Gen 13:14–15), then was geographically described (Gen 15:18–21; 17:8), and finally was included in the comprehensive statement that *"your seed shall possess the gates of their [lit., 'his'] enemies"* (Gen 22:17).

OT Israel was the "physical" fulfillment of the Abrahamic Covenant. Regarding the "seed" promise, Exod 1:6–13; Num 23:10; Deut 1:10 indicate the phenomenal expansion of the Israelites. Deut 1:10 says, *"The Lord your God has multiplied you, and behold, you are this day like the stars of heaven in number."* Similarly, the "land" promise was fulfilled at least twice, in the days of Joshua (Josh 21:43–45) and during the reign of Solomon (1 Kgs 4:20–21). Regarding the "blessing" promise, in 1 Kgs 10:1–13; 2 Chron 9:1–12 the Queen of Sheba acknowledged the great blessings that Solomon had brought to Israel and to everyone who heard his wisdom. Thus, Solomon declared in 1 Kgs 8:56, *"not one word has failed of all His good promise, which He promised through Moses His servant"* (see also Josh 21:45; 23:14).

Despite its initial physical fulfillment in OT Israel, the OT pictures the Abrahamic Covenant as ultimately unfulfilled. Regarding the "seed" promise, Deut 30:4–5; Jer 23:3; Ezek 36:10–11 promise numerical increase after God leads Israel into exile. Regarding the "land" promise, retention of Canaan was conditioned on Israel's obedience. The OT reflects a pattern of partial fulfillment, followed by dispossession and subsequent repossession. Thus, the concept of the land was never fully realized during the OT period. Regarding the "universal blessing" promise, the nations were not universally blessed during the OT period, and the prophetic literature envisaged the universal blessing as yet future.

---

4. See Williamson, "Abraham, Israel," 100–101; Kaiser, *Toward an Old,* 86; Essex, "The Abrahamic Covenant," 208; Reisinger, *Abraham's Four Seeds,* 6.

According to the NT, the fulfillment of the Abrahamic Covenant is found in the coming, atonement, and resurrection of Jesus Christ. God's mercy, and his covenant with Abraham, referred to in Jer 33:26, are cited by Mary in Luke 1:54–55 concerning the coming of Jesus. Zacharias, father of John the Baptist, likewise viewed the coming of Jesus, and his forerunner John, as fulfilling the covenant with Abraham (Luke 1:67–79). Jesus himself stressed that the Abrahamic Covenant ultimately was spiritual and that he fulfilled it (see John 8:31–58).

1. *The "seed" promise.* In many translations, the reference to Abraham's "seed"[5] is often translated "offspring" or "descendants." The Hebrew word for "seed" can denote either singular or plural. In the NT, the singular aspect of the "seed" promise is applied to Christ as the true "seed" of Abraham; Gal 3:16 says, *"Now the promises were spoken to Abraham and to his seed. He does not say, 'And to seeds,' as referring to many, but rather to one, 'And to your seed,' that is, Christ."* The plural aspect of the "seed" promise is applied to all those who are "in Christ" by faith, i.e., the church; Gal 3:29 says, *"If you belong to Christ, then you are Abraham's descendants, heirs according to promise."* This latter point is made by virtually all of the major figures of the NT:

   - *John the Baptist.* John the Baptist downplayed physical descent from Abraham by saying, *"do not suppose that you can say to yourselves, 'We have Abraham for our father'; for I say to you that from these stones God is able to raise up children to Abraham"* (Matt 3:9; Luke 3:8).

   - *Jesus Christ.* Jesus distinguished between the *physical* descendants of Abraham (who are *not* the true fulfillment of the Abrahamic Covenant) and the *spiritual* descendants of Abraham (who *are* the true fulfillment of the Abrahamic Covenant). He indicated that since the Jews were slaves of sin, they were not truly Abraham's sons (John 8:33–36). If they were children of Abraham they would do the deeds of Abraham, but their attempt to kill him was proof that they do not. Thus, their true father is not Abraham, but the devil (John 8:39–41, 44); if God were their Father, they would love Jesus and hear his word (John 8:42).

   - *The Apostle Peter.* In Acts 3:25–26 Peter specifies that it is believers in Christ *"who are the sons of the prophets and of the covenant which God made with your fathers."*

---

5. Gen 13:15; 15:3, 5, 18; 17:7, 9, 19; 22:17, 18.

Christ and the Church Fulfill the Abrahamic, Davidic, and New Covenants 141

- *The Apostle Paul.* Paul echoes what Jesus said in John 8:34–44 concerning who are the true children of Abraham. In Rom 4:11–18 he points out that the promise to Abraham was made *"not through the Law, but through the righteousness of faith"* (see also Gal 3:6–9, 14). He reiterates that in Rom 9:6–8, where he says that *"they are not all Israel who are descended from Israel,"* and *"it is not the children of flesh who are the children of God, but the children of the promise are regarded as descendants."* The argument of Galatians 3–4 as a whole is that Christ and the church are the true fulfillment of the Abrahamic Covenant.[6]

2 *The "land" promise.* The land of OT Israel was a "type," pointing to *"the city which has foundations, whose architect and builder is God . . . a better country, that is, a heavenly one,"* which even Abraham and the OT saints were looking for (Heb 11:10, 16).[7] That "better, heavenly country" is the heavenly city, the New Jerusalem (Revelation 21–22). The OT picture of the *"mountain of God"* (see, e.g., Ps 2:6; Isa 56:7) was a "shadow" or "copy," using physical language, to denote the greater living and spiritual reality of Christ himself (Col 2:16–17; Heb 8:1—10:22). Thus, in Christ we have *"not come to a mountain that can be touched . . . but you have come to Mount Zion and to the city of the living God, the heavenly Jerusalem"* (Heb 12:18, 22; 13:14). Paul made the same point in Gal 4:21–31, where he said that the physical Mount Sinai and physical Jerusalem were in slavery, but *"the Jerusalem above"* is free and *"she is our mother."* In his discussion of the "two Jerusalems," Paul quoted Isa 54:1, which originally had applied to *earthly* Jerusalem, and applied it to the "Jerusalem above"; he also denied that earthly Jerusalem was in any way connected to the "Jerusalem above."

This typological interpretation of the "land" is found elsewhere. For example, possessing the land did not constitute the final Sabbath rest, but was a foretaste of it. Heb 3:7—4:11 transforms the meaning of the promise of the "land" given in the Abrahamic Covenant, which is equated and fulfilled with the everlasting possession of our eternal salvation.[8] Similarly, Rom 4:13 expands and universalizes the "land" promise to include Abraham and his descendants as *"heir of the world."* In Rom 4:13 the word for "world" is the Greek word *kosmos*, which is global in scale, rather than *ge*, which had indicated the land of OT

---

6. See Burke, *Adopted*, 112, 114n.33.

7. See Poythress, *Shadow of Christ*, 106.

8. Lehrer, *New Covenant Theology*, 36; see below, chapter 14—Christ Fulfills and Replaces the OT Sabbath.

Israel in the accounts of the Abrahamic Covenant (Gen 12:1; 13:15, LXX). Additionally, when Paul quotes the command to *"honor your father and mother,"* he expands the OT promise associated with it (that *"it may go well with you on the land which the Lord your God gives you,"* Deut 5:16), to read, *"so that . . . you may live long on the earth"* (Eph 6:2–3).

3   *The "blessing" promise.* In Gal 3:8–9, 14 Paul quotes the "blessing" promise of Gen 12:3 but explains that *"the blessing of Abraham"* is our justification through faith which is only found *"in Christ Jesus."* Likewise, in Acts 3:25, Peter quotes the "blessing" promise given to Abraham in Gen 22:18 and applies it to all who are saved by faith in Christ, declaring, *"It is you who are the sons of the prophets and of the covenant which God made with your fathers, saying to Abraham, 'and in your seed all the families of the earth shall be blessed.'"* Thus, as with the "seed" promise and the "land" promise, the "blessing" was always intended to be fulfilled, not in a "physical" way, but spiritually in Christ.

THE DAVIDIC COVENANT IS FULFILLED IN CHRIST AND THE CHURCH[9]

Second Sam 7:1–17 contains the "Davidic Covenant" in which God promised to raise up David's seed after him and *"establish the throne of his kingdom forever"* (2 Sam 7:12–13, 16; see also Ps 89:29, 36–37).[10] The Davidic Covenant refined the Abrahamic Covenant and specified, in part, how God was going to fulfill his promises to Abraham. As a result, the two covenants are linked. That was indicated in Jer 33:23–26, which connects the fulfillment of the Abrahamic and Davidic Covenants. In fact, Mary's Magnificat (Luke 1:46–55) and Zacharias's prophecy (Luke 1:67–79) "collapse the Davidic and Abrahamic covenants together into one. . . . And in the progressive discovery of the unfolding narrative, readers catch that Gabriel's promise about Jesus on the throne of David is grounded in God's promise to Abraham."[11]

---

9. See also chapter 5 regarding The Messiah and chapter 7 regarding David and Solomon.

10. The context of the covenant had to do with the construction of the temple. Thus, the covenant in the first instance related to David's son Solomon, who built the temple, but in stating that he would *"establish the throne of his kingdom forever,"* God was making clear that the covenant extended far beyond Solomon and the entire Davidic line.

11. Brawley, "For Blessing," 20; see also Goldsworthy, *According to Plan*, 56.

The Abrahamic and Davidic Covenants both find their fulfillment in Jesus Christ and the New Covenant he inaugurated. This pivotal linkage of Abraham, David, and Jesus is seen in Matthew's genealogy of Jesus, which shows a direct line between Abraham to David to Jesus: *"The record of the genealogy of Jesus the Messiah, the son of David, the son of Abraham"* (Matt 1:1).[12] Similarly, Peter (Acts 2:22–36) and Paul (Acts 13:17–23) both directly link David and Jesus, who was the fulfillment of the prophetic expectations foreshadowed in David's kingdom.[13] Jesus' genealogy and birth indicate that he fulfills the Davidic Covenant:

- *The angel Gabriel's announcement.* Even before Jesus was born, the angel Gabriel alluded to 2 Sam 7:12–13 and Isa 9:6–7, and said that Jesus would fulfill the Davidic Covenant when he told Mary that Jesus *"will be great and will be called the Son of the Most High; and the Lord God will give him the throne of his father David; and he will reign over the house of Jacob forever, and his kingdom will have no end"* (Luke 1:31–33).

- *The term "son of David" is a Messianic term.*[14] People who recognized Jesus' power and uniqueness as the promised Messiah applied the term *"Son of David"* to him.[15] Jesus applied the term to himself (Matt 22:41–46; Mark 12:35–37). "By healing the blind man from Jericho who addressed him as the Son of David, Jesus publicly acknowledged this role."[16]

---

12. Often in the Bible, genealogies are "telescoped" (i.e., certain names are omitted) for "didactic or instructional purposes," such as to "legitimate claims to position, authority, or power in various political and societal contexts." Younger, *Judges and Ruth*, 403, 404. Matthew's genealogy of Jesus does this. His genealogy concludes by referring to fourteen generations from Abraham to David, fourteen from David to the deportation to Babylon, and fourteen from the deportation to the Messiah (Matt 1:17). Certain names are omitted, and even his last set of fourteen generations achieves the number fourteen by repeating Jeconiah. All of this suggests that the "fourteens" are symbolic. "Many have suggested that Matthew's schematic division of Jesus' genealogy into three sets of fourteen (1:17) may also contain a hint of its Davidic character since the numerical value of David's name in Hebrew (the consonants *d, w,* and *d*) is fourteen ($d = 4$, $w = 6$)." Holwerda, *Jesus and Israel*, 33n.10. Carson adds that this symbolism "points out that the promised 'son of David' (1:1), the Messiah, has come. And if the third set of fourteen is short one member, perhaps it will suggest to some readers that just as God cuts short the time of distress for the sake of his elect (24:22), so he mercifully shortens the period from the Exile to Jesus the Messiah." Carson, "Matthew," 69.

13. Goldsworthy, *Preaching the Whole Bible*, 89, 108.

14. See Matt 22:42; Mark 12:35.

15. Matt 9:27; 12:23; 15:22; 20:30–31; 21:9; Mark 10:47–48; Luke 18:38–39.

16. Goppelt, *Typos*, 87.

- *The "father-son" promise of the Davidic Covenant.* The promise *"I will be a father to him and he will be a son to me"* (2 Sam 7:14) is applied to Jesus in Heb 1:5.[17] In light of 2 Sam 7:14, the phrase *"Son of God"* was a messianic phrase denoting the promised Davidic king. Thus, to indicate fulfillment of the Davidic Covenant, Jesus frequently is called the *"Son of God."*[18] Jesus also referred to himself as the *"Son of God."*[19]

- *Micah's prophecy.* Micah prophesied that the Messiah would be born in Bethlehem (Micah 5:2), where David also was from (Ruth 4:11, 22; 1 Sam 16:1–13). In fulfillment of Micah's prophecy, Jesus was born in Bethlehem (Mic 5:2; Matt 2:1–6; John 7:42). Luke carefully records that Joseph (Jesus' putative father) was *"of the house and family of David,"* and that Bethlehem, where Jesus was born, was *"the city of David"* (Luke 2:4).[20]

Jesus' position as the foretold Davidic king of Israel[21] is seen during each stage of his earthly life and now in his resurrection glory:

- *Jesus' early life.* The magi who came from the east after Jesus' birth knew this from having read the OT (see Matt 2:1–6). Their question was, *"Where is he who has been born King of the Jews? For we saw his star in the east and have come to worship him"* (Matt 2:2).

- *Jesus' baptism.* At Jesus' baptism and transfiguration the Father's declaration, *"You are my beloved son, in you I am well-pleased"* (Matt 3:17; Mark 1:11; Luke 3:22) echoes Ps 2:7. Psalm 2 is "an inauguration psalm

---

17. Immediately after the reference to the son, v. 14 goes on to say that *"when he commits iniquity, I will correct him with the rod of men and the strokes of the sons of men."* Committing iniquity cannot apply to Jesus, since he never sinned. The prophecy does not, on its face, refer to Jesus in person, but the prophecy finds its fulfillment in Jesus as the culmination of David's line. As Charles Briggs points out, "The paternal mercy and chastisement were realized in the history of the Davidic dynasty, but that mercy was first made sure for ever in the suffering of Jesus Christ when He was chastised, not for His own sins, but for the sins of the Davidic dynasty, of Israel and the world." Briggs, *Messianic Prophecy,* 130.

18. Matt 4:3, 6; 8:29; 26:63; 27:40, 54; Mark 1:1; 3:11; 15:39; Luke 1:35; 3:38; 4:3, 9, 41; John 1:34, 49; 11:27; 20:31; Acts 8:37; 9:20; Rom 1:4; 2 Cor 1:19; Gal 2:20; Eph 4:13; Heb 4:14; 6:6; 7:3; 10:29; 1 John 3:8; 4:15; 5:5, 10, 12, 13, 20.

19. Matt 26:63–64; 27:43; Mark 14:61–62; Luke 22:70; John 3:18; 5:25; 10:36; 11:4; 19:7; Rev 2:18.

20. The NT writers stress the fact that Jesus was *"a descendant of David"* (John 7:42; Acts 13:22–23; Rom 1:3; 2 Tim 2:8). Jesus himself asserts both his Davidic authority and lineage (Rev 3:7; 5:5; 22:16).

21. See chapter 5, particularly the sections concerning "The Blessing of Judah" and "The Shoot and the Branch."

Christ and the Church Fulfill the Abrahamic, Davidic, and New Covenants 145

for the Israelite kings—the public declaration of kingship."[22] Although one can view Jesus' resurrection and ascension as his enthronement as the true king,[23] the baptismal announcement from God of Jesus' sonship, which echoed Ps 2:7, can be viewed as a proleptic announcement of that enthronement as the true Davidic king.[24]

- *The beginning of Jesus' ministry.* When Nathanael first met Jesus he said, *"Rabbi, you are the Son of God; you are the King of Israel"* (John 1:49).

- *Jesus' ministry in Galilee.* When Jesus began his ministry in Galilee, Matt 4:14–16 places it in the light of fulfilled prophecy by quoting Isa 9:1–2 (*"The land of Zebulun and the land of Naphtali . . . saw a great light"*). The context of Isa 9:1–2 is that this "light" will be from the promised Davidic king. Thus, the fact that Jesus began his ministry in Galilee is not just a matter of geography, "but also [is] a revelation that the zeal of Yahweh is now at work in history establishing the rule of justice and righteousness of the promised Davidic kingdom (Isaiah 9:6f.)."[25]

- *Jesus' entry into Jerusalem for the last time.* Zeph 3:8–20 is an oracle of judgment and salvation, which ends with *"the King of Israel, the Lord, is in your midst"* (Zeph 3:14–17). Zech 9:8–17 gives a similar oracle of the salvation of Israel, where the king is described as *"coming to you . . . humble, and mounted on a donkey, even on a colt, the foal of a donkey"* (Zech 9:9). When Jesus entered Jerusalem the final time, all four Gospels interpret that as the coming of the prophesied Davidic king.[26] Mark 11:10 explicitly says, *"Blessed is the coming kingdom of our father David."*

- *Jesus' trial and death.* Jesus himself confirmed that he was the *"King of the Jews."*[27] In John 18:33–37, however, while confirming that he was, indeed, a king, Jesus also indicated that the nature of his kingdom was not the physical, earthly kingdom that most of the people were expecting or assuming. When he was crucified, a sign was placed over him declaring that he was the *"King of the Jews."*[28]

22. Katz, "You are," n.p.
23. See the discussion of Psalm 2 in chapter 5.
24. See Walker, *Jesus and the Holy City*, 2.
25. Holwerda, *Jesus and Israel*, 49.
26. Matt 21:1–11; Mark 11:1–11; Luke 19:28–40; John 12:12–16.
27. Matt 27:11; Mark 15:2; Luke 23:3.
28. Matt 27:37; Mark 15:26; Luke 23:38; John 19:19–20; see also Matt 27:42; Mark 15:32; Luke 23:37; John 19:21–22.

- *Jesus' resurrection.* In Acts 2:29–36 Peter quoted the Davidic Covenant that *"God had sworn an oath to seat one of [David's] descendants on his throne"* (Acts 2:30; see also Ps 132:11) and also quoted Ps 16:10 that God *"will not allow your holy one to undergo decay"* (Acts 2:27, 31). He then said those prophecies *"looked ahead and spoke of the resurrection of Christ"* (Acts 2:31). All of the everlasting promises, blessings, and mercies shown to David were summarized by Isaiah's phrase *"the sure mercies of David"* (Isa 55:3). The essential promise and blessing to David was, *"Your house and your kingdom shall endure before me forever; your throne shall be established forever"* (2 Sam 7:16). In Acts 13:34 Paul quotes the Septuagint version of Isa 55:3 and says that the promise of *"the holy and sure blessings of David"* have been fulfilled in the resurrection of Jesus. Thus, Christ's resurrection from the dead and his ascension back to the Father are the way God fulfilled his promise to establish David's throne forever, from which Jesus is reigning now over the entire universe with all power and authority.[29]

There is one other aspect to the fulfillment of the Davidic Covenant. Specifically, since Christ is said to be "in" believers, and believers are said to be "in" Christ,[30] Paul alludes to 2 Sam 7:14 in 2 Cor 6:18 and applies the Davidic Covenant to the church. Significantly, Paul changes the wording of the promise God made concerning David's son Solomon (*"I will be a father to him and he will be a son to Me"*) to *"I will be a father to you, and you shall be sons and daughters to Me."* That demonstrates that the Davidic Covenant extended far beyond David and Solomon and finds its ultimate fulfillment in Christ and the church.

THE NEW COVENANT IS FULFILLED IN CHRIST AND THE CHURCH

Jer 31:31–34 had promised a New Covenant *"with the house of Israel and with the house of Judah."* The New Covenant would be an everlasting covenant in which God would write his law in his people's hearts, his people

---

29. See Mark 16:19; Luke 22:69; Acts 2:29–36; Eph 1:20–23; Col 3:1; Heb 1:3; 1 Pet 3:21–22; Rev 1:5; 3:21

30. Christ is "in" believers (John 14:20; 17:23; Rom 8:10; Gal 2:20; Eph 3:17; Col 1:27; 1 John 3:24; Rev 3:20); believers are "in Christ" (e.g., Rom 8:1; 12:5; 16:6, 7, 9–10; 1 Cor 1:2, 30; 4:10, 15; 15:18, 22; 2 Cor 1:21; 5:17; 12:2; Gal 1:22; 3:28; 6:15; Eph 1:3; 2:6, 10; Phil 1:1; Col 1:2; 1 Thess 2:14; 4:16; 1 Tim 3:13; 2 Tim 3:12; Phlm 23; 1 Pet 5:14).

would truly know the Lord, and he would forgive their sins and remember them no more.[31]

At the Last Supper, Jesus explicitly stated that he was inaugurating the New Covenant in his blood.[32] "The allusions to both the forgiveness anticipated by Jeremiah (Matt. 26:28; Jer. 31:34) and the blood associated with the establishment of the original Mosaic covenant (Luke 22:20; Exod. 24:7) further underline that Jesus understood his death as the inauguration of the new covenant."[33] When Jesus initiated the New Covenant at the Last Supper, his reference to "the" New Covenant could only refer to the New Covenant promised by Jeremiah, because Jer 31:31 is the only place where the expression "New Covenant" had been explicitly mentioned in Scripture prior to Jesus' reference to it at the Last Supper. The covenant was confirmed and finalized on the cross (Heb 9:12–17). It was ratified when Jesus rose from the dead, then ascended to heaven and sat down on the throne with the Father (Heb 10:11–18). Thus, "He is not simply the mediator of God's New Covenant; he is the incarnation of it."[34]

Although in its *form* as originally given to Jeremiah, the New Covenant was *"with the house of Israel and with the house of Judah,"* as is true with the Abrahamic and Davidic Covenants, the NT affirms that the New Covenant actually is fulfilled in Christ and the church, not with the physical nation(s) of Israel and Judah. Heb 8:8–12 quotes the New Covenant of Jer 31:31–34 in full (including the reference to *"the house of Israel and the house of Judah"*). Hebrews 8–10 then specifically apply the New Covenant to Christ and the church. The whole argument of Hebrews 8–10 is that the Mosaic Covenant, the temple, priesthood, law, and the entire Israelite sacrificial system, were simply the "symbol" (Heb 9:9), or "copies" (Heb 9:23–24), or "shadow" (Heb 10:1) of the *"better covenant"* which is based on *"better promises"* (Heb 8:6), i.e., the true and permanent reality found in Christ and the New Covenant. Heb 10:15–18 quotes from the New Covenant and applies it to "us," i.e., Christians, the church. Heb 8:6, 9:15, and 12:24 all state that Christ is the mediator of the New Covenant. The fact that he "is" (present tense) the

---

31. See also Jer 32:38–40; 50:4–5; Ezek 11:14–20; 36:24–32; 37:15–28) Ezek 11:14–20 speaks of the return of Israel from exile but concludes with New Covenant language (*"I will give them one heart and put a new spirit within them. And I will take the heart of stone out of their flesh and give them a heart of flesh, that they may walk in My statutes and keep My ordinances and do them. Then they will be My people, and I shall be their God,"* Ezek 11:19–20). Thus, the return from exile to the land is itself a "type" of the New Covenant.

32. Luke 22:20; see 1 Cor 11:25.

33. Williamson, *Sealed*, 184; see also Peterson, "Prophecy," 77.

34. Goppelt, *Typos*, 116.

mediator shows that the New Covenant is now in effect. Heb 9:12–17 points out that Christ's blood confirmed and finalized the New Covenant. Heb 8:13 concludes that the New Covenant has made the first covenant (i.e., the Old, or Mosaic Covenant [see Heb 8:9]) obsolete.[35] Heb 10:9 similarly says that *"He takes away the first in order to establish the second."* This also is indicated in that the New Covenant is called "an everlasting covenant" whereas the Mosaic (Old) Covenant is never called "everlasting."[36]

Elsewhere the New Covenant is applied to the church. Paul quotes Jesus' words inaugurating the New Covenant to the largely Gentile church at Corinth in 1 Cor 11:25. In 2 Cor 3:5–6, Paul says that *"God . . . made us [i.e., the church] . . . servants of a new covenant."* The entire argument of 2 Corinthians 3 contrasts the Mosaic Covenant with the New Covenant: (1) It is the difference between the letter and the Spirit (2 Cor 3:3, 6, 17–18). (2) The first is the ministry of death and condemnation; the second is life, hope, liberty, and Spirit (2 Cor 3:6–9, 12, 17). (3) It is the difference between something written on tablets of stone and the writing on human hearts (2 Cor 3:2–3, 7). (4) Each has its own glory, but the second has an incomparably greater glory (2 Cor 3:7–11, 18). (5) The first fades away, but the second remains forever (2 Cor 3:7, 11, 13). (6) The first is veiled, but in the second the veil is taken away (2 Cor 3:13–16, 18). Consequently, only the New Covenant gives us boldness and transforms us into the image of Christ (2 Cor 3:2–3, 12, 18). In Gal 4:21–31, Hagar and Sarah "are two covenants" (Gal 4:24): Hagar represents the Mosaic covenant (Gal. 4:24–25); Sarah represents the New Covenant (Gal 4:26–27). Paul's argument is that Hagar, the Old Covenant, is a covenant of enslavement (Gal. 4:25), whereas Sarah represents a covenant of freedom, and *"she is our mother"* (Gal 4:26, 31).

The Old Covenant was based on external, ritual activities that the people were required to perform. As such, it had a great weakness: it could not change people from the inside-out; it could not change their hearts or their

---

35. The last phrase of Heb 8:13 (*"ready to disappear"*) in Greek is *eggus aphanismou*. "Though the word *aphanismos* occurs only here in the NT, it is used frequently in the LXX (56x) to describe the physical destruction of Israel (Je. 12:11; Ezk. 6:14; Mi. 7:13; Joel 2:13), Jerusalem (Je. 19:8) and the Temple (Dn. 9:26; Jdt. 4:12). It is never used to denote a gradual disappearance as suggested by most English renderings of Hebrews 8:13 (e.g. 'ready to disappear' NASB). To the contrary, it always denotes the demise of persons or things by violent means usually due to God's judgement. The author's point is that the superiority of the New Covenant would soon be sealed by the complete destruction of the Old Covenant including its priests, sacrifices and Temple." Gleason, "Eschatology," 108–9.

36. Gentry, "Daniel's Seventy Weeks," 38; see also at 43n.33 ("Nowhere is the Sinai covenant called a 'permanent' covenant"). See Isa 55:3; 61:8; Jer 32:40; 50:5; Ezek 16:60; 37:26 regarding the everlasting covenant.

Christ and the Church Fulfill the Abrahamic, Davidic, and New Covenants 149

consciences. Heb 9:9–10 says that under the Old Covenant *"both gifts and sacrifices are offered which cannot make the worshiper perfect in conscience, since they relate only to food and drink and various washings, regulations for the body imposed until a time of reformation."* Thus, under the Old Covenant people had hearts of stone (Zech 7:12). The New Covenant changes people from the inside-out. In the New Covenant, God promised to *"sprinkle clean water on you, and you will be clean,"* and said, *"I will give you a new heart and put a new spirit within you; and I will remove the heart of stone from your flesh and give you a heart of flesh,"* and *"I will put My Spirit within you"* (Ezek 36:25–27). Heb 10:22 alludes to Ezek 36:25 by speaking of *"having our hearts sprinkled clean from an evil conscience and our bodies washed with pure water."* Second Cor 3:3 alludes to Ezek 36:26 when Paul says, *"you are a letter of Christ, cared for by us, written not with ink but with the Spirit of the living God, not on tablets of stone but on tablets of human hearts."* In the New Covenant *"the blood of Christ . . . cleanse[s] your conscience from dead works to serve the living God"* (Heb 9:14) and *"has perfected for all time those who are sanctified"* (Heb 10:14).

The New Covenant also fulfills the promise of the Holy Spirit. Jesus promised to send the Holy Spirit who would *"be with you forever"* and who *"will be in you"* (John 14:16–17). Beginning on the Day of Pentecost, he has done that. No longer is the Spirit or his gifts limited to the few, but now in the New Covenant God has poured out his Spirit on all of his people, regardless of age, sex, race, or tribe.[37] Now, *"all who are being led by the Spirit of God, these are sons of God"* (Rom 8:14). The Spirit "seals" his people, unlike the case in the OT (Eph 1:13–14). "Paul goes even further to state that the Spirit now enables God's people to do what the Law could never accomplish: 'in order that the righteous requirements of the law might be fully met in us' (Rom. 8:4)."[38]

Finally, the New Covenant is the only one of God's covenants which provides for the forgiveness of sins. That is accomplished through Christ, *"the lamb of God who takes away the sin of the world"* (John 1:29).[39] Consequently, proclaiming the forgiveness of sins through Christ is central to the Gospel.[40] In short, the New Covenant does for us what we are unable to do for ourselves, because it is based on what God through Christ has done for us, rather than what we have done or have to do. In fact, so profound is the change between what the New Covenant in Christ accomplishes compared

---

37. Acts 2:14–18; see also Rom 8:9; 1 Cor 3:16; 6:19.
38. Burke, *Adopted*, 133–34.
39. See also Matt 1:21; Acts 5:31; 1 John 3:5.
40. See Luke 24:44–49; Acts 2:38; 10:43; 13:38–39; 26:15–18.

to the Old Covenant that 2 Cor 5:17 concludes, *"Therefore if anyone is in Christ, he is a new creature; the old things passed away; behold, new things have come."*

10

Christ and the Church are the New, True, Spiritual Israel

JESUS IS THE NEW, TRUE, FAITHFUL ISRAEL

PAUL SAID IN GAL 3:16 that Jesus is the true seed of Abraham. Jesus succeeds where Adam, Abraham, Isaac, Moses, and Israel failed. "Jesus, then, is true Israel, the one who does everything that Israel was supposed to do and who is everything that Israel was supposed to be."[1] This is seen in several ways.

Jesus recapitulates the history of Israel

Examples of Jesus as the true Israel, recapitulating the history of Israel, and fulfilling what Israel was designed to be are found from his birth to his resurrection:

1   *Jesus' birth and Herod's attempt on his life.* In connection with Herod's slaughter of the infants after Jesus' birth, Matthew quotes Jer 31:15 (*"A voice is heard in Ramah . . . Rachel weeping for her children"*) and says *"what had been spoken through Jeremiah the prophet was fulfilled"* (Matt 2:17–18). Ramah is where the captives of Judah were gathered in chains to be sent to exile in Babylon (see Jer 40:1). Matthew's use of *"Rachel weeping"* signifies that, although Rachel had died long before Israel was sent into exile, Jeremiah "hears" Rachel weeping for those in exile. However, the Lord instructed Rachel to stop weeping, because there was hope for the future and her children would return to Israel

---

1. Holwerda, *Jesus and Israel*, 33.

(Jer 31:16–17). Although Israel did return from exile, the hope promised to Rachel had not been fully realized. Matthew quotes Jer 31:15 "not only to establish the continuity of Israel's grief but also to signal the fulfillment of Israel's hope contained in its context. Jesus escapes the slaughter, and therein lies the fulfillment of Israel's hope. Since Jesus is now Israel, Abraham's true seed and God's true Son, God's promise to Rachel of a restored family is now on the way to fulfillment. The hope promised for her future is now being realized. Jesus relives Israel's history and thereby restores Israel."[2]

2. *Jesus and the Exodus.* Matt 2:15 quotes Hos 11:1, "*Out of Egypt I called my son*," and applies it to Jesus. God had first called Israel his "son" at the time of the exodus (Exod 4:22, "*Israel is my son, my firstborn*"). Matthew is showing how OT Israel's history is being re-enacted by Jesus "because he is Israel's fulfillment."[3] Hos 11:1–11 both recounts Israel's exodus and hints at a second exodus because Israel's disobedience after the first exodus thwarted God's intention to create a holy people. Although the physical nation returned to the land after the exile in Babylon, it remained under the control of foreign powers, and the "holy nation" never truly existed. By applying Hos 11:1 to Jesus, Matthew not only is saying that Jesus is the true fulfillment of Israel, but also that "the long awaited [second] exodus has begun."[4] That Jesus was recapitulating Israel's exodus in his own life was indicated by Jesus himself on the Mount of Transfiguration. There he spoke of his own "exodus" (the Greek term translated as "departure" in Luke 9:30–31). Further, his own death occurred on Passover, which marked the beginning of Israel's exodus from Egypt.

3. *Jesus' baptism.* When John the Baptist baptized people, his baptism signified washing away sin away from people who acknowledged their sinfulness (Matt 3:6). Jesus did not sin and, therefore, did not need to be baptized. When Jesus came to John to be baptized, John recognized the incongruity of the situation and tried to prevent it. Nevertheless,

---

2. Holwerda, *Jesus and Israel*, 42.
3. Johnson, *Him We Proclaim*, 208, emph. in orig.
4. Holwerda, *Jesus and Israel*, 40. Greg Beale is in accord. He states that Matthew's use of Hosea is an application of typological principles. Beale, *Handbook*, 60–64. The quotation from Hos 11:1 "is to be seen within the repeated references throughout the book [of Hosea] to a past exodus *and* Israel's future *reentering and subsequent return out of* Egypt." Beale, *Handbook*, 62, emph. in orig. In that subsequent return, Israel would be led by a latter-day Davidic king (Hos 1:11; 3:5), "which enhances further why Matthew could take the corporate national language of Hos 11:1 and apply it to an individual king, Jesus." Beale, *Handbook*, 64.

Jesus told him, *"Permit it at this time; for in this way it is fitting for us to fulfill all righteousness"* (Matt 3:15). The key word is *fulfill*. "Jesus the sinless One is identifying Himself with the sinful position of His fellow Israelites by being baptized like them. His identification with them here anticipates His complete identification with sinners when He bears their sins on the cross."[5] Jesus' baptism also is a re-enactment of the crossing of the Red Sea and the Jordan River, which is where he was baptized.

4 *Jesus in the wilderness.* In Jesus' experience of being tempted by Satan in the wilderness, we see a clear typological relationship between OT Israel and Jesus. Jesus' forty days in the wilderness (Matt 4:1–2) are a miniature of the forty years which Israel spent in the wilderness. Just as God led Israel in the wilderness (Exod 13:17–18, 21), the Holy Spirit led Jesus in the wilderness (Luke 4:1). The temptations Jesus faced in the wilderness (Matt 4:1–11; Luke 4:1–13) paralleled Israel's temptations in the wilderness. "In the first temptation and Jesus' response there are several interesting and significant parallels centering on the common theme of the sonship of both Jesus and the nation of Israel. Both are 'sons' (Deut. 8:5; cf. Matt. 4:3, 6); both are 'led' (Deut. 8:2; cf. Matt. 4:1); both are taken to the desert/wilderness (Deut. 8:2; cf. Matt. 4:1); and both hunger (Deut. 8:3; cf. Matt. 4:2)."[6] Where Israel had been dissatisfied with God's provision of manna (Num 11:1–6), Jesus was tempted to turn stones into bread (Matt 4:3; Luke 4:3). Where Israel put God to the test at Massah and Meribah demanding proof of his presence and power (Exod 17:1–7), Jesus was tempted to jump from the temple's pinnacle to force God to honor his promises (Matt 4:5–6; Luke 4:9–11). Where Israel turned from God to a molten calf (Exod 32:1–6), Jesus was tempted to fall down and worship Satan (Matt 4:8–9; Luke 4:5–7). Further, Jesus met the temptations by deliberately quoting from Moses's summary of Israel's history in the wilderness (Deut 8:3; 6:13, 16). His selecting those three texts indicates that he saw a parallel between Israel's experience in the wilderness and his own.

5 *Jesus' resurrection.* In Luke 24:46, Jesus said, *"Thus it is written, that the Christ would suffer and rise again from the dead the third day."* Jesus saw Jonah's three days in the belly of the great fish as a type of his own being in the grave and then rising on the third day (Matt 12:40). Additionally, Hosea 6:2 speaks of the restoration of Israel by saying, *"He will revive us after two days; He will raise us up on the third day."* With

---

5. Poythress, *Shadow of Christ*, 253.
6. Burke, *Adopted*, 173–74n.55.

respect to Jesus' statement that it was "written" in the OT that Christ would rise from the dead on the *"third day,"* P. W. L. Walker says that the most likely reference is Hosea 6:2, which "originally referred to the restoration or revival of Israel," but Jesus "applied it instead to himself as Israel's Messiah. . . . As Dodd rightly concluded: 'the resurrection of Christ *is* the resurrection of Israel of which the prophets spoke.'"[7]

The NT applies terms and titles for OT Israel to Jesus

Just as Exod 4:22 and Hos 11:1 called Israel *"my son,"* so the Father confirms that Jesus is the true, final, and supreme Son by calling him *"my beloved son,"* at Jesus' baptism (Matt 3:17; Mark 1:11; Luke 3:22) and transfiguration (Matt 17:5; Mark 9:7; Luke 9:35).[8] The voice from heaven at Jesus' baptism "combines the language of Psalm 2:7; Isaiah 42:1; and possibly Genesis 22:2. It shows that the Law (Genesis 22:2), the Prophets (Isaiah 42:1), and the Writings (Psalm 2:7) simultaneously come to focus in Jesus."[9]

The vine was a common symbol for OT Israel.[10] Jesus called himself *"the true vine"* (John 15:1). Remarkably, "whenever historic Israel is referred to under this figure it is the vine's *failure* to produce good fruit that is emphasized, along with the corresponding threat of God's judgment on the nation."[11] Jesus' claim to be the *"true vine"* indicates a contrast with faithless Israel; he is the one who brings forth good fruit.

Titles of persons who represent Israel—King, God's Servant, Son of Man—were applied to Jesus. One of the charges against Jesus was that he was the "king of the Jews" (John 18:33–37; 19:14–15). "Just as the king was Israel, so the Servant is addressed as 'Israel',[12] and the Son of Man turns out in the latter part of the chapter to be a figure for 'the saints of the Most High' [Dan 7:18, 22, 25, 27]. Jesus' frequent allusions to these two figures [the Servant and the Son of Man] suggests that he saw it as his mission to represent Israel, to

---

7. Walker, *Jesus and the Holy City*, 285; see also France, *Jesus and*, 54–55.

8. See also Matt 4:3; 14:33; Mark 3:11; Luke 1:35; John 1:34, 49; Acts 9:20; Gal 2:22 for Jesus as the *"Son of God."*

9. Poythress, *Shadow of Christ*, 254.

10. See Ps 80:9–16; Isa 5:1–7; 27:2; Jer 2:21; 12:10; Ezek 15:1–8; 17:1–21; 19:10–14; Hosea 10:1–2.

11. Carson, *Gospel*, 513–14.

12. Isa 49:3 explicitly says, *"You are My Servant, Israel."*

sum up Israel's ideals in himself."[13] Jesus also applied psalms which originally related to the suffering and vindication of Israel to himself.[14]

In Jesus the OT promises of the restoration of Israel are fulfilled

The prophets had prophesied the restoration of Israel under the leadership of God's anointed king, who would reign from Jerusalem or Mount Zion.[15] Although the people had returned from the exile in Babylon approximately 500 years before Jesus, "in Jesus' day many, if not most, Jews regarded the exile as still continuing. The people had returned in a geographical sense, but the great prophecies of restoration had not yet come true."[16] Thus, restoration was still hoped for.[17] In Jesus, those prophecies of restoration are fulfilled (Luke 1:68) but in an unexpected way: the new Zion, the restored Israel, is not identified with a place or a nation-state but with the person of Christ and his people.

Jesus' ministry was intimately linked with the restoration or redemption of Israel. When Jesus was brought to the temple to be circumcised, the Holy Spirit came upon a man named Simeon who was *"looking for the consolation of Israel"* (Luke 2:25). That same day, the prophetess Anna began to *"speak of Him [i.e., Jesus] to all those who were looking for the redemption of Jerusalem"* (Luke 2:38). Simeon and Anna were both expressing the eschatological hope of Israel's deliverance by the promised Messiah. Darrel Bock notes:

> Israel's consolation . . . was a key element in many strands of OT and Jewish eschatology, referring to the hope of deliverance for the nation (Isa. 40:1; 49:13; 51:3; 57:18; 61:2; 2 Bar. 44.7). . . . The phrase ["redemption of Jerusalem"] refers to the redemption of Israel, since the capital stands for the nation. Equivalent to the phrase *consolation of Israel* (2:25), it has OT background in that it refers to God's decisive salvific act for his people (Isa. 40:9; 52:9; 63:4).[18]

---

13. France, "Old Testament Prophecy," 67.

14. See Matt 23:39; Mark 12:10–11, which quote from Psalm 118 and Mark 15:34; 14:18; 14:34, which quote or allude to Psalms 22, 41–43.

15. E.g., Isaiah 60–62; Jeremiah 30–33; Ezekiel 34–37.

16. Wright, *Jesus and the Victory*, 126; see also Patton, "End of Exile: The Old"; Patton, "End of Exile: Jesus."

17. Luke 2:25, 38; 19:11; 24:21; Acts 1:6.

18. Bock, *Luke 1:1—9:50*, 238, 253.

Both Simeon and Anna had used phrases concerning Messiah's deliverance of Israel that had nationalistic connotations, but when they saw Jesus their focus was on *him*. Thus, Simeon's remarks concentrate on who Jesus is and what he will do (Luke 2:30–35). Anna likewise *"continued to speak of Him"* (Luke 2:38). This all indicates that, even before Jesus began his public ministry, the Holy Spirit was revealing that God's plan for the consolation and redemption of Israel was not a political or nationalistic program. Instead, the real work of the Messiah was of a fundamentally different, far deeper and broader nature, encompassing *"all peoples"* including the Gentiles (Luke 2:31–32), designed to bring about the forgiveness of sin and the inauguration of God's true kingdom. Although it was deeper and broader than the Jews were expecting, God's program in Christ did have national implications for Israel. N. T. Wright observes that "exile" primarily was related to Israel's failure to repent and obey God with her whole heart; Israel's longing for forgiveness of her sins applied to more than simply individuals, but was "the great, unrepeatable, eschatological and national blessing" promised by God.[19]

Given that context, when John the Baptist preached *"a baptism of repentance for the forgiveness of sins"* (Mark 1:4; Luke 3:3) and then declared *"Behold, the Lamb of God who takes away the sin of the world"* (John 1:29), what John was preparing the way for was what Jesus was then offering in his call to *"repent, for the kingdom of heaven is at hand"* (Matt 4:17; see also Mark 1:15) and his claim that *"the Son of Man has authority on earth to forgive sins"* (Matt 9:6; Mark 2:10); this was nothing less than "the redemption for which Israel was longing . . . a new world order, the end of Israel's long desolation, the true and final 'forgiveness of sins', the inauguration of the kingdom of god."[20] Jesus' identification of John the Baptist with Elijah in Matt 17:11–13 was indicating that the longed-for age of "restoration" had begun (Mal 4:5–6).

Jesus' restoration of Israel is seen in other ways. Jesus chose twelve disciples (Matt 10:1–2; Mark 3:13–19; Luke 6:12–26), which alludes to the twelve tribes and symbolizes the restoration of Israel.[21] Since Israel had not had twelve visible tribes since the northern kingdom of Israel had been deported by Assyria in 722 BC, Jesus' calling of the Twelve and, especially, his telling them that they would sit on thrones and judge the twelve tribes of

---

19. Wright, *Jesus and the Victory*, 271; see, e.g., Isa 40:1–2; 43:25—44:3; Jer 31:31–34; 33:4–11; Lam 4:22; see also Patton, "End of Exile: The Old"; Patton, "End of Exile: Jesus."

20. Wright, *Jesus and the Victory*, 271–72.

21. See Schnabel, "Israel, the People," 45.

Christ and the Church are the New, True, Spiritual Israel

Israel (Matt 19:28; Luke 22:28–30), indicates that "he was thinking in terms of the eschatological restoration of Israel."[22]

Jesus' healings and other mighty works also were signs that Israel was being restored and the kingdom of God was being inaugurated. The prophecies regarding the return from exile and God's returning to Zion saw those events as a restoration of creation, marked by healing.[23] In assuring the imprisoned John the Baptist when he wondered if Jesus truly was the Messiah, Jesus alluded to those very prophecies as being fulfilled (Matt 11:4–6). Jesus' exercising power over nature, including the extraordinary catch of fish (Luke 5:4–11; John 21:1–14), stilling storms,[24] walking on water,[25] miraculously feeding thousands,[26] turning water into wine (John 2:1–11), and cursing the fig tree,[27] all show that nature itself was being restored. Thus, the kingdom of God was present (Matt 12:28; Luke 11:20)

Immediately after his resurrection, Jesus met two of his disciples on the road to Emmaus. They did not recognize him but said they had been *"hoping that it was he who was going to redeem Israel"* (Luke 24:21). Jesus rebuked them, saying, *"O foolish men and slow of heart to believe in all that the prophets have spoken! Was it not necessary for the Christ to suffer these things and to enter into his glory?"* (Luke 24:25–26) Jesus was saying that the "restoration of Israel" was a spiritual restoration finding fulfillment in his resurrection, not a physical or political restoration of Israel as a nation-state. In other words, Jesus' resurrection is Israel's restoration.

Before Pentecost and their receipt of the power of the Holy Spirit, Jesus' disciples did not understand how Jesus had redefined what the "restoration of the kingdom of Israel" was all about. They were still thinking in geographical and political terms, not spiritually. However, his answer to their question about *"restoring the kingdom to Israel"* reoriented them to a very different idea of what the "restored kingdom of Israel" really is: it is not a political nation-state but is spiritual and worldwide (Acts 1:6–8). Israel would, indeed, be restored and become prominent, but through the reign of Israel's Messiah. This reign would be implemented through the disciples' Holy Spirit-empowered mission of proclaiming the gospel to people

---

22. Wright, *Jesus and the Victory*, 300.

23. E.g., Isa 35:5–6, "Then the eyes of the blind will be opened and the ears of the deaf will be unstopped. Then the lame will leap like a deer, and the tongue of the mute will shout for joy."

24. Matt 8:23–27; 14:32; Mark 4:35–41; 6:51; Luke 8:22–25.

25. Matt 14:22–31; Mark 6:45–50; John 6:16–21.

26. Matt 14:13–21; 15:32–38; Mark 6:32–44; 8:1–9; Luke 9:12–17; John 6:1–14.

27. Matt 21:18–19; Mark 11:12–14, 20–21.

from every tribe, tongue, and nation in the entire world.[28] His ascension to heaven (Acts 1:9-11), which immediately follows his explanation of the true nature of the kingdom, graphically illustrates what "restoration" means, i.e., "This is how the kingdom is being restored to Israel: by its representative Messiah being enthroned as the world's true lord."[29]

The spiritual nature of the restoration of Israel was confirmed at the Council of Jerusalem in Acts 15. Although David had been promised an everlasting kingdom, Israel had been divided, then exiled. God, through the prophet Amos, had promised restoration: *"In that day I will raise up the fallen tabernacle of David,"* after which the Gentile nations would seek or be subject to the Lord (Amos 9:11-12). Beginning in Acts 10, God showed Peter that no nation, tribe, or people group was now to be considered "unclean." As a result, large numbers of Gentiles began to be converted but were not being circumcised or living according to Jewish law. The issue of the Council at Jerusalem in Acts 15 was whether Gentiles had to conform to OT Jewish rites and laws. The Council concluded that Gentiles were *not* subject to the OT rites and laws.

In making this ruling, in Acts 15:15-18, the apostle James quoted from Amos 9:11-12 (LXX) but began and ended his OT quotation with wording from Hos 3:5, Jer 12:15, and Isa 45:21. Those verses put the main quotation from Amos in the context of the conversion of the Gentiles in the messianic age. James concludes that the ingathering of the Gentiles into the church *is* the rebuilding of the *"tabernacle of David"* (i.e., restoration of Israel). In fact, the coming to faith by the Gentiles shows that the "tabernacle of David," i.e., Israel, *already had been rebuilt*, since the tabernacle of David had to be restored first, *"so that the rest of mankind may seek the Lord, and all the Gentiles who are called by My name"* (Acts 15:17).

Similarly, in Acts 13:32-34, 38-39 Paul equated *"the sure blessings of David"* with the resurrection of Jesus. "These promises and blessings, further, are interpreted as meaning, not a future Jewish kingdom in the millennium, but forgiveness of sins and salvation. The promises made to Israel, therefore, are fulfilled in the New Testament church."[30] In Rom 4:11 and Gal 3:29 he points out that Abraham is the father of all who believe, and all who belong to Christ are Abraham's children. The old distinction

---

28. See Goldsworthy, *Preaching the Whole Bible*, 238; Peterson, *The Acts*, 109-10 ("Through the witness of Jesus' apostles, 'the kingdom' would be restored to Israel, but not in nationalistic or political terms"); Wright, *Jesus and the Victory*, 383-90 ("He was *affirming* Israel's election even as he *redefined* it," i.e., to now consist of everyone who heard his words and followed him).

29. Wright, *Resurrection*, 655.

30. Hoekema, *Bible and the Future*, 197.

between Jews and Gentiles, "insiders" and "outsiders," has been eliminated in Christ.[31] In making these statements, Paul "expresses his conviction that the church, consisting of believing Jews and [Gentile] Christians, represents the eschatological restoration of Israel."[32]

Finally, while the Old Covenant was still in effect, even during Jesus' earthly ministry, Jerusalem was called the "holy city."[33] However, after Jesus' resurrection and ascension, Jerusalem never again is called the "holy city." The reason is that God, in the person of the Holy Spirit, indwelt, not Jerusalem or the temple, but the church (Acts 2:1–4, 38–39). In Revelation it is the *"new Jerusalem,"* the *"bride of the Lamb,"* that is called the *"holy city"* (Rev 21:2, 9–10; 22:19; see also Gal 4:21–31; Heb 12:18, 22).

BECAUSE THE CHURCH IS "IN CHRIST," THE CHURCH IS THE NEW, TRUE, SPIRITUAL ISRAEL

Leonard Goppelt states that "the church is not only the new humanity and the promised children of Abraham; it is also the true Israel. The church is the Israel of God (Gal 6:16; cf Rom 9:6; Eph 2:12); the Jews are only Israel according to the flesh."[34] This is seen in many ways.

OT Israel and the church: physical and spiritual grace, election, and faith in the OT

God chose Israel (Deut 7:6–8), redeemed Israel out of slavery (Exodus 13–15), gave Israel its own land (Joshua 1–21), and entered into covenants with Israel.[35] However, being chosen in the sense of being set apart as a nation-state (i.e., "physical election") is not the same as being eternally saved (i.e., "spiritual election"). Even in the OT, God's method of eternal, spiritual salvation was only by grace through faith, not simply a matter or externally obeying the Law of Moses.[36] Despite all that God did for Israel, throughout its entire history the nation as a whole was largely unbelieving

---

31. 1 Cor 5:12; Gal 3:28; Eph 2:14–19; Col 3:11; 1 Thess 4:12.
32. Schnabel, "Israel, the People," 54.
33. Isa 48:2; Dan 9:24; Neh 11:1, 18; Matt 4:4; 27:53.
34. Goppelt, *Typos*, 140.
35. Gen 12:1–3; 13:14–17; 15:1–21; 17:1–21; 22:15–18; Exodus 19–24; 2 Sam 7:8–17; 1 Chron 17:3–15.
36. Gen 15:6; Deut 10:16; 30:6; Hos 6:6; Hab 2:4; Rom 1:16–17; 4:13–24; 9:27–33; 11:17–23; Heb 11:1—12:2.

(see Neh 9:1–37; Acts 7:1–53). Jesus' parable of the landowner and the vineyard[37] summarized Israel's history as rejection of God's prophets and rejection of God's Son. The physical choosing and redemption of OT Israel by God's grace was typological of our spiritual choosing and redemption by God's grace.

Rather than distinguishing between Israel and the church, "the Bible places the crucial division within Israel itself—a division between the remnant, who are the faithful of God, and the apostate, who according to Jesus are the children of Satan (Jn 8:44)."[38] Romans 9–11 deals with the issue of whether God has broken his Word and Covenants with Israel. Paul's entire argument is that, while God granted great privileges to Israel (Rom 9:4–5), he never promised spiritual benefits or eternal life to anyone based on physical birth or descent. Every promise of God that brings spiritual blessing to anyone "requires that individual to personally believe the promise. Israel never inherited the promised blessing because they 'sought it not in faith' (Romans 9:32)."[39]

The relationship between OT Israel and the church

The church is both new and, in another sense, not new. "The New Testament actually speaks not so much of the Old Testament saints being admitted to the church, but of the Gentile believers of the New Testament age being admitted to Israel."[40] The church is not new in that the church is "remnant Israel" (Rom 9:27; 11:1–7) and represents a great worldwide expansion of "remnant Israel," now encompassing elect Jews and Gentiles who, together, constitute the *"Israel of God"* (Gal 6:16).[41] Paul illustrates this in Romans 11. First, he argues in Rom 11:1–6 that God has not rejected Israel, because *"I too am an Israelite"* (Rom 11:1). He then cites the case of Elijah, who thought he was the only faithful Israelite left, but God told him that, by God's gracious choice, God had kept seven thousand men who had not bowed the knee to Baal (Rom 11:2–4). He then concludes, *"In the same way then, there has also come to be at the present time a remnant according to God's gracious choice"* (Rom 11:5). Second, Paul uses the example of the "olive tree" in Rom 11:17–24. Because the church—consisting of believing Jews and Gentiles alike—is remnant Israel, Paul could say that there is only

---

37. Matt 21:22–46; Mark 12:1–12; Luke 20:9–19.
38. Grenz, *Millennial*, 125.
39. Reisinger, *Abraham's Four Seeds*, 47.
40. Bell, "Critical Evaluation," 102.
41. See Matt 13:31–32, 47–48; 16:18; Heb 11:40; Rev 5:9; 7:9.

one olive tree. The Jews were the "natural" branches, but many of them had been cut off because of their *unbelief*; the Gentiles were "wild" olives who were "grafted in" because of their *belief*. Both believing Jews and Gentiles are part of the same olive tree because of faith alone and equally partake of *"the rich root of the olive tree"* (Rom 11:17).

Elsewhere, Paul again speaks of the commonality of faithful Jews and Gentiles as the true "remnant Israel," when he discusses the *"commonwealth of Israel"* (Eph 2:11–22). Before the coming of Christ, Gentiles had been *"excluded from the commonwealth"* and were *"strangers to the covenants"* (Eph 2:12). However, Eph 2:19 says that "in Christ" the Gentiles *"are no longer strangers and aliens, but are fellow citizens with the [Jewish] saints."* The passage makes clear that, "Believing Gentiles, members of the church, have been admitted as citizens to the commonwealth of Israel, from which they had been aliens previously, and thus share in the covenants made by God with Israel in Old Testament times."[42]

The church is new in that Jesus said, *"You are Peter, and upon this rock I will build my church; and the gates of hell will not overpower it"* (Matt 16:18). Jesus' statement is in the future tense (*"will build"*) which indicates that the church was a new entity, yet to be built. The church is new for at least two reasons: First, the church is based on the death and resurrection of Christ. That had been prophesied in the OT but did not actually take place until Christ came incarnate to the earth. Second, the church is the recipient of the indwelling Holy Spirit. In the OT, the Spirit was with the people and temporarily came upon various people for particular reasons.[43] However, the Spirit does not appear to have permanently indwelt OT believers. In Ezek 36:26–27, God had promised to put the Holy Spirit within us as part of the New Covenant (see also John 14:17). The outpouring of the Spirit occurred on the day of Pentecost. Peter was amazed at the newness of what God was doing in that Gentile believers received the Holy Spirit just as Jewish believers had (Acts 10:45, 15:8). He recognized the "newness" of the New Covenant and the centrality of the operation of the Holy Spirit in the New Covenant.

---

42. Bell, "Critical Evaluation," 105.

43. Hamilton, "Were Old Covenant Believers"; see Gen 41:38; Exod 31:3; 356:31; Num 11:29; 1 Kgs 7:4; Ps 51:11.

Jesus rejected the nation of Israel as the vehicle for building God's kingdom and gave that role to his own followers, the church

The Gospels depict Jesus as the fulfillment of covenantal blessings on believing Israel and that true, believing, remnant Israel includes both believing Jews and Gentiles. The Gospels also reveal another theme, namely, the fulfillment of covenantal curses on unbelieving Israel.[44]

Regarding the Roman (Gentile) centurion's faith, Jesus said, *"I have not found such great faith with anyone in Israel! I say to you many will come from east and west, and recline at the table with Abraham, Isaac and Jacob in the kingdom of heaven; but the sons of the kingdom will be cast into the outer darkness"* (Matt 8:10–12). Jesus' statement about people coming *"from east and west"* alludes to passages such as Ps 107:3 and Isa 43:5 which spoke of *Jews* returning from exile. "Yet here is Jesus applying it to Gentiles, included among the people of God. The Jews' *special* status as people of God is ended. The privilege of belonging to that people is open to all—Jew and Gentile alike—who have faith in Jesus."[45] In his explanation of the parable of the sower (Matt 13:10–17), Jesus contrasted the deafness and blindness of Israel with his own disciples. Earlier, we saw how both Jesus and Paul used Isa 6:9–10 as a prophecy to condemn Israel for its rejection of Christ.[46]

Jesus signaled his rejection of the nation of Israel when he cursed the fig tree.[47] Cursing the fig tree was an "acted out parable." The fig tree was a symbol for the nation of Israel.[48] In cursing the fig tree, Jesus was condemning outward religious "show" that lacks true, spiritual fruit. However, he was doing more than that. Jer 5:17, 8:13, Hos 2:12; Amos 4:9, and Mic 7:1–6 all speak of judgments on fig trees as part of God's judgment on Israel. In Micah 7:1, Micah expressed his anger over Israel's corruption as his failure to find "the first-ripe fig which I crave." Jesus' being hungry and failing to find any edible figs alludes to Micah 7. Jesus then combined his cursing of the fig tree with the statement, *"No longer shall there ever be any fruit from you"* (Matt 21:19). By that statement, Jesus was not merely attacking religious hypocrisy (since hypocrites might possibly repent and change). Instead, he was demonstrating that the *nation* as the vehicle for spreading God's kingdom had been permanently rejected.

---

44. See Matt 8:12; 13:12–14; 21:43; 23:37–39; Luke 16:19–31.
45. Travis, *I Believe*, 129.
46. See chapter 5 regarding Isaiah.
47. Matt 21:18–22; Mark 11:12–14, 20–24.
48. Hos 9:10; Nah 3:12; Zech 3:10.

Jesus' parable of the landowner and the vineyard draws on Isa 5:1-7 where *"the vineyard of the Lord of hosts is the house of Israel"* (Isa 5:7). The parable recounts the history of Israel's relationship with God. In the parable, Jesus both condemned Israel's leaders and concluded that *"the kingdom of God will be taken away from you and given to a people, producing the fruit of it"* (Matt 21:33-46; see also Mark 12:1-11; Luke 20:9-18). In Matt 21:43, he used the singular *ethnos* ("people" or "nation"). It reveals that the true Israel consists of all those—and only those—who are followers of Christ; that is not determined by physical descent, but by God's grace through faith. As Donald Hagner states, "This setting aside of the privilege of Israel as the unique people of God in favor of another people, namely, the church . . . is of course nothing short of revolutionary."[49]

Following his triumphal entry into Jerusalem, the totality of Jesus' words and actions show that he rejected Israel and pronounced the destruction of Jerusalem and the temple because Israel had rejected him. Jesus' actions of cleansing of the temple[50] was another acted out parable of judgment against Israel. The same is true of the oral parables he told. Craig Blomberg concludes, "In context, the parables of the two sons (Matt 21:28-33), the vineyard,[51] and the marriage feast (Matt 22:1-14) function as "three parables that sequentially depict Israel's indictment (21:28-32), sentence (21:33-46), and execution (22:1-14)."[52] His condemning the scribes, Pharisees, Jerusalem, and his pronouncement of the doom of the temple in Matthew 23-24 show the finality of his rejection of the physical nation of OT Israel. In short, God, in the person of Jesus, had returned to Zion but, as Jesus lamented when he entered Jerusalem for the last time, *"you did not recognize the time of your visitation"* (Luke 21:44).[53]

The church is the new, true, people of God—spiritual Israel

> The first Christians did not think of the Church primarily as an organized society; to them it was the faithful Remnant consisting of the heirs to the divine promises; it was the New Israel and its members were therefore the elect or chosen of God; it was the

---

49. Hagner, *Matthew 14-28*, 623.
50. Matt 21:12-17; Mark 11:15-18; Luke 19:45-48.
51. Matt 21:33-46; Mark 12:1-12; Luke 20:9-18.
52. Blomberg, "Matthew," 74.

53. Jesus even reiterated the connection between rejection of himself and the judgment that would soon fall on Jerusalem and the temple as he was being led to his crucifixion (Luke 23:28-31).

Temple of the divine presence indwelt by the Spirit; it was the body of Christ, a new creation transcending distinctions of race, class or sex. It was a divine-human organism, established by the direct action of God in history.[54]

OT Israel was a type of the church.[55] This is seen in that the NT takes the great OT covenant ideas and terms which had described Israel and applies them to the church:

- *A chosen race, a royal priesthood, a holy nation, a people for God's own possession.*[56]
- *The people of God.*[57]
- *The sons or children of God.*[58]
- *My people.*[59]
- *The seed (descendants) of Abraham.*[60]
- *"I will be their God, and they shall be My people."*[61]
- *The wife of God.*[62]
- *The household of God.*[63]
- *The flock of God.*[64]

---

54. Davies, *Early*, 46.
55. See Goppelt, *Typos*, 109.
56. Eph 1:4–5; Col 3:12; Titus 2:14; 1 Pet 2:5, 9; Rev 1:6; 5:10; compare Exod 19:5–6; Deut 4:20; 7:6–7; 14:2; Isa 43:20–21.
57. Rom 9:22–26; 1 Pet 2:10; compare Hos 1:10; 2:23. In Rom 9:24–26 Paul not only quotes Hosea but specifically says that Hosea (who was talking about Israel) applies to "us" (i.e., the church).
58. Rom 8:14, 16; 9:26; Gal 3:26; 1 John 3:1–2; compare Exod 4:22; Deut 14:1.
59. Rom 9:25; 2 Cor 6:16; Heb 8:10; Rev 18:4.
60. Rom 4:13–16; Gal 3:29; compare Ps 105:6–7.
61. 2 Cor 6:16; Heb 8:10; Rev 21:3; compare Gen 17:8; Exod 6:7; 29:45; Lev 26:12; Jer 7:23; 11:4; 24:7; 30:22; 31:1, 33; 32:38; Ezek 11:19–20; 14:10–11; 36:28; 37:23, 27; Hos 2:23; Zech 8:8; 13:9.
62. Eph 5:25–32; Rev 21:9–14; compare Isa 54:4–7.
63. Eph 2:19; 1 Tim 3:15; compare Num 12:7.
64. Luke 12:32; John 10:15–16; 1 Pet 5:2–3; compare Ezek 34:12–16. Jesus "takes up Zechariah's picture of the smitten shepherd, and applies it to himself and to his disciples as 'the scattered sheep' (Mark 14:27, quoting Zechariah 13:7). Thus an Old Testament figure for Israel is applied specifically and exclusively to the disciples." France, "Old Testament Prophecy," 69.

Christ and the Church are the New, True, Spiritual Israel

- *God's field.*[65]
- *Use of the Greek word "ekklēsia" for the church.*[66]
- *The (true) circumcision.*[67]
- *The olive tree.*[68]
- *God's vine.*[69]
- *A kingdom of priests.*[70]
- *"The Israel of God."*[71]

The NT also takes OT signs and prophecies which related to Israel and applies them to the church:

- *Circumcision.* Circumcision was the sign of the covenant God made with Abraham (Gen 17:9–14). That outward, physical sign really pointed to an inward, spiritual state—"circumcision of the heart."[72]

---

65. 1 Cor 3:9; compare Jer 12:10.

66. "The Hebrew term *qāhāl*, commonly rendered *ekklēsia* in the Septuagint is applied to Israel in the Old Testament. To give just a few examples, we find the word *qāhāl* used of the assembly or congregation of Israel in Exodus 12:6, Numbers 14:5, Deuteronomy 5:22, Joshua 8:35, Ezra 2:64, and Joel 2:16. Since the Septuagint was the Bible of the Apostles, their use of the Greek word *ekklēsia*, the Septuagint equivalent of *qāhāl*, for the New Testament church clearly indicates continuity between the church and Old Testament Israel." Hoekema, *Bible and the Future*, 215.

67. Rom 2:28–29; Phil 3:3; Col 2:11; compare Gen 17:9–15; Deut 30:6; Acts 7:51; Eph 2:11; Phil 3:2.

68. Rom 11:17–24; compare Jer 11:16; Hos 14:6.

69. John 15:1–5; compare Hos 10:1.

70. 1 Pet 2:5, 9; Rev 1:6; 5:10; compare Exod 19:6; Isa 61:6.

71. Gal 6:16. This phrase occurs only here in the NT. Who it is referring to is disputed. Some hold that the phrase refers to believing Jews. However, in the context of Galatians as a whole, *"the Israel of God"* probably refers to the entire church (i.e., Jewish and Gentile believers). "What avails in Christ, Paul argues, is the cross and the new creation, not circumcision.... If this expression meant the Jewish people, or even Jewish Christians, he would be directly contradicting himself.... It is inescapable that the *Israel of God* means the true people of God (in contrast to the Judaizers) who glory in the cross and count the new birth as that saving act of God and not circumcision." Ramm, *Protestant Biblical*, 263–64. Further, "Since the dominant message [in Galatians] is one of doing away with national distinctions among God's people (3.7–8, 26–29; 4.26–31; 5.2–12), it would seem unlikely that Paul would conclude the epistle by referring to those in the church according to their ethnic distinctives. This idea is especially unlikely since 6.11–18, as the conclusion of the epistle, is intended by Paul to summarize its major themes." Beale, "Peace and Mercy," 205; see also LaRondelle, *Israel of God*, 108–14; Cole, *Letter*, 235–37; McKnight, *Galatians*, 302–4; Longenecker, *Galatians*, 297–99.

72. See Deut 10:16; 30:6; Jer 4:4.

The NT says, "*He is a Jew who is one inwardly; and the circumcision is that which is of the heart, by the Spirit, not by the letter; and his praise is not from men, but from God*" (Rom 2:29). Phil 3:3 adds, "*We are the true circumcision, who worship in the Spirit of God and glory in Christ Jesus and put no confidence in the flesh.*" Similarly, Col 2:11 says, "*In Him you were also circumcised with a circumcision made without hands, in the removal of the body of flesh by the circumcision of Christ.*"

- *The New Covenant.* As we saw in chapter 9, at the Last Supper, Jesus explicitly stated that he was inaugurating the New Covenant in his blood (Luke 22:20; see 1 Cor 11:25). Multiple places in the NT apply the New Covenant to the church.

- *Ezekiel's vision of the dry bones and the two sticks* (Ezekiel 37). The vision given to Ezekiel of the dry bones coming to life (Ezek 37:1–14) occurred when the kingdom of Judah was in exile in Babylon. "*These bones are the whole house of Israel*" (Ezek 37:11). The prophecy promised, "*I will open your graves, My people, and I will bring you to the land of Israel. . . . I will put my Spirit within you and you will come to life*" (Ezek 37:12, 14). The vision of the two sticks (Ezek 37:15–28), which represented the house of Judah and the house of Israel, also occurred at that time. In the prophecy, God promised to "*make them one stick . . . and I will make them one nation in the land . . . My servant David will be king over them, and they will have one shepherd; . . . I will make a covenant of peace with them; it will be an everlasting covenant . . . and I will be their God, and they will be my people*" (Ezek 37:19, 22, 24, 26–27). Although Israel returned to its land from Babylon after the exile, the "dry bones" prophecy pointed to a spiritual, not physical, fulfillment, because, at the time of Ezekiel's vision, the nation was not physically dead, but was alive, although "entombed" in Babylon. Ephesians 2 exactly parallels Ezekiel 37. Robert Suh[73] shows this:

Ezekiel 37	Ephesians 2
37:1–10—Bringing alive the dead bones	2:1–7—Bringing alive sinners who were once dead for their sins
37:11–14—Explanation	2:8–10—Explanation
37:15–23—Unification of Judah and Israel	2:11–18—Unification of Jews and Gentiles
37:24–28—Looking forward to the establishment of the new sanctuary in a single Davidic rulership	2:19–22—Looking forward to the final establishment of the new sanctuary in the rulership of Christ

73. Suh, "Use of Ezekiel 37," 723–24.

This is reaffirmed in the book of Revelation. Rev 7:15-17 and 21:3-6 quote or allude to Ezek 37:26-28 and apply Ezekiel's prophecy of Israel's restoration to the church.

- *Hosea's prophecy of the restoration of Israel* (Hos 2:23). In Hosea, God says, *"I will say to those who were not My people, 'You are My people!'"* (Hos 2:23). In context, that was talking about the restoration of Israel. Both Paul (Rom 9:25-26) and Peter (1 Pet 2:10) quote that verse and apply it to the church, particularly the calling of the Gentiles into the church.

- *Joel's prophecy of the outpouring of the Spirit* (Joel 2:28-32). In Joel's prophecy, God promised to *"pour out My Spirit on all mankind"* (Joel 2:28). According to the form of the prophecy, God was speaking only to Israel (Joel 2:27; 3:1-2). On the Day of Pentecost, however, Peter quoted that prophecy and specifically said that it was fulfilled by the pouring out of the Holy Spirit on the believers in Jesus Christ, which had caused them to speak in other languages (Acts 2:14-21). Joel 2:32 also says those *"on Mount Zion and in Jerusalem"* who *"call upon the name of the Lord"* will escape God's judgment. Heb 12:22 says that those in Christ *"have come to Mount Zion and to the city of the living God, the heavenly Jerusalem"* (see also Gal 4:21-31). Rom 10:13 quotes Joel 2:32 and applies it to Jesus and the preaching of the gospel.

- *Amos' prophecy of the "rebuilding of the tabernacle of David"* (Amos 9:11-12). The context of Amos' prophecy was the restoration of Israel following God's judgment and Israel's captivity (Amos 9:7-10, 13-15). At the Council of Jerusalem in Acts 15, the issue was whether or not the Gentiles who were turning in faith to Jesus Christ needed to submit to the Mosaic Law and be circumcised. In holding that they did not, in Acts 15:13-19 the apostle James quoted Amos 9:11-12 and said that the prophecy was not about the restoration of physical Israel or the physical rebuilding of David's throne or Israel's tabernacle but was fulfilled by the Gentiles becoming part of the church.

In addition to the above OT descriptions, signs, and prophecies concerning Israel that the NT applies to the church, a number of other factors show that the church is the new, true, spiritual Israel. For example, Jesus' founding the church on the basis of twelve disciples/twelve apostles symbolized that He was founding a new, spiritual Israel. The twelve disciples/twelve apostles are symbolic of the twelve tribes of Israel: "They are the representatives of and the active nucleus for the formation of the twelve new tribes."[74] James recognizes this by beginning his letter *"to the twelve tribes who are dispersed abroad"* (Jas 1:1). That letter was written to Christians (see Jas 2:1). "In using the phrase [*ai dōdeka phulai;* "the twelve tribes"], the author looks on the recipients of the epistle as the true Israel. The church has quite naturally appropriated the title, for it was the work of the Messiah to reestablish the twelve tribes (Je. 3:18; Ezk. 37:19–24; Pss. Sol. 17:28), and Christians recognized themselves as the true heirs of the Jewish faith (Romans 4; 1 Cor. 10:18; Gal. 4:21–31; Phil. 3:3)."[75]

The beginning of the church also parallels the beginning of OT Israel in the land. Each began with an outpouring of God's wrath in punishing disobedience, covetousness, and sin. In the case of Israel, it was Achan's sin of taking from Jericho items God had prohibited the people to take (Josh 7:1–26); in the case of the church, it was Ananias and Sapphira's keeping for themselves some of the money for property they had sold and then lying about it (Acts 5:1–11). God was giving a poignant object lesson that, just as he was Lord over Israel, so is he Lord over the new, true, spiritual Israel, the church.

In Matt 19:28 Jesus says, *"In the regeneration [or, renewal of all things] when the Son of Man will sit on his glorious throne, you also shall sit upon twelve thrones, judging the twelve tribes of Israel"* (see also Luke 22:29–30). The reference to the *"Son of Man"* alludes to Dan 7:13. "In Daniel 7 it is *Israel* 'the saints of the Most High' [Dan 7:22, 27] who receives the kingdom and rules over the *nations,* whereas Jesus asserts that it will be the *twelve disciples* who will judge the *twelve tribes of Israel.* This transfer highlights the role of the disciples for the spiritual state and the eschatological fate of Israel."[76] In short, just as Christ is the new, true, faithful Israel, so are all those who are united with Christ through faith, i.e., the church.

---

74. Goppelt, *Typos,* 108.

75. Davids, *Epistle,* 63. Typologically, the church far surpasses Israel. This is seen in the fact that the church will judge the twelve tribes of Israel (Matt 19:27–28; Luke 22:29–30) and consists of people from every tribe, tongue, nation, and people of the world (Rev 5:9; 7:9). It is even seen in the language used in Mark 3:14 when Christ *"appointed"* the twelve. The word translated "appointed" is the Greek word *"epoiēsen,"* which is the same word translated "created" in Gen 1:1, LXX. In other words, Christ was creating the new, worldwide people of God.

76. Schnabel, "Israel, the People," 45; see also Marshall, "Church," 123.

11

Christ and the Church Fulfill and Replace the Old Testament Tabernacle and Temple

IN HIS FAMOUS SPEECH in Acts 7, Stephen pointed out that the tabernacle and temple were only models or shadows of true reality because *"the Most High does not dwell in houses made by human hands"* (Acts 7:44–50). Heb 9:1–2, 11–12, 24 contrast the earthly tabernacle/temple which was a mere "copy" of the true one. In Heb 9:24, the Greek word translated as "copy" is "antitype" (*antitupa*). The typological nature of the tabernacle and temple is also indicated in Heb 8:5 which quotes Exod 25:40 regarding the tabernacle, *"See that you make them after the pattern for them, which was shown to you on the mountain."*[1] The Greek word for "pattern" is "type" (*tupon*). Christ and heaven are the true "holy place," of which the earthly tabernacle and temple were earthly replicas.

JESUS IS THE TRUE TABERNACLE/TEMPLE

The primary point of the tabernacle and the temple was that "it was the place where God's glorious presence was manifested on earth to his people."[2]

---

1. Significantly, Hebrews never specifically refers to the "temple" but always to the "tabernacle." Walker points out that the author was "making a far more fundamental point concerning the very essence of the Temple. By concentrating his attention on the 'tabernacle' in the wilderness, he could argue that the Tabernacle system of worship, even when considered in its most pristine and pure form under Moses (before any human sin might have twisted the divine intention), had been declared redundant by God through Jesus." Walker, *Jesus and the Holy City*, 207–8.

2. Beale, *Temple*, 276.

Jesus, like the tabernacle and temple, was the unique dwelling place of God on the earth. Jesus was called "Emmanuel" which means "God with us" (Matt 1:23). In John 1:51 Jesus said, *"You will see the heavens opened and the angels of God ascending and descending on the Son of Man."* That is an allusion to Gen 28:12 in which Jacob's temporary sanctuary memorialized a link between heaven and earth. That was a precursor to the tabernacle, where God's presence in heaven was linked to earth. Jesus' identification of himself as the stairway of Genesis 28 is another way of claiming that he, not the tabernacle or temple, is the primary link between heaven and earth.

The name "tabernacle" foreshadowed that Christ would become incarnate and dwell among us. John 1:14 says, *"The Word became flesh and dwelt among us."* The word *"dwelt"* (*eskēnōsen*, past tense of the verb *skēnoō*) is the verbal form of the noun "tent" or "tabernacle" (*skēnos*). It literally means that he "tabernacled" among us. Just as God filled the tabernacle and the temple,[3] the Holy Spirit publicly came down upon Jesus and filled Him.[4] Unlike God's leaving the temple,[5] the Holy Spirit remained with Jesus until Jesus released him on the cross (Luke 23:46).

Jesus expressly declared the typological nature of the temple when he said, *"'Destroy this temple, and in three days I will raise it up.' The Jews then said, 'It took forty-six years to build this temple, and will You raise it up in three days?' But He was speaking of the temple of His body."* (John 2:19–21)[6] In the account of Jesus' trial in Mark 14:57–58, it says that some gave *"false testimony"* against Jesus saying, *"We heard him say, 'I will destroy this temple made with hands, and in three days I will build another made without hands.'"* The falsehood of the testimony probably is the accusation that Jesus personally would destroy the temple. The phrase *"made with hands . . . made without hands"* contrasts the temple building with Jesus. Describing the temple as *"made with hands"* is "a strong means of playing down its significance. This had been a way of belittling the pagan idols (*e.g.* Ps. 15:4; *cf.* Isa. 46:6)."[7] The last book of the Bible again confirms the typological nature of the temple and its ultimate fulfillment in the person of Jesus. In speaking of the New Jerusalem, Rev 21:22 says, *"I saw no temple in it, for the Lord God the Almighty and the Lamb are its temple."*

The typology or symbolism of the tabernacle and temple also is seen in that the throne of God was symbolized by the "mercy seat" (the lid of the

---

3. Exod 40:34–38; Num 9:15–23; 1 Kgs 8:10–11; 2 Chron 5:11–14; 7:1–2.
4. Matt 3:16–17; Mark 1:10–11; Luke 3:21–22; John 1:32–34.
5. See Ezek 9:3; 10:1–19; 11:22–23.
6. See also Matt 26:60–61; Mark 15:29.
7. Walker, *Jesus and the Holy City*, 10.

ark of the covenant in the tabernacle and temple, which was sprinkled with the blood of the sin offering on the Day of Atonement) (Exod 25:17–22). The Septuagint translates the word for "mercy seat" as "*hilastērion*" (Exod 25:17, LXX).[8] Rom 3:25 calls Jesus' sacrifice on the cross a "propitiation." The word used for "propitiation" is *hilastērion*.

Other correspondences show the typological nature of the tabernacle and temple. There was only one gate to the court of the tabernacle. Just as Jesus said, *"I am the door"* (John 10:7), so he is the gate.[9] He said, *"Enter through the narrow gate; for the gate is wide and the way is broad that leads to destruction, and there are many who enter through it. For the gate is small and the way is narrow that leads to life, and there are few who find it."* (Matt 7:13–14) The interior of the tabernacle had a Holy Place and a Holy of Holies; the temple followed the same pattern (1 Kgs 6:16–20; 2 Chron 3:3–8). The Holy Place and the Holy of Holies were separated by a great veil (Exod 26:31–34; 2 Chron 3:14). Behind the veil was the ark of the covenant and the mercy seat (Exod 25:10–22). When Jesus was crucified *"the veil of the temple was torn in two from top to bottom"* (Matt 27:51; Mark 15:38; Luke 23:45). The tearing of the veil symbolized the destruction of the temple and the free access that people now have through Jesus to God. As a result of Jesus' sacrifice, we now have *"confidence to enter the holy place by the blood of Jesus, by a new and living way which He inaugurated for us through the veil, that is, His flesh"* (Heb 10:19–20). In other words, "In Christ is realization. It is not so much that Christ fulfills what the temple means; rather Christ is the meaning for which the temple existed. . . . The coming of the true supersedes

---

8. See also Heb 9:5 which refers to the mercy seat as the *hilastērion*.

9. Steve Lehrer cautions, "When Jesus Christ says, 'I am the gate' (John 10:7), He is saying that he is like the gate only in a particular sense, which is clearly laid out in the context in which He uses the metaphor. We are not supposed to speculate about the meaning of the hinges on the gate. Christ only intended those aspects of the metaphor to have meaning that he specified to have meaning." Lehrer, *New Covenant Theology*, 21n.6.

Some people see symbolism or typology in every, or virtually every, aspect of the tabernacle and temple, e.g., the linen fence, the outer covering of porpoise skins, the colors of the gate and veil, the gold and the wood of various items in the tabernacle, all of the articles in the tabernacle, the showbread, the altar and the laver in the court. See Booker, *Miracle*, 59–86; Habershon, *Study*, 53–70; Epp, *Portraits of Christ*; McLaughlin, "What is the Tabernacle?"; "Jesus In The Tabernacle." Fritsch is probably on safer ground in saying, "Wherein does the typological character of the tabernacle lie? Is it in the material out of which it was constructed, or is it in the prophetic, parabolic purpose which is carried out in the disposition of the furniture and the ministrations of the priesthood within its courts? We would certainly say the latter. The boards and sockets and skins of the tabernacle are not types in themselves, but they are necessary materials out of which the type is made. In other words, is it not necessary to distinguish in the type between the eternal and the contingent?" Fritsch, "Biblical Typology," 221.

the figurative. The veil of the temple made with hands is destroyed, for its symbolism is fulfilled."[10]

Jesus fulfilled the role of the tabernacle and temple in a greater way than ever could occur through OT rituals. Jesus had the unique ability to forgive people's sins on his own, without their having to offer any sacrifices or take part in any OT tabernacle and temple rituals at all.[11] In Rom 9:4–5, Paul declares that Jesus is qualitatively superior to all of Israel's other blessings and advantages, including temple worship. In Rom 9:4 *"the service"* (*hē latreia*) "likely refers to 'the *temple* service' (so NASB, NASB update) or 'the temple worship.'"[12] Thus, Jesus not only was the perfect sacrifice for sin, but also is the perfect high priest who made the sacrifices.[13]

Jesus asserted his superiority and authority over the temple. In Matt 12:6 Jesus said, *"I say to you that something greater than the temple is here."* Jesus is *"greater than the temple"* because the temple was simply a building made by men, which pointed to God and the created universe. On the other hand, Jesus is God himself and is the one who both created and sustains the universe (Heb 1:1–3). In his parable of the landowner and the vine-growers (Matt 21:33–46; Mark 12:1–12; Luke 20:9–19), Jesus quoted Ps 118:22, *"the stone which the builders rejected, this became the chief cornerstone"* (Matt 21:42). In do that, he implied that "rejection of Jesus as the 'cornerstone' of the temple . . . is equivalent to rejection of Jesus as the true temple."[14] Later NT writers explicitly identify Jesus as the "cornerstone" upon which the new, true temple (the church) is built.[15]

In John 4:21–26 Jesus reaffirmed that he, not the temple in Jerusalem, is the one to establish true worship of God. The Samaritan woman had asked whether the correct temple where worship should be conducted was the temple in Jerusalem or the one on Mount Gerizim (John 4:20). In John 4:22 Jesus said, *"You worship what you do not know; we worship what we know, for salvation is from the Jews."* In other words, *now,* according to the Law of Moses, the correct temple is the one in Jerusalem. But in John 4:21, 23 Jesus said, *"An hour is coming when neither in this mountain or in Jerusalem will you worship the Father . . . [but] true worshipers will worship the Father in spirit and in truth."* When Jesus refers to his "hour" in the book of John, he is

---

10. Clowney, "Final Temple," 177, 183.
11. See Matt 9:2–6; Mark 2:1–12; Luke 5:17–25; 7:40–50; John 8:1–11.
12. Sweeney, "Jesus, Paul," 608n.16.
13. Heb 2:17; 4:14—5:10; 7:1—8:6; 10:11–22.
14. Beale, *Temple,* 184.
15. Acts 4:10–11; Eph 2:20–22; 1 Pet 2:4–8 (which quotes Ps 118:22).

referring to his death on the cross.[16] He was saying that, although there is a temple in Jerusalem where priests make sacrifices, they were only pointing to him—he was about to make the one true sacrifice to atone for all sin; when he did that there would no longer be any need for temples (because he is the true temple), or priests (because he is the priest to end all priests), or sacrifices (because his is the sacrifice to end all sacrifices). By saying *"neither on this mountain nor in Jerusalem will you worship the Father"* (John 4:21), Jesus was saying that from now on true worship may take place anywhere in the world as long as one has Jesus.

Jesus also judged the temple. Jesus drove out the moneychangers from the temple.[17] In doing that, Jesus quoted from Isa 56:7 (*"my house will be called a house of prayer"*), which is part of a prophecy (Isa 56:3–8) that God would call the Gentiles to himself in his "temple" (*"holy mountain"*). He also quoted from Jer 7:11 (*"den of robbers"*), which is part of a word from the Lord (Jer 7:1–11) that God has seen how Israel has not practiced justice, has oppressed foreigners and the helpless, has shed innocent blood, and has gone after other gods. Jesus' point is that, just as God rejected the first temple in 586 BC because it had become corrupt, so the physical temple in Jerusalem had to be replaced with a greater "temple" because it was corrupt and not fulfilling its role. Additionally, when Jesus cast out the moneychangers, *"the blind and the lame came to him in the temple, and he healed them"* (Matt 21:14). That again indicates that Jesus was fulfilling the prophecy of Isa 56:3–8 that there would be a new people of God *"in My house,"* since that prophecy had indicated that eunuchs would be able to worship with Gentiles.[18] We see the new people of God as prophesied by Isaiah also fulfilled in Acts 8:26–38 when the Ethiopian eunuch converted to Christ and was baptized. With the coming of the Gentiles to faith in Christ, all believers in Christ, regardless of physical defects or ethnic background, are now "priests" in the new, true, house of God.[19]

Jesus prophesied the destruction of the temple. In Matt 21:18–22 (Mark 11:12–14, 20–24) Jesus cursed the fig tree. The fig tree clearly represents God's rejection of Israel (as it did in Jer 8:11–13 to which it alludes). Central to the rejection of Israel is rejection of the temple. That is corroborated by Jesus' remark about casting *"this mountain"* into the sea. The "mountain" probably referred to the temple mount, since that was the most

16. See John 2:4; 4:21, 23; 5:25, 28; 12:23, 27; 13:1; 16:32; 17:1; see also 7:30; 8:20; 16:21.

17. Matt 21:12–13; Mark 11:15–18; Luke 19:45–46; John 2:13–16.

18. This was contrary to OT law, in which anyone who had a physical defect had not been permitted to serve in the temple (Lev 21:16–24).

19. Eph 2:19–22; 1 Pet 2:5, 9; Rev 1:6; 5:10.

important mountain in Jerusalem, and the temple was often synonymous with the mountain on which it was located. "The saying is not simply a miscellaneous comment on how prayer and faith can do such things as curse fig trees. It is a very specific word of judgment: the temple mountain is, figuratively speaking, to be taken up and cast into the sea."[20]

Although Jesus affirmed the temple as the traditional dwelling place of God on the earth (Matt 23:21), in that same discourse he called it *"your house"* and said that it *"is being left to you desolate"* (Matt 23:38). Those statements indicate that, because of Israel's sin and disobedience to God—preeminently in rejecting Jesus as their Messiah—the temple was no longer fulfilling its role. Thus, it was no longer "God's" temple and would be destroyed. In several of his statements that Jerusalem and the temple would be destroyed, Jesus contrasted the temple's destruction with his own kingdom and coming.[21]

AS THE VISIBLE REPRESENTATION OF CHRIST ON THE EARTH, THE CHURCH IS GOD'S "TEMPLE" ON THE EARTH

The early church recognized the significance of the destruction of the physical temple in Jerusalem in AD 70 and the fact that God has created his church to be the new, true, spiritual temple. After mentioning the destruction of the temple in AD 70, the *Epistle of Barnabas*, 16.1–10 (c.70–131) stated:

> But let us inquire whether there is in fact a temple of God. There is—where he himself says he is building and completing it! . . . How then will it be built in the name of the Lord? . . . By receiving the forgiveness of sins and setting our hope on the Name, we become new, created again from the beginning. Consequently, God truly dwells in our dwelling-place—that is, in us. . . . This is the spiritual temple that is being built for the Lord.

The phrase *"temple of God"* is found eleven times in the NT.[22] Other than in Matt 26:61, where Jesus uses it to refer to his body, it always refers to the church.[23] Significantly, in 1–2 Corinthians "Paul was able to refer

---

20. Wright, *Jesus and the Victory*, 422.

21. Matt 24:1–2; Mark 13:1–2; Luke 21:20–24; see also Matt 26:61; Mark 14:58; Acts 6:13–14.

22. Matt 26:61; 1 Cor 3:16, 17a, 17b; 2 Cor 6:16a, 16b; 2 Thess 2:4; Rev 3:12; 7:15; 11:1, 19.

23. 1 Cor 3:9, 16–17; 2 Cor 6:16—7:1; Eph 2:21; 1 Pet 2:5; Rev 3:12; see also Rev

Christ and the Church Fulfill and Replace the Old Testament Tabernacle 175

to believers in the 50s AD, *while the Jerusalem temple was still standing*, as the temple of God indwelt by the Spirit."[24] Thus, in God's eyes the temple had already been replaced even before it was physically destroyed by the Romans in AD 70.

In 2 Cor 6:16—7:1, after comparing the church to a temple, Paul concludes by saying, *"Therefore, having these promises."* The promises from which he quotes in 2 Cor 6:16-18 include Lev 26:11-12, 2 Sam 7:14, and Ezek 37:27, where God promises to build a house (temple), establish David's throne forever, and establish his sanctuary and dwelling place forever with his people. By referring to those promises in the context of calling the church *"the temple of the living God"* (2 Cor 6:16) Paul is saying, "The fullest realization of God's covenant, the eternal and abiding presence of God, binding his people to himself and himself to them forever: these are the promises that are fulfilled in the church—we *are* a temple of the living God."[25] Because the church is a living temple not made by hands, we are called "living stones" that *"are being built up as a spiritual house"* (1 Pet 2:5; see also Eph 2:21-22). In 2 Cor 5:1 Paul uses both "temple" and "tabernacle" language by calling our bodies *"our earthly house of a tent."* Further, individual believers are called a temple in 1 Cor 6:19.

When the tabernacle and Solomon's temple were dedicated, *"fire came down from heaven and consumed the burnt offering and the sacrifices, and the glory of the Lord filled the house"* (2 Chron 7:1; see also Lev 9:24). Likewise, the church received the "fire" of God at its beginning. On the Day of Pentecost *"suddenly there came from heaven a noise like a violent rushing wind, and it filled the whole house where they were sitting. And there appeared to them tongues as of fire distributing themselves, and they rested on each one of them. And they were all filled with the Holy Spirit and began to speak with other tongues, as the Spirit was giving them utterance."* (Acts 2:2-4) Those *"tongues as of fire"* were the outward, visible sign that John the Baptist's prophecy, that Jesus *"will baptize you with the Holy Spirit and fire"* (Matt 3:11; Luke 3:16), had been fulfilled. Significantly, whereas the burnt offerings in the tabernacle and temple were consumed by the fire, the fire did not consume the disciples on the Day of Pentecost, because we are to be *"a living and holy sacrifice"* (Rom 12:1).[26]

13:6 where the church is called "His tabernacle".

24. Sweeney, "Jesus, Paul," 629). "The dating of 1 Corinthians in the fifth decade of the first century is not greatly debated." Sweeney, "Jesus, Paul," 629n.116.

25. Clowney, "Final Temple," 186.

26. For Christians, this means that "the new age begun in [Jesus] requires that the chaff of our lives be burned away. That fire, the fire of the Holy Spirit, is the fire of a love so intense that we fear its grasp. Yet it is the love unleashed in Jesus' life—the

Just as the glory of the Lord filled the tabernacle and temple, so it filled the church. When the tabernacle was erected, *"the glory of the Lord filled the tabernacle. Moses was not able to enter the tent of meeting because the cloud had settled on it, and the glory of the Lord filled the tabernacle."* (Exod 40:34–35) When the temple was dedicated, *"the house of the Lord was filled with a cloud so that the priests could not stand to minister because of the cloud, for the glory of the Lord filled the house of God"* (2 Chron 5:13–14). On the Day of Pentecost, the glory of the Lord filled the house where the disciples were, *"and they were all filled with the Holy Spirit and began to speak with other tongues, as the Spirit was giving them utterance"* (Acts 2:4). In the Old Covenant, when the glory of the Lord filled the tabernacle and temple the priests could *not* minister; in the New Covenant, the church is *in Christ*; thus, the glory of the Lord, the fullness of the Spirit, *empowers* the church for ministry! As the unique dwelling place of God on the earth, the church has been filled with the presence of God.[27]

Peter uses language reminiscent of the Shekinah glory of God coming upon the OT tabernacle and temple when he says, *"The Spirit of glory and of God rests on you"* (1 Pet 4:14). That verse echoes Isa 11:2 which says, *"The Spirit of the Lord will rest on Him."* There is likely another strand of OT background to the passage: "the motif of the temple sanctuary as the 'resting place' of Yahweh (1 Chr 6:31; 28:2; 2 Chr 6:41; Ps 132:7–8, 14; Isa 66:1–2).... Further confirmation for the temple imagery that underlies this reference to the Spirit's resting upon believers is to be found in Peter's earlier description of the Church as a 'spiritual house' in which 'spiritual sacrifices' are offered by a holy priesthood ([1 Pet] 2:5)."[28] Because the church is the greater antitype, God no longer just dwells *among* his people, but he now dwells *within* his people. Further, the Spirit "seals" his people *"for the day of redemption"* (Eph 1:13–14; 4:30). Thus, God will *never leave* the new, true temple of the church, as he did with respect to the old, physical temple.[29]

Like the OT temple, the church, as the new, true temple of God, is characterized by its gold, silver, and precious stones. First Cor 3:10–12,

---

life into which we are baptized—that, as Paul tells us in Rom. 6, frees us from the sin revealed through the law but from which the law cannot in itself deliver us." Hauerwas, *Matthew,* 48.

27. Matt 18:20; 28:20; John 14:17, 23; 20:22; Acts 1:8; 2:1–11, 38–39; 4:31; 8:14–17; 10:44–47; Eph 3:19; 5:18; 1 Cor 3:16; 6:19.

28. Johnson, "Fire in God's House," 289–90.

29. Matt 18:20; 28:20; Rom 8:33–39; compare Ezek 9:3; 10:1–19; 11:22–23. There is no reference to the Shekinah's returning or to fire coming from heaven when the new temple was constructed by Zerubbabel following the exile. See Ezra 3–6; Haggai 1–2; Zechariah 2–4.

in discussing Christ and acts of faith, talks about a "foundation" and then building on it with "gold, silver, precious stones." The only other place in Scripture where a "foundation" of a building is laid and "gold," "silver," and "precious stones" are "built" upon it is Solomon's temple (1 Kgs 5:17—6:36; 1 Chron 29:1–9). Since the new, true temple is a living temple, the gold, silver, and precious stones are the works which we do in this life to build the kingdom and help the poor and needy (1 Cor 3:9–17). If we do not, we will be judged like God judged the old temple. Peter's use of Shekinah language for the church was made in the context of the church's "ordeal," "testing," "sufferings," and being "reviled" (1 Pet 4:12–16). Peter concludes, *"For it is time for judgment to begin with the household [or house] of God"* (1 Pet 4:17). P. W. L. Walker summarizes the significance of this,

> The imagery is drawn from two Old Testament passages which speak of God's work of judgement beginning in the Jerusalem Temple (Ezek. 9; Mal. 3:1–5). . . . The Christian community thus inherits not just the privileges but also the demanding responsibilities of the Jerusalem Temple (the first place to witness God's judgement). This was a clear example of how the Church needed to eschew triumphalism and always apply the biblical theme of judgement in the first instance to itself. It also made quite plain that the Church had the right to see itself as the true inheritor of these Old Testament realities. Christians were the new Temple.[30]

---

30. Walker, *Jesus and the Holy City*, 311; see also Johnson, "Fire in God's House," 285–94.

12

Christ Fulfills and Replaces the Old Testament Sacrificial System and Priesthood

HEB 8:4–6 EXPLICITLY SAYS that the priests and the sacrifices and offerings they made according to the Law were *"a copy and shadow of the heavenly things"* which find their fulfillment in Christ. Heb 10:11–12, 14 adds, *"Every priest stands daily ministering and offering time after time the same sacrifices, which can never take away sins; but He [Christ], having offered one sacrifice for sins for all time, sat down at the right hand of God, . . . for by one offering He has perfected for all time those who are sanctified."*

OT ISRAEL'S SACRIFICIAL SYSTEM

OT Israel had three categories of offerings or sacrifices. All involved the sacrifice of animals except the grain and drink offerings (but those normally accompanied the burnt and peace offerings).

1. *Expiatory offerings* (i.e., satisfying the wrath of God). These consisted of sin offerings,[1] to atone for sins where restitution was not possible; and trespass/guilt offerings,[2] to atone for sins where restitution could be made to an aggrieved party (the offending party had to make the aggrieved party whole, plus pay an additional 20 percent).

---

1. Lev 4:1—5:13; 6:24–30; 8:14–17; 16:3–22.
2. Lev 5:14—6:7; 7:1–8; Num 5:5–10.

2   *Consecratory offerings* (i.e., dedicating and/or expressing sincerity to God). These consisted of burnt offerings,[3] to consecrate yourself or a building to God or to show the sincerity of other sacrifices; grain offerings,[4] given for thanksgiving and securing divine goodwill; and drink offerings,[5] given for consecration.

3   *Peace offerings* (i.e., establishing deeper intimacy with God).[6] These consisted of thank offerings,[7] for gratitude to God or fellowship with God or for an unexpected blessing already received; votive offerings,[8] for a blessing or deliverance already granted when a vow had been made in support of the petition; and freewill offerings,[9] to express general thankfulness and love toward God without regard to specific blessings.

The Levitical sacrificial system was not a complete and final scheme whereby all forms of sin could be removed. The sacrificial system was mainly concerned with sins of ignorance, carelessness, accident, and omission, including ritual defilement and misdemeanors that violated property rights. "Highhanded sins," including all those requiring the death penalty, could not be atoned for by sacrificial ritual (see Num 15:30–31). Such sins done in defiance of the Lord and his commands could be forgiven only by God himself on the basis of unqualified grace in response to faith and repentance (see Psalms 32, 51).

JESUS FULFILLED AND SUPERSEDED OT ISRAEL'S ENTIRE SACRIFICIAL SYSTEM

Jesus' death on the cross fulfilled the underlying basis of the Levitical sacrifices. "The fundamental idea of sacrifice in the Old Testament is that of substitution, which again seems to imply everything else—atonement and redemption, vicarious punishment and forgiveness."[10] Thus, underlying all blood sacrifices was the substitution of an innocent life (the sacrificial animal) for that of the guilty party. Nevertheless, animal sacrifices were inadequate to remove the guilt of an obstinate and rebellious heart (1 Sam 15:22).

3. Lev 1:1–17; 6:8–13; 8:18–21; 16:24.
4. Lev 2:1–16; 6:14–23; 7:9–10.
5. Lev 23:37; Num 15:1–10.
6. Lev 3:1–17; 7:11–34; 19:5–8; 22:18–30.
7. Lev 7:12–15; 22:29–30.
8. Lev 7:16–18; 22:18–25.
9. Lev 7:16–18; 22:18–26.
10. Edersheim, *Temple*, 107; see also Poythress, *Shadow of Christ*, 107.

"Later Scripture corrects Israel's failure to recognize the depth to which the slain animals pointed (Ps. 40:6–8; 50:7–15; 51:16–17), and prophets pointed to a Servant who would justify many by bearing their sin and guilt as a silent lamb (Isa. 53)."[11]

Christ fulfilled the entire basis of the sacrificial system because he alone had the capacity to act as our sacrificial substitute, since he alone was without sin.[12] Christ fulfilled the concepts of the expiatory offerings,[13] the consecratory offerings,[14] and the peace offerings.[15] Poythress summarizes:

> Christ bore the punishment for our sins (1 Peter 2:24; Isaiah 53:5). Thus He is the final sin [expiatory] offering. Christ was wholly consecrated to God. He suffered death and destruction for sin, and also brings about our death to sin (Romans 6:2–7). Thus He is the final burnt [consecratory] offering. Christ in His perfect obedience gave to God the honor and thanks that are due to Him. Thus He is the final grain offering. Christ now offers us His flesh to eat (John 6:54–58). By partaking of His flesh and blood we have eternal life, we have communion with the Father, and we are transformed into Christ's image (2 Corinthians 3:18). Thus Christ is the final fellowship [peace] offering.[16]

The NT links Passover, the Day of Atonement, and the entire sacrificial system, and says that Jesus' death on the cross fulfilled and replaced them all. In Rom 3:25, Jesus' death was described as a "propitiation" or "atoning sacrifice." That is the same Greek term (*hilastērion*) used for the "mercy seat" which covered the ark of the covenant in the holy of holies (Exod 25:17, LXX; see also Heb 9:5 which refers to the mercy seat as the *hilastērion*) and was particularly associated with the Day of Atonement. That, combined with the references to Christ's "blood"[17] and the statement that Christ is "*our Passover*" (1 Cor 5:7), shows that Christ's work connected and fulfilled the two chief festivals associated with the temple: Passover and the "Day of Atonement."

---

11. Johnson, *Him We Proclaim*, 236.

12. Isa 53:4–12; Luke 23:41, 47; Acts 3:14–15; 2 Cor 5:21; Heb 4:15; 7:26; 1 Pet 2:21–24; 1 John 3:5.

13. See Isa 53:4–8, 10; Rom 8:1–4; 2 Cor 5:18–21; Heb 9:11–28; 10:11–12; 13:10–15.

14. See Matt 26:39; Mark 14:36; Luke 22:42; John 4:34; 5:17–20, 30; 6:38; 8:28–29; 10:18; 12:49–50; 14:10, 24, 31; 17:1–26.

15. See John 14:27; 16:33; Rom 5:1–11; Eph 2:13–18; Col 1:18–20.

16. Poythress, *Shadow of Christ*, 49.

17. See Rom 3:25; 5:9; 1 Cor 11:25; Eph 1:7; 2:13; Col 1:14, 20.

JESUS FULFILLED AND SUPERSEDED THE ENTIRE OT PRIESTHOOD

Because of human sin, including his own, the high priest on the Day of Atonement had to first make a sin offering for himself and then for the people (Lev 9:7; 16:6, 11, 15-16, 19-22, 24). Because of the imperfections of the Aaronic priesthood, Heb 7:1—8:6 tells us there was need for a new and greater priesthood according to the order of Melchizedek. Therefore, Heb 7:28 says, *"The Law appoints men as high priests who are weak, but the word of the oath, which came after the Law, appoints a Son, made perfect forever."* Since the Son is *"perfect forever,"* the "weak" OT priesthood has been forever superseded. Jesus is a priest *"according to the order of Melchizedek, and not . . . according to the order of Aaron"* (Ps 110:4; Heb 5:6; 7:11). Heb 7:12 says that, because the coming of Christ resulted in a new priesthood, *"when the priesthood is changed, of necessity there takes place a change of law also."* T. D. Alexander summarizes that "the reference here to 'a change in the law' indicates that the regulations associated with the Levitical priesthood were no longer in force once the church became the new temple of God."[18] The fact that Jesus is called both a "priest" and a "high priest"[19] indicates that the entire OT sacrificial system and priesthood have been replaced because, according to the OT law, Jesus was not able to be a priest at all since he was not descended from Aaron or the tribe of Levi but from the tribe of Judah.[20] Instead of an entire priesthood acting as mediators between God and mankind, now there is *"one God, and one mediator also between God and men, the man Christ Jesus"* (1 Tim 2:5). In contrast to the OT priesthood being limited to the tribe of Levi (Num 18:1-24; Jer 33:19-22), as a result of the sacrifice of Christ, *all* believers in Jesus Christ are now priests in the eyes of God (1 Pet 2:5, 9; Rev 1:6; 5:10).

HEBREWS CONTRASTS ISRAEL'S ENTIRE SACRIFICIAL SYSTEM AND PRIESTHOOD WITH CHRIST

The book of Hebrews repeatedly demonstrates that Christ's sacrifice on the cross, and his resurrection and ascension, far exceed what all of Israel's sacrifices and priests, including the high priest on the Day of Atonement, could ever have hoped to achieve:[21]

---

18. Alexander, *From Eden*, 150.
19. Heb 2:17; 3:1; 4:14-15; 7:11, 15-17, 24, 26, 28; 8:1-2; 9:11.
20. Heb 8:4; see Matt 1:2-3; Luke 3:33-34.
21. See Nelson, "He Offered Himself," 251.

- *The old sacrificial system required multiple sacrifices and priests* (Heb 7:23; 9:25; 10:1, 11). The former priests existed in great numbers *"because they were prevented by death from continuing"* (Heb 7:23). But *"because [Jesus] continues forever, [he] holds His priesthood permanently"* (Heb 7:24), and he had to make only one sacrifice for all people and for all time.[22]

- *The old sacrificial system could not change people on the inside or make them perfect.* By his sacrifice, Christ does that.[23]

- *The Day of Atonement served as a "reminder" of sins every year.* Through Christ's sacrifice, the Father *"will remember their sins and lawless deeds no more"* (Heb 10:3, 16–18).

- *Christ did what no earthly priest could do.* He ascended into heaven itself, where he continually intercedes for his people with the Father (Heb 7:24–25) and not just as a priest but as a high priest.[24]

- *By his death, resurrection, and ascension Christ now enables every believer to do what only the OT priests could do.* In the OT only the priests could enter the holy place of the Temple. Jesus has enabled all of his people with *"confidence to enter the holy place by the blood of Jesus"* all of the time (Heb 10:19–22; 4:16).

In addition to the above, Heb 13:10–14 shows that continuing to worship in the OT manner in the physical temple and worshiping Jesus are *mutually exclusive*. Verse 10 indicates that Jesus inaugurated a new system (the word "altar") in contrast to the Old Covenant system (the word "tabernacle"). By saying that *"those who serve the tabernacle have no right to eat"* from the altar Jesus established, v. 10 is saying that Old Covenant and New Covenant worship are mutually exclusive. This mutual exclusivity is reinforced by highlighting that, in Old Covenant worship, the blood of the sacrificial animals *"is brought into the holy place by the high priest as an offering for sin"* (v. 11), whereas Jesus suffered *"outside the gate"* as our atoning sacrifice (v. 12); the passage then states, *"So, let us go out to Him outside the camp, bearing His reproach"* (v. 13). In other words, with the coming of Jesus, a choice is now required: one must either go to Jesus "outside" the camp where *"we do not have a lasting city, but we are seeking the city which*

---

22. Heb 7:24, 27; 9:12, 25–28; 10:10–14.
23. Heb 7:11; 9:9–10; 10:1–2, 14–16.
24. Heb 4:14–15; 7:26; 8:1–2.

is to come" (v. 14) or remain "inside" the existing city, focused on the old, physical temple and its rituals.[25]

The finality and perfection of Christ's Atonement—and thus the complete and permanent elimination of the entire OT sacrificial system and priesthood—is seen in the fact that he *"sat down at the right hand of God"* in the true heavenly holy of holies.[26] "Because sacrificial service entailed the posture of *standing* before God or at the altar ([Heb] 10:11; Deut 10:8; 18:7), the contrasting act of *sitting down* indicates the termination of Christ's sacrificial act ([Heb] 10:12). Yet, at the same time, his enthronement at God's right side gives him the access and status appropriate for ongoing, effective intercession."[27]

---

25. See Walker, *Jesus and the Holy City*, 207.

26. Heb 1:3; 10:12, 14; see also Ps 110:1; Mark 16:19; Luke 22:69; Rom 8:34; Eph 1:20–21; Col 3:1; 1 Pet 3:21–22.

27. Nelson, "He Offered Himself," 257.

13

Christ Fulfills and Replaces the Old Testament Law

THE CONTRAST BETWEEN THE Mosaic Law and the incomparable greatness of Christ is made clear in John 1:17: *"For the Law was given through Moses; grace and truth were realized through Jesus Christ."* To understand the epoch-changing significance of the coming of Jesus, of central importance is the effect Christ, his teaching, and his announcement of the kingdom had with respect to OT law (Torah). When Jesus appeared, he forced his contemporaries to make a choice: What constitutes loyalty to God, adherence to Torah or following Jesus? The same issue—our understanding of the Christ's effect on the OT—still faces us today.

THE OT LAW WAS PART OF THE MOSAIC (OLD) COVENANT

The Mosaic Covenant and Law were designed to regulate the nation of Israel in the land. Hence, God's blessings and curses were tied in a physical way directly to Israel's obedience or disobedience to Mosaic Law.[1] Although the Law itself was holy, spiritual, and good (Rom 7:12, 14, 16), it was not designed or able to impart life (Gal 3:21). It could not justify people (Rom 3:21; Gal 3:11). It was not a basis for righteousness (Gal 3:21). If the Law *could* have been the means of life, then Christ did not need to come (see Gal 3:11-13, 19-24; 4:4-5). Mosaic Law was instituted because of the people's sin (Gal 3:19). It revealed people's sinfulness (Rom 3:19-20; 7:7-12). It even

---

1. See Leviticus 26; Deuteronomy 4; 6-9; 11; 27-29.

aroused or increased sin.² It imprisoned people under sin.³ It brought death and condemned people for their sinful behavior (Rom 7:5, 9–11; 2 Cor 3:7–9). It proved to be *"a yoke which neither our fathers nor we have been able to bear"* (Acts 15:10).

THE OT LAW WAS TEMPORARY

The Law showed people that, if they were to have right standing with God, it could not be on the basis of Law-keeping (since they could not perfectly keep the Law) but would have to be through some other means (i.e., through Jesus Christ who *could and did* perfectly keep the Law and through the *grace* of God who graciously imputed Christ's perfect righteousness to those who are united to Christ by faith). The Law thereby prepared people for Christ (Gal 3:15—4:31; see also Rom 7:24–25).

In light of the pre-existing Abrahamic covenant, the OT Law was only temporary until the coming of Christ.⁴ In Gal 3:1–19 Paul discusses the relationship of the Abrahamic Covenant, the Mosaic Covenant and Law, and Christ. Paul argues that Abraham was justified by faith, not by the works of the Law (Gal 3:6, quoting Gen 15:6). Further, God's covenant with and promises to Abraham were given 430 years before the Law was given to Moses, and the Law *"does not invalidate a covenant previously ratified by God, so as to nullify the promise"* (Gal 3:17). The Law was added *"because of transgressions"* (Gal 3:19a). The OT Law acted as a "guardian" (pedagogue) (Gal 3:24–25; 4:2) over "minor children" (Gal 4:1–3) until sonship came with Christ (Gal 3:26; 4:4–7). A pedagogue (Greek = *paidagōgos*) was a domestic slave within the household, whose task was to oversee and regulate children from their infancy until they reached puberty. Linda Belleville summarizes:

> The life of a child under the control of a *paidagōgos* was strictly supervised. It was without any measure of freedom. . . . The tightly knit structure of [Paul's] argument [in Gal 3—4:7] and the broad pattern of chiasm in these verses points to a single function of the Law. This function is that of a custodian who closely regulates and supervises God's people in a period of spiritual minority. Like the elementary principles of the world

---

2. Rom 4:15; 5:13–14, 20; 7:5; 1 Cor 15:56.

3. Rom 7:6, 23; 8:2–3; Gal 3:23; 5:1; Col 2:14.

4. Significantly, although the covenants with Noah (Gen 9:16, Isa 24:5), Abraham (Gen 17:7, 19; Ps 105:10; 1 Chron 16:17), David (2 Sam 23:5; 2 Chron 13:5), and the New Covenant (Isa 55:3; 61:8; Jer 32:40; 50:5; Ezek 16:60; 37:26) are all called "everlasting" covenants, the covenant with Moses is never called "everlasting" or "permanent."

[Gal 4:3, 9], the Law orders the daily affairs of its wards until sonship is realized.... With the coming of faith in Christ, the Law's function as guardian and custodian ceases and the Spirit becomes the internal guiding principle.[5]

Gal 3:23 and 3:25 show the contrast: *"Before faith came in, we were kept in custody under the law,"* but *"Now that faith has come, we are no longer under a pedagogue."* The "faith" is found in Jesus Christ (3:24).

THE OT LAW WAS SYMBOLIC

The Mosaic Law had symbolic purposes that pointed to and are fulfilled in Christ and the church. Several examples of this are food laws, laws relating to ceremonial uncleanness, laws relating to yoking and muzzling animals, and criminal laws.

1. *Food laws.* After the Flood, God told Noah that people could eat animals of *all kinds,* without restriction (Gen 9:3–4). Only with the Mosaic Covenant came the prohibition against eating certain "unclean" animals (Lev 11:1–23, 41–47; Deut 14:1–21). This suggests that the law was symbolic.[6] Because these laws were symbolic—a "type" and "shadow" that was pointing forward to Christ and heavenly realities (Heb 10:1–2)—they were fulfilled when the Christ, the reality to which they pointed, appeared.

    That the food laws were symbolic of the *heart* or inner state of a person is made clear by Christ in Mark 7:14–23, where he says that it is not what goes into a person (i.e., certain kinds of food) that defiles the person, but what comes out of the person's heart defiles the person. That the food laws were symbolic of *people* was further made clear in the vision God gave Peter in Acts 10:9–20. Three times Peter saw a sheet filled with "unclean" animals, and God told Peter to *"kill and eat"* them. Peter thought that only animals were being talked about, but God told him, *"What God has cleansed, no longer consider unholy"* (Acts 10:15). Peter then understood that God meant that all human beings of whatever tribe or ethnic group are equally "clean."[7] The

---

5. Belleville, "Under Law," 59, 60, 70. By using "we" in 4:3, Paul was including himself with the Galatian Christians and also was indicating that the Mosaic Law was one of the enslaving elements of the cosmos. The pre-Christian, pagan, Gentile Galatians had been just as "enslaved in their pagan idolatry as the Jews had been in their servitude to the Law," and equally in need of salvation. Burke, *Adopted,* 86–87.

6. See Poythress, *Shadow of Christ,* 85–86.

7. Acts 10:28, 34–35; 11:1–18; 15:7–9.

symbolism of the OT food laws has been fulfilled in that those who are Christ's have feasted on the ultimate, life-giving food: the body and blood of Christ himself (John 6:51–58). Therefore, in Christ all the lesser symbols have been done away with. Now that Christ has come and fulfilled the Law, to require a person to abstain from certain "unclean" foods amounts to a form of falling away from the faith, because God has created all food *"to be gratefully shared in by those who believe and know the truth. For everything created by God is good, and nothing is to be rejected if it is received with gratitude; for it is sanctified by means of the word of God and prayer."* (1 Tim 4:3–5)

2   *Laws relating to ceremonial uncleanness.* Israelites were not to touch human corpses (Num 19:11–22) or the carcasses of certain animals (Lev 11:24–40), because they would thereby become "unclean" for a period of time and have to perform various purification rituals. These, and other such prohibitions, were based on the fact that *"you are a holy people to the Lord your God"* (Deut 14:21). The distinction between the clean and the unclean dramatized the prevailing power of sin: the unclean pollutes the clean; the clean does not purify the unclean (Hag 2:10–14). "Such uncleanness is not in itself sin. It is merely *symbolic* of sin. And separation from uncleanness accompanies *symbolic* holiness."[8]

Christ is the fulfillment of what the cleanliness laws symbolized, since he is the only completely pure and holy being who ever lived, and he triumphed over sin and death.[9] Therefore, the prevailing power of Christ reverses the principle of the cleanliness laws. When Jesus touched a leper, Jesus was not defiled, but the leper was cleansed.[10] Through his sacrifice on the cross Jesus sanctifies all who are united to him by faith (Heb 10:10). This same principle applies in practical ways in our lives: although OT Israelites who married unbelievers were supposed to separate from their pagan spouses (Ezra 9:1—10:14), Christians are not required to separate from their unbelieving spouses (1 Cor 7:10–13). Instead, the unbelieving spouse and children of the marriage are deemed "clean" by virtue of their connection with the Christian (1 Cor 7:14).[11]

---

8. Poythress, *Shadow of Christ*, 84.

9. See Mark 1:24; Luke 4:34; Acts 3:14; 4:27, 30; Rom 5:19; 6:6; 1 Cor 15:21–22; 1 Pet 3:18; 1 John 2:20.

10. Matt 8:1–4; Mark 1:40–44; Luke 5:12–14.

11. Paul's discussion in 1 Cor 7:14 assumes that the marriage to the unbeliever took place before the believing spouse became a Christian, since believers are always to marry *"in the Lord"* (1 Cor 7:39). Thus, in 2 Cor 6:15–17 Paul asks, *"What has a believer*

3   *Laws relating to yoking and muzzling animals.* Deut 22:10 says, "You shall not plow with an ox and a donkey together."[12] Paul applies this concept to people in 1 and 2 Corinthians: do not *"associate with any so-called brother if he is an immoral person"* (1 Cor 5:11); marry *"only in the Lord"* (1 Cor 7:39); *"Do not be bound together [lit. 'unequally yoked'] with unbelievers"* (2 Cor 6:14). Similarly, Deut 25:4 says, "You shall not muzzle the ox while he is threshing." In 1 Cor 9:9-10 Paul quotes this law and then comments, *"God is not concerned about oxen, is He? Or is He speaking altogether for our sake? Yes, for our sake it was written."* He quotes this law again in 1 Tim 5:17-18 as the reason why the church should pay its pastor. In other words, these laws relating to animals applied to animals in the OT but were typological and symbolic of human relationships.

4   *Laws relating to manslaughter.* If a person accidentally killed someone, he could flee to a city of refuge and thereby escape the family members of the deceased person seeking to avenge the death.[13] The person would have to remain in the city of refuge until the high priest died (Num 35:25-27). The reason for this "incarceration" of the manslayer is that even accidentally spilled blood *"pollutes the land"* (Num 35:32-34).[14] The death of Christ fulfilled what such laws pointed to and, thereby, superseded such laws and practices. The reason is that Christ died as the great High Priest.[15] His death permanently, once and for all, atoned for blood spilled on the ground.... The only permanently defiled place in God's universe any more is hell, and in hell the great Avenger of Blood pours out eternal wrath on those who refused to flee to Jesus Christ, our City of Refuge (Heb. 6:18)."[16]

5   *Laws relating to capital punishment.* God cannot abide in the presence of sin (see Isa 59:1-2; Hab 1:13). The Law required the death penalty for certain sexual sins, idolatry, and other matters, to signify God's holiness and the standard of holiness he requires of his people, i.e., "Be holy, for I am holy" (Lev 11:44-45; 19:2; 20:26). The NT takes the

---

in common with an unbeliever?" and quotes Isa 52:11 (*"Do not touch what is unclean"*) to emphasize that the *principle* of separation from sinfulness which was at the heart of the OT cleanliness laws still applies to Christians in their marital and other relationships.

12. See also Lev 19:19; Deut 22:9, 11 for other forbidden mixtures.

13. See Num 35:1-34; Deut 19:1-10.

14. See also Gen 4:10-11 (*"The voice of [Abel's] blood is crying to Me from the ground"*).

15. Heb 2:17; 4:14—5:10; 7:1—8:6; 10:11-22.

16. Jordan, *Law*, 101-2.

principle of holiness and purity but reapplies it in the church, which again shows that the OT Law is superseded when the reality to which it pointed has arrived. In applying OT Law to the church, however, the NT changes the meaning or, perhaps more accurately, shows what the OT Law was pointing to all along. For example, Lev 20:11 required that a man who had sexual relations with his father's wife be put to death. Paul addressed that very situation in 1 Cor 5:1–13 but instructed the church excommunicate the man, not execution him. Although excommunication is very serious, Paul recognized that God may work in the offender's life so that *"his spirit may be saved in the day of the Lord Jesus"* (1 Cor 5:5). He ended his discussion of this issue in 1 Cor 5:13 by quoting Deut 22:22, 24, which also talked about capital punishment for sexual and other sins. Dennis Johnson points out that "the rationale for so severe a punishment is not an abstract principle of justice among the nations at large, but rather the preservation of Israel's purity as God's covenant people. The procedures of church discipline specified by Jesus (Matt. 18:15–20) and his apostles (1 Cor. 5:1–13; 1 Tim. 5:20–25; etc.) are the means by which God now calls his new covenant people to protect its purity."[17]

THE OT LAW WAS PROPHETIC

In Luke 16:16 (*"The Law and the Prophets were proclaimed until John; since that time the gospel of the kingdom of God has been preached"*), Jesus announced a fundamental change in the OT Law (see also Matt 11:13, *"the Law prophesied until John"*). Jesus was saying that, because the Mosaic Law (and the OT in general) had a typological and prophetic function which pointed to Jesus and his teaching, when the fulfillment came, the type ceased to exist and was superseded by the reality which had been prophesied.[18]

JESUS CAME TO FULFILL THE LAW

Jesus said, *"Do not think that I came to abolish the Law or the Prophets; I did not come to abolish but to fulfill, for truly I say to you, until heaven and earth pass away, not the smallest letter or stroke shall pass from the Law until all is accomplished"* (Matt 5:17–18). "The Law or the Prophets" refers to the entire OT.

17. Johnson, *Him We Proclaim*, 281–82.
18. See Moo, "Jesus and the Authority," 23.

Jesus was *"born under the Law"* (Gal 4:4). He perfectly complied with all the demands of the Old Covenant and Law.[19] In Matt 5:17, the word "fulfill" (Greek = *plēroō*) normally means "to bring to its intended meaning,"[20] or to "bring something to completion."[21] When Jesus said that he came to "fulfill" the Law, he was saying that the Law and the Prophets were incomplete in themselves, but he—his life, his death, and his teaching—completed and fulfilled what the Law and the Prophets pointed to. Jesus' work on the cross brought the *purpose* and the *binding nature* of OT (Mosaic) law to an end. When Matt 5:18 says that nothing of the Law shall pass away *"until all is accomplished,"* Jesus' death and resurrection are that accomplishment. In Matt 5:18, v. 18d (*"until all is accomplished"*) "reinterprets the apocalyptic language of 18b [*"until heaven and earth pass away"*] in terms of the fulfillment of all prophecy in Christ (culminating in his death-resurrection). In short, 18d says that 18b takes place at the death-resurrection of Jesus, which is the fulfillment of OT prophecies; vs. 18b says that 18d is the apocalyptic event ushering in the new aeon. The two clauses have a reciprocal relationship."[22] Thus, Jesus' last words from the cross immediately before he died were *"It is finished!"* (John 19:30).

JESUS ASSERTED AND DEMONSTRATED HIS AUTHORITY OVER THE ENTIRE OT LAW

Jesus taught on his own independent authority, not dependent on either the oral laws or traditions, or even the written OT law.[23] His statements, *"You have heard it said . . . But I say to you,"*[24] emphasize "a new and startling focus on the authority of this Jesus of Nazareth, an authority that goes far beyond a restatement of the OT law."[25] Indeed, "Jesus' own demands go considerably beyond any fair exegesis of the actual texts he quotes; nor do most of his

---

19. See Isa 53:9; Luke 23:40–41; John 8:46; Heb 4:15. He was not even accused of law-breaking at his trial. See Matt 26:57–68; Mark 14:53–65; Luke 22:66–71; John 18:19–24.
20. Hays, "Applying," 29.
21. Poythress, *Shadow of Christ*, 368.
22. Meier, *Law and History*, 64–65.
23. Matt 7:28–29; 13:54; Mark 1:21–22; Luke 4:31–32; John 7:46.
24. Matt 5:21–22, 27–28, 31–32, 33–34, 38–39, 43–44.
25. Moo, "Law of Moses," 205.

demands find support anywhere in the OT."[26] He confirmed this authority by the miraculous signs he performed.[27]

The Jews believed that the "oral law" (*Halakah*) had been given at Mount Sinai along with the written law (*Torah*). The oral law was accepted as authoritative, even if its authority did not match that of the written law.[28] Jesus' life demonstrated a clear distinction between the written law and the oral law. "There is no undisputed example of a specific precept of the written Torah that He Himself actually contravened."[29] On the other hand, Jesus clearly rejected the authoritativeness of the oral law. Examples of Jesus' attacks on, or violations of, the oral law include "corban" (money dedicated to the temple);[30] non-emergency healings on the Sabbath;[31] and eating with unwashed hands.[32]

JESUS LIVED UNDER THE OLD COVENANT BUT WAS A MESSENGER OF THE NEW COVENANT

Although Jesus himself lived under the Old Covenant, his teachings struck at the heart of the Mosaic Law and ushered in the New Covenant. In Mark 7:14–23 Jesus asserted a principle (*"whatever goes into the man from outside cannot defile him, [but] that which proceeds out of the man, that is what defiles the man,"* v. 15) that was "destined to abrogate large segments of Pentateuchal laws."[33] By asserting that principle, Jesus thereby *"declared all foods clean"* (Mark 7:19), thus striking at the heart of the OT food laws.[34]

The major issue at the Council of Jerusalem (Acts 15) was whether or not new believers in Christ were required to be circumcised and obey the Law of Moses (Acts 15:1–2, 5–6). The Council concluded that circumcision and being bound by the Law of Moses were *not* required (Acts 15:7–11, 19–20, 28–29; see Gal 5:1–6). Christ had made baptism, not circumcision, the essential rite of initiation into the faith and the church (Matt 28:19).

26. Moo, "Law of Moses," 205.
27. Matt 9:2–8; Mark 2:1–12; Luke 5:18–26.
28. Carson, "Jesus and the Sabath," 76; Moo, "Jesus and the Authority," 18.
29. Carson, "Jesus and the Sabbath," 79.
30. Matt 15:5–12; Mark 7:9–13.
31. Matt 12:9–14; Luke 13:10–17; John 5:1–17.
32. Matt 15:1–3; Mark 7:1–9.
33. Moo, "Jesus and the Authority," 28.
34. See also Acts 10:9–16; Rom 14:1–17 (*"the kingdom of God is not eating and drinking"*); 1 Cor 8:1—9:4; 10:23–30; Col 2:16–17 (*"no one is to act as your judge in regard to food or drink"*); 1 Tim 4:3–5.

The church, in conformity with the teaching of Christ, realized that it was no longer bound by the Mosaic Law and, therefore, no longer commanded obedience to the Mosaic Law.

Christ had said, *"Not the smallest letter or stroke shall pass from the law until all is accomplished"* (Matt 5:18). The food laws and circumcision were not "minor" matters (*"the smallest letter or stroke"*) but went to the very heart of the Law.[35] By no longer requiring adherence to the food laws or circumcision, the church recognized that, in his life and in his death on the cross, Christ had "accomplished all" the Law had foreshadowed. Therefore, to be a follower of Christ means that one is no longer under the Law of Moses.

CHRISTIANS ARE NOT BOUND BY THE MOSAIC COVENANT OR ANY OF THE OT LAWS BUT ARE UNDER THE "LAW OF CHRIST"

The entire OT Law hangs together. Either Christ superseded the entire OT Law or the entire OT Law is still in effect. Thus, in connection with circumcision, Paul said that for someone to go back and put himself under the authority of one part of the OT law means that he is thereby subject to the *entire* OT law: *"It was for freedom that Christ set us free; therefore keep standing firm and do not be subject again to a yoke of slavery. Behold I, Paul, say to you that if you receive circumcision, Christ will be of no benefit to you. And I testify again to every man who receives circumcision, that he is under obligation to keep the whole Law."* (Gal 5:1-3)

The result of the change of redemptive eras (i.e., from the Old Covenant to the coming of Christ) is that no Mosaic commandment is directly applicable to believers. Rom 6:14 says, *"Sin shall not be master over you, for you are not under law but under grace."* In Rom 7:1-6, Paul argues that *"the law has jurisdiction over a person as long as he lives"* (7:1). However, we *"were made to die to the Law through the body of Christ"* (7:4). Therefore, *"we have been released from the Law, having died to that by which we were bound, so that we serve in newness of the Spirit and not in oldness of the letter"* (7:6). Gal 3:13 says, *"Christ redeemed us from the curse of the Law."* Eph 2:14-15 says, *"The Law of commandments contained in ordinances,"* which distinguished between and separated Jews from Gentiles, was *"broken down"* and *"abolished"* in Christ. Col 2:13-14 says, *"The certificate of debt consisting of decrees against us, which was hostile to us"* was *"canceled,"* *"taken out of the way"* and

---

35. See Lev 11:44-47; Deut 14:21 (the distinction between "clean" and "unclean" foods symbolized holiness); Gen 17:9-14 (circumcision was the sign of the Abrahamic Covenant); Lev 12:3 (circumcision was necessary for all Jewish male children); Josh 5:2-9 (circumcision was necessary for Israel to enter the promised land).

Christ Fulfills and Replaces the Old Testament Law

"*nailed to the cross.*" Heb 7:11–12 says that the coming of Christ resulted in a new priesthood, and *"when the priesthood is changed, of necessity there takes place a change of law also."* In short, the *entire* Old Covenant is *"obsolete"* (Heb 8:13). Heb 10:9 adds, *"He takes away the first [Old, Mosaic Covenant] in order to establish the second [New Covenant]."*

Jesus is the true interpreter of the OT and is the ultimate source of authoritative teaching. Thus, "Jesus is to Moses what the butterfly is to the caterpillar. . . . In Christ Moses reaches maturity and emerges in full bloom."[36] In other words, the OT Law and the Prophets are "fulfilled" and thereby superseded by Jesus—who he is, what he did, and what he taught. Since the entire OT was pointing to Jesus, only through him can we know the will of God truly and authoritatively. Instead of being subject to the Old Covenant, Christians are now subject to the New Covenant—the "law of Christ."[37]

The NT writers never appealed to the Ten Commandments as the basis for our moral or ethical decisions. Instead, they appealed to Christ and to the gospel (see, e.g., Gal 2:14; Eph 4:17—5:21). The "law of Christ" is not only the teachings of Jesus but also that of the NT writers.[38] Jesus said that if we "abide" or "continue in" his word, then we *"will know the truth, and the truth will make you free"* (John 8:31–32). His word transforms us from the "inside-out" into the image of Christ himself (see Rom 8:29; 12:2). The OT Law never could do what Jesus and the law of Christ can do (see also Acts 15:10–11). Although the OT law has been superseded by Christ, it may still have symbolic applications. For example, in 2 Cor 6:14–17 Paul refers to the OT prohibition against touching unclean things in order to underscore the general principle of separation from sinfulness. In other words, although Christians are no longer directly under any OT law or command, the OT may have helpful principles for us but, as Wells and Zaspel caution us, when Christians read the OT today, particularly its laws, commands, and rules, they "must wear their Christian lenses."[39]

---

36. Wells and Zaspel, *New Covenant*, 157.

37. Luke 22:20; 1 Cor 11:25; 2 Cor 3:6; Heb 8:8–13; 9:15. Or, as Wells and Zaspel put it, "Jesus came to bring about what Moses' law anticipated. The law pointed forward to him all along; he is its eschatological goal. Only in him does it find its full significance and continuing validity; apart from Jesus' interpretation of it, it has precisely no enduring use. . . . Accordingly, the church is not at all obliged to follow the old law in its older form. We are required to follow the law only as it comes to us through the grid of Jesus Christ, the law's Lord and fulfiller." Wells and Zaspel, *New Covenant*, 118, 130.

38. See, e.g., John 14:24–26; 16:12–15; 17:8, 18–20; 1 Cor 14:37; Gal 1:11–12; Eph 2:20; 1 Thess 2:13; 2 Thess 2:15; 3:6, 14; Heb 2:3; Rev 1:11.

39. Wells and Zaspel, *New Covenant*, 157. Application of OT law and principles today is discussed in detail in Menn, *Biblical Interpretation* at pages 39–56 and Appendices C and D.

14

Christ Fulfills and Replaces the Old Testament Sabbath

In Col 2:13–15 Paul argues that Christ cancelled our debt of sin on the cross and made us alive together with him. In Col 2:16–17 he concludes, *"Therefore, no one is to act as your judge in regard to food or drink or in respect to a festival or a new moon or a Sabbath day—things which are a mere shadow of what is to come; but the substance belongs to Christ"* (see also Gal 4:9–11).[1]

JESUS ASSERTED AND DEMONSTRATED HIS AUTHORITY OVER THE SABBATH

The Pharisees claimed that Jesus' disciples were guilty of breaking the Sabbath because they picked heads of grain on the Sabbath. In response, Jesus answered that the disciples were innocent because he, as the Son of Man, is *"Lord of the Sabbath"* (Matt 12:8; Mark 2:28; Luke 6:5). Jesus made a similar claim in John 5:17–18 when he healed a man on the Sabbath and told him to *"pick up your pallet and walk,"* in violation of Sabbath regulations. Thus, Jesus' claim to be *"Lord of the Sabbath"* relates not only to his own conduct but also affects the conduct of others (i.e., made it lawful for the man to carry his pallet when that was prohibited). Because the law of the Sabbath was part of the Ten Commandments, "Jesus' authority as the law's fulfiller stands even

---

1. By calling the Sabbath *"a mere shadow,"* Paul was explicitly denoting its typological nature.

Christ Fulfills and Replaces the Old Testament Sabbath

over the Decalogue."[2] Further, his claim to be Lord of the Sabbath "is not only a messianic claim of grand proportions, but it raises the possibility of a future change or reinterpretation of the Sabbath."[3]

THE NT TRANSFORMS THE SIGNIFICANCE OF THE SABBATH

God's blessing and sanctifying the seventh day, because that is when he finished his work of creation (Gen 2:1–3), did not establish a religious significance for the seventh day or an obligation of mankind to worship on or otherwise observe the seventh day. "There is no record, for the first several thousand years of human history, that **anyone** kept the sabbath as a day of religious worship, as such was authorized under the Mosaic system. There is not a solitary passage in Genesis that mentions any of the patriarchs observing the Sabbath, as a holy day or otherwise."[4] Any Sabbath regulations came later in connection with, and limited to, the nation of Israel.[5] The Sabbath was the sign of the Old Covenant (Exod 31:12–17). The Fourth Commandment regarding the Sabbath (Exod 20:8–11; Deut 5:12–15) had two rationales: God's resting from his work of creation (Exod 20:11) and the exodus from Egypt (Deut 5:15). Although it may not be apparent how the exodus serves as a basis for the Sabbath, that becomes clear when one considers that the purpose of the exodus was to free Israel from its slavery in Egypt; that would become complete when Israel was in its own land, where it would find rest from its enemies (Deut 12:9–10; 25:19; Josh 11:23; Ps 106:7–12).

The Sabbath also was a "type." Charles Fritsch observes, "The ultimate goal of God's redemptive purpose is the bring men into the divine rest which is typified by the earthly Sabbath."[6] Heb 3:7—4:11 reveals that the divine "rest" finds its fulfillment in New Covenant salvation, which is our true "Sabbath rest." Heb 3:7–11, 15; 4:3, 7 all quote from Ps 95:7–11 to the effect that the generation in the wilderness following the exodus forfeited their "rest" because of rebellion and lack of faith (Heb 3:16–19). Although Joshua ultimately led the Israelites into the Promised Land, that did not constitute the Sabbath "rest" God intended, because *"if Joshua had given them rest, He*

---

2. Moo, "Jesus and the Authority," 29.
3. Carson, "Jesus and the Sabbath," 66.
4. Jackson, "Was the Sabbath," paragraph (1), bold emph. in orig.
5. See Exod 16:22–30; 31:12–17; Neh 9:13–14.
6. Fritsch, "Biblical Typology," 96; Jackson, "Was the Sabbath," paragraphs (2)–(5).

would not have spoken of another day after that" (Heb 4:8). Instead, there remains a rest for us "today" (Heb 4:7). Everyone who has faith in Christ (Heb 4:2–3) has *"rested from his works"* and *"has entered His rest"* (Heb 4:10). In other words, "the Sabbath no longer has significance *as a day*; . . . For those who rest in Christ, every day is a Sabbath (cf. Rom. 14:5)."[7] As A. T. Lincoln concludes, since the OT Sabbath day was a type that pointed to the true Sabbath, namely, our salvation rest in Christ, "Christ brings the spiritual reality; His work fulfills the intent of the Sabbath, and with Christ comes that for which the Sabbath existed. The reality of salvation rest supersedes the sign."[8] In short, when the Old Covenant was superseded by the New Covenant, so was the sign of the Old Covenant; thus, under the New Covenant the Sabbath and other "special days" of the OT are no longer binding.[9] As Col 2:16–17 puts it, *"Therefore no one is to act as your judge in regard to . . . a new moon or a Sabbath day—things which are a mere shadow of what is to come; but the substance belongs to Christ."*

The argument in Hebrews 3–4 is very similar to Paul's argument concerning faith and the law in Galatians 3–4. In Galatians, Abraham was justified by faith, not by the law (Gal 3:6–11), and the promised blessings through Abraham accrue only to those who believe in Jesus Christ (Gal 3:14, 16, 18, 22, 29). The law was only temporary until the coming of Christ (Gal 3:23–25). Likewise, Hebrews argues that because of unbelief, OT Israel never truly entered the "rest" God had promised (Heb 3:7–12, 16–19; 4:2, 5–6). Although Israel ultimately entered the promised land, it never found rest and peace but continued to experience war, oppression, and exile. In the OT, refraining from work one day per week (i.e., "keeping the Sabbath") reflected the temporary and partial nature of Israel's rest from her enemies. On the other hand, Christ defeated our only permanent enemies—sin, Satan, and death. Because Christ has done all the work needed to secure our *permanent* salvation, *our "rest" is permanent.* Consequently, early church father Justin Martyr recognized that Christianity does *not* require keeping one particular Sabbath day; instead, we are living in a "perpetual Sabbath."[10]

The fact that the Sabbath Day was a "type" which finds its true fulfillment in the permanence of our Sabbath rest in Christ is even hinted at in the first mention of God's resting on the seventh day in Gen 2:1–3. William Dumbrell observes that it is "most remarkable" that "unlike the previous six days, the seventh day is without beginning and end [compare Gen 1:5, 8,

---

7. Wells and Zaspel, *New Covenant*, 236.
8. Lincoln, "Sabbath, Rest," 215.
9. Rom 14:5; Gal 4:8–11; Col 2:15–17.
10. Justin Martyr, *Dialogue with Trypho*, 12; see also *Epistle of Barnabas*, 15.8–9.

13, 19, 23, 31 with 2:2–3]. The intention of the narrative seems to be to underline the distinctly special and unending place of the seventh day.... The unending Sabbath day provides the context in which the ideal life of the garden is to take place and is to be perpetuated in human society."[11] The consummation of the believers' rest, that "ideal life," will be experienced on the new heaven and new earth, where *"they may rest from their labors"* (Rev 14:13), as opposed to the unbelievers, *"who have no rest day and night"* (Rev 14:11).[12]

THE FULFILLMENT OF THE SABBATH IN CHRIST MEANS THAT SUNDAY IS NOT SIMPLY A "CHRISTIAN SABBATH" DAY OF REST EQUIVALENT TO SATURDAY AS THE JEWISH SABBATH

Christians early-on recognized the significance of the end of the Old Covenant by transforming their understanding of the Sabbath and no longer "honoring the seventh day" as a day of rest and worship. At the Jerusalem Council (Acts 15) the whole point was whether it is necessary to circumcise new Gentile believers and require them to observe the Law of Moses (Acts 15:5). The answer was a resounding "No!" Sabbath observance (or even some alternative "Sabbath day" for Gentiles) was not required of Gentile believers by the apostolic decree of Acts 15.

"One of the Jewish beliefs held with most tenacity is observance of the Sabbath, and yet Christian Jews transferred their worship from Saturday to Sunday, which they termed 'the Lord's Day' [Rev 1:10]."[13] Christians began gathering for worship on Sundays in honor of Christ's resurrection, and that happened early-on (Acts 20:7; 1 Cor 16:2). This is confirmed by the early church fathers. Ignatius of Antioch said, "Let every friend of Christ keep the Lord's Day as a festival, the resurrection-day, the queen and chief of all the days."[14] Justin Martyr similarly said, "We all hold this common gathering on Sunday, since it is the first day, on which God transforming darkness and matter made the universe, and Jesus Christ our Saviour rose from the dead on the

---

11. Dumbrell, "Genesis 2:1–3," 220–21.

12. This is corroborated by the fact that the new heaven and new earth is the consummation of the biblical theme of God's dwelling with mankind which began in the garden. See chapter 3—Two Biblical Themes Concerning God's Relationship with Mankind.

13. Maier, *First Easter*, 122; see also *Didache*, 14.1.

14. Ignatius, "To the Magnesians," 9.

same day."[15] Evidence from the second century reveals "no trace whatever of any controversy as to whether Christians should worship on Sunday, and no record of any Christian group that did not worship on Sunday."[16]

Christians are not "commanded" to worship on Sundays. They are free to worship any day of the week. However, Christian worship on Sunday ("the Lord's Day") underscores the different basis of Christian worship and worship on the Jewish Sabbath. Because Christ's resurrection fulfills the rest signified by the OT Sabbath, there is a link between the seventh day (the Sabbath) and the first day of the week on which Christians worship. That link is *not* turning the first day of the week into a day of physical rest but into a day of "celebration of the true Sabbath rest of salvation brought by Christ whom believers worshipped and with whom they had fellowship."[17] There is no warrant for applying the OT Sabbath requirement of physical rest to the NT Lord's Day.

---

15. Justin Martyr, *First Apology*, 67.

16. Bauckham, "Lord's Day," 236.

17. Lincoln, "Sabbath, Rest," 205, 215–16. Walter Martin, *Kingdom*, 459–73 provides a detailed biblical and historical refutation of the claim by Seventh Day Adventists that seventh day (Sabbath) worship is required of Christians; see also Martin, "Sabbath," n.p. It is a fact little noted by Christian "Sabbatarians" that, both when God rested on and sanctified the seventh day in Gen 2:1–3, there is no command about Sabbath-day worship or observation, "nor is there any religious significance attached to the day, so far as man's obligations or behavior are concerned." Wells and Zaspel, *New Covenant*, 214n.292. The Fourth Commandment regarding the Sabbath merely says that the Israelites were to *"observe the Sabbath day," "keep it holy,"* and *"not do any work"* on that day. No specific prescriptions regarding attending worship services or other behaviors are given.

15

Christ and the Church Fulfill and Replace the Old Testament Feasts

COL 2:16–17 SAYS THAT *"no one is to act as your judge . . . in respect to a festival or a new moon . . . things which are a mere shadow of what is to come, but the substance belongs to Christ"* (see also Gal 4:9–11).[1] Sacrifices were a required part of all of the OT feasts and festivals. Because Christ is the one, permanent sacrifice which fulfilled the entire sacrificial system, he thereby fulfilled all of the feasts and festivals. If Christ did not fulfill all of the OT feasts and other ceremonies, then we should still be keeping them, because they were said to be *"perpetual statutes."*[2] The fact that the church has never kept these OT customs shows that it has recognized that all the feasts pointed to Christ and that their substance has been fulfilled in Christ. We keep the feasts forever "in Christ," and therefore do not have to observe the outward forms as required by the Old Covenant Mosaic Law. How Jesus fulfilled each of the feasts and festivals is discussed below.

OT ISRAEL'S CALENDAR

OT Israel used a lunar calendar; each new day began and ended at sundown.[3] Because the lunar calendar was 360 days (12x30), every so often they had to add a "leap month." OT Israel had a civil calendar and a sacred calendar. The first month of the civil calendar (Tishri, which corresponds to September-October) was the seventh month of the sacred calendar (Abib

---

1. By calling these things *"a mere shadow,"* Paul is explicitly denoting their typological nature.
2. See Exod 12:14; Lev 23:14, 21, 31, 41.
3. See Gen 1:1, 8, 19, 23, 31.

[or, after the exile, called Nisan], which corresponds to March-April), and *vice versa*.[4] Each month began with a new moon.[5] The first day of the new year (1 Tishri) is called *Rosh Ha-Shanah* ("head of the year") and was marked by the Feast of Trumpets. Every week ended with the Sabbath day when the Israelites were supposed to rest and do no work.[6] When the Sabbath ended at sundown, the new week began. The Jewish months corresponded to our months as follows:

Jewish Month	Begins New Moon of	Bible References
1. Abib* / Nisan	March-April	Exod 13:4; 23:15; Neh 2:1
2. Zif* / Iyyar	April-May	1 Kgs 6:1, 37
3. Sivan	May-June	Est 8:9
4. Tammuz	June-July	—
5. Ab / Av	July-August	—
6. Elul	August-September	Neh 6:15
7. Ethanim* / Tishri	September-October	1 Kgs 8:2
8. Bul* / Marheshvan / Heshvan	October-November	1 Kgs 6:38
9. Chisleu / Chislev / Kislev	November-December	Neh 1:1
10. Tebeth / Tevet	December-January	Est 2:16
11. Shebat / Shevat	January-February	Zech 1:7
12. Adar	February-March	Est 3:7
13. 2nd Adar (7 times every 19 years)	March 14,15	—
* Pre-exilic names		

Israel also had a "Sabbath year" and a "year of Jubilee." The Sabbath year was every seven years. During that year the land was to lie fallow (Exod 23:10–11; Lev 25:1–7); all debts (except from foreigners) were to be forgiven (Deut 15:1–11); and Hebrew slaves were to be set free (Exod 21:1–6; Deut 15:12–18). The year of Jubilee was every fifty years. At that time, debts were

---

4. While Israel was still in Egypt, God had changed the calendar when he established the Feast of Passover (Exod 12:2). John Sittema explains that he was "announcing to a people long structured by the agricultural calendar of the Egyptians that life would start anew with their liberation. . . . Israel was to remember—with each yearly celebration of the Feast of Passover—that her existence as the people of God began with *God's mighty deliverance from slavery.*" Sittema, *Meeting Jesus*, 45.

5. Num 10:10, 28:11, 1 Sam 20:5, Ps 81:3, Isa 66:23, Ezek 46:3, Amos 8:5, Col 2:16.

6. Gen 2:2–3; Exod 16:22–23; 20:9–11; 23:12; 31:13–17; 34:21.

Christ and the Church Fulfill and Replace the Old Testament Feasts

to be cancelled; Hebrew slaves freed; the land was to lie fallow; and each parcel was to be returned to its original owner (Lev 25:8–55). The Bible indicates that one reason for the exile in Babylon was Israel's failure to keep these required Sabbaths for the land.[7]

OT ISRAEL'S SYSTEM OF FEASTS

OT Israel had seven main feasts, celebrations, or holy days, in two sets: the Spring feasts and the Fall feasts. Hebrew males were required to appear before the Lord at the chosen place (i.e., in Jerusalem, after the conquest of the land and the building of the temple) three times per year, at the Feast of Unleavened Bread (Passover); Feast of Weeks; and Feast of Tabernacles.[8]

The Spring feasts began in the first month of the sacred calendar (Abib/Nisan [March-April]):

- *Passover (14 Abib/Nisan).* Commemorated deliverance from Egyptian bondage (i.e., God's angel of death "passed over" the Israelites). A lamb was slain, its blood was sprinkled on the lintel and doorposts of the house, and then it was roasted and eaten by the family.[9]

- *Unleavened Bread (15–22 Abib/Nisan).* Associated with Passover,[10] it commemorated the hurried flight from Egypt. Holy convocations on 15 and 22 Abib counted as Sabbaths. Burnt offerings and sin offerings were made. All leaven was to be removed from one's house at the beginning of the week, and unleavened bread was to be eaten during the week.[11]

---

7. See Lev 26:34–35; 2 Chron 36:20–21; Jer 25:11–12; 29:10.
8. Exod 23:14–17; 34:23–24; Deut 16:16.
9. Exod 12:1–13, 21–27; Lev 23:5; Num 28:16; Deut 16:1–8. After Israel left Egypt and entered the promised land, modifications from the "Egyptian" manner of observing Passover were made, including no longer sprinkling the blood on the lintel and doorposts. Edersheim, *Temple,* 212–18.
10. See Matt 26:17; Mark 14:12; Luke 22:1. Passover and Unleavened Bread are so closely associated because the Passover lamb was to be killed at twilight, at the close of 14 Nisan (Lev 23:5–6); there was "no interval between the killing of the lamb and the keeping of the Feast of Unleavened Bread, though the one belonged to the fourteenth day and the other to the fifteenth." Holiday, *Feasts,* 27. "From their close connection [Passover and Unleavened Bread] are generally treated as one, both in the Old and in the New Testament." Edersheim, *Temple,* 208. Confusingly, "Passover" and "Unleavened Bread" are sometimes *both* used to describe the combination of 14 Nisan (Passover) and the subsequent week-long Feast of Unleavened Bread. When this is done, the "first day of Unleavened Bread" would then be referring to 14 Nisan, not 15 Nisan (see Matt 26:17; Mark 14:12; Luke 22:2, 7–8).
11. Exod 12:14–20; 34:18; Lev 23:6–8; Num 28:17–25.

- *First Fruits (16 Abib/Nisan).* Celebrated the first fruit of the barley harvest. A sheaf of the barley harvest was to be waved by the priest and a burnt offering made.[12]
- *Feast of Weeks (also called Feast of the Harvest; Day of the First Fruits; and Pentecost) (6 Sivan [May–June]).* Celebrated the first fruits of the wheat harvest and how the Lord brought Israel out of slavery in Egypt. It occurred fifty days after First Fruits (hence the name Pentecost ["fiftieth"]).[13] A holy convocation counted as a Sabbath; wave, burnt, sin, and peace offerings were made.[14]

The Fall feasts began on the first month of the civil calendar (Tishri [September–October]):

- *Feast of Trumpets (Rosh Ha-Shanah) (1 Tishri).* Celebrated the beginning of the seventh month (civil New Year) and heralded the coming Day of Atonement, nine days later. A holy convocation, trumpets were blown, and burnt, grain, and sin offerings made.[15]
- *Day of Atonement (Yom Kippur) (10 Tishri).* The holiest day of the year. The sins of the people were covered and cleansed for the year. A holy convocation, burnt, grain, and sin offerings were made. After making offerings for himself the high priest was allowed to enter the holy of holies in the temple and sprinkle blood on the mercy seat as an atonement for the sins of the people. The atonement procedure involved two goats: one was killed and its blood sprinkled on the mercy seat; the other (the "scapegoat") had Israel's sins confessed over it and then was sent into the wilderness.[16]
- *Feast of Tabernacles (Booths) (also called Feast of the Ingathering) (15–22 Tishri).* Commemorated the wandering in the wilderness and celebrated the completion of all the harvests. Holy convocations on 15 and 22 Tishri counted as Sabbaths. Burnt, grain, and sin offerings were made. Participants were to live in temporary booths and joyfully celebrate with palm and willow branches.[17]

Israel also celebrated two other minor festivals: Purim and Hanukkah. These two festivals are not part of the system of festivals, Sabbath years,

---

12. Exod 34:26; Lev 23:10–14.
13. Acts 2:1; 20:16; 1 Cor 16:8.
14. Exod 23:16; 34:21–24; Lev 23:15–21; Num 28:26–31; Deut 16:9–12.
15. Lev 23:23–25; Num 29:1–6.
16. Lev 16:1–34; 23:27–32; Num 29:7–11.
17. Exod 23:16; 34:22; Lev 23:33–43; Num 29:12–38; Deut 16:13–15.

Christ and the Church Fulfill and Replace the Old Testament Feasts 203

and years of Jubilee established in the Torah (the Mosaic Law). They were established later. Although they are important festivals in Judaism, they are called "minor" festivals because work is permitted on them.[18]

- *Purim (14–15 Adar; in leap years, 14–15 2nd Adar).* Celebrates the saving of the Jewish people from Haman's attempt to destroy them, as recorded in Est 7:1—9:32. Fasting is done on 13 Adar in commemoration of Esther's three-day fast (Est 4:15–17). Then, on 14–15 Adar, Scripture verses are read, gift-giving is "an essential part of the celebration," and "it is obligatory to eat, drink and be merry on Purim."[19]

- *Hanukkah (also called the Feast of Lights and Feast of Dedication) (25 Kislev–2 or 3 Tevet).* Celebrates the rededication of the temple in Jerusalem at the time of the Maccabean Revolt (167–160 BC). According to the Talmud, the Temple was purified and the wicks of the menorah miraculously burned for eight days even though there was only enough sacred oil for one day's lighting. The rededication is discussed in the apocryphal books of 1–2 Maccabees (see 1 Macc 4:36–59 and 2 Macc 1:18–36). Candles are lit for 8 nights, songs are sung, special foods are eaten, and games are played.

JESUS FULFILLED PASSOVER AND THE FEAST OF UNLEAVENED BREAD

The NT identifies Jesus with the Passover lamb. At the beginning of Jesus' public ministry, John the Baptist recognized who Jesus was and identified him as *"the Lamb of God who takes away the sin of the world"* (John 1:29, 36). By this identification, John was joining Passover (which required the sacrifice of a lamb) and the Day of Atonement (in which Israel's sins were covered). The identification of Jesus with the sacrificial Lamb is reaffirmed in 1 Pet 1:19; Rev 5:6, 8. Christ was crucified at the time of Passover when the Passover lamb was killed (Luke 22:1; John 19:14, 31).[20] The NT says that

18. Lehrman, *Guide,* 70.

19. Lehrman, *Guide,* 60, 65.

20. Orthodox Christianity holds that Jesus was crucified on Friday and resurrected on Sunday morning. However, there is controversy about on which *Hebrew day* the last supper occurred. The traditional Passover meal "would begin just before sundown on Nisan 14 but would *continue* into the new day of Nisan 15." Parsons, "When does Passover," Passover at the Temple. There is also controversy about whether Jesus was crucified on 14 or 15 Nisan (remember that Hebrew days include part of two Roman days because Hebrew days began at sundown, not midnight, and continue until the next sundown). Michael Scheifler sets forth the basis for a 13–14 Nisan last supper and

Passover was prophetic of the sacrifice of Christ. John 19:36 quotes Exod 12:46 and Num 9:12 (which specify that the bones of the Passover lambs are not to be broken) and says, "*These things* [i.e., the soldiers not breaking Christ's legs as they did to the men crucified with Jesus] *came to pass to fulfill the Scripture, 'Not a bone of him shall be broken.'*" First Cor 5:7 says, "*Christ our Passover also has been sacrificed.*"

At the Last Supper Jesus instituted a new Passover—the Lord's Supper.[21] The meal itself was a Passover meal (Luke 22:15), and many of the specifics of the meal as recorded in the Gospels reflect that, e.g., the wine, it's taking place in the evening, and interpretive sayings drawn from redemptive history.[22] Bretscher lists eleven comparisons between the original Passover/Unleavened Bread and the Lord's Supper:[23]

- *Each feast was instituted at the command of God* (Exod 12:1; 1 Cor 11:23).
- *Each feast involved the sacrifice of a lamb* (Exod 12:3; 1 Cor 5:7).
- *In each feast the lamb was without blemish* (Exod 12:5; 1 Pet 1:19).
- *In each feast no bone of the sacrificial lamb was broken* (Exod 12:46; John 19:31–36).
- *In each feast it is by eating of the flesh of the sacrificial lamb that the individual participates in the sacrifice and personally receives its benefits* (Exod 12:47; John 6:52–57; 1 Cor 10:18; Matt 26:26; Mark 14:22; Luke 22:17–19; 1 Cor 11:24).
- *In each feast the blood that is shed plays a central part of the ceremony.* In Passover, the blood of the lamb was to be placed on the doorposts and lintel of the house (Exod 12:7, 22); in the Lord's Supper, the blood becomes a part of the feast itself (Matt 26:27–29; Mark 14:23–25; Luke 22:17–20; 1 Cor 11:25–26).
- *To each feast God attaches his promise.* In Passover, God promised to spare his people the plague of the death of the first-born child (Exod 12:13, 23). In the Lord's Supper, Christ promises the forgiveness of sins (Matt 26:28; see Mark 14:24; Luke 22:20). The Lord's Supper is thus a far more powerful and effective feast, because it is not limited

---

a 14 Nisan crucifixion. Scheifler, "Was Jesus," n.p.; Alfred Edersheim sets forth the basis for a 14–15 Nisan last supper and a 15 Nisan crucifixion. Edersheim, *Temple*, 244–59, 389–401.

21. Matt 26:20–29; Mark 14:12–25; Luke 22:1–22; John 13:1–2; 1 Cor 11:23–32.
22. Behm, "Klaō," 734; Goppelt, *Typos*, 110–12.
23. Bretscher, "Covenant," 199–209.

- *Both feasts are given as a memorial to be celebrated from generation to generation.* Passover memorializes the deliverance of Israel from the Egyptians (Exod 12:14, 24–27). The Lord's Supper memorializes Christ who, in his death, *"takes away the sin of the world"* (1 Cor 11:25–26).

- *Both feasts imply the necessity of faith.* The Israelites' obedience to God at the time of the Passover demonstrated their faith and trust in what he said (Exod 12:27–28) and thereby spared them from death. In the Lord's Supper, the participants likewise must examine themselves and take the Supper in a worthy manner; failure to do so results in judgment, even to death (1 Cor 11:27–32).

- *Real blood underlies both feasts, but the blood that underlies the Lord's Supper has infinite, intrinsic worth and power, whereas the blood that underlies Passover does not.* The blood of the lamb in Passover was merely a "sign" that God would see as his death angel moved through Egypt but had no intrinsic power to spare men's lives in itself (Exod 12:13). On the other hand, the blood of Christ which underlies the Lord's Supper is the very blood of the Son of God, which alone is intrinsically able and sufficient to *"take away the sin of the world"* (Matt 26:28). Thus, Jesus could say, *"This . . . is the new covenant in my blood"* (Luke 22:20), not merely that his blood was a "sign" of the new covenant.

- *Both feasts are exclusive.* Passover was only for Hebrews; non-Israelites had to go through the rite of circumcision in order to partake (Exod 12:43–45, 48). The Lord's Supper is for the body of Christ (1 Cor 10:16–17, 20–21); we are the true circumcision (Rom 2:28–29; Phil 3:3).

Jesus' instituting a "new" Passover in Jerusalem was implying that *even in Jerusalem* Israel was still in slavery in Egypt. Mark corroborates this idea in that, in Mark 15;20, when he describes Jesus being "led out" to be crucified, he uses the Greek word *eksagō* for "led out." Elsewhere in the NT, that word "is regularly used to describe the 'leading out' of the Israelites from Egypt under Moses."[24] It is only through Jesus' sacrificial death that Israel, and anyone else who "eats his flesh and drinks his blood," is freed from slavery.[25] The Lord's Supper itself is typological. It is telling us that the church in history is not yet the consummation but is pointing to the consummation. It "points to the joyous banquet in the future that Christ will celebrate with his

---

24. Walker, *Jesus and the Holy City*, 14; see Acts 7:36, 40; 13:17; Heb 8:9.
25. See John 8:31–36; Rom 6:1–23; Heb 2:14–15.

disciples in the kingdom of God (Luke 22:15–18; Mark 14:25; Matt 26:29; 1 Cor 11:26)."[26]

Jesus' burial fulfilled the Feast of Unleavened Bread. Although Jesus was crucified and died on Passover, since each day began at sundown, he was buried as the Feast of Unleavened Bread began. This fulfilled the requirement of Exod 12:15 that *"on the first day you shall remove leaven from your houses."* John Sittema explains that Jesus did not just keep the feast of Unleavened Bread, but he *"became the leaven, and his entombment was the cleansing of our lives."*[27]

Christ's fulfillment of Passover and Unleavened Bread have practical implications for the lives of Christians. Leaven was symbolic of the Hebrews' old life of slavery in Egypt; unleavened bread symbolized their putting off their old life, as they left Egypt for their new life in the promised land (Exod 13:3–10). We, like the Hebrews, also were slaves—slaves of sin (Rom 6:6–20), but now, in Christ, we are to put off our old self and put on the new self of Christlikeness (Eph 4:22–24). In 1 Cor 5:6–8 Paul associates both Passover and Unleavened Bread in discussing how we should live our lives. He argues that *because* Christ *"our Passover"* has been sacrificed for us, *therefore* we should *"clean out the old leaven so that you may become a new lump, just as you are in fact unleavened"*; we should not live with *"the leaven of malice and wickedness, but with the unleavened bread of sincerity and truth."* Passover and Unleavened Bread are intimately united, as are Christ and the church: our redemption is secured by the blood of the Passover Lamb, and we are united with Christ in his death (Gal 2:20); but we are also united with him in his burial as the leaven (Rom 6:4). Since the leaven of our sin has been removed by Christ, the week-long Feast of Unleavened Bread pictures the character of how our new lives in Christ should now be lived.

---

26. Goppelt, *Typos*, 116.

27. Sittema, *Meeting Jesus*, 61. It appears that Jesus was buried the same Hebrew day he was crucified, i.e., before sundown which would begin a new day. The reason is that the next day was a Sabbath on which no work (such as burying a body) could be done (see Matt 27:57–62; Mark 15:42–47; Luke 23:50–56; John 19:14, 30–42). If Sittema is correct, then Jesus' crucifixion and burial both occurred on 15 Nisan. However, if Jesus was crucified and buried on 14 Nisan, then Sittema is technically incorrect if he means that Jesus was *placed in the tomb* on 15 Nisan. However, the typology is preserved in that 15 Nisan is the only *entire day* in which Jesus would have been *in the tomb*. When the Jews cleansed their homes of leaven, "traditionally the 'leaven package' is burned at the time of morning prayer on Nisan 14 . . . the exact day in which the Mashiach Yeshua was crucified, removing our sin and spiritual leaven forever." Parsons, "Chag HaMatzot," Leaven and the Sacrifice of Yeshua.

JESUS FULFILLED THE FEASTS OF FIRST FRUITS AND WEEKS

"First Fruits" celebrated the first fruits of the barley harvest and was part of the week-long Passover/Unleavened Bread celebration (Exod 34:26; Lev 23:10–14). A sheaf of the first fruits of the harvest were joyously waved on the day of First Fruits (Lev 23:11–12). First Fruits also marked the first day of the fifty-day period which culminated in the Feast of Weeks (hence, Weeks was also called "Pentecost," i.e., "fiftieth"; Lev 23:15–16). Weeks celebrated the first fruits of the wheat harvest. Thus, Weeks was also called the Feast of the Harvest (Exod 23:16; 34:22), and the first day of the Feast was called the *"day of the first fruits"* (Num 28:26). Both feasts celebrated the bounty that God had given to the nation, of which the "first fruits" were a token.

Just as Jesus in his death was our Passover, so in his resurrection he is our First Fruits. Jesus was offered up as the Passover Lamb on Passover (14 Nisan); he spent the first day of Unleavened Bread (15 Nisan) in the grave; and he rose from the dead the next day (16 Nisan), the day of First Fruits.[28] As a result, in 1 Cor 15:20, 23 Christ is specifically called the *"first fruits"* for all of those who are in Christ: we will be resurrected just as he has been resurrected from the dead (Rom 8:11; 1 Cor 15:20–58). The waving of the sheaf of the first fruits of the harvest—which was done on the very day Jesus rose from the dead—is a fitting symbol of the resurrection.

The sending of the Holy Spirit on the day of Pentecost (the *"day of first fruits"*) fulfilled the Feast of Weeks. Christ rose from the dead early Sunday morning after the Passover Sabbath.[29] He appeared for forty days to various groups of people (Acts 1:3). He then ascended into heaven but told his disciples to wait in Jerusalem for the promise of the Father to baptize them with the Holy Spirit (Acts 1:4–5). Ten days later (i.e., fifty days after the

---

28. See "Was Jesus resurrected," *NeverThirsty*; Gordon, "resurrection"; Craham, "Christ Rose"; see also the discussion of the *"Three days and three nights"* in connection with Jonah, in chapter 7. Others maintain that Jesus was crucified on Thursday, 14 Nisan (Passover), was in the grave Friday, 15 Nisan (first day of Unleavened Bread and a High Sabbath) and Saturday, 16 Nisan (regular weekly sabbath), and rose early Sunday morning, 17 Nisan (Day of First Fruits). See Turner, "Feast of First Fruits"; Parsons, "Yom HaBikkurim." The dispute arises from the interpretation of Lev 23:11, concerning the Day of First Fruits, *"He shall wave the sheaf before the Lord for you to be accepted; on the day after the sabbath the priest shall wave it."* Even in Jesus' day, the issue was disputed. The issue was whether the verse is referring to the weekly sabbath or the special sabbath of the first day of Unleavened Bread. The Sadducees held that *"the day after the sabbath"* was always a Sunday, whereas the Pharisees held that the verse referred to the day after the first day of Unleavened Bread (15 Nisan), so *"the day after the sabbath"* would always be 16 Nisan, regardless of which day of the week it fell on.

29. Lev 23:15–16; Matt 28:1–6; Mark 16:1–6; Luke 24:1–6; John 20:1–2.

resurrection) *"when the day of Pentecost had come"* the Holy Spirit came down and filled Jesus' disciples (Acts 2:1–4). By sending the Holy Spirit, Christ fulfilled the true spiritual meaning and purpose of the Feast of Weeks, which commemorated the first fruits of the wheat harvest. Jesus had compared himself to a grain of wheat and said that *"if it dies, it bears much fruit"* (John 12:24). The pouring out of the Holy Spirit on Pentecost led to the great "first fruits" of the harvest of souls into the kingdom—three thousand on that day alone (Acts 2:37–41). The first fruits of the harvest represented the entire harvest (see Num 18:29–30). In other words, giving the first fruits to God at the Feast showed the people's reliance on God to provide the rest of the harvest. In Rom 8:23 Paul says that we have *"the first fruits of the Spirit."* In 2 Cor 1:22; 5:5; Eph 1:13–14; 5:5, Paul says that—like the first fruits of the wheat harvest given on the day of Pentecost—the Holy Spirit has been given to us as a "pledge" or "guarantee" of our resurrection, entire sanctification, and the presence of the Lord with us forever. As a result, Jas 1:18 says, *"In the exercise of His will He brought us forth by the word of truth, so that we would be a kind of first fruits among His creatures."*

Over time, the meaning of the Feast of Weeks was transformed. It became a commemoration of the giving of the Torah (Law) on Mount Sinai.[30] Just as God *"descended upon [Mount Sinai] in fire"* (Exod 19:18), so on Pentecost *"there appeared to the disciples tongues as of fire distributing themselves, and they rested on each one of them"* (Acts 2:3). More importantly, Jewish writer Tracey Rich says that counting the fifty days before the Feast of Weeks (Lev 23:15–16) "is intended to remind us of the link between Passover, which commemorates the Exodus, and Shavu'ot [Weeks], which commemorates the giving of the Torah. It reminds us that the redemption from slavery was not complete until we received the Torah."[31]

This purpose of the Feast of Weeks was fulfilled in a far deeper way by the giving of the Holy Spirit on Pentecost as opposed to the giving of the Torah. The Law (Torah)—like the Holy Spirit (see John 14:26; 16:8, 13)—tells us how we should live, but the Law does not give us the power to do what we should. As Paul argues in Gal 3:21–25, the Law was never able to impart life and was only a temporary guardian until Christ came who would give us his righteousness. We receive Christ—and the righteousness he imputes to us—by faith. But Christ knew that even faith on its own does not give us the transforming power we need to live holy lives. Consequently, he told the disciples to wait to receive the *"power when the Holy Spirit has come upon*

---

30. Rich, "Shavu'ot," n.p.; Malabuyo, "Gift," Waiting for the Gift. There may be a basis for this later tradition from the text of Exod 19:1–11; see Cassuto, *Commentary*, 229.

31. Rich, "Counting," n.p.

you" (Acts 1:8). That happened on the Day of Pentecost. When the Holy Spirit was poured out on Pentecost, our "redemption from slavery" truly became complete. The OT Law was external, written on tablets of stone. Now, the Holy Spirit lives inside us (Ezek 36:26–27; John 14:16–17), the law of Christ is written on our heart (Jer 31:33; Heb 8:10), and we ourselves are *"a letter of Christ . . . written not with ink but with the Spirit of the living God, not on tablets of stone but on tablets of human hearts"* (2 Cor 3:3). Linda Belleville summarizes, "With the coming of faith in Christ, the Law's function as guardian and custodian ceases and the Spirit becomes the internal guiding principle."[32]

JESUS FULFILLED THE FEAST OF TRUMPETS

The Feast of Trumpets was the first of the three Fall feasts. It was instituted in Lev 23:23–25; Num 29:1–6 as *"a reminder [or 'memorial']"* (Lev 23:24), but Scripture is silent as to what it was memorializing. Although both Lev 23:24 and Num 29:1 specify that the Feast of Trumpets was to take place on the first day of the *seventh month*, other ancient peoples "thought of the year beginning in the autumn, at the time of the late harvest. It is highly plausible, therefore, to see the Biblical festival as a harvest feast, marking the beginning of the agricultural year."[33] Hence, Trumpets became known as *Rosh Ha-Shanah* ("head of the year") and announced the civil new year and anticipated *Yom Kippur* (the Day of Atonement). The days between *Rosh Ha-Shanah* and *Yom Kippur* "are commonly known as the Days of Awe (*Yamim Noraim*) or the Days of Repentance. This is a time for serious introspection, a time to consider the sins of the previous year and repent before Yom Kippur."[34]

The Feast of Trumpets was fulfilled at Christ's first coming.[35] Trumpets' primary role was to announce a turning point in time—the beginning of the new year. Jesus' first coming did that. Jesus himself implicitly announced that in Luke 4:18–19 when he quoted from Isa 61:1–2 that he had been sent *"to proclaim the acceptable year of the Lord."* In Luke 4:21 he then declared, *"Today this Scripture has been fulfilled in your hearing."* The fact that Christ's

---

32. Belleville, "Under Law," 70.

33. Jacobs, *Guide*, 4.

34. Rich, "Days of Awe," n.p.

35. Many people speculate that Trumpets relates only to the second coming of Christ, because various passages indicate that the second coming and the resurrection of the dead will be heralded by angelic "trumpets" (see Matt 24:31; 1 Cor 15:52; 1 Thess 4:16). Other people say that Trumpets is somehow related to the "trumpet judgments" of Rev 8:1—9:21; 11:15–19. Both views overlook the points discussed in this section.

first coming marks a new time of human history is confirmed by the fact that his first coming marks the beginning of the "last days" which we are now in and which will continue until his return.[36] Second Cor 5:17 further confirms the "newness" that Christ brings by stating, *"Therefore, if anyone is in Christ, he is a new creature* [or, *'creation'*]; *the old things have passed away; behold, new things have come."*

The first coming of Jesus has changed time from BC ("before Christ") to AD (which is an abbreviation of the Latin *anno domini,* "in the year of our Lord"). Even those who do not use the BC and AD labels—but use the "Common Era" abbreviations, "BCE" and "CE"—are implicitly acknowledging the epoch-changing nature of Christ's first coming. The dates are the same as the BC and AD dates, but those using the BCE and CE abbreviations do not want to acknowledge that Jesus is, in fact, Lord.

Jesus fulfilled traditional Jewish reasons for blowing the *shofar* ("ram's horn trumpet") on the Feast of Trumpets. In AD 942, a famous Babylonian teacher, Saadi Gaon, listed ten reasons why the Jews blew the *shofar* during the Feast of Trumpets.[37] They all, directly or indirectly, relate to Christ:

- *God is acclaimed as King on the New Year.* Christ is the King of Kings and Lord of Lords and has all authority.[38] At his crucifixion, the sign placed over Jesus declared that Jesus is *"the king of the Jews."*[39]

- *Rosh Ha-Shanah is the beginning of the Ten Days of Penitence.* Christ fulfilled the Day of Atonement, to which the Ten Days of Penitence were directed.

- *The Torah was given on Sinai accompanied by the sound of the shofar.* Christ is the new law giver, greater than Moses (Matt 5:1–48).

- *The prophets compare their admonitions to the sound of the shofar.* Jesus is the prophet like Moses, who had been promised by God.[40]

- *The temple in Jerusalem was destroyed amid trumpet blasts, and at the new year the Jews look forward to the restoration of the ancient glories.* Jesus fulfilled and replaced both the temple and the nation itself.

---

36. See Acts 2:16–17; Heb 1:2; Jas 5:1–3; 1 Pet 1:20; 1 John 2:18.

37. Jacobs, *Guide*, 44–48.

38. Matt 28:18; Acts 2:36; Eph 1:20–22; Phil 2:9–11; Col 2:9–10; 1 Pet 3:22; Rev 17:14; 19:16.

39. Matt 27:37; Mark 15:26; Luke 23:28; John 19:19.

40. See Deut 18:15, 18–19; John 1:45; 6:14; Acts 3:20–23 and the discussion of "A Prophet like Moses" in chapter 5.

- *In Genesis 22 a ram was substituted for Isaac.* On Rosh Ha-Shanah, Jews remember the merit of their righteous ancestors by sounding the ram's horn to remind them that to give the self in service to God is the essence of true religion.[41] Jesus was our substitute, who paid the price for our sins.

- *Amos 3:6 asks, "Shall the shofar be blown in the city and the people not be afraid?"* Feelings of seriousness, reverence, and respect for life and for him who gave it are awakened by the sound of the *shofar.* Jesus sustains our lives and is *"the radiance of His glory and the exact representation of His nature, and upholds all things by the word of His power"* (Heb 1:3).

- *Zeph 1:16 speaks of Judgment Day as a "day of the shofar and alarm."* It is Christ who will judge both the living and the dead.[42] In a real sense that judgment has already occurred as a result of people's responses to Jesus (John 3:17–19), although that judgment will be finalized at the second coming.[43]

- *Isa 27:13 speaks of the shofar that will herald the coming of Messiah to bring the scattered ones of Israel back to their land.* Jesus is the Messiah (John 4:25–26). He has brought the new, true Israel to the "land" of their rest and salvation.

- *The shofar is to be sounded at the Resurrection.* Jesus is the resurrection and the life (John 11:25). Jesus' own resurrection is the *"first fruits"* of the general resurrection (1 Cor 15:22) which will occur *"at the last trumpet"* (1 Cor 15:51–52).

Two other, spiritual reasons have been advanced for Trumpets which, likewise, point to Christ and the church:

1. *The Lord's Supper.* Lev 23:24 said that the Feast of Trumpets was to be a "reminder" or "remembrance." That indicates that the event to be remembered had taken place before God called for this remembrance. The great event requiring memorialization, which itself was connected with the blowing of trumpets, was God's giving the Mosaic Covenant to the people on Mount Sinai: trumpets sounded, and God manifested himself in an awesome display of smoke, fire, thunder, and lightning (Exod

---

41. See the discussion concerning Issac in chapter 7.

42. Matt 7:22–23; John 5:22; Acts 10:42; 17:31; Rom 14:10; 2 Cor 5:10; 2 Tim 4:1; Jude 14–15; Rev 19:11.

43. Matt 13:24–30, 36–43, 47–50; 16:27; 25:31–46; John 12:48; Rom 2:1–16; 1 Cor 4:5; 2 Thess 1:6–10; Rev 22:12.

19:3–20). "At the Feast of Trumpets, the sound of the shofar ... reminds Israel that they are a people under covenant, a nation who has accepted the responsibilities of being God's people."[44] Although Trumpets is not specifically mentioned in the NT, it finds a New Covenant analog. Specifically, when we partake in the Lord's Supper—the "remembrance" established by Jesus (Luke 22:19; 1 Cor 11:24–25)—we remember the cataclysmic events of the Lord's death and resurrection, that we have received atonement for our sins, and that we have entered into the responsibilities of being New Covenant people.

2. *The witness of the church.* Trumpets in the OT were used for multiple purposes, including summoning the people, signaling triumph in war, announcing good news, praising the Lord, and sounding alarm.[45] The trumpet did not stand alone but was connected to the proclamation of the herald, warner, or worshippers.[46] John Sittema suggests that Trumpets was a type that finds its fulfillment in the "trumpet call" of the witness and preaching of the church.[47]

JESUS FULFILLED THE DAY OF ATONEMENT

All of the major elements of the rituals performed on the Day of Atonement were "types" that pointed to Christ: the rites were performed at the temple (Lev 16:23, 20, 33)—Christ is the true temple (John 1:14; 2:18–22); the high priest performed the rites (Lev 16:2–3, 32–33)—Christ is our high priest (Heb 4:14–15; 5:5–10; 8:1–6; 9:11; 10:21); a bull and a goat were sacrificed as sin offerings and their blood was shed (Lev 16:8–9, 15)—Christ was sacrificed for our sins and his blood was shed (Heb 7:27; 9:12, 14, 26, 28); the high priest entered the holy of holies behind the veil (Lev 16:12–15)—Christ's body is the true veil (Heb 10:19–20) and he entered the true holy of holies (Heb 8:1–2; 9:11–12, 24); the blood of the goat was sprinkled on the mercy seat (Lev 16:14–15)—Christ is the mercy seat (Rom 3:25; compare Exod 25:17, LXX); the sins of the nation were imputed to the scapegoat (Lev 16:20–21)—Christ bore our sins (Isa 53:4–5; Heb 9:28; 1 Pet 2:24) and

---

44. Jews for Jesus, "Feast," n.p.

45. See, e.g., Num 10:1–10; Josh 6:4–20; Judg 6:34; 7:16–22; 1 Sam 13:3; 2 Sam 6:15; 15:10; 20:22; 1 Kgs 1:34–39; 2 Chron 5:13; 7:6; 29:27–28; Neh 4:20; Ps 98:6; 150:3; Jer 4:5; Ezek 33:1–9; Amos 3:6.

46. See Josh 6:5, 20; Judg 6:34; 7:16–20; 1 Sam 13:3; 2 Sam 6:15; 15:10; 1 Kgs 1:34, 39; 2 Chron 5:13; 7:6; 29:27–28; Ps 98:6; Jer 4:5; Ezek 33:3, 7.

47. Sittema, *Meeting Jesus*, 99.

became sin for us (2 Cor 5:21); the scapegoat was led into the wilderness (Lev 16:21–22)—Christ was led into the ultimate wilderness of separation from God (Isa 53:8; Matt 27:46); the bodies of the slain animals were burned outside the camp (Heb 13:11)[48]—Christ *"suffered outside the gate"* (Heb 13:12).

Leviticus 16–17 stresses the importance of sacrificial blood to make atonement for sin. The sacrificial animal's blood was necessary for the high priest to bring into the holy of holies and sprinkle on the mercy seat. Hebrews 7–10 demonstrates that Christ's sacrifice on the cross was what the Day of Atonement had always pointed to. Christ's own blood infinitely exceeded in value the blood of animals: The OT rites, using animal blood, had to be endlessly repeated (Heb 10:1–4); Christ's sacrifice involved his own blood and only had to be done once (Heb 7:27; 9:25–26). Further, his blood is "the polar opposite of anything physical or temporary ([Heb] 9:12). The redeeming and purifying effect of his blood is interior and eternal rather than external and impermanent ([Heb] 9:12–14; cf. 10:1–4)."[49]

The essential element on the Day of Atonement was the high priest's entering God's presence in the holy of holies, behind the curtain, and applying the sacrificial blood to the mercy seat to purify the holy things and the nation from pollution and sin (Lev 16:2–19). By contrast, through his resurrection and ascension, Christ entered *"heaven itself"* (Heb 9:24; see also Heb 4:14; 8:1–2), into *"the inner shrine behind the curtain"* (Heb 6:19–20, RSV). Thus, Christ acts both as victim and as high priest: as victim, his blood was perfect because he led a perfect life and was without sin (Heb 9:12–14; 10:4–10); as high priest, he was also perfect because he did not have to atone for himself (Heb 7:26–27; 9:7). The high priest sprinkled the blood in the holy of holies behind the veil; Jesus died in full public view, and at his death *"the veil of the temple was torn in two from top to bottom"* (Matt 27:51). These facts signify that Jesus achieved atonement for sins for everyone who has faith in him, instead of just covering the sins of the nation for a year.

The scapegoat was unique to the Day of Atonement. The blood of one goat was brought into the Holy of Holies, the sins of the nation were symbolically transferred onto the scapegoat, and it was "driven to the furthest point from God (the wilderness)."[50] On the cross, Jesus bore our sins (Isa 53:4–5), and *"By oppression and judgment He was taken away [and] was cut off out of the land of the living"* (Isa 53:8). The essence of hell is separation from God. Jesus' cry from the cross, *"My God, My God, why have you*

---

48. See Edersheim, *Temple*, 324.
49. Nelson, "He Offered Himself," 256.
50. Williamson, *Sealed*, 110.

forsaken me?" (Matt 27:46; Mark 15:34), indicates that he was experiencing hell itself. The scapegoat's being driven into the wilderness pales in comparison to Jesus' being driven from the presence of the Father.

Heb 9:9 says that the gifts and sacrifices offered at the temple—including the sacrifices on the Day of Atonement—*"cannot make the worshiper perfect in conscience."* On the other hand, Heb 9:14 says, *"How much more will the blood of Christ, who through the eternal Spirit offered Himself without blemish to God, cleanse your conscience from dead works to serve the living God?"* In other words, the sacrifices offered on the Day of Atonement could not make a person clean *on the inside*. Only Christ can bring about true inner change.

JESUS FULFILLED THE FEAST OF TABERNACLES

The Feast of Tabernacles (Booths) was the last of the fall feasts. It lasted a week and commemorated the wandering in the wilderness. It also celebrated the completion of the fall harvest. To commemorate the wandering in the wilderness, the people were to make and live in temporary booths (tabernacles) during the week of the feast.[51] The Feast of Tabernacles was fulfilled by Christ at his first coming.

John 1:14 says that *"the Word [i.e., Jesus] became flesh and dwelt among us."* The word "dwelt" is the verbal form (*skēnoō*) of the word for "tabernacle" (*skēnē*). Thus, the NASB has a note to John 1:14 that says, "or *tabernacled*; i.e., lived temporarily." Just as the booths the people made were not fancy or attractive structures, there was nothing about Jesus' earthly appearance that would attract us to him (Isa 53:2).

The Feast of Tabernacles commemorated God's delivering Israel from bondage in Egypt and their wandering in the wilderness on the way to the promised land (Lev 23:42–43). Jesus not only delivers people from physical bondage, but from spiritual slavery to sin and death so that *"we too might walk in newness of life"* (John 1:29; Rom 6:3–23). Jesus was tempted by Satan in the wilderness just as Israel was tempted (Matt 4:1–11; Luke 4:1–13). However, unlike Israel, Jesus did not succumb to the temptations. When he was tempted, Jesus even responded to Satan by deliberately quoting from Moses' summary of the history of Israel's history in the wilderness (Deut 8:3; 6:13, 16). Thus, in his life Jesus fulfilled everything of which Tabernacles was a "type."

At the time Jesus lived on earth, a central part of the celebration of the Feast of Tabernacles in Jerusalem was a "water pouring" ceremony in which

---

51. Exod 23:16–17; 34:22–23; Lev 23:33–43; Num 29:12–38; Deut 16:13–15.

the priests would fill a golden flask from the Pool of Siloam and then pour out water and wine to the Lord at the temple.[52] "The Jews referred to water from springs or streams fit for drinking as 'living water.' Living water was considered the most superior form of water for ritual purification."[53] The ceremony evoked God's provision of water in the desert (Exod 17:1–6), to his pouring out of his Spirit in the last days, and symbolically to the messianic age when water would flow from Jerusalem to the eastern and western seas (Zech 14:8). That is the context—at the temple during the Feast of Tabernacles itself (John 7:2, 37)—in which Jesus *"stood and cried out, saying, 'If anyone is thirsty, let him come to Me and drink. He who believes in Me, as the Scripture said, From his innermost being will flow rivers of living water.'"* (John 7:37–38) Jesus is saying that he is the one who provides the true, living water; he is the fulfillment of the Feast of Tabernacles.

At the time Jesus lived on earth, another ceremony was performed at the temple to celebrate the Feast of Tabernacles: four huge lamps were lit, and at night the people celebrated holding burning torches; the light from the temple area shone all over Jerusalem.[54] It is in that context that Jesus said, *"I am the Light of the world; he who follows Me will not walk in the darkness, but will have the Light of life"* (John 8:12).[55] Again, Jesus was saying that the Feast of Tabernacles was fulfilled in him.[56]

The connection of the Feast of Tabernacles with the harvest and the completion of Israel's mission of gathering the nations to the Lord (Zech 14:16–21) also finds its fulfillment in Jesus. As we have seen, Jesus *is* the new, true Israel. John 11:52 makes clear that Jesus is gathering his people now.[57] His gathering does not involve geographical relocation to Israel or Jerusalem. Instead, Jesus said that his being lifted up by his death on the cross *"will draw all men to Myself"* (John 12:32). The harvest is people *"from every tribe and tongue and people and nation"* in the world.[58] He said the fields now *"are white for harvest"* (John 4:35), and *"the harvest is plentiful, but the workers are few. Therefore beseech the Lord of the harvest to send out workers into his harvest."* (Matt 9:37–38; Luke 10:2) In the "Great

---

52. Carson, *Gospel*, 321–22; Hillyer, "First Peter," 46–48.

53. Satterfield, "John 7–9," 5.

54. Carson, *Gospel*, 337; Hillyer, "First Peter," 49–50.

55. The earliest Greek NT manuscripts do not include John 7:53—8:11. Instead, John 8:12 immediately follows after John 7:52. Thus, the context of 8:12 appears to be connected with the Feast of Tabernacles. Carson, *Gospel*, 333–37.

56. See also John 3:19–21; 1 John 1:5–7.

57. Matt 3:12; 12:30; 13:30, 47–48; 18:20; 22:10; 23:37; 24:31; Mark 13:27; Luke 3:17; 11:23; 13:34.

58. Matt 9:36; Luke 10:1; Rev 5:9; 7:9.

Commission" (Matt 28:18–20) Jesus commissioned his followers to go into all the world and make disciples. Thus, believers are both the workers in the harvest fields and the "first fruits" of the harvest (Jas 1:18; Rev 14:4).

Because it was related to the completion of the harvest, the Feast of Tabernacles also took on an eschatological meaning. Tabernacles "looked forward to the final joyful harvest, when Israel's mission on earth should be completed by gathering all the nations of the world to the Lord, as prophesied by Zechariah (14:16)."[59] In his parable of the wheat and the tares, Jesus said that *"the harvest is the end of the age"* (Matt 13:24–30, 36–43). Believers now are living in their temporary tabernacles, awaiting their permanent, glorified, eternal bodies (see 2 Cor 5:1–4; 2 Pet 1:14). When Jesus comes again, the age of temporary tabernacles will be over, the harvest will be complete; the judgment will reveal who are the wheat and who are the tares.

JESUS FULFILLED THE SABBATH YEAR

During the Sabbath year, the land was to lie fallow *"so that the needy of your people may eat"* (Exod 23:11). Slaves were to be freed (Exod 21:2) and debts forgiven (Deut 15:1–2). God specifically cautioned the people not to have a hard heart as the year of remission approached but to give generously to the poor (Deut 15:7–11).

Jesus fulfilled all of the requirements of the Sabbath year. With respect to the fallow land, so that the needy could eat, just as God promised to bless the harvest of the sixth year so that it would be sufficient for three years (Lev 25:20–22), so Jesus miraculously multiplied a few fish and loaves of bread to feed thousands of people.[60] Jesus *is* the *"bread of life"* (John 6:35, 48), and those who feast on him will never hunger or thirst or die.[61] With respect to slaves being freed, we all were *"slaves to sin"* and *"slaves to impurity and to lawlessness"* (Rom 6:17–20). As a result of Christ's sacrifice of himself in our place, we have been *"freed from sin and enslaved to God . . . resulting in sanctification, and the outcome, eternal life"* (Rom 6:22; see also John 8:31–32). With respect to debts being cancelled, Jesus has cancelled the greatest debt that anyone could possibly have—our debt of sin that results in our death: *"When you were dead in your transgressions and the uncircumcision of your flesh, He made you alive together with Him, having forgiven us all our transgressions, having canceled out the certificate of debt consisting of decrees*

---

59. Hillyer, "First Peter," 40. Probably in light of its harvest connection, Zechariah 14 was read on the first day of the feast. Carson, *Gospel*, 322; Balfour, "Jewishness," 376.

60. Matt 14:13–21; 15:32–38; Mark 6:30–44; 8:1–10; Luke 9:10–17; John 6:1–14.

61. John 4:13–14; 6:41–58; 7:37–38.

against us, which was hostile to us; and He has taken it out of the way, having nailed it to the cross" (Col 2:13–14).

The particular concern of the Sabbath year was for the poor and needy. In connection with the Sabbath year, Deut 15:11 says, *"For the poor will never cease to be in the land; therefore I command you, saying, 'You shall freely open your hand to your brother, to your needy and poor in your land.'"* Jesus identified himself as the true "Sabbath year" by quoting or alluding to that verse in connection with himself: *"For you always have the poor with you; but you do not always have Me"* (Matt 26:11; see also Mark 14:7; John 12:8). Jesus did not just "freely open his hand" to his brother, but on the cross opened both arms, freely giving all he had, including his life, for those who were so poor and needy that they could do nothing to save themselves. And he did this not just for his "brothers" but for his *enemies*!

JESUS FULFILLED THE YEAR OF JUBILEE

The Sabbath year and the Year of Jubilee are related. They are discussed together in Leviticus 25. The theme of the year of Jubilee was liberty: *"You shall consecrate the fiftieth year and proclaim liberty throughout the land to all its inhabitants"* (Lev 25:10, ESV). Debts were to be cancelled, slaves were to be freed, and each parcel of land was to be returned to its original owner (Lev 25:8–55). OT Israel never celebrated the Year of Jubilee—but Jesus inaugurated the real Jubilee.

Jesus announced that he was inaugurating the Year of Jubilee at the beginning of his public ministry. In Luke 4:16–21, in his hometown of Nazareth, Jesus spoke in the synagogue and read from Isa 61:1–2, a passage that alludes to the Year of Jubilee. He quoted, *"The Spirit of the Lord is upon me, because He appointed me to preach the gospel to the poor. He has sent me to proclaim release to the captives, and recovery of sight to the blind, to set free those who are oppressed, to proclaim the favorable year of the Lord"* (Luke 4:18–19). The word "release" in Isa 61:1 (Luke 4:18) is the same word found in Lev 25:10. The verbs in this passage (*"preach the gospel to the poor," "proclaim release to the captives," "set free [the] oppressed"*) refer to "the practice of the jubilee year authorized in Leviticus 25, when all properties lost in economic transactions will be returned in order to permit a stable, functioning community. Thus, the series of verbs is taken to be an announcement of the jubilee."[62] *"The favorable year of the Lord"* alludes to the Year of Jubilee which is "now made symbolic by his [Jesus'] own saving acts."[63] When Jesus

---

62. Brueggemann, *Isaiah 40–66*, 214.

63. Marshall, *Gospel*, 184; see also Motyer, *Isaiah*, 426; Bock, *Luke 1:1—9:50*, 410;

quoted Isa 61:1–2 and then said, *"Today this Scripture has been fulfilled in your hearing"* (Luke 4:21), in substance he was saying, "I am the fulfillment of what that always pointed to; in me the ultimate Jubilee is now here."

Immediately upon leaving Nazareth and for the rest of his earthly ministry, in both word and deed, Jesus demonstrated the truth of what he had told the synagogue by preaching the gospel to the poor, proclaiming release to the captives, restoring sight to the blind, and setting free the oppressed.[64] While Isaiah prophesied an anointed one proclaiming deliverance, Jesus actually brings that deliverance and brings it in a far deeper and more permanent way than Isaiah could have envisioned: he frees people from their spiritual blindness and from their captivity to, and oppression by, sin. In Luke and elsewhere, the blind have both literal and symbolic meaning. Thus, while Jesus literally healed the blind, salvation also is called "seeing" (Luke 2:29–32; 3:6). The poor similarly may have a broader and spiritual meaning (compare Matt 5:3 and Luke 6:20). In other words, physical healing and deliverance were the outward, visible signs of the vastly more important spiritual healing and deliverance Jesus brings.

What was unique about the Year of Jubilee was that each parcel of land was to be returned to its original owner. The "redemption of the land" in the Year of Jubilee (Lev 25:24) reflected the fact that *"the land is Mine [and] you are but aliens and sojourners with Me"* (Lev 25:23). This rationale points us to the fact that *we* are not the ultimate creators, sustainers, or owners of the land—God is. This should point us to Jesus, who is the agent through whom God created the world (Heb 1:2), who *"upholds all things [including the earth] by the word of His power"* (Heb 1:3), and who has *"all authority . . . in heaven and on earth"* (Matt 28:18; see also Eph 1:18–23). The consummation of the Jubilee, when *"the creation itself also will be set free from its slavery to corruption"* (Rom 8:21), will occur when Christ returns (see Acts 3:19–21; 2 Pet 3:3–15; Rev 21:1–5).

JESUS FULFILLED THE FESTIVALS OF PURIM AND HANUKKAH

Although they were not part of the system of feasts set forth in the Mosaic Law, both Purim and Hanukkah are important in Jewish life and have important spiritual implications which Jesus fulfills.

Lenski, *Interpretation*, 252.

64. See Luke 4:31–44; 5:12–26; 6:6–10, 17–26; 7:1–15, 36–50; 8:1–2, 22–56; 9:12–17; 10:17–24; 13:10–17; 14:1–6; 17:11–19; 18:35–43.

1. *Purim.* Purim celebrates the Jewish victory over Haman as a result of Esther's going into the king's inner court at the risk of her life and inviting the king and Haman to a banquet at which she revealed the plot against the Jews; that caused the king to hang Haman and permit the Jews to defend themselves (Est 4:1—9:17). Timothy Keller notes that "Jesus is the true and better Esther, who didn't just risk losing an earthly palace but lost the ultimate heavenly one, who didn't just risk his life but gave his life—to save his people."[65]

2. *Hanukkah.* Hanukkah celebrates the rededication of the temple during the Maccabean Revolt and is celebrated for eight days based on the (perhaps legendary) account that, although there was only enough sacred oil to light the menorah in the temple for one day, it miraculously burned for eight days until additional oil could be obtained. As was discussed in chapter 11, Jesus is the true temple. Additionally, Rabbi S. M. Lehrman states, "The celebration of Hanukkah calls attention to the significant place occupied by lights in our faith. . . . In Messianic times, the Lord alone will be our everlasting light [Isa 60:19–20]."[66] Jesus said, "*I am the light of the world*" (John 8:12); he is the "*light of revelation to the Gentiles*" (Luke 2:32) and is "*the radiance of His [God's] glory*" (Heb 1:3). The prophecy of Isaiah referred to by Rabbi Lehrman is specifically fulfilled on the new earth by God and Christ. Rev 21:23 says, "*The city has no need of the sun or of the moon to shine on it, for the glory of God has illumined it, and its lamp is the Lamb*" (see also Rev 22:5). When Hanukkah is celebrated, a special nine-branched candelabra is used; the middle candle is known as the "servant" candle.[67] Jesus is the prophesied "Servant of the Lord"[68] and said, "*the Son of Man did not come to be served, but to serve, and to give His life a ransom for many*" (Matt 20:28). Finally, "the date of the Feast of the Dedication [Hanukkah]—the 25th of Chislev—seems to have been adopted by the ancient Church as that of the birth of our blessed Lord—Christmas—the Dedication of the true Temple, which is the body of Jesus."[69]

---

65. Keller, *Preaching*, 78.
66. Lehrman, *Guide*, 19.
67. Chosen People Ministries, *Gospel*, 11.
68. See chapter 6—Christ and Church are the prophesied Servant of the Lord.
69. Edersheim, *Temple*, 334.

Appendix 1

Jesus Is Fully God and Fully Man

Because Jesus Christ is at the very heart of the Bible, is its main character, and holds the biblical story together, it is vital to have a clear understanding of who he is. We have seen indications, in his pre-incarnate OT appearances, prophecy, and typology, that Jesus is both a human being but also, at the same time, he is God. It is important to explicitly consider the identity of Jesus, why that is important, and the implications of the fact that Jesus is both fully God and fully man.

THE IMPORTANCE OF CHRISTOLOGY

Historic Christianity espouses "the Christology stated in The Apostle's Creed, refined in the Nicean-Constantinople Creed, elaborated in the Chalcedonian Creed, and finally summed up in the Creed of Athanasius. . . . Christology is so central to Christian theology that to alter Christology is to alter all else. . . . To abandon historic Christology is to abandon the concept of heresy. But if there is no heresy it follows logically that there is no truth."[1]

---

1. Ramm, *Evangelical*, 15–17.

Appendix 1

HISTORIC, ORTHODOX CHRISTOLOGY AS STATED IN THE HISTORIC, ECUMENICAL CREEDS

Apostles' Creed (c. 2nd century AD)

I believe in God the Father, Almighty, Maker of heaven and earth, and in Jesus Christ, his only begotten Son, our Lord; who was conceived by the Holy Ghost, born of the Virgin Mary, suffered under Pontius Pilate, was crucified, dead and buried; He descended into hell; the third day he rose again from the dead; He ascended into heaven, and sits at the right hand of God the Father Almighty; from thence he shall come to judge the quick and the dead.

I believe in the Holy Ghost. I believe in the holy catholic church,[2] the communion of saints, the forgiveness of sins, the resurrection of the body, and the life everlasting. Amen.

Nicene-Constantinople Creed (AD 325/381)

I believe in one God, the Father Almighty, Maker of heaven and earth, and of all things visible and invisible, and in one Lord Jesus Christ, the only-begotten Son of God, begotten of the Father before all worlds; God of God, Light of Light, very God of very God; begotten, not made, being of one substance with the Father, by whom all things were made. Who, for us men for our salvation, came down from heaven, and was incarnate by the Holy Spirit of the virgin Mary, and was made man; and was crucified also for us under Pontius Pilate; He suffered and was buried; and the third day He rose again, according to the Scriptures; and ascended into heaven, and sits on the right hand of the Father; and He shall come again, with glory, to judge the quick and the dead; whose kingdom shall have no end.

And I believe in the Holy Ghost, the Lord and Giver of Life; who proceeds from the Father [and the Son]; who with the Father and the Son together is worshipped and glorified; who spoke by the prophets.

And I believe one holy catholic and apostolic Church. I acknowledge one baptism for the remission of sins; and I look for the resurrection of the dead, and the life of the world to come. Amen.

---

2. The term "catholic" means "universal," and must be distinguished from the modern Roman Catholic Church. "Catholic" is the term generally used for approximately the first 1000 years of church history to describe the orthodox Christian faith, particularly as that faith was defined in the universal creeds and developed at the ecumenical councils.

Chalcedonian Creed (AD 451)

We, then, following the holy Fathers, all with one consent, teach people to confess one and the same Son, our Lord Jesus Christ, the same perfect in Godhead and also perfect in manhood; truly God and truly man, of a reasonable [rational] soul and body; consubstantial [co-essential] with the Father according to the Godhead, and consubstantial with us according to the Manhood; in all things like unto us, without sin; begotten before all ages of the Father according to the Godhead, and in these latter days, for us and for our salvation, born of the Virgin Mary, the Mother of God, according to the Manhood; one and the same Christ, Son, Lord, only begotten, to be acknowledged in two natures, inconfusedly, unchangeably, indivisibly, inseparably; the distinction of natures being by no means taken away by the union, but rather the property of each nature being preserved, and concurring in one Person and one Subsistence, not parted or divided into two persons, but one and the same Son, and only begotten God, the Word, the Lord Jesus Christ; as the prophets from the beginning [have declared] concerning Him, and the Lord Jesus Christ Himself has taught us, and the Creed of the holy Fathers has handed down to us.

Athanasian Creed (c. late 5th–early 6th century AD)

Whosoever will be saved, before all things it is necessary that he hold the Catholic Faith. Which Faith except every one do keep whole and undefiled; without doubt he shall perish everlastingly. And the Catholic Faith is this: That we worship one God in Trinity, and Trinity in Unity; Neither confounding the Persons; nor dividing the Essence. For there is one Person of the Father; another of the Son; and another of the Holy Ghost. But the Godhead of the Father, of the Son, and of the Holy Ghost, is all one; the Glory equal, the Majesty coeternal. Such as the Father is; such is the Son; and such is the Holy Ghost. The Father uncreated; the Son uncreated; and the Holy Ghost uncreated. The Father unlimited; the Son unlimited; and the Holy Ghost unlimited. The Father eternal; the Son eternal; and the Holy Ghost eternal. And yet they are not three eternals; but one eternal. As also there are not three uncreated; nor three infinites, but one uncreated; and one infinite. So likewise the Father is Almighty; the Son Almighty; and the Holy Ghost Almighty. And yet they are not three Almighties; but one Almighty. So the Father is God; the Son is God; and the Holy Ghost is God. And yet they are not three Gods; but one God. So likewise the Father is Lord; the Son Lord; and the Holy Ghost Lord. And yet not three Lords; but one Lord.

For like as we are compelled by the Christian verity; to acknowledge every Person by himself to be God and Lord; so are we forbidden by the Catholic Religion; to say, There are three Gods, or three Lords. The Father is made of none; neither created, nor begotten. The Son is of the Father alone; not made, nor created; but begotten. The Holy Ghost is of the Father and of the Son; neither made, nor created, nor begotten; but proceeding. So there is one Father, not three Fathers; one Son, not three Sons; one Holy Ghost, not three Holy Ghosts. And in this Trinity none is before, or after another; none is greater, or less than another. But the whole three Persons are coeternal, and coequal. So that in all things, as aforesaid; the Unity in Trinity, and the Trinity in Unity, is to be worshipped. He therefore that will be saved, let him thus think of the Trinity.

Furthermore it is necessary to everlasting salvation; that he also believe faithfully the Incarnation of our Lord Jesus Christ. For the right Faith is, that we believe and confess; that our Lord Jesus Christ, the Son of God, is God and Man; God, of the Essence of the Father; begotten before the worlds; and Man, of the Essence of his Mother, born in the world. Perfect God; and perfect Man, of a reasonable soul and human flesh subsisting. Equal to the Father, as touching his Godhead; and inferior to the Father as touching his Manhood. Who although he is God and Man; yet he is not two, but one Christ. One; not by conversion of the Godhead into flesh; but by assumption of the Manhood into God. One altogether; not by confusion of Essence; but by unity of Person. For as the reasonable soul and flesh is one man; so God and Man is one Christ; Who suffered for our salvation; descended into hell; rose again the third day from the dead. He ascended into heaven, he sitteth on the right hand of the God the Father Almighty, from whence he will come to judge the quick and the dead. At whose coming all men will rise again with their bodies; And shall give account for their own works. And they that have done good shall go into life everlasting; and they that have done evil, into everlasting fire. This is the Catholic Faith; which except a man believe truly and firmly, he cannot be saved.

JESUS CHRIST IS FULLY GOD AND FULLY MAN: BIBLICAL EVIDENCE

Jesus Christ is fully God

Jesus was miraculously conceived by the Holy Spirit and born of a virgin (Matt 1:18–25; Luke 1:26–38). Jesus had miraculous powers: He miraculously healed people.³ He cast out demons.⁴ He gave others authority over spirits and diseases.⁵ He could read minds.⁶ He raised the dead.⁷ He miraculously fed multitudes of people.⁸ He could walk on water (Matt 14:22–33; Mark 6:45–51; John 6:16–21). He caused others to walk on water (Matt 14:28–31). He had authority over nature and the weather.⁹ He could turn water into wine (John 2:1–11). He had extraordinary knowledge and wisdom.¹⁰ The people living in Jesus' day, like people living in our day, knew that five loaves of bread and two fish cannot feed 5000 people, that great storms cannot be stopped simply at the word of a man, that many sicknesses and infirmities cannot be healed even by the best doctors, and that dead people stay dead.

The same names, titles, and other attributes that are applied to God in the OT or NT are applied to Jesus in the NT. Sometimes a passage which applied to God is alluded to or directly quoted as applying to Jesus (in the following table, $^{x,\,y,\,z}$ indicate direct quotes).

Name/Title/Attribute	Applied to God	Applied to Jesus
I AM	Exod 3:13–14	John 8:24, 28, 58; 18:5–6
Lord	Isa 40:3^x; 45:23–24^y; Joel 2:32^z	Mark 1:2–4^x; Phil 2:10–11^y; Acts 2:36; Rom 10:13^z
God	Ps 45:6–7^x	Heb 1:8–9^x; John 1:1, 18; 20:28; 2 Pet 1:1
First and Last	Isa 41:4; 44:6; 48:12	Rev 1:17; 2:8; 22:13
Alpha and Omega	Rev 1:8^x; 21:5–6^x	Rev 22:13^x
Savior	Isa 43:3, 11; 1 Tim 4:10	Matt 1:21; Luke 2:11; John 4:42; Titus 2:13

3. Matt 8:1–17; 9:1–8, 20–22, 27–31; 12:9–15, 22; 14:35–36; 15:29–31; 19:1–2; 20:29–34; 21:14; Mark 1:29–34, 40–42; 2:1–12; 3:1–5, 10; 5:25–34; 6:5, 53–56; 7:31–35; 8:22–25; 10:46–52; Luke 4:38–41; 5:12–15, 17–26; 6:6–10, 17–19; 7:1–10, 21–22; 8:43–48; 13:10–13; 14:1–4; 18:35–43; 22:50–51; John 4:46–54; 5:2–9; 9:1–7; Acts 10:38.

4. Matt 8:28–34; 9:32–33; 12:22–29; 15:21–28; 17:14–18; Mark 1:23–28, 34, 39; 3:11, 22–27; 5:1–13; 7:24–30; 9:17–27; Luke 4:31–36, 41; 8:26–36; 9:37–42; 11:14–22.

5. Matt 10:1; Mark 6:7; Luke 9:1; 10:17–19.

6. Matt 9:4; 12:25; Mark 2:8; Luke 5:22; 6:8; 9:46–48; John 13:10–11.

7. Matt 9:18, 23–25; Mark 5:35–42; Luke 7:11–15; 8:49–55; John 11:11–44.

8. Matt 14:13–21; 15:32–38; Mark 6:33–44; 8:1–9; Luke 9:12–17; John 6:1–13.

9. Matt 8:23–27; 21:18–19; Mark 4:35–41; 11:12–14, 20–21; Luke 8:22–25.

10. Matt 13:54; John 1:48; 2:24–25; 4:16–19, 28–29; 6:64; 13:10–11; 16:30; 18:4; 21:17; 1 Cor 1:24; Col 2:2–3; Rev 2:23; 5:12.

Name/Title/Attribute	Applied to God	Applied to Jesus
Judge	Gen 18:25; Ps 50:4-6; 96:13	John 5:22; 2 Cor 5:10; 2 Tim 4:1
King	Ps 95:3	Rev 17:14; 19:16
King of Israel	Isa 43:15; 44:6; Zeph 3:15	John 1:49; 12:13
Light	Ps 27:1; Isa 60:20; Mic 7:8	John 1:4-5, 9; 3:19; 8:12; 9:5
Rock	Deut 32:4; 2 Sam 22:32; Ps 89:26	1 Cor 10:4; 1 Pet 2:4-8
Bridegroom	Isa 62:5	Matt 9:15; Mark 2:19-20; Luke 5:34-35
Husband	Isa 54:5; Hos 2:16	Mark 2:18-19; 2 Cor 11:2; Rev 21:2
Shepherd	Ps 23:1; 80:1; Isa 40:11	John 10:11, 16; Heb 13:20; 1 Pet 2:25; 5:4
Creator	Gen 1:1; Ps 102:25-27^x; Isa 40:28	John 1:3, 10; Col 1:16; Heb 1:10-12^x
Giver of life	Deut 32:39; 1 Sam 2:6; Ps 36:9	John 5:22; 10:28; 11:25
Searches hearts & minds	1 Chron 28:9; Ps 7:9; 139:23; Jer 17:10	Rev 2:23
Rewards according to their deeds	Ps 62:12^x; Jer 17:10; 32:19	Matt 16:27^x; Rev 2:23

Jesus claimed to have the attributes of God and in fact has them: He claimed to be pre-existent, i.e., to have existed before he became a man (John 8:58; 17:5, 24) and is in fact pre-existent.[11] He claimed to come from the Father in heaven[12] and in fact did so.[13] He created the world.[14] He claimed to be the only one who knows the Father and can reveal the Father (Matt 11:27; John 6:46; 17:25); that is true (John 1:18; Heb 1:1-2; 1 John 5:20). He claimed to have the power to give people eternal life[15] and in fact does so.[16] He claimed to be the author of life itself (John 11:25) and in fact is (John 1:4;

---

11. John 1:1-2, 14-15, 30; 8:58; 1 Cor 8:6; Phil 2:6-7; Col 1:15-17; Heb 1:2; 1 John 2:13-14.

12. John 3:13; 5:23-24; 6:29, 32-39, 41-42, 46, 50-51, 57-58, 62; 7:33; 8:23, 42; 11:41-42; 16:5, 27-28; 17:3, 5, 8, 18, 23, 25.

13. John 3:31; 13:3; 29-30; 1 Cor 15:47; 1 John 4:9-10, 14.

14. John 1:3, 10; Rom 11:36; 1 Cor 8:6; Eph 3:9; Col 1:15-17; Heb 1:2, 10.

15. John 3:16; 4:14; 5:25-29, 40; 6:27, 32-40, 44, 47-58, 68; 10:10, 27-28; 11:25-26; 14:6, 19; 17:1-3; Rev 1:18.

16. Rom 6:23; 2 Tim 1:10; 1 John 5:11-13, 20; Rev 21:27.

Jesus Is Fully God and Fully Man

5:26; Rev 1:18). He holds the world together (Col 1:17; Heb 1:3). He claimed to have all authority[17] and in fact has all authority and rules as King of Kings and Lord of Lords.[18] He says he will judge the world[19] and in fact will do so.[20]

Jesus lived a perfectly holy and sinless life and is the perfect manifestation of the Father.[21] He taught with divine authority. He would quote God's Word (*"you have heard that it was said"*) but then clarify, modify, extend, deepen, or revoke it *on his own authority* by saying *"but I say to you."*[22] He equated his own words with the law of God and said that his words will never pass away (compare Matt 5:18; 24:35). The Bible says that God sends the prophets (2 Chron 36:15; Jer 26:5; Luke 11:49–51); to show that he is God come to earth, Jesus said that he was the one sending the prophets (Matt 23:34–35). He claimed to send and baptize with the Holy Spirit (Luke 24:49; John 15:26; 16:7; 20:22); he in fact does so.[23] He knows and can foretell the future.[24] He is the Lord of the Sabbath (Matt 12:8; Mark 2:28; Luke 6:5). "For Jesus to give an authoritative interpretation of the Sabbath, which originated in the Ten Commandments, is virtually to teach with the identical authority of God. He speaks with the same authority as the One who originally gave the law (cf. Mark 2:28, Luke 6:5)."[25]

---

17. Matt 11:27; 19:28; 26:64; 28:18; Mark 14:62; Luke 10:22; 22:29–30, 69; John 17:2; 18:36–37

18. Luke 1:32–33; 2:11; 19:37–38; 23:42; John 3:31; 13:3; Acts 2:30–36; 5:31; 10:36; Rom 9:5; 14:9; 1 Cor 15:23–28; Eph 1:20–22; Phil 2:9–11; Col 2:10, 15; 1 Tim 6:15–16; 2 Tim 4:8; Heb 2:7–8; 10:12–13; 1 Pet 3:22; Rev 1:5; 5:12; 11:15; 12:10; 14:14; 17:14; 19:11–16; 20:4–6.

19. Matt 7:21–23; 13:41; 16:27; 25:31–46; John 5:22, 27–29; Rev 2:23; 22:12.

20. Matt 3:12; Luke 3:17; Acts 10:42; 17:31; Rom 2:16; 14:10; 1 Cor 4:4–5; 2 Cor 5:10; 2 Tim 4:1, 8; 1 Pet 4:5.

21. Matt 1:22–23; 27:3–4; Mark 1:24; Luke 1:35; 4:34; 23:22, 40–41, 47; John 5:30; 7:18; 8:29, 46; 14:6–11; 17:6; Acts 3:14; 4:27, 30; 13:28, 35; 2 Cor 4:4; 5:21; Col 1:15, 19; 2:9; 1 Tim 3:16; Heb 1:3, 9; 3:2; 4:15; 7:26–28; 9:14; 1 Pet 1:19; 2:22; 1 John 2:29; 3:5; Rev 3:7; 5:1–8.

22. Matt 5:21–22, 27–28, 31–32, 33–34, 38–39, 43–44; 7:28–29; see also Heb 1:1–2.

23. Matt 3:11; Mark 1:8; Luke 3:16; John 1:33; Acts 1:8; 2:1–21.

24. Matt 10:17–23; 12:40; 16:21; 17:9, 22–27; 20:17–19; 21:1–7; 23:34–36; 24:1–31; 26:1–2, 13, 20–25, 31–34, 69–75; Mark 8:31; 9:1, 9, 30–31; 10:32–34; 11:1–7; 13:1–27; 14:9, 12–21, 27–30, 66–72; 16:6–7; Luke 8:49–56; 9:22, 43–44; 17:22–36; 18:31–33; 19:29–35, 41–44; 21:7–28; 22:7–13, 20–23, 31–34, 54–62; 24:6–8; John 2:18–22; 4:21; 6:70–71; 11:23, 43–44; 12:27–33; 13:18–28, 36–38; 16:4, 16–20, 32; 18:4, 25–27; 21:4–6, 18–19; Acts 1:5, 8.

25. Ramm, *Evangelical*, 43.

He claimed the authority to forgive people of their sins.[26] He, in fact, is the savior who alone can save people from their sins.[27] We all understand that a person has the right and authority to forgive someone who has offended or hurt the forgiver personally; but what right or authority does someone have to forgive a person for treading on other men's toes and stealing other men's money?

> Yet this is what Jesus did. He told people that their sins were forgiven, and never waited to consult all the other people whom their sins had undoubtedly injured. He unhesitatingly behaved as if He was the party chiefly concerned, the person chiefly offended in all offences. This makes sense only if He really was the God whose laws are broken and whose love is wounded in every sin. In the mouth of any speaker who is not God, these words would imply what I can only regard as silliness and conceit unrivalled by any other character in history.[28]

When Jesus told a crippled man in the presence of Jewish leaders, *"Son, your sins are forgiven"* (Mark 2:5; see also Matt 9:2), the Jewish leaders recognized the significance of this and reasoned to themselves, *"Why does this man speak that way? He is blaspheming; who can forgive sins but God alone?"* (Mark 2:7; see also Matt 9:3)

Jesus claimed to have a unique relationship with God the Father, calling Him "My Father,"[29] not "our Father," which he taught his disciples to say when praying to God.[30] Further, Jesus addressed the Father directly, using the Aramaic word "Abba," a term of close, personal affection (Mark 14:62). Although there are very rare instances of other Jews *describing* God as Abba, "We have no evidence that others before Jesus *addressed* God as Abba."[31] Rom 8:15 and Gal 4:6 indicate that Jesus taught his disciples to use his own

---

26. Matt 9:2–8, 12–13; Mark 2:3–12; Luke 5:17–26, 31–32; 7:47–50; 9:56; 19:10; John 5:33–34; 8:1–11; 10:7–9; 12:47.

27. Matt 1:21; Luke 2:11; John 1:29; 3:17; 4:42; Acts 3:26; 4:12; 5:31; 13:23, 38–39; 15:11; 16:31; Rom 3:24–26; 4:25; 5:1, 6–11, 15–21; 8:2; 10:9; 1 Cor 1:30; 6:11; 15:17; 2 Cor 5:18–21; Gal 1:3–4; Eph 2:13–16; 4:32; 5:2, 25–26; Phil 3:20; Col 1:12–14; 3:13; 1 Thess 1:10; 5:9–10; 1 Tim 1:15; 2 Tim 2:10; 3:15; Titus 1:4; 2:13–14; Heb 2:17; 5:9; 7:25; 13:20; 1 Pet 1:18–19; 3:18; 2 Pet 1:11; 1 John 3:5; 4:9–10, 14; Rev 5:9; 14:4.

28. Lewis, *Mere Christianity*, 55.

29. Matt 7:21; 10:32–33; 11:27; 12:50; 16:17; 18:10, 19; 20:23; 25:34; 26:39, 42, 53; Luke 2:49; 10:22; 22:29; 24:49; John 2:16; 5:17, 43; 6:32, 40; 8:19, 38, 49, 54; 10:18, 25, 29, 37; 14:2, 7, 20, 21, 23; 15:1, 8, 10, 15, 23, 24; 20:17; Rev 2:27; 3:5, 21.

30. Matt 6:9; see also Luke 11:2; Rom 1:7; 1 Cor 1:3; 2 Cor 1:2; Gal 1:3; Eph 1:2; Phil 1:2; Col 1:2; 2 Thess 1:1; Phlm 3.

31. Bauckham, "Sonship," 249, emph. added.

Jesus Is Fully God and Fully Man

distinctive address of God as Abba. That unique form of address "was Jesus' own relationship to God as Abba which he shared with his disciples: their sonship derived from his own."[32]

Jesus equated and identified himself with God in general.[33] He said that whatever he taught came from God and had absolute and final authority.[34] He said that he does in like manner whatever the Father does (John 5:19). He and the Father are one (John 10:30). All will honor him even as they honor the Father, and to not honor him is to not honor the Father who sent him (John 5:23). Only he has seen the Father (John 6:46). To see him is to see the Father who sent him (John 12:45; 14:9). To receive him is to receive the Father (Mark 9:37). To know him is to know the Father (John 8:19). To believe in him is to believe in the one who sent him (John 12:44). To hate him is to hate the Father (John 15:23).[35] Jesus proved that He is God by doing what only God could do: he rose from the dead.[36] He appeared to many witnesses in bodily form after rising from the dead and could communicate with them.[37] He could appear and disappear in bodily form at will.[38] He ascended to heaven in the presence of witnesses.[39] He was seen in heaven by witnesses on earth (Acts 7:55–56; Rev 4:1—5:10).

The magnitude of the claims Jesus made about himself is astounding. The magnitude of Jesus' claim to be God is enhanced by the context: Jesus was not a pantheist who held that that God is all and all is God. He was a first-century Jew who held that God was a being different from and outside the world, who made the world, and that to worship any human being as God was blasphemy. The magnitude of the claims themselves, made in that context, should cause any reasonable person to seriously investigate the truth of who Jesus is. This is particularly the case since, although anyone

---

32. Bauckham, "Sonship," 248.

33. E.g., John 5:17–23; 10:30, 34–38; 14:6–11; 17:21–23.

34. Matt 5:21–48; 7:24–26; 24:35; John 5:24; 8:26–28; 12:48–50.

35. In addition to all of the above, Jesus demonstrated his deity by performing multiple, public miracles or "signs" (see above discussion).

36. Matt 28:1–7; Mark 16:1–7; Luke 24:1–7; John 2:18–22; Acts 2:29–32; 3:15; 4:10; 5:30; 13:26–37; 17:31; 26:22–23; Rom 1:4; 4:24–25; 6:4–10; 8:11, 34; 14:9; 1 Cor 6:14; 15:4, 20–23; 2 Cor 4:14; 5:15; 13:4; Gal 1:1; Eph 1:20; Phil 3:10; Col 1:18; 2:12; 1 Thess 1:10; 2 Tim 2:8; Heb 13:20; 1 Pet 1:3, 21; 3:21; Rev 1:5, 18.

37. Matt 28:8–10, 16–20; Mark 16:9–14; Luke 24:13–49; John 20:11–29; 21:1–14; Acts 1:1–8; 5:30–32; 9:1–7, 10–17; 10:40–41; 13:30–31; 22:17–21; 23:11; 26:12–18; 1 Cor 9:1; 15:5–8; Rev 1:9—3:22; 22:12–13, 16, 20.

38. Luke 24:30–31, 36–43; John 20:19–20, 26–29.

39. Mark 16:19; Luke 24:50–51; Acts 1:9–11; see also Acts 1:1–2; 2:33–35; 3:20–21; Rom 8:34; Eph 1:20—2:6; 4:10; Col 3:1; 1 Tim 3:16; Heb 1:3; 4:14; 7:26; 8:1; 9:24; 10:12; 12:2; 1 Pet 3:22.

can claim to be God, and a few people (generally "cranks") have done so, there is nothing of the "crank" about Jesus. He has persuaded billions of people from all walks of life, education, and position, throughout the world, over the last 2000 years, that he is exactly who he claimed to be. Of course, billions of people could all be wrong in their conclusion. But that level of acceptance should at least raise the issue that there are good reasons why so many people, in so many places, and for so long, have accepted Jesus' claims.

Further, the last people on earth who are likely to worship someone as God are those closest to the person, i.e., family and close friends. The reason, of course, is that family and close friends know all about what the person is "really" like. They can see what a person tries to hide from the public; and they can see the unintentional "slips" of anger, pettiness, selfishness, and other character flaws that those who have more remote contact with a person cannot see. Yet those closest to Jesus worshipped him because they saw his true character, namely, that Jesus had no "slips" into anger, pettiness, selfishness, or other character flaws: he was, in fact, sinless in thought, word, and deed. Jesus had the character of God, because he was God come to earth as a man. Any reasonable person should seriously investigate the truth of who Jesus is because, if he is right, then one's eternal destiny hangs on one's answer to the question of who Jesus is and what that entails for our lives.

In light of Jesus' first-century Jewish context and his conception of the nature of who God is, C. S. Lewis summarizes the significance of the above claims by Jesus,

> A man who was merely a man and said the sort of things Jesus said would not be a great moral teacher. He would either be a lunatic—on a level with the man who says he is a poached egg—or else he would be the Devil of Hell. You must make your choice. Either this man was, and is, the Son of God; or else a madman or something worse. You can shut Him up for a fool, you can spit at Him and kill Him as a demon; or you can fall at His feet and call Him Lord and God. But let us not come with any patronizing nonsense about His being a great moral teacher. He has not left that open to us. He did not intend to.[40]

---

40. Lewis, *Mere Christianity*, 55–56; see also Lewis, "What are We," 157–58. The validity of Lewis's "trilemma" (i.e., Jesus' claim confronts us with only three possibilities: he was either a liar, or insane, or was, indeed, the Son of God) is indicated by the speciousness of Richard Dawkins' positing a fourth possibility, "that Jesus was honestly mistaken." Dawkins, *God Delusion*, 92. A person cannot be "honestly mistaken" if he believes and announces himself to be God Almighty, creator of heaven and earth! Only severe mental illness would lead a person to say such a thing (assuming he was not consciously lying) unless, of course, he was telling the truth about himself.

Jesus Christ is fully man

Jesus identified himself as a "man" (John 8:40) and was recognized as a "man" by others.[41] Jesus had a human genealogy.[42] Jesus had a human gestation and birth.[43] Jesus had a human body of flesh, blood, and bone.[44] Jesus experienced all the normal human, bodily experiences: He grew (Luke 2:40, 52). He was hungry and thirsty, ate and drank.[45] He became tired and slept (Matt 8:24; Mark 4:38; Luke 8:24). He experienced weariness and weakness.[46] He suffered.[47] He died and was buried.[48]

Jesus had a normal human mind and a normal human will.[49] He had normal human emotions and expressed them: He felt compassion.[50] He loved.[51] He got angry.[52] He felt sorrow (Matt 26:38). He marveled (Matt 8:10; Mark 6:6). He rejoiced and experienced joy (Luke 10:21; John 13:11). He was moved and troubled in spirit and experienced grief, agony, and distress.[53] He wept (Luke 19:41; John 11:35; Heb 5:7).

Jesus experienced a normal human spiritual life: He was circumcised (Luke 2:21). He was baptized.[54] He prayed.[55] He fasted (Matt 4:2; Luke 4:2). He kept the Jewish religious ceremonies and worshiped in the temple and

---

41. Matt 8:9, 27; 12:23–24; 13:54, 56; 26:61, 71–72, 74; Mark 2:7; 6:2; 14:71; 15:39; Luke 5:21; 7:8, 39, 49; 9:9; 15:2; 23:2, 4, 6, 14, 18, 22, 41, 47; John 1:30; 4:29; 6:52; 7:12, 15, 25, 27, 35, 46, 51; 9:11, 16, 29, 33; 10:33; 11:37, 47, 50; 18:14, 17, 40; 19:5, 12; Acts 2:22–23; 5:28; 6:13; 17:31; 25:19; Rom 5:15; 1 Cor 15:21, 47; Gal 2:20; Eph 5:2; Phil 2:8; 1 Tim 2:5.

42. Matt 1:1–17; Luke 3:23–38; John 7:42; Rom 1:3; 9:5; Gal 3:16; 2 Tim 2:8.

43. Matt 1:18—2:1; Luke 1:31; 2:1–20; 11:27; Rom 1:3; Gal 4:4.

44. Luke 22:44; 24:39–40; John 1:14; 19:34; 20:19–29; Rom 1:3; 8:3; Phil 2:7; Col 2:9; 1 Tim 3:16; Heb 2:14; 10:5; 1 Pet 2:24; 1 John 1:1–3; 4:2; 2 John 7.

45. Matt 4:2; 21:18; 27:48; Mark 11:12; 15:36; Luke 4:2; 24:41–43; John 4:6; 19:28–30.

46. Matt 4:11; 27:32; Mark 15:21; Luke 23:26; John 4:6.

47. Matt 20:17–19; 26:67; 27:26–31; Mark 9:12; 10:32–34; 14:65; 15:16–20; Luke 22:63–64; 23:11; John 4:6; 18:22; 19:1–3; Heb 5:8.

48. Matt 27:50, 57–66; Mark 15:37, 39, 42–47; Luke 23:46, 50–56; John 19:30–42; Acts 25:19; Rom 5:8; 1 Cor 15:3–4; Phil 2:8; Heb 2:14.

49. Matt 26:39; Mark 13:32; Luke 2:40, 52; John 4:1; 5:6; 6:38; 7:1; Heb 5:8–9.

50. Matt 9:36; 14:14; 15:32; 20:34; Mark 1:41; 6:34; 8:2; Luke 7:13.

51. Mark 10:21; John 11:5, 36; 13:23; 15:10, 12; 21:20.

52. Matt 21:12–13; Mark 3:5; 11:15–17; Luke 19:45–46; John 2:13–16.

53. Matt 26:37–38; Mark 3:5; 14:33–34; Luke 22:44; John 11:33, 38; 12:27; 13:21.

54. Matt 3:13–17; Mark 1:9–11; Luke 3:21–22; John 1:29–34.

55. Matt 26:36–44; Mark 14:35–36, 39; Luke 9:18; 10:21; 11:1; 22:41–45; John 17:1–26; Heb 5:7.

synagogue.[56] He read and memorized Scripture.[57] He observed the Sabbath and obeyed the OT laws.[58] He received the fullness of the Spirit.[59]

In Rom 8:3, Paul says that God sent his Son into the world *"in the likeness of sinful flesh"* (*en homoiōmati sarkos hamartias*). However, he does not say that Christ came *en sarkos hamartias* (*"in sinful flesh"*). That distinction is emphasizing that Christ was a real man with a real human body but, at the same time, did not succumb to the power of sin and did not in fact sin (2 Cor 5:21), even though he was *"tempted in all things as we are"* (Heb 4:15).[60] This is highly significant. Historically, people have been called "sinners" because they have yielded to temptation and "saints" because they have resisted the lure of temptation enough to defeat it. Bernard Ramm observes that the essence of temptation is to present evil as good; to be tempted is

> to enter into the gravitational field of seduction, for temptation is but a species of seduction. . . . The essence of temptation is then how the tempted person manages the gravitational pull of seduction and not whether or not such a person may sin. If this is the nature of temptation then a sinless person who is at the same time genuinely human (and capable of entering realistically into such a gravitational field) can have genuine temptations without yielding to sin.[61]

The fact that Christ was tempted in all ways like we are yet never sinned means that he experienced the *full power and pull* of temptation because he resisted the temptation all the way to the end—unlike those who give in to the temptation before it has reached its full force.

IMPLICATIONS OF THE FACT THAT JESUS CHRIST IS FULLY GOD AND FULLY MAN

God can be truly and personally known in Christ

In other monotheistic religions, God is essentially an abstract idea. In polytheistic religions, the gods are simply spirits. In neither case can God's (or

---

56. Mark 1:39; Luke 2:41–49; 4:16, 44; John 2:23.

57. Matt 4:4–10; 11:10; 21:42; 22:41–45; Mark 12:10–11, 35–37; Luke 4:4–12, 18–19; 7:27; 20:41–44; 22:37; John 6:45; 15:25.

58. Matt 5:17; 17:24–27; 22:15–21; Luke 4:16; 20:20–25; John 7:10–14; 15:10.

59. Matt 3:16—4:1; Mark 1:10–12; Luke 3:22; 4:1.

60. See also Heb 2:18; Matt 4:1–10; Mark 1:12–13; Luke 4:1–12.

61. Ramm, *Evangelical*, 81–82.

the gods') true nature be known in a definitive and personal way. However, Christ is *"the image of the invisible God"* (Col 1:15); he is *"the radiance of His glory and the exact representation of His nature"* (Heb 1:3); and in Christ *"all the fullness of Deity dwells in bodily form"* (Col 2:9). Through Jesus, finite human beings can have some understanding of the infinite God that would not be possible if God had not become a human being and lived among us:

> If Jesus had been "only" a man or created being, then the hugeness of the gulf between God and humanity—the infinite and the finite, the Creator and the created, the Holy and the unholy—would have remained. . . . No created being could have bridged the gigantic gap between God and human beings any more than a piece of clay could aspire to understand and reach the level of the sculptor. Out of love, God took that step down to us. He wanted to open a way that all might come to know Him.[62]

Only in Christ can God be *truly* known. Further, the fact that God became a man and lived among us means that we can know Him *personally*. This makes Christianity unique among all the religions of the world.

Christ shows us what God's true nature is and thereby is our true example of how to live

Because Jesus is God, it is appropriate and necessary to believe in him and worship him. In fact, he equated faith in God with faith in himself (John 14:1; see also Acts 16:31). However, because he is man, he also is a true example for our character and how we should live our lives here on earth: *"By this we know that we are in Him: the one who says he abides in Him ought himself to walk in the same manner as He walked"* (1 John 2:5–6). With respect to patiently enduring unjust suffering for doing what is right, Peter says, *"This finds favor with God. For you have been called for this purpose, since Christ also suffered for you, leaving you an example for you to follow in His steps"* (1 Pet 2:20–21). It is here that Christ's divinity and humanity converge in a profound way, both for our understanding of who God is and what he is really like, and for our understanding of how we should then live. Phil 2:5–11 describes how Christ was God (vv. 5–6) but emptied himself to become a man, even a slave (v. 7) who was obedient to the point of death on a cross (v. 8); therefore, God highly exalted him such that everyone will worship him as Lord of all (vv. 9–11).

---

62. McDowell and Larson, *Jesus: A Biblical Defense*, 19.

This passage amounts to a Christological statement of the identity of God. The exaltation of Christ to participation in the unique divine sovereignty shows him to be included in the unique divine identity. But since the exalted Christ is first the humiliated Christ, since indeed it is *because* of his self-abnegation that he is exalted, his humiliation belongs to the identity of God as truly as his exaltation does. The identity of God—who God is—is revealed as much in self-abasement and service as it is in exaltation and rule. The God who is high can also be low, because God is God not in seeking his own advantage but in self-giving."[63]

The fact that God's true nature is revealed as much in self-abasement and service as it is in exaltation and rule has important practical implications for how God personally identifies with us in our human condition. Christ *"was despised and forsaken of men, a man of sorrows and acquainted with grief"* (Isa 53:3). That means God knows pain, sorrow, grief, rejection, and betrayal personally and experientially. As a result, "God enters into the hurts of those who suffer so that from inside those hurts, being fully identified with them to the point of communicating his divinity through them, he heals them."[64] God's personal identification with us in Christ then leads us to identify with others since we have received the mind of Christ (1 Cor 2:16) and the Spirit of Christ (Rom 8:1–17). We treat others with love and forgiveness because that is the way Christ has treated us (Eph 4:32; 1 John 4:7–21). Our lives and actions become more and more like Christ's as we are conformed to his image (Rom 8:29; 12:1–2). As with everything else, Christianity is unlike any other religion in the world. The Christian God is unlike any other god—and it is only Christ who reveals this.

Redemption from our sin is possible only because Christ is both fully God and fully man

All people intuitively know that we have a problem: we are separated from God because he is holy and perfect, but we are sinful. The Bible correctly sees that mankind has a fatal flaw, an inner corruption known as indwelling sin.[65] The Bible also correctly sees that *"the wages of sin is death."*[66] All other religions in the world try to bridge the gap between people and God

---

63. Bauckham, *God Crucified*, 61.
64. Carter, *Race*, 368.
65. E.g., Gen 6:5; Ps 51:5; Jer 17:9; Rom 3:9–18, 23; 7:14–24; Gal 3:21–22.
66. Rom 6:23; see also Gen 2:17; Ezek 18:4, 20; Rom 5:12.

by making one's salvation or acceptance by God dependent on what the individual person *does:* each person must try to "establish his own righteousness" (Rom 10:3) by performing certain religious rituals, making certain sacrifices, doing enough good deeds, etc. However, all such religions are doomed to failure because they all have a defective view of the nature of mankind. No amount of desire, willing, rituals, sacrifices, or other actions can change the fundamental problem of our inner corruption and the sinfulness of mankind's heart. Consequently, we can *never* "establish our own righteousness" or "earn" our way to heaven, salvation, or acceptance by God by any amount of rituals, sacrifices, or other actions we may do (Gal 2:16). Out of all the religions in the world, Christianity alone recognizes that all people have a fundamental problem of a sinful nature, cannot change that, and cannot save themselves. Consequently, God chose to do for mankind what mankind could not do for itself. That is why God became a man in the person of Jesus Christ.

Christ lived the life we should have lived. He was *"tempted in all things as we are, yet without sin"* (Heb 4:15; see also Heb 2:18). That qualified him to be our representative with the Father, to die the death we should have died, and pay the penalty for our sins that otherwise we would have to pay but never could (Rom 8:3–4). First Tim 2:5 says, *"There is one God, and one mediator also between God and man, the man Christ Jesus."* A mediator is someone who brings together two parties who are opposed to each other. A mediator therefore has to identify with each of the parties. Because he is God, Christ identifies with God the Father. Because he is man, Christ identifies with us. Because he did not sin, he did not have to atone for his own sin. Instead, Christ could take our sin onto himself, pay the price for our sin that we should have paid, and also impute to us his righteousness so that we could stand before God.[67] He alone can thereby reconcile us to God (Col 1:19–20).

Timothy Keller points out, "All other major faiths have founders who are teachers that show the way to salvation. Only Jesus claimed to actually *be* the way of salvation himself."[68] That is why the fact that Jesus was fully man but also was fully God not only is important but is absolutely necessary to salvation. Gleason Archer states,

> God as God could not forgive us for our sins unless our sins were fully paid for; otherwise He could have been a condoner and protector of the violation of His own holy law. It was only as a man that God in Christ could furnish a satisfaction sufficient

---

67. Isa 53:5–6, 10–11; Rom 10:4; 2 Cor 5:21; Heb 2:17–18; 1 Pet 2:4; 3:18.
68. Keller, *Reason*, 174.

to atone for the sins of mankind; for only a man, a true human being, could properly represent the human race. But our Redeemer also had to be God, for only God could furnish a sacrifice of infinite value, to compensate for the penalty of eternal hell that our sin demands, according to the righteous claims of divine justice."[69]

Christ bore our punishment on the cross so that we do not have to face God's punishment for our sin; he was forsaken on the cross so that we can be accepted. In Christ, we are as free from the guilt and penalty of sin as if we had paid the full price for our sin ourselves (Rom 6:3-7; Gal 2:20).

No one else who has ever lived—neither Muhammad, nor Buddha, nor anyone else—ever claimed to redeem people from their sins. And no one else who has ever lived was *qualified* to redeem people from their sins even if he wanted to do so because: (1) no one else who has ever lived was both God and man like Christ is; and (2) everyone else who has ever lived has had his own sinful nature and actual sins to deal with (Acts 4:12; Rom 3:9-18). Consequently, Christianity alone recognizes that salvation is not, *and cannot be,* based on what we do, but is, *and can only be,* based solely on what Christ has done for us. Salvation cannot be earned by us but is a gift given to us by the grace of God through Christ (Rom 5:18-21; 6:23; Eph 1:7; 2:4-5, 8-9). Therefore, if we have turned to Christ as our Lord and received what he has done on our behalf, we can have confidence to approach God, because Christ is our advocate who intercedes for us with the Father (Rom 8:34; Heb 4:16; 7:25; 10:19-22; 1 John 2:1).

---

69. Archer, *Encyclopedia*, 323.

APPENDIX 2

The Trinity

THE CHRISTIAN DOCTRINE OF the Trinity is that there is only one God, but he consists of three distinct persons: Father, Son, and Holy Spirit. Throughout this book, we have seen indications of the Trinity: in Christ's pre-incarnate appearances; in certain prophesies; in certain cases of typology; and in the great ecumenical creeds and other factors discussed in Appendix 1. Christians do not now and never have believed in three gods. Both the OT and NT emphatically and repeatedly assert that there is only one God.[1] God is not *part* of a Trinity, he *is* Trinity. The Trinity is *not* an assertion that there are three gods or that the one God has two partners; rather, the Trinity is an assertion of God's *oneness*—one God in Three Persons—but a oneness that is rich and complex.

Because the Trinity is the central and unique conception of the nature of God according to Christianity, it should be explained and understood. We will do that here. As we do so, we will see that the concept of the Trinity not only emerges from the Bible but is the only thing that corresponds to reality and can explain reality as it exists.

OBJECTIONS TO THE TRINITY

Alhaj A. D. Ajijola is typical of Muslim apologists who attack the idea of the Trinity when he states, "Jesus was subject to and sought the fulfillment of human needs. Finally, as the Christian version goes, enemies nailed him to

---

1. Deut 4:35, 39; 6:4; 32:39; 1 Kgs 8:59–60; Ps 86:10; Isa 43:10–13; 44:6; 45:14, 18, 21–22; 46:9; Mark 12:29, 32; John 17:3; Rom 3:29–30; 1 Cor 8:4; Eph 4:3–6; 1 Tim 2:5; Jas 2:19.

death. Can a person of the limited dimensions and characteristics that the Holy Bible itself has shown Jesus to be, be the True God?"[2] In fact, *because God is Trinity*, God in the person of the Son (Jesus) could indeed become incarnate and limited as a man and yet continue to exist as God and could die as a man yet continue to exist as God (who cannot die). Death does not mean that a person ceases to exist; rather, it effects a separation of the spirit from the body. Sam Shamoun states, "The one true God always exists as three distinct Persons even during the entombment of Christ's physical body. And, even as his body lay buried, Christ was alive and sovereignly sustaining the universe along with the Father and the Holy Spirit."[3] Only this mysterious union of God and man in the person of Jesus enabled God both to inflict and endure the spiritual punishment of humanity's sins on the cross.

Some people, who have a simplistic view of God's "oneness," might make statements like, "Everyone knows that 1+1+1=3, but in the Trinity, Christians would have us believe that 1+1+1=1."[4] That mathematical equation is a *false comparison* with the Trinity. It *assumes in advance* that the three persons of the Trinity are three gods (or one god with two partners). It does not take into account that *"God is Spirit"* (John 4:24), and Spirit cannot be divided into parts. W. A. Pratney points out, "The unity of the Godhead is not a simple unity but an interdependent unity. Expressed mathematically it would never be 1 + 1 + 1 = 1, for independent unity never gives true equality; but 1 x 1 x 1 = 1, for interdependent unity gives an exact correspondence of equality, and the omission of one part of such an interdependent unity leads to the loss of the entire product (1 x 1 x 0 = 0)."[5] Further, Abbas Sundiata asks, "Why should the numerical figure one (1) be the expression in mathematics that represents God? If any mathematical expression could represent the Christian concept of God, it would be infinity! And as far as we know, infinity x infinity x infinity = infinity, and infinity + infinity + infinity = infinity, just like God x God x God = God, and God + God + God = God."[6]

THE DOCTRINE OF THE TRINITY

God is a being unlike anything else and unlike anything that could have been dreamed up by finite humans. The doctrine of the Trinity is an attempt to understand or describe the nature of God who, by his very nature,

2. Ajijola, *Myth*, 27.
3. Shamoun, "If Jesus," n.p.
4. See Sundiata, *Look Behind*, 195.
5. Pratney, *Nature and Character*, 261.
6. Sundiata, *Look Behind*, 196.

is unique and beyond our finite ability to fully understand and describe. Christians have always believed—based upon what the Bible says about God—that God is Trinity; this belief was not invented or derived from other sources. One indication that this idea was not "made up" is the fact that the concept of the Trinity is *not* easy for many to conceptualize. People would not make up a conceptualization of God that others find hard to believe or even irrational; however, as we will see, the concept of the Trinity clearly arises from the Bible itself.

"Briefly stated, the doctrine of the Trinity claims that God is one as to essence [Greek = *ousia*] and three as to persons [Greek = *hypostasis*]."[7] Ghabril explains, "God's essence is not material but spiritual. Spirit does not, under any circumstances, permit division. Thus the Father, the Son and the Holy Spirit are in respect to their hypostasis of the same essence. Each of them enjoys the essence of one deity without division or separation. In our language there is no equivalent to the meaning of hypostasis in order to be able to describe the Holy Trinity more easily."[8] Cornelius Van Til adds, "In God the one and the many are equally ultimate. Unity in God is no more fundamental than diversity, and diversity in God is no more fundamental than unity. The persons of the Trinity are mutually exhaustive of one another. The Son and the Spirit are ontologically [i.e., in the nature of their existence or being] on par with the Father."[9] Elsewhere he says, "When Scripture ascribes certain works specifically to the Father, others specifically to the Son, and still others specifically to the Holy Spirit, we are compelled to presuppose a genuine distinction within the Godhead back of that ascription. On the other hand, the work ascribed to any of the persons is the work of one absolute person.[10] As to this last point, John Feinberg explains:

> Since there is only one divine essence shared equally by all three persons, there is a sense in which all three persons "do" whatever any of them does. On the other hand, insofar as it makes any sense to speak of distinct persons, i.e., distinct ways in which that divine essence is manifest, it also makes sense to attribute specific actions to only one of the three members. Hence, it is the second member of the Godhead (not the others) who becomes incarnate as Jesus of Nazareth, the Christ.[11]

---

7. Feinberg, *No One*, 437.
8. Ghabril, *Themes*, 39.
9. Van Til, *Defense*, 25.
10. Van Til, *Introduction*, 210, 215, 220, 228.
11. Feinberg, *No One*, 495.

Appendix 2

THE DOCTRINE OF THE TRINITY NECESSARILY ARISES FROM THE DATA GIVEN US IN THE BIBLE

The word "Trinity" is not in the Bible but is based on the teachings of the Bible. We mentioned above that the Bible clearly and repeatedly affirms that there is only "one God." However, as W. A. Pratney points out, "There are two kinds of unity or 'oneness' in both English and Hebrew; an *absolute unity* and *compound unity*. Absolute unity is that of singularity; I give you one apple, and you get a single apple. But if you ask for 'one' bunch of grapes, you don't simply get one grape! 'One' in this case is a word of compound unity, the many in the one."[12]

This is significant, because there are multiple indications in the OT that the Godhead, Yahweh, is a plural form of unity, not a simplistic form of unity. The OT is consistent with the Trinity in that it describes God using terms that indicate unity in plurality and plurality in unity. The NT makes this clear by revealing that the unity in plurality and plurality in unity are found in the three persons of the Trinity: the Father, Son, and Holy Spirit.

1. *The Hebrew word for "one" used to describe God. Yachead* is the Hebrew word for an absolute or mathematical numeral one. It is used about 12 times in the OT but is never used to describe the oneness of God. *Echad* is the Hebrew word for a compound or collective oneness (e.g., *"the two shall be one flesh,"* Gen 2:24). This is the word always used in the OT when God is called "one" Lord.

2. *The Hebrew word for "God."* The typical OT word for the God of Israel is *Elohim*; it is a plural noun. It is used approximately 2500 times in the OT.[13] There are three interesting aspects of this. First, the singular of *elohim* is *eloah* which is occasionally used to refer to God. "Unless the intent is to make a point about plurality, why not just use the singular *eloah*?"[14] Second, while the plural *elohim* typically is used for God, it is most often used with a singular verb. Normally, nouns and verbs agree in number, so this is grammatically unusual. Third, while generally singular pronouns (e.g., "I," "He," "My") are used to refer to God, sometimes *plural* pronouns are used, which "seem to suggest plurality of some sort in the Godhead."[15] For example, in Gen 1:26 (*"Let us make man in our image"*) "the verb 'make' (*na'áśeh*) is plural,

---

12. Pratney, *Nature and Character*, 258–59.
13. Pratney, *Nature and Character*, 259.
14. Feinberg, *No One*, 449.
15. Feinberg, *No One*, 449.

and so is 'our.'"¹⁶ Although some might suggest that *elohim* is a "plural of majesty," that concept was entirely unknown to the Hebrews and is found nowhere else in biblical Hebrew.¹⁷

3 *With the full revelation of the NT, the Bible makes clear that God is Trinity, consisting of the Father, the Son, and the Holy Spirit.* The Bible does this by attributing the same names, titles, and attributes of Godhood to each one of them. In the following table, $^{x, y}$ indicate direct quotes.

Name/Title/Attribute	God the Father	God the Son	God the Holy Spirit
God	Ps 45:6–7^x; 1 Cor 8:6	Heb 1:8–9^x; John 1:1, 14, 18; 20:28	Acts 5:3–4
Lord	Isa 40:3^x; 45:23–24^y	Mark 1:2–4^x; Phil 2:10–11^y	2 Cor 3:17–18
Eternal	Ps 90:2; Isa 43:10, 13	Micah 5:2	Heb 9:14
Creator	Gen 1:1; Ps 102:25–27^x	John 1:10; Col 1:16; Heb 1:10–12^x	Gen 1:2; Job 33:4; Ps 104:30
Omniscient	Job 21:22; Ps 33:13–15	John 16:30; 21:17	John 16:13; 1 Cor 2:10–11
Omnipotent	Isa 46:9–11; Nah 1:3–6	Eph 1:20–22; Heb 1:3	Luke 1:35
Omnipresent	Prov 15:3; Jer 23:24	Matt 18:20; 28:20; Eph 4:10	Ps 139:7–10
Does miraculous signs	Exod 14:22; Dan 3:23–27	Mark 6:45–52; John 20:30	Rom 15:19; 1 Cor 12:7–11
Raised Jesus from the dead	Gal 1:1; Eph 1:17, 20	John 2:19	Rom 8:11
Loves	John 3:16; 1 John 3:1	John 11:36; 13:1	Rom 15:30
Has his own will	Matt 26:39; Eph 1:11	Matt 11:27; Luke 10:22	1 Cor 12:11
Has knowledge	1 Sam 2:3; Matt 11:27	Matt 11:27; John 6:64; 21:17	1 Cor 2:10–11
Chooses	Rom 9:15–18	Luke 6:13	Acts 13:2
Is True	John 7:28	John 14:6	1 John 5:6

16. Feinberg, *No One*, 450; see also Gen 3:22; 11:7; Isa 6:8.
17. Runia, "Trinity," 166; Archer, *Encyclopedia*, 359.

Name/Title/Attribute	God the Father	God the Son	God the Holy Spirit
Is Holy	1 Sam 2:2; John 17:11	Acts 3:14; Heb 7:26	John 14:26
Is Good	Ps 34:8	John 10:11	Ps 143:10
Gives spiritual life	Eph 2:4–5	John 1:4; 5:21	John 3:8; Rom 8:10
Strengthens people	Ps 28:7–8; 46:1–2; 133:3	Phil 4:13	Eph 3:16
Indwells believers	2 Cor 6:16	Eph 3:17; Col 1:27	John 14:17; Rom 8:9
Fellowships with believers	1 John 1:3	1 John 1:3	2 Cor 13:14
Sanctifies believers	John 17:17	Eph 5:26; Heb 10:10	1 Pet 1:2
Speaks to people	Matt 3:17; Luke 9:35	John 12:48–50; 16:1, 4, 19–25	John 16:13; Acts 8:29; 13:2
Teaches	Isa 48:17	Matt 5:1–2	John 14:26
May be grieved	Gen 6:6; Ps 78:40	Isa 53:3; Mark 3:5	Isa 63:10; Acts 4:30

Note that the last fifteen of these attributes are personal and relational. This indicates that the Father, Son, and Holy Spirit are "persons," not just "forces" or attributes of a remote or impersonal god.[18]

4   All three Persons in the Godhead are referred to and linked together in various passages.

- Isa 61:1: "The Spirit of the Lord God *is upon* me, *because* the Lord has anointed me."[19]

- Matt 28:19: "*Go therefore and make disciples of all the nations, baptizing them in the name of* the Father *and* the Son *and* the Holy Spirit."

18. Some people think that the Holy Spirit is simply a "force" or the "power of God," based on verses like Micah 3:8 ("*On the other hand, I am filled with power—with the Spirit of the Lord*"). As the above table makes clear, the Holy Spirit is a person, not a force or power. Further, in John 15:26, Jesus says, "*When the Helper comes, whom I will send to you from the Father, that is the Spirit of truth who proceeds from the Father, He will testify about Me.*" First, Jesus is using a personal pronoun ("He"), not an impersonal pronoun ("It"), to describe the Holy Spirit. Second, the Holy Spirit is said to do what only persons can do, namely, "testify."

19. Jesus quoted Isa 61:1–2 in Luke 4:18–21 as specifically applying to himself, i.e., he is the "me" referred to.

- Luke 3:21–22: *"Now when all the people were baptized, Jesus was also baptized, and while He was praying, heaven was opened, and the Holy Spirit descended upon Him in bodily form like a dove, and a voice came out of heaven, 'You are My beloved Son, in You I am well-pleased'"* (see also Matt 3:16–17; Mark 1:10–11).

- John 14:26: *"But the Helper, the Holy Spirit, whom the Father will send in My name, He will teach you all things, and bring to your remembrance all that I said to you."*

- John 15:26: *"When the Helper comes, whom I will send to you from the Father, that is the Spirit of truth who proceeds from the Father, He will testify about Me, and you will testify also, because you have been with Me from the beginning."*

- Rom 8:8–9: *"And those who are in the flesh cannot please God. However, you are not in the flesh but in the Spirit, if indeed the Spirit of God dwells in you. But if anyone does not have the Spirit of Christ, he does not belong to Him."*

- Eph 4:4–6: *"There is one body and one Spirit, just as also you were called in one hope of your calling; one Lord, one faith, one baptism, one God and Father of all who is over all and through all and in all."*

- Titus 3:4–6: *"But when the kindness of God our Savior and His love for mankind appeared He saved us, not on the basis of deeds which we have done in righteousness, but according to His mercy, by the washing of regeneration and renewing by the Holy Spirit, whom He poured out upon us richly through Jesus Christ our Savior."*

- Jude 20–21: *"But you, beloved, building yourselves up on your most holy faith, praying in the Holy Spirit, keep yourselves in the love of God, waiting anxiously for the mercy of our Lord Jesus Christ to eternal life."*

THE CONCEPT OF THE TRINITY IS NOT ILLOGICAL AND IS REASONABLY UNDERSTANDABLE

The doctrine of the Trinity is neither incoherent (i.e., internally self-contradictory) nor illogical. The late Coptic Pope Shenuda III began the explanation of how the triune God does not involve separation into three gods with this example:

As Christ said in the Gospel of John, "I and the Father are one." (John 10:30) The Son comes from the Father without leaving Him. He comes out of Him and yet remains in Him, which leads to the enquiry, how? I shall explain to you with the help of an example: When you think and your thought emerges as sound, that thought reaches the ears of people, yet thought is still in your mind. It is also possible for the thought to leave your mind and enter a book which is distributed in America where many read it. In that sense the thought came out from you and yet remains with you.[20]

Various analogies may make the nature of the Trinity more understandable:[21]

1. *The number of airline passengers and persons.* If an airline passenger takes three trips on the same airline to the same place, he counts as three separate *passengers* but is still only one *person*. Similarly, the Father, Son, and Holy Spirit are all divine persons, "but that doesn't mean there are as many gods as divine persons. It is the same God manifested in three distinct persons, just as it is the same person 'manifested' on three separate passenger lists and flights."[22]

2. *A marble statue that is used as a pillar in a building.* A building contractor fashions a marble statue that is to be used as a pillar in the building:

    The statue and the pillar are one and the same material object, not two. And yet they are distinct. Surface erosion will destroy

---

20. Shenuda, *Trinity and Unity*, 4.

21. No analogy is perfect. That is particularly true when trying to describe the infinite God! Two popular analogies are water, which can take three forms (liquid, vapor, and ice), which is analogous to God taking three forms (Father, Son, and Holy Spirit) and an egg, which consists of shell, yolk, and albumen, analogous to God consisting of three persons. Brower and Rea point out the flaws of both analogies: "The problem with both analogies is that instead of explaining the orthodox view, they actually lead us *away* from it. Liquid, vapor, and ice are three *states* or *manifestations* of a single substance, water; thus to say that the Persons of God are like them is to fall into modalism [the view that God is not three persons but is only one person who appears in different "modes" at different times]. On the other hand, shell, yolk, and albumen are three *parts* of an egg; but neither shell, yolk, nor albumen *is* an egg. So this analogy suggests that neither Father, Son, nor Holy Spirit is God—they are merely parts of God." Brower and Rea, "Understanding the Trinity," 4. Despite the inherent limitation of analogies, the analogies in the text at minimum help us see that the biblical concept of one God consisting of three persons is neither incoherent nor irrational.

22. Feinberg, *No One*, 497–98.

the statue without destroying the pillar. Internal corruption that preserves the surface but undermines the statue's capacity to support the weight of a building will destroy the pillar but (if the statue is removed from its position as a load-bearing structure) will not destroy the statue. Thus, what we want to say is that the statue and the pillar are the *same material object*, even though they are *not identical*. . . . By now the relevance of all this to the Trinity should be clear: . . . Each divine person . . . is distinct from the other [so modalism is avoided]. But they are nevertheless the *same* substance.[23]

3. *A liquid solution.* A solution is two or more different elements or compounds that are mixed together but are not chemically bonded. Examples would be saltwater and lemon tea. In saltwater, salt is dissolved in the water. Both the water and the dissolved salt cannot be separated; they both fill the entire area containing the saltwater, yet both are distinct. Similarly, lemon tea consists of water, tea, and lemon juice. They cannot be separated; nevertheless, they are distinct. All three are necessary: to remove one of them means that lemon tea no longer exists (to remove the tea leaves only lemon water; to remove the lemon leaves only simple tea). Thus, there is only one cup of tea, but it consists of three distinct elements, each of which permeates the entire cup, and each of which plays a unique role in making the lemon tea what it is.

4. *A three-note musical chord.* Musicologist Victor Zuckerkandl describes a musical chord:

> Three tones sound. . . . None of them is in a place; or better, they are all in the same place, namely, everywhere. . . . Yet there is order here, unmistakable and undeniable: a triad. Order of simultaneous sensations involving space, order that we hear, not merely think: spatial order without different places, without juxtaposition. . . The first tone, as it sounds, spreads through all space. Joining the first, the second tone, however much it might wish to, could find no room to take a place beside it: all available space is already occupied by the first. Nevertheless, it is not covered by the first: the first turns out to be, as it were, transparent for it. The second tone is and remains audible *through the first*. The same is true of the third tone: the tones connected in the

---

23. Rea, "Trinity," 712–15, emph. in orig.

triad sound *through one another.* Or let us say they interpenetrate one another.[24]

5   *The nature of space: the difference between one, two, and three-dimensional objects.*

For any three-dimensional object, each of the three dimensions—length, height, and width—is not just a "part" of the object but pervades the entire object. Even though we can speak of and measure length, height, and width as if they were separate entities, if any one of them is removed from the object you do not get a smaller object; rather, the object ceases to exist entirely. To determine the space or any three-dimensional object, you do not add height + length + width; you multiply them (height x length x width). To add height + length + width would imply that each such dimension was only a third of the whole. In fact, each dimension permeates the entire whole, but until one has all three dimensions multiplied by each other, there is no space at all.[25]

6   *The nature of the universe.* The universe is composed of space, time, and matter (energy). None of these entities created the others or exists apart from the others. Yet, each is distinct and can be measured separately. As with length, height, and width in a three-dimensional object, or the elements constituting a liquid solution, space, time, and matter permeate and fill the entire universe. To remove any one of them would result, not in a smaller universe, but in no universe at all. Henry Morris adds:

> Note the parallels between the divine trinity and the tri-universe in terms of the logical order of its three components. Space is the invisible, omnipresent background of everything in the universe. Matter-and-Energy reveal the reality of the universe. Time makes the universe understandable in the events occurring in it. Note that exactly the same sentence will apply if the words Father, Son, and Holy Spirit replace the words, Space, Matter, and Time.[26]

---

24. Zuckerkandl, *Sound and Symbol*, 297, 299, emph. in orig.; see also Williams, "Understanding the Trinity," Trinitarian Analogies.

25. See Wood, *Trinity*, 175–77.

26. Morris, "Tri-Universe," n.p.

7   *Light.* Although light appears simple, colorless, and the same to us, it actually consists of three types of spectra: *a continuous spectrum* (or continuum emission), *an emission line spectrum,* and *an absorption line spectrum.*[27] One manifestation of this is that a prism disperses a beam of transparent or "white" light into a rainbow of colors that were present in the light all along. Additionally,

> Light behaves as both particles and waves at the same time, and scientists have been able to observe this duality in action using an ultrafast electron microscope.... Waves are very distinct phenomena in our universe, as are particles. And we have different sets of mathematics to describe each of them.... A particle is, as best as I can put it, a thing. It's a small, single, finite object.... On the other hand, waves are almost completely different. They're not localized.[28]

In other words, light mirrors the Trinity in that God could act both as a "particle" (a finite object, i.e., the man Jesus Christ) and yet *at the same time* act as a "wave" (i.e., Spirit).[29]

8   *The triple point of water.* The "triple point" is "the point where the solid, liquid, and gaseous forms of a substance coexist in equilibrium.... This means that coexistence of ice, steam, and water can occur only at one specific temperature and one specific pressure."[30] The triple point "shows how one substance can exist in three fundamental forms concurrently, each fully the same in nature yet clearly distinct to the extent of having a real interaction with each other, different properties, and different applications"[31]

9   *Molecular resonance.* The basic "building block" of any physical object is the atom. Atoms bond to one another by sharing electrons, thus forming a molecule. "Different arrangements of the electrons in certain molecules are called 'resonance structures.' Some molecules, like water, have no resonance while others have three resonance structures or more, like [nitrate]."[32] "The nitrate ion can be viewed *as if* it resonates

---

27. Evans, "Three types," n.p.
28. Sutter, "Is it," n.p.
29. Bozack lists seven points of similarity between the hypostatic union of Christ's divine and human natures and the dual nature of waves and particles. Bozack, "Physics," 72–76.
30. Bozack "Thermodynamical," 39.
31. Bozack, "Physics," 67.
32. Qureshi, *Seeking Allah*, 194.

between ... three different structures. ... The hypothetical switching from one resonance structure to another is called *resonance*. ... It is important to stress that the nitrate ion is not really changing from one resonance structure to another. ... In actuality, the ion behaves as if it were a blend of the three resonance structures."[33]

In other words, resonating molecules exist in multiple forms *simultaneously*, each form having the same chemical composition. Thus, nitrate has three resonance structures and exists in all of these forms simultaneously. This is the phenomenon that caused then-Muslim Nabel Qureshi to see that the idea of the Trinity was plausible. He wrote, "One molecule of nitrate is all three resonance structures all the time and never just one of them. The three are separate but all the same, and they are one. They are three in one. That's when it clicked: if there are things in this world that can be three in one, even incomprehensively so, then why cannot God?"[34]

10 *Triune patterns of reality.* The three persons of the Godhead (Father, Son, and Holy Spirit), although sharing the same essence with the other two, manifest different roles, particularly in their interaction with the world and with people, e.g., the Father sent the Son to be the savior of the world (1 John 4:14), the Son alone became incarnate in the person of Jesus Christ (Phil 2:5–8), and the Holy Spirit comes to indwell and guide believers (John 14:16–17, 26).[35] Because God is triune, it is not surprising that virtually every aspect of reality in some way reflects a triune pattern—in many ways mirroring the roles of the Father, Son, and Holy Spirit. Examples include:

- *The Sun.* The sun consists of fire (technically, plasma), light, and heat. All three pervade the entire sun, yet each is distinct. Without any one of them the sun would cease to exist.

- *Matter.* Matter consists of energy (the universal, unseen source, potentiality), motion (particular embodiment of that energy), and phenomena (particular motion in contact with other existences):

---

33. "Resonance," n.p.
34. Qureshi, *Seeking Allah*, 195–96.
35. This is something like a man who can be a father, a son, and a husband at the same time. There is only one man. He is not partly father, partly son, and partly husband. All of him is father, all of him is son, and all of him is husband, all of the time. Nevertheless, his roles, particularly in their interaction with the world and with people, differ as father, son, and husband.

It is the nature of energy to beget motion. As for motion, it cannot exist without energy back of it. Neither can it take place without phenomena inevitably issuing from it. It can hardly be motion without different *kinds* of motion, and that means phenomena. And in turn phenomena cannot exist without motion, and back of the motion the energy, from which the phenomena issue. . . . Each of the three is inevitable with the others. None of the three can be without the others. No two can exist without the third.[36]

- *Time.* Time consists of future (the universal potentiality of events), present (particular embodiment, realization of future things we know and touch), and past (the present after it has related itself to others). As with the other examples we have discussed, none of these aspects of time can exist without the others: "If there is no past, time has never existed until this instant, and a little later this instant also never will have existed. If there is no present, there will never be any instant in which time exists. If there is no future, time ceases now, and indeed ceased long ago. . . . It is an absolute threeness."[37]

    Further, all of time is or has been future; all of time is or has been or will be present; and all of time is or will be past. At the beginning, all of time was future; now, all of time is present; and at the end, all of time will be past. Each one is the whole of time.[38]

- *A human person.* A person consists of soul (the person's unique non-physical nature [mind, emotions, personality]), body (the person's unique physical nature [form, sex, DNA]), and spirit (that which enables the person to relate to God). Each aspect is intimately related to and influences the others. All three must co-exist or the "humanity" of the person ceases to exist (inanimate objects have only a body; animals have only a body and a soul; only humans consist of body, soul, and spirit). Nevertheless, they constitute only one person, not three people.[39]

36. Wood, *Trinity*, 35.
37. Wood, *Trinity*, 41.
38. See Wood, *Trinity*, 41.
39. Geisler and Saleeb provide a caveat to this "trichotomous" understanding of human beings, "Even if true (and many Christians reject it for a dichotomy of just body and soul), it would be a bad illustration. Body and soul can be and are separated at death (2 Cor. 5:8; Phil. 1:23; Rev. 6:9), but the nature and persons of the Trinity cannot he separated." Geisler and Saleeb, *Answering Islam*, 276.

These examples indicate that the pattern of the Trinity appears to be designed into the universe and human life. That is not by accident. The Bible says, *"The heavens declare the glory of God"* (Ps 19:1, ESV). The nature of reality does this by reflecting the nature of God. Granted, there is a mysterious element to this, but "Mystery is not the absence of meaning, but the presence of more meaning than we can comprehend."[40] When we begin to grasp the idea of the Trinity, "we are then, for the first time in our lives, getting some positive idea, however faint, of something supra-personal—something more than a person."[41] That "something" is the true God: Father, Son, and Holy Spirit: one God in three persons.

IMPLICATIONS OF THE TRINITY

That the God of the Bible is Trinity has important implications, including the following:

Because he is Trinity, God alone is self-sufficient

If God were a simplistic singularity like the Islamic conception of Allah and not a Trinity, he would not be self-sufficient. If God were a simplistic singularity he would have *needed* to create other beings in order to have relationship. However, because God is Trinity, he did not need to create anything (see Acts 17:24–26). This necessarily means that any "god," such as Allah, who is a simplistic, not a triune, unity is an *insufficient being who is dependent upon creation*. In other words, a "god" who is a "bare unity" that lacks intrinsic plurality necessarily "cannot function without the supplementation supplied by the plurality of the world."[42] Of necessity, therefore, such a "god" cannot be the true God over the universe.

Because he is Trinity, God alone is personal and relational at the core of his being

The Bible tells us that *"God is love"* (1 John 4:8). That stems from the fact that God is Trinity and for all eternity had a perfect love relationship among the Father, Son, and Holy Spirit. Because he is Trinity, God is by nature a *personal* God; in other words, all of God's "personal" or "relational" attributes

40. Yancey, *Reaching*, 96.
41. Lewis, *Mere Christianity*, 143.
42. Frame, *Cornelius Van Til*, 64.

derive from and are an intrinsic part of his being. On the other hand, any "god," such as Allah, that has a simplistic unitary nature, *could not have any relationship* until he created other beings with whom he could then be in relationship; he could not *experience or express* any "personal" or "relational" attribute unless and until he created the world. Consequently, none of the "personal" or "relational" attributes are, *or could be, an intrinsic part* of such a god's being. This means that, in and of himself, such a "god" necessarily is an *impersonal* being (like a force or a force-field), not a personal one. However, a force or force-field or any impersonal entity *cannot create, relate to, or have relationship with "personality" or "personal" beings*, because personality cannot come from impersonality. Therefore, such a simplistic god cannot account for the personality of human beings, since human beings are "personal" beings.

There is a practical implication of this for human relationships. John 16:14; 17:4–5 say that the Holy Spirit, the Son, and the Father all "glorify" each other. Keller observes, "To glorify something or someone is to praise, enjoy, and delight in them. . . . To glorify someone is also to serve or defer to him or her. . . . Each person of the Trinity loves, adores, defers to, and rejoices in the others. That creates a dynamic, pulsating dance of joy and love."[43] The Trinity's relationship of interpersonal deference and love (see Matt 26:39) should be the model for our own interpersonal relationships.[44]

Because God is Trinity, we can have assurance of our salvation

According to the Bible, no human being can atone for his own sins, because of his or her inherent sinfulness. But God in Christ chose to do for us what we could not do for ourselves: live the life we should have lived, die the death we should have died, and pay the price for sin that otherwise we would have to pay but never could. In this regard, not only is the doctrine of the Trinity important, it is absolutely necessary: "If Jesus is less than God . . . how can he serve as the atoning sacrifice for all? . . . As to the Holy Spirit, . . . Scripture teaches that the Holy Spirit regenerates believers and indwells and fills them, but if the Holy Spirit is a lesser God or no God at all, how can we be sure that he can do any of these things?"[45]

---

43. Keller, *Reason*, 214–15.
44. See Feinberg, *No One*, 441–42.
45. Feinberg, *No One*, 440–41.

The Trinity alone provides the answer to the ultimate questions of existence and of humanity

The universe includes both non-living and living matter, impersonal beings and personality (i.e., beings that have consciousness, perception, self-awareness). Additionally, unity (with an underlying rationality that can be perceived and studied) and diversity (particularity, individuation) are found at all levels of the universe. That is true for living and non-living beings and from the atomic level to the largest star systems in the universe. To account for existence as it is, consisting of unity and diversity along with personality, the cause must be at least as great as the universe and its components.[46] As Francis Schaeffer puts it, in order to have a cause sufficient to account for existence, "we need two things. We need a personal-infinite God (or an infinite-personal God), and we need a personal unity and diversity in God."[47]

The God of the Bible meets the need of existence as it is, in both its unity and diversity, its personality and impersonality. Schaeffer concludes, God is "personal unity and diversity on the high order of Trinity.... Without the high order of personal unity and diversity as given in the Trinity, *there are no answers.*"[48] Only the triune God of the Bible is an adequate cause for and explanation of existence as it is, including its unity, diversity, and personality.

CONCLUSION

Although there is an element of mystery to the idea of the Trinity, the concept of the Trinity clearly emerges from the Bible. The concept of Trinity is neither irrational nor illogical. Only God as Trinity can account for reality as it exists. Indeed, the concept of Trinity is clearly woven into all levels of reality, from the microscopic to the macroscopic. This fact may be one of the things behind the Bible's statement, *"The heavens are telling of the glory of God; And their expanse is declaring the work of His hands"* (Ps 19:1).

---

46. Wood, *Trinity*, 22–23.
47. Schaeffer, "He Is There," 286.
48. Schaeffer, "He Is There," 287–88, emph. in orig.

Bibliography

"13 Reasons Why Melchizedek Was Actually the Pre-Incarnate Word of God." *The Christ Plus Zero Movement*. 2014. https://christpluszero.wordpress.com/2014/12/13/10-reasons-why-melchizedek-was-actually-the-pre-incarnate-word-of-god/.
Ajijola, Alhaj A. D. *The Myth of the Cross*. Mafmdeen [online publisher], 1972. http://www.scribd.com/doc/14956531/The-Myth-of-the-Cross.
Alexander, T. Desmond. *From Eden to the New Jerusalem: Exploring God's plan for life on earth*. Nottingham, England: Inter-Varsity, 2008.
———. "Genealogies, Seed and the Compositional Unity of Genesis." *Tyndale Bulletin* 44 (1993) 255–70. http://www.biblicalstudies.org.uk/pdf/tb/genealogies_alexander.pdf.
Alter, Robert. *Genesis*. New York: W. W. Norton, 1996. https://archive.org/details/genesisoooounse_h9l6.
Archer, Gleason. *Encyclopedia of Bible Difficulties*. Grand Rapids: Zondervan, 1982. http://sent2all.com/Archer-Introduction%20to%20Bible%20Difficulties.pdf.
Augustine. *The City of God*. New York: Random House, 1950 (reprint).
———. *The City of God*. http://www.ccel.org/ccel/schaff/npnf102.iv.html.
Baker, David. "Typology and the Christian Use of the Old Testament." *Scottish Journal of Theology* 29 (1976) 137–57.
Balfour, Glenn. "The Jewishness of John's Use of the Scriptures in John 6:31 and 7:37–38." *Tyndale Bulletin* 46 (1995) 357–80. http://www.tyndalehouse.com/tynbul/library/TynBull_1995_46_2_08_Balfour_John6_7.pdf.
Bartholomew, Craig. "Biblical Theology." In *Dictionary for Theological Interpretation of the Bible*, edited by Kevin Vanhoozer, 84–90. Grand Rapids: Baker Academic, 2005. https://archive.org/details/dictionaryfortheoooounse.
Bartholomew, Craig, and Michael Goheen. "The Story-Line of the Bible." Not dated. https://missionworldview.com/wp-content/uploads/2020/06/ea8a85_7f07978cf7244bf7a24cbccoba1178c7.pdf.
Bartlett, John. "Maccabees, The Books of the." In *The Oxford Companion to the Bible*, edited by Bruce Metzger and Michael Coogan, 475–82. New York: Oxford, 1993. https://archive.org/details/isbn_9780965072595.
Bauckham, Richard. *God Crucified: Monotheism and Christology in the New Testament*. Grand Rapids: Eerdmans, 1998.
———. "The Lord's Day." In *From Sabbath to Lord's Day: A Biblical, Historical and Theological Investigation*, edited by D. A. Carson, 221–50. Grand Rapids: Zondervan, 1982. https://archive.org/details/fromsabbathtolor1982unse.

———. "The Sonship of the Historical Jesus in Christology." *Scottish Journal of Theology* 31 (1978) 245–60.

Beale, G. K. *Handbook on the New Testament Use of the Old Testament*. Grand Rapids: Baker Academic, 2012.

———. "Peace and Mercy Upon the Israel of God: The Old Testament Background of Galatians 6,16b." *Biblica* 80 (1999) 204–23. http://www.bsw.org/Biblica/Vol-80-1999/Peace-And-Mercy-Upon-The-Israel-Of-God-The-Old-Testament-Background-Of-Galatians-6-16b/320/.

———. *The Temple and the Church's Mission: A Biblical Theology of the Dwelling Place of God* (NSBT 17). Downers Grove, IL: InterVarsity, 2004.

———. *We Become What We Worship: A Biblical Theology of Idolatry*. Downers Grove, IL: IVP Academic, 2008. https://archive.org/details/we-become-what-we-worship-a-biblical-theology-of-idolatry-g.-k.-beale.

Beare, Francis. "The Sabbath Was Made for Man?" *Journal for Biblical Literature* 79 (1960) 130–36.

Beckwith, Roger. "The Unity and Diversity of God's Covenants." *Tyndale Bulletin* 38 (1987) 93–118. http://www.tyndalehouse.com/TynBul/Library/TynBull_1987_38_04_Beckwith_GodsCovenant.pdf.

Behm, Johannes. "Klaō." In *Theological Dictionary of the New Testament*, vol. 3, edited by Gerhard Kittel, 722–43, translated by Geoffrey Bromiley. Grand Rapids: Eerdmans, 1965.

Bell, William Everett, Jr. "A Critical Evaluation of the Pretribulation Rapture Doctrine in Christian Eschatology." Ph.D. diss., New York University, 1967.

Belleville, Linda. "'Under Law': Structural Analysis and the Pauline Concept of Law in Galatians 3:21—4:11." *Journal for the Study of the New Testament* 26 (1986) 53–78.

Blocher, Henri. *Original Sin: Illuminating the Riddle*. Leicester, England: Apollos, 1997.

Blomberg, Craig. "Matthew." In *Commentary on the New Testament Use of the Old Testament*, edited by G. K. Beale and D. A. Carson, 1–109. Grand Rapids: Baker Academic, 2007.

Bock, Darrell. *Luke 1:1—9:50* (BECNT). Grand Rapids: Baker, 1994.

Boice, James. *Foundations of the Christian Faith*, rev. ed. Downers Grove, IL: InterVarsity, 1986.

Booker, Richard. *The Miracle of the Scarlet Thread*. Plainfield, NJ: Logos, 1981. https://archive.org/details/miracleofscarletoobook.

Bozack, Michael. "Physics in the Theological Seminary." *Journal of the Evangelical Theological Society* 36 (1993) 65–76. https://www.etsjets.org/files/JETS-PDFs/36/36-31/JETS_36-1_065-76_Bozack.pdf.

———. "The Thermodynamical Triple Point: Implications for the Trinity." *Perspectives on Science and Christian Faith* 39 (1987) 39–41. https://www.asa3.org/ASA/PSCF/1987/PSCF3-87Bozack.html.

Brawley, Robert. "For Blessing All Families of the Earth: Covenant Traditions in Luke-Acts," *Currents in Theology and Mission* 22 (1995) 18–26.

Bretscher, Paul. "The Covenant of Blood." *Concordia Theological Monthly* 25 (1954) 199–209.

Briggs, Charles, *Messianic Prophecy*. New York: Charles Scribner's Sons, 1886. Reprint, Peabody, MA: Hendrickson, 1988. https://archive.org/details/messianicprophecooobrig/page/n5/mode/2up.

Brower, Jeffrey, and Michael Rea. "Understanding the Trinity." *Logos: A Journal of Catholic Thought and Culture* 8:1 (2005) 145–57.
Brueggemann, Walter. *Isaiah 40–66.* Louisville KY: Westminster John Knox, 1998.
Burke, Trevor. *Adopted into God's Family: Exploring a Pauline Metaphor* (NSBT 22). Nottingham, England: Apollos, 2006.
Busenitz, Irvin. "Woman's Desire for Man: Genesis 3:16 Reconsidered." *Grace Theological Journal* 7 (1986) 203–12. http://faculty.gordon.edu/hu/bi/Ted_Hildebrandt/OTeSources/01-Genesis/Text/Articles-Books/Busenitz-Gen3-GTJ.pdf.
Carson, D. A. "Getting Excited About Melchizedek; Psalm 110." In *The Scriptures Testify About Me,* edited by D. A. Carson, 145–74. Wheaton, IL: Crossway, 2013.
———. *The Gospel According to John* (PNTC). Grand Rapids: Eerdmans, 1991.
———. "Jesus and the Sabbath in the Four Gospels." In *From Sabbath to Lord's Day: A Biblical, Historical and Theological Investigation,* edited by D. A. Carson, 57–97. Grand Rapids: Zondervan, 1982. https://archive.org/details/fromsabbathtolor1982unse.
———. "Matthew." In *Expositor's Bible Commentary,* vol. 8, edited by Frank Gaebelein, 1–599. Grand Rapids: Zondervan, 1984.
Carter, J. Kameron. *Race: A Theological Account.* Oxford: Oxford University Press, 2008.
Cassuto, Umberto. *A Commentary on the Book of Exodus,* translated by Israel Abrahams. Jerusalem: Magnes, 1967.
———. *A Commentary on the Book of Genesis,* Part I, translated by Israel Abrahams. Jerusalem: Magnes, 1961.
Chosen People Ministries. *The Gospel According to Hanukkah.* New York: Chosen People Ministries, not dated. https://archive.chosenpeople.com/the-gospel-according-to-hanukkah/.
Clement of Alexandria. *Stromata.* In *The Ante-Nicene Fathers,* vol. 2, edited by Alexander Roberts and James Donaldson, revised by A. Cleveland Coxe, 299–567. New York: Christian Literature, 1885. Reprint, Peabody, MA: Hendrickson, 1994. http://www.ccel.org/ccel/schaff/anf02.vi.iv.html.
Clement of Rome. *First Epistle of Clement to the Corinthians.* In *The Ante-Nicene Fathers,* vol. 1, edited by Alexander Roberts and James Donaldson, revised by A. Cleveland Coxe, 1–22. New York: Christian Literature, 1885. Reprint, Peabody, MA: Hendrickson, 1994. http://www.ccel.org/ccel/schaff/anf01.viii.iv.html.
Clowney, Edmund. "The Final Temple." *Westminster Theological Journal* 35 (1972–73) 156–89. http://www.beginningwithmoses.org/articles/finaltemple.htm.
———. "Preaching Christ From All the Scriptures." In *The Preacher and Preaching,* edited by Samuel Logan, 163–91. Philipsburg, NJ: Presbyterian and Reformed, 1986.
———. *Preaching Christ in All of Scripture.* Wheaton, IL: Crossway, 2003.
Cole, Graham. *IG 500,* unpublished class notes. Deerfield, IL: Trinity Evangelical Divinity School, 2006.
Cole, R. A. *The Letter of Paul to the Galatians,* 2nd ed. Leicester, England: Inter-Varsity, 1989.
Cross, John. *The Stranger on the Road to Emmaus,* 3rd ed. Olds, AB, Canada: GoodSeed, 2003. https://archive.org/details/strangeronroadtooocros_0/mode/2up.
———. "Where in the Scriptures does it say that God told Cain and Abel to bring a blood sacrifice?" 2014. http://www.goodseed.com/blog/2014/01/02/where-in-the-scriptures-does-it-say-that-god-told-cain-and-abel-to-bring-a-blood-sacrifice/.

"(Dan. 3:25) Who is the fourth man in the fire? Was it Jesus? Or an angel?" *Evidence Unseen*. 2024. https://www.evidenceunseen.com/bible-difficulties-2/ot-difficulties/daniel-amos/dan-325-who-is-the-fourth-man-in-the-fire-was-it-jesus-or-an-angel/.

Danielou, Jean. *From Shadows to Reality: Studies in the Biblical Typology of the Fathers*. Westminster, MD: Newman, 1960. https://archive.org/details/fromshadowstoreaooooodani_b2k8/page/n3/mode/2up.

Danker, Frederick, ed. *A Greek-English Lexicon of the New Testament and Other Early Christian Literature*. Chicago: The University of Chicago Press, 2000. https://archive.org/details/a-greek-english-lexicon-of-the-new-testament-and-other-early-christian-literatur/page/675/mode/2up.

Davids, Peter. *The Epistle of James* (NIGTC). Grand Rapids: Eerdmans, 1982.

Davidson, Richard. *Typology in Scripture: A Study of Hermeneutical Tupos Structures*. Berrien Springs, MI: Andrews University Press, 1981.

Davies, J. G. *The Early Christian Church*. Grand Rapids: Baker, 1965. https://archive.org/details/earlychristianchoooodavi.

Davis, C. Truman. "The Anatomical And Physiological Details Of Death By Crucifixion." *New Wine Magazine*. 1982. https://thecatholicmanshow.com/55-meditations-on-the-crucifixion-of-jesus/.

———. "A Physician Analyzes the Crucifixion." *New Wine Magazine*. 1982. http://www.thecross-photo.com/Dr_C._Truman_Davis_Analyzes_the_Crucifixion.htm.

Dawkins, Richard. *The God Delusion*. Boston: Houghton Mifflin, 2006. https://archive.org/details/isbn_9780552773317.

DeHaan, M. R. *Portraits of Christ in Genesis*. Grand Rapids, Zondervan: 1988. https://archive.org/details/portraitsofchrisoooomrde.

Delling, Gerhard. "Hē[set macron over e]mera." In *Theological Dictionary of the New Testament*, vol. 2, edited by Gerhard Kittel, 943–53, translated by Geoffrey Bromiley. Grand Rapids: Eerdmans, 1964.

Didache. c.70–110. http://www.ccel.org/ccel/richardson/fathers.viii.i.html.

Dumbrell, William. "Genesis 2:1–3: Biblical Theology of Creation Covenant." *Evangelical Review of Theology* 25 (2001) 219–30.

Duncan, Ligon. "Jesus and Melchizedek." *RTS*. 2013. https://rts.edu/resources/jesus-and-melchizedek/.

Edersheim, Alfred. *The Temple*. Grand Rapids: Eerdmans, 1988 (reprint). https://books.google.com/books?id=XFc-AAAAYAAJ.

Edwards, Jonathan. *The Works of Jonathan Edwards*. Vol. 1, *A Careful and Strict Inquiry into the Prevailing Notions of the Freedom of Will; Dissertation on the End for which God Created the World; The Great Christian Doctrine of Original Sin Defended; A History of the Work of Redemption*. Carlisle, PA: The Banner of Truth, 1984 (reprint). http://www.ccel.org/ccel/edwards/works1.html.

Epistle of Barnabas. In *The Apostolic Fathers*, 2nd ed., edited and revised by Michael Holmes, translated by J. B. Lightfoot and J. R. Harmer, 159–88. Grand Rapids: Baker, 1989, http://www.ccel.org/ccel/schaff/anf01/Page_137.html.

Epp, Theodore. *Portraits of Christ in the Tabernacle*. Lincoln, NE: Back to the Bible, 1976. https://archive.org/details/portraitsofchrisooootheo.

Essex, Keith. "The Abrahamic Covenant." *The Master's Seminary Journal* 10 (1999) 191–212. http://www.ondoctrine.com/2esso001.pdf.

Eusebius. *The Ecclesiastical History of Eusebius Pamphilus*. Grand Rapids: Baker, 1988 (reprint). http://www.ccel.org/ccel/schaff/npnf201.toc.html.

Evans, Rhodri. "Three types of spectrums (spectra)." *The Curious Astronomer*. 2013. https://thecuriousastronomer.wordpress.com/2013/07/09/three-types-of-spectrums-spectra/.

Evans, William. "WRF Member Dr. William Evans Asks, 'How Much Did the Old Testament Writers Know?'" *World Reformed Fellowship*. 2014. https://wrf.global/theological-education/wrf-member-dr-william-evans-asks-how-much-did-old-testament-writers-know.

Fairbairn, Patrick. *The Typology of Scripture*. Grand Rapids: Zondervan, 1963. https://archive.org/details/typologyofscriptoooopatr.

Feinberg, John. *No One Like Him*. Wheaton, IL: Crossway, 2001.

FIRM Staff. "Fulfillment Theology: The Theology I Didn't Know I Had." *Fellowship of Israel Related Ministries*. 2017. https://firmisrael.org/learn/fulfillment-theology-theology-didnt-know/.

Foh, Susan. "What Is the Woman's Desire?" *Westminster Theological Journal* 37 (1974–75) 376–83. http://faculty.gordon.edu/hu/bi/Ted_Hildebrandt/OTeSources/01-Genesis/Text/Articles-Books/Foh-WomansDesire-WTJ.pdf.

Ford, Desmond. *The Abomination of Desolation in Biblical Eschatology*. Washington, DC: University Press of America, 1979. https://archive.org/details/abominationofdesooooford.

Frame, John. *Cornelius Van Til: An Analysis of His Thought*. Phillipsburg, NJ: P&R, 1995. https://archive.org/details/corneliusvantilaooofram.

France, R. T. *The Gospel of Matthew* (NICNT). Grand Rapids: Eerdmans, 2007.

———. *Jesus and the Old Testament*. London: Tyndale, 1971. https://archive.org/details/jesusoldtestamenoooofran.

———. "Old Testament Prophecy and the Future of Israel: A Study of the Teaching of Jesus." *Tyndale Bulletin* 26 (1975) 53–78. https://www.tyndalebulletin.org/article/30633.

Fritsch, Charles. "Biblical Typology." *Bibliotheca Sacra* 104 (1947) 87–100, 214–22.

Geisler, Norman. *Christian Apologetics*. Grand Rapids: Baker, 1976. https://archive.org/details/christianapologeooogeis.

Geisler, Norman, and Abdul Saleeb. *Answering Islam*. Grand Rapids: Baker, 2002. https://archive.org/stream/pppp8888212/1#page/n0/mode/2up.

Gentry, Peter. "Daniel's Seventy Weeks and the New Exodus." *Southern Baptist Journal of Theology* 14 (2010) 26–44. http://www.sbts.edu/resources/files/2010/05/sbjt_v14_n1_gentry.pdf.

Ghabril, Nicola Yacoub. *Themes for the Diligent*. Rikon, Switzerland: The Good Way, 2003. http://www.the-good-way.com/eng/books.

Gidley, Robert. "The facts of crucifixion." *Catholic Education Resource Center*. 2000. https://catholiceducation.org/en/controversy/the-facts-of-crucifixion.html.

Gleason, Randall. "The Eschatology of the Warning in Hebrews 10:26–31." *Tyndale Bulletin* 53 (2002) 97–120. http://www.tyndalehouse.com/tynbul/library/TynBull_2002_53_1_06_Gleason_Hebrews10Warning.pdf.

Goldsworthy, Graeme. *According to Plan: The Unfolding Revelation of God in the Bible*. Downers Grove, IL: InterVarsity, 1991.

———. *Preaching the Whole Bible as Christian Scripture*. Grand Rapids: Eerdmans, 2000.

Goppelt, Leonhard. "Tupos." *Theological Dictionary of the New Testament,* vol 8, edited by Gerhard Friedrich, translated by Geoffery Bromiley, 246–59. Grand Rapids: Eerdmans, 1964.

———. *Typos: The Typological Interpretation of the Old Testament in the New* translated by Donald Madvig. Grand Rapids: Eerdmans, 1982.

Gordon, I. "The Resurrection—Jesus in the Feast of First Fruits Bible Study." *Jesusplusnothing.com.* 2025. https://jesusplusnothing.com/series/post/FeastOfFirstFruits.

Graham, Wyatt. "Christ Rose So that We Might Rise in Him." *The Gospel Coalition.* 2020. https://ca.thegospelcoalition.org/columns/detrinitate/christ-rose-so-that-we-might-rise-in-him/.

Greidanus, Sidney, *Preaching Christ from the Old Testament.* Grand Rapids: Eerdmans, 1999.

Grenz, Stanley. *The Millennial Maze.* Downers Grove, IL: InterVarsity, 1992.

Grudem, Wayne. *1 Peter* (TNTC). Grand Rapids: Eerdmans, 1988.

Gundry, Robert. "The New Jerusalem: People as Place, Not Place for People." *Novum Testamentum* 29 (1987) 254–64.

———. *The Use of the Old Testament in St. Matthew's Gospel.* Leiden: E. J. Brill, 1967. https://archive.org/details/useofoldtestamenooogund.

Guthrie, George. "Hebrews." In *Commentary on the New Testament Use of the Old Testament,* edited by G. K. Beale and D. A. Carson, 919–95. Grand Rapids: Baker Academic, 2007.

Habershon, Ada. *The Study of the Types: Priests and Levites,* new enlarged ed. Grand Rapids: Kregel, 1974. https://archive.org/details/studyoftypesoohabe.

Hagopian, David G., ed. *The Genesis Debate: Three Views on the Days of Creation.* Mission Viejo, CA: Crux, 2001.

Hagner, Donald. *Matthew 14–28* (WBC 33B). Dallas: Word, 1995.

Hamilton, James. "Were Old Covenant Believers Indwelt by the Holy Spirit?" *Themelios* 30 (2004) 12–22. https://media.thegospelcoalition.org/documents/themelios/Themelios30.1.pdf.

Hamstra, Sam. "An Idealist View of Revelation." In *Four Views on the Book of Revelation,* edited by C. Marvin Pate, 95–131. Grand Rapids: Zondervan, 1998. https://books.google.com/books?isbn=0310872391.

Hanson, Anthony. *Jesus Christ in the Old Testament.* London: SPCK, 1965.

Harrison, Everett. *Interpreting Acts: The Expanding Church.* Grand Rapids: Academie, 1986. https://archive.org/details/interpretingactsoooharr.

Hartzler, H. Harold. "Foreword." In *Science Speaks,* rev. online ed., by Peter Stoner, 4–5. Chicago: Moody, 2005. https://archive.org/details/sciencespeakspeterw.stoner/mode/2up?view=theater.

Hauerwas, Stanley. *Matthew* (BTCB). Grand Rapids: Brazos, 2006.

Hays, Richard. "Christ Prays the Psalms: Paul's Use of an Early Christian Exegetical Convention." In *The Future of Christology,* edited by Abraham Malherbe and Wayne Meeks, 122–36. Minneapolis: Fortress, 1993.

Hengstenberg, E. W. *Christology of the Old Testament.* Grand Rapids: Kregel, 1970 (reprint). https://archive.org/details/christologyofold01heng/mode/2up.

Hillyer, Norman. "First Peter and the Feast of Tabernacles," *Tyndale Bulletin* 21 (1970) 39–70. http://www.tyndalehouse.com/tynbul/library/TynBull_1970_21_02_Hillyer_1PeterFeastTabernacles.pdf.

"The Historical and Spiritual Significance of Shiloh in the Bible." *Sar-El Tours & Conferences.* 2020. https://sareltours.com/article/shiloh-in-the-bible.

Hoekema, Anthony. *The Bible and the Future.* Grand Rapids: Eerdmans, 1979.

Holiday, Alfred. *The Feasts of the Lord.* London: Pickering & Inglis, not dated. https://www.brethrenarchive.org/media/361356/holiday-a-j-_-feasts-of-the-lord.pdf.

Holwerda, David. *Jesus and Israel: One Covenant or Two?* Grand Rapids: Eerdmans, 1995.

Hugenberger, G. P. "Introductory Notes on Typology." In *The Right Doctrine from the Wrong Texts?*, edited by G. K. Beale, 331–41. Grand Rapids: Baker, 1994.

Ignatius. "To the Magnesians." In *The Apostolic Fathers*, 2nd ed., edited and revised by Michael Holmes, translated by J. B. Lightfoot and J. R. Harmer, 93–97. Grand Rapids: Baker, 1989. http://www.ccel.org/ccel/lightfoot/fathers.ii.iv.html.

Jackson, Wayne. "Was Melchizedek the Preincarnate Christ?" *Christian Courier.* 2025. https://christiancourier.com/articles/was-melchizedek-the-preincarnate-christ.

———. "Was the Sabbath a Divine Requirement from the Time of Creation?" *Christian Courier.* 2025. https://christiancourier.com/articles/was-the-sabbath-a-divine-requirement-from-the-time-of-creation.

Jacobs, Louis, *A Guide to Rosh Ha-Shanah.* London: Jewish Chronicle, 1959. =

———. "Messiah." *Jewish Virtual Library*, 2013. https://www.jewishvirtuallibrary.org/jsource/judaica/ejud_0002_0014_0_13744.html.

"Jesus In The Tabernacle—How Does The Old Testament Tabernacle Point To Jesus?" *studyandobey.com.* 2012–2022. https://studyandobey.com/jesus-in-the-tabernacle/.

"Jesus Is Better Than Melchizedek." *Israel My Glory.* 1993–1994. https://israelmyglory.org/article/jesus-is-better-than-melchizedek/.

Jews for Jesus. "The Feast of Trumpets: Background and Fulfillment." 2000. https://jewsforjesus.org/blog/the-feast-of-trumpets.

Johnson, Dennis. "Fire in God's House: Imagery from Malachi 3 in Peter's Theology of Suffering (1 Pet. 4:12–19)." *Journal of the Evangelical Theological Society* 29 (1986) 285–94. http://www.etsjets.org/files/JETS-PDFs/29/29-23/29-23-pp285-294_JETS.pdf.

———. *Him We Proclaim: Preaching Christ from All the Scriptures.* Phillipsburg, NJ: P&R, 2007.

———. "Jesus Against the Idols: The use of Isaianic Servant Songs in the Missiology of Acts." *Westminster Theological Journal* 52 (1990) 343–53.

———. *Triumph of the Lamb: A Commentary on Revelation.* Phillipsburg, NJ: P&R, 2001.

Johnson, S. Lewis. "Romans 5:12—An Exercise in Exegesis and Theology." In *New Dimensions in New Testament Study,* edited by Richard Longenecker and Merrill Tenney, 298–316. Grand Rapids: Zondervan, 1974. https://archive.org/details/new-dimension-in-new-testament-study.

Jordan, James. *The Law of the Covenant.* Tyler, TX: Institute for Christian Economics, 1984. http://www.garynorth.com/freebooks/docs/pdf/the_law_of_the_covenant.pdf.

———. *Through New Eyes: Developing a Biblical View of the World.* Brentwood, TN: Wolgemuth & Hyatt, 1988. http://www.garynorth.com/freebooks/docs/pdf/through_new_eyes.pdf.

Josephus. *The Antiquities of the Jews*. In *The Works of Josephus Complete and Unabridged*, translated by William Whiston, 27–542. Peabody, MA: Hendrickson, 1987. http://www.ccel.org/ccel/josephus/works/files/works.html.

———. *The Wars of the Jews*. In *The Works of Josephus Complete and Unabridged*, translated by William Whiston, 543–772. Peabody, MA: Hendrickson, 1987. http://www.ccel.org/ccel/josephus/works/files/works.html.

Justin Martyr. *Dialogue with Trypho*. In *The Ante-Nicene Fathers*, vol. 1, edited by Alexander Roberts and James Donaldson, revised by A. Cleveland Coxe, 194–270. New York: Christian Literature. Reprint, Peabody, MA: Hendrickson, 1994. http://www.ccel.org/ccel/schaff/anf01.viii.iv.html.

———. *First Apology*. In *The Ante-Nicene Fathers*, vol. 1, edited by Alexander Roberts and James Donaldson, revised by A. Cleveland Coxe, 159–87. New York: Christian Literature. Reprint, Peabody, MA: Hendrickson, 1994. http://www.ccel.org/ccel/schaff/anf01.viii.ii.html.

Kagin, Josiah. "The Crucifixion of Jesus from a Doctor's Perspective." 2022. https://josiahkagin.com/2022/04/13/the-crucifixion-of-jesus-from-a-doctors-perspective/.

Kaiser, Walter. *The Messiah in the Old Testament*. Grand Rapids: Zondervan, 1995. https://archive.org/details/messiahinoldtestooookais.

———. *The Old Testament Documents: Are They Reliable and Relevant?* Downers Grove, IL: InterVarsity, 2001. https://archive.org/details/oldtestamentdocuooookais.

———. *Toward an Old Testament Theology*. Grand Rapids: Zondervan, 1978.

Katz, Jochen. "You are my Son, today I have begotten you." *Answering Islam*. Not dated. http://www.answering-islam.org/BibleCom/ps2-7.html.

Keller, Timothy. "Getting Out (Exodus 14)." In *The Scriptures Testify About Me*, edited by D. A. Carson, 33–53. Wheaton, IL: Crossway, 2013.

———. *Preaching: Communicating Faith in an Age of Skepticism*. New York: Viking, 2015.

———. *The Reason for God*. New York: Dutton, 2008.

———. *Walking with God through Pain and Suffering*. New York: Riverhead, 2013.

Kepple, Robert. "The Hope of Israel, the Resurrection of the Dead, and Jesus: A Study of Their Relationship in Acts with Particular Regard to the Understanding of Paul's Trial Defense." *Journal of the Evangelical Theological Society* 20 (1977) 231–41. http://www.etsjets.org/files/JETS-PDFs/20/20-23/20-23-pp231-240_JETS.pdf.

Kistemaker, Simon. "The Temple in the Apocalypse." *Journal of the Evangelical Theological Society* 43 (2000) 433–41. http://www.etsjets.org/files/JETS-PDFs/43/43-43/43-43-pp433-441_JETS.pdf.

Klooster, Fred. "The Biblical Method of Salvation: A Case for Continuity." In *Continuity and Discontinuity: Perspectives on the Relationship Between the Old and New Testaments*, edited by John Feinberg, 132–60. Westchester, IL: Crossway, 1988.

Knowles, Michael. *Jeremiah in Matthew's Gospel* (JSNTSup 68). Sheffield, England: Sheffield Academic, 1993.

Koehler, Ludwig, and Walter Baumgartner, *The Hebrew and Aramaic Lexicon of the Old Testament*, vol 1, translated and edited under the supervision of M. E. J. Richardson. Leiden: Brill, 2001. https://archive.org/details/hebrewaramaiclex0001kohl.

Köstenberger, Andreas, and David Jones. *God, Marriage, and Family: Rebuilding the Biblical Foundation*, 2nd ed. Wheaton, IL: Crossway, 2010.

Lampe, G. W. H. "The Reasonableness of Typology." In *Essays on Typology*, edited by G. W. H. Lampe and K. J. Woollcombe, 9–38. Naperville, IL: Alec R. Allenson, 1957. https://archive.org/details/essaysontypology0000unse_i7e1/page/n9/mode/2up.

LaRondelle, Hans. *The Israel of God in Prophecy: Principles of Prophetic Interpretation*. Berrien Springs, MI: Andrews University Press, 1983. https://archive.org/details/israelofgodinpro0000laro.

Lehrer, Steve. *New Covenant Theology: Questions Answered*. Steve Lehrer, 2006. https://archive.org/details/newcovenanttheolo000stev.

Lehrman, S. M. *A Guide to Hanukkah and Purim*. London: Jewish Chronicle, 1958. https://archive.org/details/guidetohanukkahp0000rabb.

Leithart, Peter. "The Kingdom of God." Not dated. http://www.beginningwithmoses.org/articles/leithartkingdomofgod.htm.

Lenski, R. C. H. *The Interpretation of St. Luke's Gospel*. Minneapolis: Augsburg, 1946. https://archive.org/details/interpretationof0000rchl_h1p2.

Lessing, Reed. "Dying to Live: God's Judgment of Jonah, Jesus, and the Baptized." *Concordia Journal* 33 (2007) 9–25. http://deimos3.apple.com/WebObjects/Core.woa/DownloadTrackPreview/csl-public.1572099114.01572099121.1572651714.pdf.

Levenson, Jon. *Creation and the Persistence of Evil*. San Francisco: Harper & Row, 1988.

Lewis, C. S. *Mere Christianity*. New York: Touchstone, 1996 (reprint). https://www.dacc.edu/assets/pdfs/PCM/merechristianitylewis.pdf.

———. "What Are We to Make of Jesus Christ?" In *God in the Dock*, edited by Walter Hooper, 156–60. Grand Rapids: Eerdmans, 1970. https://archive.org/details/collectedworksofoocsle/mode/2up.

Lincoln, A. T. "Sabbath, Rest, and Eschatology in the New Testament." In *From Sabbath to Lord's Day: A Biblical, Historical and Theological Investigation*, edited by D. A. Carson, 197–220. Grand Rapids: Zondervan, 1982. https://archive.org/details/fromsabbathtolor1982unse.

Longenecker, Richard. *Galatians* (WBC 41). Nashville: Thomas Nelson, 1990. https://archive.org/details/galatians-volume-41-richard-n.-longenecker.

Lunn, Nick. *Jesus in the Jewish Scriptures*. Pontypool, Wales: Faithbuilders, 2020.

Luther, Martin. *Luther's Works*, American Edition, vol. 2, edited by Jaroslav Pelikan, translated by Martin Bertram. St. Louis: Concordia, 1957 (reprint).

Maier, Paul. *First Easter*. New York: Harper & Row, 1973. https://archive.org/details/firsteastertrueu0omaie.

Malabuyo, Nollie. "The Gift of Pentecost (Feast of Weeks)." 2013. http://www.twoagespilgrims.com/pasigucrc/2013/10/29/the-gift-of-pentecost-feast-of-weeks/.

Marsh, Herbert. *Lectures on the Criticism and Interpretation of the Bible*. London: Gilbert & Rivington, 1842. https://archive.org/details/lecturesonthebib0omarsuoft.

Marshall, I. Howard. *The Acts of the Apostles* (TNTC). Grand Rapids: Eerdmans, 1980.

———. "Church." In *Dictionary of Jesus and the Gospels*, edited by Joel Green, Scot McKnight, and I. Howard Marshall, 122–25. Downers Grove, IL: InterVarsity, 1992.

———. *The Gospel of Luke* (NIGTC). Grand Rapids: Eerdmans, 1978.

Martin, J. Mark. "The Sabbath & Sunday." 1999. http://www.exadventist.com/Home/Sabbath/SabbathSunday/tabid/516/Default.aspx.

Martin, R. A. "The Earliest Messianic Interpretation of Genesis 3:15." *Journal of Biblical Literature* 84 (1965) 425–27.

Martin, Walter. *The Kingdom of the Cults,* revised and expanded ed. Minneapolis: Bethany, 1985.

Mbewe, Conrad. "The Righteous Branch." In *The Scriptures Testify About Me,* edited by D. A. Carson, 93–102. Wheaton, IL: Crossway, 2013.

McCartney, Dan, and Charles Clayton. *Let the Reader Understand.* Wheaton, IL: BridgePoint, 1994. https://archive.org/details/letreaderunderstoooomcca/mode/2up.

McDermott, Gerald. "Gerald McDermott on Why the Lad Promises Belong to Ethnic Israel." *The Gospel Coalition.* 2023. https://www.thegospelcoalition.org/article/israel-land-promise-mcdermott/.

McDowell, Josh. *The Resurrection Factor.* San Bernardino, CA: Here's Life, 1981. https://archive.org/details/resurrectionfactoomcdo.

McDowell, Josh, and Bart Larson. *Jesus: A Biblical Defense of His Deity.* San Bernardino, CA: Here's Life, 1983. https://archive.org/details/jesusbiblicaldefoooomcdo.

McKnight, Scot. *Galatians* (NIVAC). Grand Rapids: Zondervan, 1995.

McLaughlin, Melissa. "What Is the Tabernacle? 8 Ways Jesus is Our Tabernacle." *Truthful Grace.* 2019. https://melissamclaughlin.org/2019/04/30/what-is-the-tabernacle-8-ways-jesus-is-our-tabernacle/.

Meier, John. *Law and History in Matthew's Gospel* (AnBib 71). Rome: Biblical Institute, 1976. https://archive.org/details/meier-john-p.-law-and-history-in-matthews-gospel.-a-redactional-study-of-mt.-5-1/mode/2up?view=theater.

Menn, Jonathan. *Biblical Eschatology,* 2nd ed. Eugene, OR: Resource, 2018.

———. *Biblical Interpretation.* 2008–2017. http://www.eclea.net/courses.html.

Merrill, Eugene. "The Sign of Jonah." *Journal of the Evangelical Theological Society* 23 (1980) 23–30. http://www.etsjets.org/files/JETS-PDFs/23/23-21/23-21-pp023-30_JETS.pdf.

Metzger, Bruce. *An Introduction to the Apocrypha.* New York: Oxford, 1957. https://archive.org/details/introductiontoapoooomtz_e6j7.

Miller, Kirk. "In Pursuit of Something More than an Analogical Interpretation." *kirkmillerblog.com.* 2013. https://kirkmillerblog.com/2013/08/22/in-pursuit-of-responsibly-typology/.

Miller, Stephen. *Daniel* (NAC 18). Nashville: B&H, 1994.

Montgomery, James. *A Critical and Exegetical Commentary on the Book of Daniel* (ICC). New York: Chrales Scribner's Sons, 1927. https://archive.org/details/criticalexegeticoooomont_b9d5/mode/2up?view=theater.

Moo, Douglas. "Jesus and the Authority of the Mosaic Law." *Journal for the Study of the New Testament* 20 (1984) 3–49. www.djmoo.com/articles/jesusandauthority.pdf.

———. "The Law of Moses or the Law of Christ." In *Continuity and Discontinuity: Perspectives on the Relationship Between the Old and New Testaments,* edited by John Feinberg, 203–18. Westchester, IL: Crossway, 1988.

Moo, Jonathan. "The Sea that Is No More: Rev 21:1 and the Function of Sea Imagery in the Apocalypse of John." *Novum Testamentum* 51 (2009) 148–67.

Morris, Henry. "The Tri-Universe." *Acts & Facts* 34 (2005). http://www.icr.org/article/2590/.

Motyer, J. Alec. *Isaiah* (TOTC 20). Nottingham, England: Inter-Varsity, 1999. https://archive.org/details/isaiahintroductioooomoty.

Myers, Jeremy. "Crucifixion—The Physical Suffering of Jesus." *Redeeming God*. 2011. https://redeeminggod.com/crucifixion-physical-suffering-jesus/.

Nelson, Richard. "'He Offered Himself': Sacrifice in Hebrews." *Interpretation* 57 (2003) 251–65.

Nelson, William. "Melchizedek." In *The Oxford Companion to the Bible*, edited by Bruce Metzger and Michael Coogan, 511–12. New York: Oxford University Press, 1993. https://archive.org/details/isbn_9780965072595.

Ortlund, Raymond. *God's Unfaithful Wife: A Biblical Theology of Spiritual Adultery* (NSBT 2). Downers Grove, IL: InterVarsity, 1996. https://archive.org/details/whoredomgodsunfaooooortl.

Osborne, Grant. *Matthew* (ZECNT). Grand Rapids: Zondervan, 2010.

Owen, John. *An Exposition of the Epistle to the Hebrews*, vol. 1, edited by W. H. Goold. Grand Rapids: Baker, 1980 (reprint). https://archive.org/details/expositionofepis00010wen/mode/2up?view=theater&q=%22true+and+only+Messiah%22.

———. *Indwelling Sin in Believers*. Grand Rapids: Baker, 1979 (reprint). http://www.godrules.net/library/owen/131-2950wen_f4.htm.

Parsons, John. "Chag HaMatzot—Unleavened Bread." *Hebrew for Christians*. 2016. http://www.hebrew4christians.com/Holidays/Spring_Holidays/Unleavened_Bread/unleavened_bread.html.

———. "When Does Passover begin?" *Hebrew for Christians*. 2016. http://www.hebrew4christians.com/Holidays/Spring_Holidays/Pesach/Zman_Seder/zman_seder.html.

———. "Yom HaBikkurim—Messiah as the First of the Harvest." *Hebrew for Christians*. Not dated. https://hebrew4christians.com/Holidays/Spring_Holidays/First_Fruits/first_fruits.html.

Payne, J. Barton. *Encyclopedia of Biblical Prophecy*. Grand Rapids: Baker, 1980 (reprint). https://archive.org/details/encyclopediaofbioooopayn/page/n5/mode/2up.

Peterson, David. *The Acts of the Apostles* (PNTC). Grand Rapids: Eerdmans, 2009.

———. "The Prophecy of the New Covenant in the Argument of Hebrews." *Reformed Theological Review* 38 (1979) 74–81.

Piper, John. *Brothers, We Are Not Professionals*. Nashville: B&H, 2013. https://document.desiringgod.org/brothers-we-are-not-professionals-en.pdf?1439242057.

Powell, Mark. "Echoes of Jonah in the New Testament." *World & Word* 27 (2007) 157–64. http://wordandworld.luthersem.edu/issues.aspx?article_id=979.

Poythress, Vern. *The Shadow of Christ in the Law of Moses*. Brentwood, TN: Wolgemuth & Hyatt, 1991. http://frame-poythress.org/ebooks/the-shadow-of-christ-in-the-law-of-moses/.

Pratney, W. A. *The Nature and Character of God*. Minneapolis: Bethany, 1988. http://www.moh.org/PDF_Files/CharactrerAndNatureOutline.pdf.

Qureshi, Nabeel. *Seeking Allah, Finding Jesus*. Grand Rapids: Zondervan, 2016. https://www.academia.edu/35321484/Seeking_Allah_Finding_Jesus_-_Nabeel_Qureshi.

Ramm, Bernard. *An Evangelical Christology*. Nashville, TN: Thomas Nelson, 1985. https://archive.org/details/evangelicalchrisooramm/mode/2up.

———. *Protestant Biblical Interpretation*, 3rd ed. Grand Rapids: Baker, 1970. http://www.glasovipisma.pbf.rs/phocadownload/knjige/bernard%20ramm%20protestant%20biblical%20interpretation.pdf.

Rea, Michael. "The Trinity." In *The Oxford Handbook of Philosophical Theology*, edited by Thomas Flint and Michael Rea, 689–734. New York: Oxford University Press, 2009. https://www3.nd.edu/~mrea/papers/The%20Trinity.pdf.

Reasons to Believe. *Why the Bible Can be Trusted*. Not dated. https://mcusercontent.com/8906841e0b76067a1c57df68d/files/7cf8e606-563b-8d85-b509-51619057b825/WhytheBible_EBook_2022_V04.pdf.

Reisinger, John. *Abraham's Four Seeds*. Frederick, MD: New Covenant Media, 1998. http://www.worldwithoutend.info/bbc/books/NC/abrahams_seed/toc.htm.

"Resonance." *Mark Bishop's Chemistry Site*. Not dated. http://www.mpcfaculty.net/mark_bishop/resonance.htm.

Rich, Tracey. "The Counting of the Omer." *Judaism 101*. 1995–2011. http://www.jewfaq.org/holidayb.htm.

———. "Days of Awe." *Judaism 101*. 1995–2011. http://www.jewfaq.org/holiday3.htm.

———. "Shavu'ot. *Judaism 101*. 1995–2011. http://www.jewfaq.org/holidayc.htm.

Riddlebarger, Kim. *A Case for Amillennialism*. Grand Rapids: Baker, 2003. https://archive.org/details/kim-riddlebarger-a-case-for-amillennialism.

Roukema, Riemer. "The Good Samaritan in Ancient Christianity." *Vigiliae Christianae* 58 (2004) 56–74.

Runia, Klaas. "The Trinity." In *Eerdmans' Handbook to Christian Belief*, edited by Robin Keeley, 163–75. Grand Rapids, Eerdmans, 1982.

Sailhamer, John. "Genesis." In *Expositor's Bible Commentary*, vol. 2, edited by Frank Gaebelein, 3–284. Grand Rapids: Zondervan, 1990.

Satterfield, Bruce. "John 7–9 in Light of the Feast of Tabernacles." 1998. http://emp.byui.edu/SATTERFIELDB/Papers/John7-9.3.pdf.

Sawyer, John. "Messiah." In *The Oxford Companion to the Bible*, edited by Bruce Metzger and Michael Coogan, 513–14. New York: Oxford University Press, 1993. https://archive.org/details/isbn_9780965072595.

Schaeffer, Francis. "He Is There and He Is Not Silent." In *The Complete Works of Francis Schaeffer: A Christian Worldview, Volume One, A Christian View of Philosophy and Culture*, 273–352. Westchester, IL: Crossway, 1982. http://files.tyndale.com/thpdata/FirstChapters/978-70-8423-1413-18.pdf.

Scheifler, Michael. "Was Jesus crucified on Wednesday, Thursday, or Friday?" Not dated. http://biblelight.net/pasover.htm.

Schnabel, Eckhard. *Acts* (ZECNT). Grand Rapids: Zondervan, 2012. https://archive.org/details/acts-zondervan-exegetical-commentary-on-the-new-testament-eckhard-j.-schnabel-clinton-e.-arnold.

———. "Israel, the People of God, and the Nation." *Journal of the Evangelical Theological Society* 45 (2002) 35–57. http://www.etsjets.org/files/JETS-PDFs/45/45-41/45-41-PP035-57_JETS.pdf.

Schreiner, Thomas. "Luke." In *Evangelical Commentary on the Bible*, edited by Walter Ewell, 799–839. Grand Rapids: Baker, 1989.

Septuagint (LXX). http://www.ellopos.net/elpenor/greek-texts/septuagint/default.asp (Greek/English); http://www.ecmarsh.com/lxx/ (English only).

Shamoun, Sam. "If Jesus Is God, How Can God Die? Who was running the universe those three days that Jesus was dead?" *Answering Islam*. Not dated. http://www.answering-islam.org/Shamoun/q_god_dying.htm.

Shenuda III, Pope. *Trinity and Unity*. Rikon, Switzerland: The Good Way, 2010. http://www.the-good-way.com/eng/books.

"Shiloh." *Encyclopedia of the Bible*. Not dated. https://www.biblegateway.com/resources/encyclopedia-of-the-bible/Shiloh.

Shrier, Cahleen. "The Science of the Crucifixion." *Azusa Pacific University*. 2002. https://www.apu.edu/articles/the-science-of-the-crucifixion/.

Sittema, John. *Meeting Jesus at the Feast: Israel's Festivals and the Gospel*. Grandville, MI: Reformed Fellowship, 2013.

Smyth, Kevin. "The Prophecy Concerning Juda: Gen. 49:8–12." *The Catholic Biblical Quarterly* (1945) 290–305.

Stanton, Gerald. "The Prophet Jonah and His Message [part 1]." *Bibliotheca Sacra* 108 (1951) 237–49.

Stitzinger, Michael. "Genesis 1–3 and the Male/Female Role Relationship." *Grace Theological Journal* 22 (1981) 41–42. http://faculty.gordon.edu/hu/bi/Ted_Hildebrandt/OTeSources/01-Genesis/Text/Articles-Books/Stitzinger-Gen-1-3-GTJ-1981.htm.

Stoner, Peter. *Science Speaks*, rev. online ed. Chicago: Moody, 2005. https://archive.org/details/sciencespeakspeterw.stoner/mode/2up?view=theater.

Storms, Sam. "Replacement Theology or Inclusion Theology?" *samstorms.org*. 2017. https://www.samstorms.org/enjoying-god-blog/post/replacement-theology-or-inclusion-theology.

Suh, Robert. "The Use of Ezekiel 37 in Ephesians 2." *Journal of the Evangelical Theological Society* 50 (2007) 715–33. http://www.etsjets.org/files/JETS-PDFs/50/50-54/JETS_50-4_715-733_Suh.pdf.

Sundiata, Abbas. *Look Behind the Façade*. Xulon [online publisher], 2006.

Sutter, Paul. "Is it a Wave or a Particle? It's Both. Sort Of." 2019. https://www.space.com/wave-or-particle-ask-a-spaceman.html.

Sweeney, James. "Jesus, Paul, and the Temple: An Exploration of Some Patterns of Continuity." *Journal of the Evangelical Theological Society* 46 (2003) 605–31. http://www.etsjets.org/files/JETS-PDFs/46/46-44/46-44-pp605-631_JETS.pdf.

Sykes, Stephen. *The Story of Atonement*. London: Darton, Longman & Todd, 1997.

Targum Jerusalem. c. 380–180. https://www.sefaria.org/Targum_Jerusalem?tab=contents.

Targum Jonathan. c. 150–250. https://www.sefaria.org/Targum_Jonathan_on_Genesis?tab=contents.

"Temple of Herod." *Jewish Encyclopedia*. 2002. http://www.jewishencyclopedia.com/view.jsp?artid=123&letter=T.

"Temple, the Second." *Jewish Encyclopedia*. 2002. http://www.jewishencyclopedia.com/view.jsp?artid=128&letter=T.

Travis, Stephen. *I Believe in the Second Coming of Jesus*. Grand Rapids: Eerdmans, 1982. https://archive.org/details/ibelieveinsecondoooootrav.

Tertullian. *An Answer to the Jews*. In *The Ante-Nicene Fathers*, vol. 3, edited by Alexander Roberts and James Donaldson, revised by A. Cleveland Coxe, 151–73. New York: Christian Literature, 1885. Reprint, Peabody, MA: Hendrickson, 1994. http://www.ccel.org/ccel/schaff/anf03.iv.ix.i.html.

Turner, Joe. "Feast of First Fruits." *Easy Torah*. Not dated. https://eztorah.com/archive/feast-of-first-fruits/.

Twiss, Paul. "A Tale of Two Brothers: The Messiah in Genesis 49." *The Master's Seminary Journal* 33 (2002) 255–67.

Van de Weghe, Rob. *Prepared to Answer*. Port Hadlock, WA: Windmill Ministries, 2007. https://www.scribd.com/document/58502410/Prepared-To-Answer.

Van Til, Cornelius. *The Defense of the Faith*, 3rd ed. Phillipsburg, NJ: P&R, 1979. https://archive.org/details/defenseoffaithooooocorn.

———. *An Introduction to Systematic Theology*. Phillipsburg, NJ: P&R, 1974.

VanGemeren, Willem. *Interpreting the Prophetic Word*. Grand Rapids: Zondervan, 1990. https://archive.org/details/interpretingpropoooovang.

———. "The Sons of God in Genesis 6:1–4 (An Example of Evangelical Demythologization?)." *Westminster Theological Journal* 43 (1981) 320–48.

Venema, Cornelis. *The Promise of the Future*. Carlisle, PA: Banner of Truth, 2000. https://archive.org/details/promiseoffutureoooovene.

Veras, Richard. *Jesus of Israel*. Cincinnati: Servant, 2007. https://archive.org/details/jesusofisraelfinoooovera.

Vos, Geerhardus. *The Pauline Eschatology*. Grand Rapids: Baker, 1979 (reprint). https://archive.org/details/paulineeschatolooo06vosg.

Waldron, Samuel. "Structural Considerations." In *Lecture Notes on Eschatology*. Not dated. http://www.vor.org/truth/rbst/escatology03.html.

Walker, P. W. L. *Jesus and the Holy City: New Testament Perspectives on Jerusalem*. Grand Rapids: Eerdmans, 1996.

Walton, John. *The Lost World of Genesis One*. Downers Grove, IL: IVP Academic, 2009.

"Was Jesus resurrected on the same day Noah's ark rested on Mt. Ararat?" *Never Thirsty*. Not dated. https://www.neverthirsty.org/bible-qa/qa-archives/question/was-jesus-resurrected-on-the-same-day-noahs-ark-rested-on-mt-ararat/.

"Was Melchizedek a man or a type of Christ?" *Never Thirsty*. Not dated. https://www.neverthirsty.org/bible-qa/qa-archives/question/was-melchizedek-a-man-or-a-type-of-christ/.

Wells, Tom, and Fred Zaspel. *New Covenant Theology*. Frederick, MD: New Covenant Media, 2002.

"What is a *michtam* in the Bible?" *Got Questions*. 2025. https://www.gotquestions.org/michtam.html.

"What is the role of the Holy Spirit in our lives today?" *Got Questions*. 2022. https://www.gotquestions.org/Spirit-today.html.

"Who is Shilo?—Jewish sources: Interpretation of 'Shiloh.'" *Kol HaTor*. 2020. https://www.kolhator.com/shilo-jewish-sources-interpretation-shiloh/.

Williams, Peter. "Understanding the Trinity." *Bethinking*. 2012. http://www.bethinking.org/god/understanding-the-trinity.

Williamson, Paul. "Abraham, Israel and the Church." *Evangelical Quarterly* 72 (2000) 99–118. http://www.beginningwithmoses.org/articles/abrahamisraelchurch.htm.

———. *Sealed with an Oath: Covenant in God's Unfolding Purpose* (NSBT 23). Nottingham, England: Apollos, 2007.

Wood, Nathan. *The Trinity in the Universe*. Grand Rapids: Kregel, 1978. https://archive.org/details/trinityinuniversoooowood.

Work, Telford. "Converting God's Friends: From Jonah to Jesus." *Word & World* 27 (2007) 165–73. http://wordandworld.luthersem.edu/issues.aspx?article_id=1396.

Wright. N. T. *Jesus and the Victory of God.* Minneapolis: Fortress, 1996.
———. *The Resurrection of the Son of God.* Minneapolis: Fortress, 2003.
Yancey, Philip. *Reaching for the Invisible God.* Grand Rapids: Zondervan, 2000.
Yarbrough, Robert. "Biblical Theology." In *Evangelical Dictionary of Biblical Theology,* edited by Walter Elwell, 61–66. Grand Rapids: Baker, 1996. http://www.biblestudytools.com/dictionaries/bakers-evangelical-dictionary/biblical-theology.html.
Younger, K. Lawson. *Judges and Ruth* (NIVAC). Grand Rapids: Zondervan, 2002.
Zodhiates, Spiros. *The Complete Word Study Dictionary: New Testament,* rev. ed. Chattanooga: AMG, 1993. https://archive.org/details/completewordstudoooozodh.
Zuckerkandl, Victor. *Sound and Symbol: Music and the External World.* Princeton, NJ: Princeton University Press, 1956.

Subject and Name Index

Aaron, 39, 50, 181
Abba, 228–29
Abed-nego, 55
Abel, 6, 16n.29, 188n.14
    as a type, 107–8
Abomination of Desolation, 134–35, 135nn.102–3
Abraham (Abram), xvi, 1, 4–7, 20, 21n.50, 24, 29–30, 41, 48, 52–53, 57, 59, 62, 96, 100, 109n.39, 110, 139, 143, 143n.12, 151, 158–59, 162, 164–65, 185, 196
    as a type, 108–9
Abrahamic Covenant, xvii, 5, 18n.36, 20–21, 21n.50, 22–23, 23n.58, 24, 27, 68–69, 110, 138–42, 165, 185, 185n.4
    as fulfilled in Christ and the church, xvii, 5, 140–43, 196
Absalom, 6
Adam, xvi, 6–7, 10–14, 14n.22, 15–18, 30, 33, 37, 43, 45, 55n.20, 66–67, 103, 133, 151
    as a type, 105–6, 106n.34, 107, 107n.35, 133, 151
Ahithophel, 121
Ajijola, Alhaj A. D., 237
Alexander, T. Desmond, 34n.101, 37n.2, 40n.15, 42n.32, 181
Allah, 9, 250–51
allegory, 102–5, 105nn.28–29, 107n.35
Amelek, 104
American Scientific Affiliation, 93n.90
Amos, 25, 158, 167

analogy, 3, 102–4, 104n.25, 105, 105n.29, 125, 212, 244, 244n.21
Ancient Near East, 8, 68
"Angel of the Lord" ("Angel of God"), 48–49n.2, 49, 51, 51nn.5–6, 52–54, 54n.13–14, 55, 55n.15, 56, 56–57n.22, 60, 60n.35
angel(s), 8, 16n.32, 42, 51, 55–56, 58, 60, 60n.35, 71–73, 83–84, 87, 95, 104n.25, 116, 120, 128, 130, 143, 170, 201, 205, 209n.35
Anna, 155–56
Antiochus Epiphanes, 29, 134–35, 135n.102
apostle(s) (see also disciple(s)), 30, 82, 91, 99, 102, 107n.35, 119, 158, 158n.28, 165n.66, 167, 189
Apostles' Creed, 221–22
Ararat, 18, 128
Archer, Gleason, 235
ark (of Noah), 18, 128
    as a type, 127–29
ark of the covenant, 23, 39, 41, 41n.22, 70, 171, 180
Assyria/Assyrians, xvi, 1, 26, 45, 156
Athanasian Creed, 221, 223–24
Augustine, 109n.39

Babel, 15, 19, 19n.39, 20
Babylon/Babylonians, xvi, 1, 6, 26, 28, 41n.22, 56, 64n.5, 82, 85, 143n.12, 151–52, 155, 166, 201, 210
Babylonian Talmud, 41n.22, 70, 125

Balaam, 53
Balak, 53
baptism/baptize, 33, 72n.30, 127, 129–30, 130n.92, 131–32, 134, 173, 175, 176n.26, 191, 222, 242–43
Bauckham, Richard, 88
Beale, G. K., 37n.2, 82, 101n.5, 105n.29, 152n.4
Beelzebul (see Satan)
Belleville, Linda, 185, 209
Bethlehem, 62, 91, 92n.86, 144
Bible (see also Scripture; Septuagint (LXX)), xi–xii, xv–xviii, 1–2, 2n.5, 3–4, 6–8, 8n.2, 11, 14, 16–18, 18n.36, 19–241, 250–520, 32–34, 41n.22, 43n.34, 45, 47, 51, 54n.13, 55, 59–61, 62n.4, 66–67, 69, 93, 100, 102–3, 105, 107, 116, 125, 135–36, 148n.12, 160, 170, 200–201, 221, 227, 234, 237–41, 250–52
   New Testament (NT), xv–xvi, 1–3, 28–29, 31–33, 46, 48, 49n.2, 61n.1, 62–65, 67, 75, 81, 83, 90–91, 94, 97, 100, 100n.1, 101, 101n.3, 102–4, 109–10, 112, 117, 120–21, 135–36, 140, 144n.20, 147, 148n.35, 154, 158, 160, 164–65, 165n.66, 165n.71, 166–67, 172, 174, 180, 188–89, 193, 195, 198, 201n.10, 203, 205, 212, 215n.55, 225, 237, 240–41
   Old Testament (OT; Hebrew Bible) (see also Torah), xv–xvii, xviin.4, xviii, 1–5, 11, 20, 22, 25, 27–32, 42, 45–46, 48, 49n.2, 50n.3, 51, 57n.22, 61, 61n.1, 62–66, 70, 73, 77, 88–89, 89n.75, 91, 100, 100n.1, 101, 101n.3, 102–5, 105n.31, 109, 117–18, 120, 134–37, 93, 193n.39, 139, 141, 141n.8, 142, 144, 149, 152–55, 158–61, 163–64, 164n.64, 165, 165n.66, 167–69, 172, 173n.18, 176–79, 181–88, 188n.11, 189–93, 193n.39, 194, 196, 198–99, 201, 209, 212–13, 217, 221, 225, 232, 237, 240
   storyline, xv, 3–4, 8–35

Biblical Eschatology, 2nd ed. (Menn), xi, 32n.98, 76n.36, 89n.71
Biblical Interpretation (Menn), 193n.39
biblical theology, xi–xii, xv–xviii, 1, 4, 24
   described, 1
   presuppositions of, 2–3
   themes of, xv–xvi, 3–7, 25, 36–47, 162, 165n.71, 177 197n.12
Blomberg, Craig, 88, 163
Boaz, 104n.25
Bock, Darrel, 155
Boice, James, 12
Bozack, Michael, 247n.29
Branch, 84–86
Briggs, Charles, 75, 85, 144n.17
bronze serpent, 115, 133
Buddha/Buddhism, 8, 236

Cain, 1, 5–6, 15–16, 16n.29, 17n.32, 107–8
Calvary (Golgotha), 69
Canaan (the land)/Canaanites, 21, 38, 45, 104n.25, 139
Canaan (the person), 17, 17n.34
Captain of the Lord's host, 60, 60n.35
Capernaum, 83, 117
Carson, D. A., 58, 143n.12
"catholic," 222, 222n.2
Chalcedonian Creed, 221, 223
cherubim, 37, 39, 41–42
Christ (see Jesus Christ)
Christian/Christianity, xii, xviii, 4, 19n.39, 29–30, 70, 101, 103, 125, 177, 193, 196, 198, 198n.17, 203n.20, 221, 222n.2, 224, 233–38
Christians, xii, 30, 46, 76, 134, 147, 159, 163, 165n.71, 168, 175n.26, 177, 186n.5, 187, 187n.11, 193, 197–98, 198n.17, 206, 237–39, 249n.39
church, xvi–xvii, 5, 30–31, 33, 43, 45–47, 50n.3, 68, 73n.30, 77, 85, 94, 97–99, 102n.11, 103, 104n.25, 106–7, 107n.35, 109, 119, 137–38, 140–41, 146–48, 151, 158–64, 164n.57, 165, 165n.66, 165n. 71, 166–68, 168n.75, 169, 172, 174–75, 175n.23, 176–77,

Subject and Name Index

181, 186, 188–89, 191–92, 193n.37, 196–97, 199, 205–6, 211–12, 219, 222, 222n.2
circumcision/circumcise(d), 95, 133–34, 155, 158, 165, 165n.71, 166–67, 191–92, 192n.35, 197, 205, 216, 231
Clayton, Charles, 102
Clement of Rome, 104n.24
Cornelius, 30
Council of Jerusalem, 134, 158, 167, 191, 197
covenant(s) (see also Abrahamic Covenant; Mosaic (Old) Covenant; New Covenant; Noahic Covenant), xi, xvi–xvii, 3, 5, 17–18, 18n.36, 20–21, 21n.50, 22–23, 23n.58, 24–28, 34–36, 49, 49n.2, 53, 63, 68–69, 91, 95–96, 105, 108, 110, 110n.40, 112n.44, 113, 115, 120n.58, 127, 138, 138n.2, 139–42, 142n.10, 143–47, 147n.31, 148, 148nn.35–36, 149–50, 159–62, 164–66, 171, 175–76, 182, 184–85, 185n.4, 186, 189–92, 192n.35, 193, 195–97, 199, 205, 211–12
creation, 4, 8–10, 9nn.5–6, 13–15, 18, 22n.51, 30, 33–37, 55n.20, 106, 157, 164, 165n.71, 168n.75, 172, 187, 195, 218, 226, 230n.40, 241, 250
cross (see also Jesus Christ, crucifixion of), 9n.6, 67, 67n.12, 68–69, 79–80, 88, 90, 104, 108–9, 116, 121, 123, 125, 130, 133, 138, 147, 153, 165n.71, 170–71, 173, 179–81 187, 190, 192–93, 194, 213, 215, 217, 233, 236, 238.
Cross, John, 16n.29
curse(s), 13–15, 17, 17n.34, 23, 33–34, 44, 53, 116, 162, 173–74, 184, 192
Cyrus, 28

Daniel, 26, 55n.15, 58, 74, 86, 134–35, 135n.103

David (see also son of David; throne of David.), xvi, 1, 6, 24, 26–29, 54, 54n.14, 56, 62, 70–74, 78, 78n.42, 81, 84–85, 89–90, 120n.58, 137, 143, 143n.12, 144, 144n.20, 145–46, 158, 166, 185n.4
as a type, 79, 102, 119–21
Davidic Covenant, xvii, 5, 18n.36, 24, 27, 91, 120n.58, 142, 142n.10, 147, 185n.4
as fulfilled in Christ and the church, xvii, 5, 143–44, 144n.17, 144n.20, 145–46
Davidson, Richard, 102n.11, 106n.34
Davis, C. Truman, 79
Dawkins, Richard, 230n.40
Day of Atonement (see under feasts and festivals)
"Day of the Lord," 27–29, 116, 189
Dead Sea Scrolls, 60
death, 3–4, 12–13, 13n.16, 17, 29, 31–35, 44, 68, 78, 90, 106, 109, 111–13, 115–17, 123–24, 128–32, 136, 148, 179, 182, 185, 187–89, 196, 204–5, 214, 216, 234–35, 238, 249n.39, 251
angel of, 104n.25, 130, 201, 205
of Jesus, 9n.6, 13n.16, 19n.39, 29, 33, 61, 63, 67–68, 97, 109, 111, 113–15, 121, 123–25, 130, 133, 146–47, 152, 161, 173, 179–80, 182, 188, 190, 192, 205–7, 212–13, 215, 233, 235, 238, 251
DeHaan, M. R., 106
demon(s), 17n.32, 31, 113, 225, 230
devil (see Satan)
disciple(s) (see also apostle(s)), 30–31,b 33, 61, 64, 67n.12, 77, 80, 88, 90, 98–99, 111–12, 114–15, 117–19, 124, 156–57, 162, 164n.64, 167–68, 175–76, 194, 206–8, 216, 228–29, 242
Dodd, C. H., 154
Dumbrell, William, 196

Eden, xvi, 6–7, 10–12, 15, 18, 35–39, 41–45, 107, 197, 197n.12

Egypt/Egyptians, xvi, 6, 21, 45, 53, 69n.16, 102, 104n.25, 110–14, 130–32, 138, 152, 152n.4, 195, 200n.4, 201, 201n.9, 202, 205–6, 214,
Eli, 23
Elijah, 26, 29, 54, 117n.51, 130, 160
   as a type, 116–19, 156
Elisha, 117, 119
   as a type, 116–19
Emmanuel (see Immanuel (Emmanuel))
Enoch, 17
Ephraim (the person), 5
Ephraim (the place), 70–71
Epistle of Barnabas, 174
Equipping Church Leaders East Africa, Inc., xi
Esau, 5–6, 21, 52
Essenes, 29
Evans, William, 100n.1
Eve, xvi, 6–7, 10–13, 13n.16, 14–15, 33, 37, 43, 45, 66, 68n.13, 106–7, 107n.35, 133
exile, 6, 26, 28–29, 41n.22, 82, 85, 139, 147n.31, 151–52, 155–58, 162, 166, 176n.29, 196, 200–201
exodus, xvi, 6, 21–22, 26, 113, 195, 208
   as a type, 130–34, 152, 152n.4
Ezekiel, 27, 166–67
Ezra, 28

Fairbairn, Patrick, 101n.5, 102n.11
faith/faithful(ness), xvii, 3, 5–7, 12–13, 16n.29, 21–23, 25, 27, 30, 33–34, 46, 51, 66, 72n.30, 79, 83, 102, 104n.25, 105–6, 108, 112, 128, 130n.92, 131, 134, 137, 140–42, 151, 158–63, 167–68, 173–74, 177, 179, 185–87, 191, 195–96, 205, 208–9, 213, 219, 222n.2, 223–24, 233, 243
faithful remnant, 7, 26, 82, 94, 160–63
fall (into sin), xvi, 4, 7, 11–13, 13n.17, 14, 14n.22, 15, 16n.32, 44, 107, 133
Father, xviii, 9, 9n.6, 10n.7, 30, 33, 43, 48–49, 49n.2, 51, 56, 65, 81, 83, 87–88, 91, 95, 103, 107, 109–11, 114, 119–21, 125, 128–29, 132, 140, 144, 146, 154, 172–73, 180, 182, 207, 214, 222–24, 226–29, 235–42, 242n.18, 243–44, 244n.21, 246, 248, 250–51
feasts and festivals, xviin.4, 5, 180, 194, 197, 199, 201–3, 214, 218
   as fulfilled and replaced by Christ and the church, xi, xvii, 5, 130, 130n.93, 152, 180, 194, 199, 203–6, 206n.27, 207–9, 209n.35, 210–19
   Day of Atonement (*Yom Kippur*), 40, 43, 171, 180–82, 202–3, 209–10, 212–14
   First Fruits, 202, 207, 207n.28, 208–9
   Hanukkah, 202–3, 218–19
   Passover, xviin.4, 22, 104n.25, 112, 130, 130n.93, 152, 180, 200n.4, 201, 201nn.9–10, 203, 203n.20, 204–7, 207n.28, 208
   Purim, 202–3, 218–19
   Tabernacles (Booths), xviin.4, 201–2, 214–15, 215n.55, 216
   Trumpets (*Rosh Ha-Shanah*), 200, 202, 209, 209n.35, 210–12
   Unleavened Bread, 201, 201n.10, 203–6, 206n.27, 207, 207n.28
   Weeks (Pentecost), xviin.4, 201–2, 207–8, 208n.30, 209
Feinberg, John, 239
fig tree, 157, 162, 173–74
First Fruits, feast of (see under feasts and festivals),
Flood, xvi, 7, 17–19, 186
   as a type, 127–30
Ford, Desmond, 134
France, R. T., 118, 120
Fritsch, Charles, 171n.9, 195
fulfill/fulfillment, xi, xvii, 1, 3, 5, 8, 10n.7, 13, 19–22, 24, 26–30, 32–35, 60–64, 64n.5, 65, 67–69, 71, 72n.30, 73–76, 78–80, 82–85, 90–92, 94–97, 101, 101n.5, 104–5, 109–10, 110n.40, 117, 120–21, 127, 133–44, 144n.17,

145–58, 162, 166–67, 169–93, 193n.37, 194–99, 203–19, 237

Gabriel, 7, 72, 83–84, 95, 120, 142–43
Galilee, 63, 123, 145
Garden of Eden (see Eden)
Garden of Gethsemene, 124
Gath-hepher, 123
Gentiles, xvii, 6, 30–31, 63–64, 72–73n.30, 76, 83, 94–96, 98, 104n.25, 110, 124, 134, 148, 156, 158–62, 165n.71, 166–67, 173, 186n.5, 192, 197, 219
Ghabril, Nicola Yacoub, 239
Gibeon, 38
Gideon, 53–54
God (Lord God; Most High; Ancient of Days) (see also Father; Lord; Yahweh (YHWH)), xv–xvi, xviii, 3–19, 19n.39, 20–21, 21n.45, 21n.50, 22, 22n.51, 22–23n.58, 23–41, 41n.22, 43–48, 48–49n.2, 49–50, 50n.4, 51–54, 54n.13, 55, 55n.18, 56, 56n.20, 57, 57n.22, 58–60, 62–63, 64n.5, 65–66, 68, 68n.13, 69, 71–74, 74n.2, 75–80, 81n.51, 82–88, 89n.75, 90–93, 95–96, 98, 100–101, 103, 105, 107–11, 113–16, 120–21, 125, 127–30, 130n.92, 131–43, 145–46, 147n.31, 148–49, 152–53, 156–65, 165n.71, 166–68, 168n.75, 169n.1, 170–81, 183–89, 193, 195–97, 198n.17, 200n.4, 203–11, 213–14, 216, 218–19, 221–30, 230n.40, 232–44, 244n.21, 247–52.
  Ancient of Days, 86.
  Lord God, 34, 52, 54, 68, 71–72, 83–84, 120, 143, 170, 242.
  Most High, 55, 57, 72, 84, 120, 143, 154, 168–69.
God the Son (see Son of God)
God's people (see also church; Israelites), xvi, 4–7, 10, 10n.7, 20–22, 25–28, 28n.80, 29–30, 33, 37–38, 43–47, 74, 77, 80, 85, 103, 104n.25, 108–10, 113–16, 127, 131, 138, 146, 147n.31, 149, 152, 155, 162–64, 165n.71, 166–67, 168n.75, 169, 173, 175–76, 182, 185, 187–89, 200n.4, 204, 212, 215, 219
Goldsworthy, Graeme, xi–xii
Goppelt, Leonard, 105, 107n.35, 159
Gospel, the, 4, 30, 32–33, 66, 69, 72n.30, 77, 83, 98, 101, 104n.25, 119, 127, 133, 136–37, 149, 157, 167, 189, 193, 204, 217–18
Gospels (Matthew, Mark, Luke, John), 29–30, 57n.22, 61n.1, 86, 120–21, 125, 145, 162, 244
grace, 5, 7, 15–18, 20, 22, 28, 49, 98, 100, 107, 115, 127–28, 130, 137–38, 159–60, 163, 179, 184–85, 192, 236

Habershon, Ada, 110n.42, 112n.43
Hades (see also Sheol), 72, 78
Hagar, 52, 105, 105n.28, 148
Hagner, Donald, 163
Halakah ("oral law"), 191
Ham, 17n.34, 19
Hamstra, Sam, 34
Hanson, Anthony, 59
Hanukkah, feast of (see under feasts and festivals)
Hartzler, H. Harold, 93n.0
Hasmonean Dynasty, 29
heaven(s), 2–5, 10, 19, 19n.39, 22n.51, 31, 34, 39–40, 42n.32, 50, 56–n.22, 57, 73–74, 77, 86–88, 106, 113–14, 118–19, 122, 127, 132, 138–39, 141, 147, 154, 158, 169–70, 175, 176n.29, 178, 182–83, 186, 189–90, 207, 213, 218–19, 222, 224, 226, 229, 230n.40, 235, 243, 250, 252
hell (see also second death), 4, 13, 69, 87, 161, 188, 214, 222, 224, 230, 236
Hengstenberg, E. W., 72n.29, 76, 77n.39, 80, 85
Herod the Great, 29, 41n.22, 114, 151
Herodias, 116

high priest, 40, 43–44, 56, 59, 76, 85,
    87–88, 181–83, 188, 202, 212–13
  Jesus as, 85, 85n.61, 90, 172, 181–83,
    188, 212–13
Hinduism, 8
Holy of Holies, 38–41, 41n.22, 42–44,
    171, 180, 183, 202, 212–13
Holy Place, xvi, 37–39, 41, 41n.22, 43,
    57, 69, 135, 169, 171, 182
Holy Spirit (Spirit of God), xviii, 9,
    19n.39, 27, 30, 32–33, 41n.22,
    46–48, 48–49n.2, 51, 56, 62–63,
    72–73n.30, 77, 81, 83–84, 94–
    95, 97–98, 100, 110–11, 112n.44,
    119, 123, 134, 148–49, 153,
    155–57, 159, 161, 164, 166–67,
    170, 175, 175n.26, 176, 186, 192,
    207–9, 214–15, 217, 222, 224,
    227, 232, 234, 237–42, 242n.18,
    243–44, 244n.21, 246–48,
    250–51
  baptism with, 119, 175, 207, 227
Hosea, 25, 152n.4, 164n.57, 167
Hugenberger, G. P., 103
humanity (see mankind)

idols/idolatry, 23, 82, 133, 135n.102,
    170, 186n.5, 188
Ignatius of Antioch, 197
image of God (including image of
    Christ), 9–10, 10n.7, 18, 37–38,
    49n.2, 106, 148, 180, 193, 233–
    34, 240
Immanuel (Emmanuel), 62, 83, 170
Is Christianity True? (Menn), xi
Isaac, 5, 20–21, 41, 52–53, 62, 108, 139,
    151, 162, 211
  as a type, 57, 108–9, 109n.39, 110
Isaiah, 25–26, 50, 73, 82–84, 94, 98, 146,
    173, 218–19
Ishmael, 5, 52
Islam, 9, 250
Israel (see also Judah (the southern
    kingdom)), xi, xvi–xvii, xviin.4,
    xviii, 1, 3–7, 21–27, 29, 35, 38,
    42, 45, 49, 53–55, 60, 69n.16,
    72–74, 76, 76n.36, 77–78, 80, 82,
    87, 89, 91, 94, 101, 104, 113–18,
    125–27, 130–34, 143, 145,
    159–60, 166, 168, 173, 178, 184,
    192n.35, 195–96
  as fulfilled in Christ and the church,
    xi, xvii, 5, 91n.84, 120, 137–42,
    151–64, 164n.57, 165, 165n.66,
    165n.71, 166–68, 168n.75, 211
  calendar of, 199–201.
  restoration of, 25, 28, 46, 77, 95–96,
    152–58, 158n.28, 157–58,
    158n.28, 159, 167, 210
Israelites (Hebrews) (see also Jews/
    Jewish), 6, 21–22, 38, 53, 76, 90,
    104n.25, 114, 120, 126, 130–34,
    139, 145, 147, 153, 160, 187,
    195, 200–201, 205–6, 241

Jacob (Israel), 5–6, 20–21, 21n.45, 52–
    53, 62, 70–74, 84, 96, 112, 120,
    143, 162, 170
James, 30, 158, 167–68,
Japheth, 19
Jeconiah, 143n.12
Jeremiah, xvii, 27, 64n.5, 84, 147, 151
Jericho, 60, 103–4, 104n.25, 143, 168
Jerusalem, xviin.4, 5, 19n.39, 24, 26, 28,
    30, 38, 42, 42n.32, 51, 56, 58, 63,
    64n.5, 77, 81–82, 90–91, 96, 98,
    103, 105, 109, 119–20, 125, 130,
    141, 145, 148n.35, 155, 159, 163,
    163n.53, 167, 172–75, 177, 201,
    203, 205, 207, 210, 214–15
"Jerusalem above" ("heavenly
    Jerusalem") (see also New
    Jerusalem), 105, 141, 167
Jerusalem Talmud, 125
Jesus Christ (see also Branch; death, of
    Jesus; high priest, Jesus as; Lord,
    Jesus as; Messiah; prophecy/
    prophet(s), Jesus in prophecy;
    protoevangelium; Savior;
    Servant of the Lord (Suffering
    Servant); Shepherd; Son of
    David; Son of God; Son of Man;
    Stone (Rock); Trinity; typology;
    and Jesus' fulfillment of the
    OT, the covenants, and OT
    Israel and its persons, events,

and institutions, as discussed in chapters 8–15), xi–xii, xv–7, 9n.6, 10n.7, 11, 13n.16, 14–16, 19n.39, 20, 22, 28–33, 35–36, 41n.22, 42–47, 48–49n.2, 55n.20, 61, 61n.1, 62–67, 67n.12, 68–72, 72n.30, 73–76, 76n.36, 77–78, 80–88, 91–93, 100, 100n.1, 104, 104n.25, 105, 135, 135n.102, 221–22, 229–30, 238, 248

as fully God, xviii, 48–49, 49n.2, 64n.5, 72, 75, 77, 81, 84, 86–88, 221–30, 230n.40, 238–44, 247n.29

as fully man, xviii, 221–24, 231–32, 247n.29

ascension of, 4, 19n.39, 30, 33, 56n.22, 57, 65, 72, 83, 86, 118–20, 128, 130, 145–47, 158–59, 170, 181–82, 207, 213, 222, 224, 229

baptism of, 48n.2, 76, 84, 91, 95, 123, 144–45, 152–54, 231, 243

crucifixion of (see also cross), 9n.6, 13n.16, 19n.39, 3, 63–65, 68–69, 72, 77, 79, 79n.44, 80, 90, 222, 224

implications of the fact that Jesus Christ is fully God and fully man, 232–36

miracles (signs) of, 31, 97, 157, 191, 218, 225, 227, 229n.35, 241

parables of, 32, 63, 74, 82, 97, 103, 111, 160, 162–63, 172, 216

pre-incarnate appearances of, xvi, 3, 48–49, 49n.2, 50–56, 56–57, 57n.22, 58–60, 60n.35, 137

resurrection of, 9n.6, 19n.39, 32–33, 63–65, 72–73, 76–79, 83, 91n.84, 222, 224, 229

second coming of, 30, 31n.93, 32–33, 78, 103, 210, 218, 222, 224

transfiguration of, 75–76, 91, 95, 113, 117, 130, 144, 152, 154

Jesse, 62, 84

Jews/Jewish (see also Israelites (Hebrews)), xv, xvii, xviin.4, 28, 30–31, 40, 42, 58, 63, 70, 72–73n.30, 76–77, 82, 88–89, 98, 104n.25, 109n.39, 124–26, 134–35, 140, 144–45, 154–56, 158–62, 165n.71, 166, 168, 170, 172, 186n.5, 191–92, 192n.35, 197–98, 200, 203, 206n.27, 208, 210–11, 215, 218–19, 228–29, 231

Jezebel, 116–17

Job, 24–25

as a type, 121–22

Joel, 25, 167

John, 4, 30, 43n.34, 50, 66, 67n.12, 79, 82, 84, 86, 115,

John the Baptist, 29, 46, 66, 88, 116–17, 117n.51, 140, 152, 156–57, 175, 189, 203,

Johnson, Dennis, 133, 189

Jonah, 25, 122

"the sign of Jonah," 122–26, 126n.78, 127

Jordan River, 104n.25, 116, 133, 153

Joseph (son of Jacob), 20–21, 52, 71, 73–74, 110, 113

as a type, 110, 110n.42, 111–12

Joseph (Jesus' putative father), 75, 144

Josephus, 40, 42, 135

Joshua (Moses's successor), xvi, 23, 39, 56, 139, 195

as a type, 116

Joshua (high priest), 56, 74, 85

Jubilee, year of, 60, 200, 203

as fulfilled by Jesus, 217–18

Judah (the person and tribe), 5, 21, 25, 62, 70–72, 72n.29, 73, 146–47, 181

Judah (the southern kingdom), 25–26, 28, 64n.5, 147, 151, 166

Judaism, xviin.4, 30, 41, 134, 203

Judas, 81, 121, 124

judgment(s) of God (including God/
     Jesus as judge), 62, 74, 106, 112,
     125, 127, 129, 145, 156, 168,
     168n.75, 226
  final judgment, 4, 15, 22n.51, 28,
     30, 47, 60, 69, 73–74, 87–88,
     121–22, 125, 127–28, 167, 211,
     216, 222, 224, 227
  temporal judgments, 15, 17–19, 23,
     25–26, 28, 35, 66, 75–76, 76n.36,
     82, 113, 126–29, 131, 148n.35,
     154, 162–63, 163n.53, 167, 173–
     74, 177, 205, 209n.35, 213
Justin Martyr, 104n.24, 196–97

Kaiser, Walter, 71, 120
Katz, Jochen, 76
Keller, Timothy, 108, 124, 131, 219, 235,
     251
Kingdom of God (kingdom of heaven;
     messianic kingdom), 4, 6, 15,
     24, 29–31, 31n.93, 32–33, 50,
     72–74, 76n.36, 77n.39, 83–84,
     86–87, 89, 113, 120–21, 127,
     134, 142, 142n.10, 143, 145–46,
     156, 156–58, 158n.28, 162–63,
     174, 177, 184, 189, 191n.34, 206,
     208, 222

Laban, 52
Lamech, 16
land,. See also Promised Land.
Last Supper, 58, 113, 115, 147, 166,
     203–4n.20, 204–5, 211–12
Law
  of Christ, 114–15, 130, 190, 192–93,
     193n.37, 209–10, 227
  of God, 15, 27, 114–15, 130, 146,
     227, 235
  of Moses, 5, 22–23, 39, 57, 103,
     105n.29, 114–15, 119–20, 131,
     147, 158, 167, 173n.18, 176n.26,
     181, 184–86, 186n.5, 187–90,
     190n.19, 191–93, 193n.37,
     193n.39, 194, 196, 203, 218
  as fulfilled and replaced by Christ,
     xi, xvii, 5, 147, 149, 181, 185–93,
     193n.37, 199

leaven, 105, 201, 206, 206n.27
Lehrer, Steve, 171n.9
Lehrman, S. M., 219
Levi/Levites/Levitical, 25, 37–38, 40, 59,
     89, 103, 179, 181
Lewis, C. S., 230, 230n.40
Lincoln, A. T., 196
Lord, 15, 16n.29, 21, 23, 25–26, 28,
     35, 41n.22, 43–44, 46, 48,
     50n.4, 54n.14, 59–60, 69n.16,
     72, 74–77, 81, 84–85, 92, 107,
     111–14, 133, 139, 142–43, 147,
     151, 158, 163, 167–68, 173–76,
     179, 187–88, 201–2, 208–9, 212,
     215–17, 219, 222–25, 240–41,
     242n.18, 243
  Jesus as, 48, 48–49n.2, 49–51, 62,
     64n.5, 77, 81–83, 87–88, 111,
     116–17, 120, 128, 145, 193n.37,
     194–95, 210, 222–25, 227, 230,
     233, 236, 241, 243
Lord's Supper (see Last Supper)
Lot, 1
Luke, 4, 55
Lunn, Nick, 53
Luther, Martin, 126

Maccabean Revolt, 29, 134, 203, 219
Manasseh, 5
mankind (humanity), xv–xvi, 3–4, 1,
     6–15, 17–19, 19n.39, 35–38, 45,
     47, 56n.22, 58, 67–68, 73, 77, 82,
     87, 91, 104n.25, 105–6, 124, 136,
     157–59, 167, 181–82, 185–86,
     195, 197n.12, 233–36, 240, 243,
     248, 248n.35, 249, 252
manna, 39, 114, 132, 153
Manoah, 54
Mark, 4, 205
marriage, xvi, 13, 13n.17, 17n.32, 24,
     32, 36, 45–47, 50, 107, 128, 163,
     187, 187–88n.11, 188
Martin, R. A., 67n.8
Martin, Walter, 198n.17
Mary, xvi, 56n.22, 58, 67, 67n.12, 77,
     83–84, 95, 108, 113, 120, 137,
     140, 142–43, 222–23
Mary Magdalene, 9n.6

Subject and Name Index

Matthew, 4, 29, 64n.5, 83, 97, 121, 143, 143n.12, 151–52, 152n.4
Matthias, 81
Mbewe, Conrad, 85
McCartney, Dan, 102
Melchizedek, 57–60, 89–90, 181
mercy seat, 39–40, 43, 170–71, 171n.8, 180, 202, 212–13
Meshach, 55
Messiah, 1, 28–30, 32, 34, 55, 58–59, 61–62, 66–67, 67n.8, 70–77, 81, 81n.50, 85, 88–89, 89n.75, 90–91, 91n.84, 105, 114, 120, 120n.58, 121, 123, 133, 143, 143n.12, 144, 154–58, 168, 174, 195, 211, 219
Micah, 25, 144, 162
Michael the archangel, 56
Midian, 53
Miller, Stephen, 55
Miriam, 50
Moab, 115
monism, 8
Montgomery, James, 55
Moo, Douglas, 34
Morris, Henry, 246
Mosaic (Old) Covenant, 5, 18n.36, 22–23, 26–27, 49, 105, 115, 138, 147–48, 184–85, 185n.4, 186, 190–93, 199, 211
   as a type/fulfilled in Christ, 5, 147, 186
Moses, xvi, 3, 6, 21–22, 22–23n.58, 23, 38–39, 49–50, 53, 56, 60, 69n.6, 75, 75n.35, 90, 101, 104, 130–33, 139, 151, 169n.1, 176, 205, 210, 214
   as a type, 112, 112n.43, 113–15, 193
Mount Girizim, 172
Mount Moriah (see Mount Zion)
Mount of Transfiguration (see also Jesus, transfiguration of), 75, 113, 117, 130, 152
Mount Sinai, 49, 69n.16, 113, 141, 191, 208, 211
Mount Zion (see also Zion), 41–42, 76–77, 77n.39, 109, 141, 155, 167

Muhammad, 236

Naaman, 6, 117
Naphtali, 83, 145
Nathanael, 75, 145
Nazareth, 75, 85, 91n.84, 117, 123, 190, 217–18, 239
Nebuchadnezzar, 55, 74
Nehemiah, 28
New Covenant, xvii, 3, 5, 18n.36, 27, 49, 63, 105, 138, 146–47, 148n.36, 185n.4, 138, 146, 147n1, 148n.35, 161, 185n.4
   as fulfilled in Christ and the church, xvii, 5, 49, 105, 108, 112n.44, 113, 115, 143, 146–47, 147n.31, 148, 148n.35, 149–50, 166, 176, 182, 189, 191, 193, 195–96, 205, 212
new heaven and new earth (see also New Jerusalem; re-creation (new creation)), xv, 5–6, 27, 33–35, 43, 43n.34, 44, 47, 116, 197, 197n.12
New Jerusalem (heavenly Jerusalem; Jerusalem above) (see also new heaven and new earth.), xvi, 5, 37, 43, 43n.34, 44, 47, 105, 141, 159, 170
New Testament (NT) (see under Bible)
Nineveh/Ninevites, 25, 122, 126–27
Nicene-Constantinople Creed, 221–22
Noah, xvi, 7, 16–17, 17n.34, 18–20, 128, 186
   as a type, 128–29.
Noahic Covenant, 5, 18, 18n.36, 185n.4

Old Testament (OT; Hebrew Bible) (see under Bible)
Olivet Discourse, 135
Origen, 103

Palestine, 31, 138
pantheism/pantheist, 229
parables (see Jesus Christ, parables of)
Passover (see under feasts and festivals)
"pattern of reversal," 5–6

Paul (Saul of Tarsus), 28, 30, 46, 49, 66, 68n.13, 78, 80–82, 84, 91, 98, 105, 105nn.28–29, 106, 109, 131, 133–34, 137, 141–43, 146, 148–49, 151, 158–62, 164n.57, 165n.71, 167, 172, 174–75, 176n.26, 185, 186n.5, 187n.11, 188–89, 192–94, 194n.1, 196, 199n.1, 206, 208, 232
Payne, J. Barton, 61n.1, 71n.24, 105n.31
Pentecost (see under feasts and festivals)
Persia/Persians, xvi, 28–29, 68, 79
Peter, 30, 72, 72n.30, 75, 78, 80–81, 83, 95–96, 100, 111, 120, 129, 130n.93, 137, 140, 142–43, 146, 158, 161, 167, 176–77, 186, 233
Pharaoh, 6, 21, 111, 113–14, 130–31
Pharisees, 29, 31, 81, 119–20, 122–23, 126, 163, 194, 207n.
Philip, 75, 97
Philistines, 23
Piper, John, 130n.92
Pisidian Antioch, 78
plural/plurality, 10, 51, 55, 55n.18, 56, 73, 76, 140, 240–41, 250
Pontius Pilate, 9n.6, 31, 126, 222
Potiphar, 111
Powell, Mark, 127
Poythress, Vern, 13, 180
Pratney, W. A., 238, 240
priest(s) (including high priest)/ priesthood), xviin.4, 22–23, 38–40, 43–44, 56–57, 59, 76, 85, 87–88, 103, 111, 119, 123, 171n.9, 202, 207n.28, 212–13, 215
  as fulfilled and replaced by Christ and the church, xi, xvii, 62, 76, 85, 85n.61, 86, 89–90, 112, 147, 148n.35, 164–65, 172–73, 176, 178, 181–82, 188, 193, 212–13
Prince of Peace, 58, 70, 83, 123
probability analysis, 80, 91–93, 93n.90
Promised Land, xvi, 5, 21–22, 39, 45, 53, 60, 116, 130–31, 133, 138, 192n.35, 195–96, 201n.9, 206, 214

promise(s) of God (see also Promised Land), xvii, 5, 20–24, 27–30, 44, 53, 59, 66, 71, 72n.30, 78, 90–91, 96–98, 104–5, 108–10, 119–22, 125, 130, 133–34, 136–37, 139–43, 143n.12, 144–47, 149, 152–53, 155–61, 163, 166–67, 175, 185, 196, 204, 207, 210, 216
prophecy/prophet(s), xvii, 2, 6–7, 22–23, 25–28, 31, 53–54, 56, 69n.16, 101, 101n.5, 105, 114, 116–19, 134–35, 139–40, 142, 160, 165–67, 171n.9, 173, 189, 222, 227
  Jesus in prophecy, 3, 30, 34, 49n.2, 50, 58, 61, 61n.1, 62–64, 64n.5, 65–67, 67n.8, 68–72, 72n.29, 73–79, 79n.44, 80–89, 89n.75, 90–97, 100, 112, 120, 122–27, 137, 143–44, 144n.17, 145–46, 151, 154–58, 161–62, 173, 175, 180, 189–90, 193, 204, 210, 216, 218–19, 221, 223, 227, 237
"A Prophet like Moses," 75–76
protoevangelium, 66–68
psalms, 22n.51, 24, 59, 71, 76–78, 78n.42, 79–81, 81n.50, 82, 120n.58, 144–45, 154–55, 155n.14, 179,
Purim, feast of (see under feasts and festivals)

Queen of Sheba (Queen of the South), 121–22, 139
Qumran, 55, 70
Qureshi, Nabel, 248

Rachel, 151–52
Rahab, 104, 104n.25
Ramah, 151
Rebekah, 20
re-creation (new creation) (see also new heaven and new earth; New Jerusalem), xv, 4, 18, 43, 106, 164, 165n.71, 210, 218
Red Sea, 131, 153
redemption (including redeem; Redeemer; redemptive), 2, 4–5,

7, 19n.39, 20–22, 29, 32, 45, 47, 52–53, 55, 72n.29, 89, 100–101, 103, 128, 130n.93, 138, 155–57, 159–60, 176, 179, 192, 195, 204, 206, 208–9, 213, 218, 234, 236
Rehoboam, 25
Rich, Tracey, 208
righteous/righteousness, 16, 16n.29, 17, 21, 47, 50, 57–58, 66, 70, 72–73, 82–84, 105, 107–8, 116, 136–37, 141, 145, 149, 153, 184–85, 208, 211, 235–36, 24
Rome/Romans, 29–30, 41n.22, 79, 90, 104n.24, 135, 162, 175, 203n.20, 222n.2

Sabbath, 9n.6, 22, 87, 119, 141, 191, 194–95, 197n.17, 200–202, 206n.27, 207, 207n.28, 232
   as fulfilled and replaced by Christ, xi, xvii, 120, 194, 194n.1, 195–97, 197n.17, 227
Sabbath year, 200–202, 216–17
   as fulfilled by Jesus, 216–17
sacrifices/sacrificial system, xviin.4, 5, 7, 16n.29, 19n.39, 22–23, 38, 41, 46, 52, 59, 85, 107–9, 109n.39, 115, 124, 134, 148n.35, 175, 178–79, 182, 199, 204, 212–14, 235
   as fulfilled and replaced by Christ, xi, xvii, 5, 108–9, 109n.39, 115, 124, 128, 130, 133, 147, 148n.35, 149, 171–73, 175–76, 178–83, 187, 199, 203–6, 212–14, 216, 236, 251
Sadducees, 29, 122, 207n.28
Sailhamer, John, 71
Salmon, 104n.25
salvation/save(d) (see also Savior), 7, 10n.7, 13n.16, 22n.51, 25–26, 28n.80, 32, 51, 55, 60, 87, 90–91, 94–96, 98, 104n.25, 107, 110–12, 115–16, 119, 124, 127–30, 130n.92, 131, 133, 138, 141–42, 145, 158–59, 165n.71, 172, 186n.5, 189, 195–96, 198, 203, 205, 211, 217–19, 222–24, 228, 235–36, 243, 251
Samaria/Samaritans, 30, 89–90, 103, 119, 172
Samuel, 23–24
Samson, 54
Sanhedrin, 76
Sarah (Sarai), 20, 52, 105, 105n.28, 108, 148
Satan (Beelzebul; the devil; the dragon), 11–13, 15, 29, 56, 66–68, 68n.13, 90, 98, 107n.35, 113–14, 116, 131, 140, 153, 160, 196, 214, 230
Saul, 1, 6, 24
Savior, 7, 89–91, 103, 110, 197, 225, 228, 243, 248
scapegoat, 202, 212–14
scarlet thread, 104, 104n.25
Schaeffer, Francis, 252
Scharf, Greg, xii
Schreiner, Thomas, 88
Scripture (see also Bible), xv, 2–3, 21, 66–67, 79, 83, 91, 95, 97, 101, 103, 119, 132–33, 137–38, 147, 177, 180, 203–4, 209, 215, 218, 222, 232, 239, 251
second death (see also hell), 115, 124
"seed" (human offspring), 14, 20, 24, 30, 35, 62, 66–67, 67n.8, 70, 109, 120, 120n.58, 121, 138–40, 142, 151–52, 164
Septuagint (LXX), 50, 50n.3, 51, 67n.8, 78, 98, 101n.3, 111, 118, 124–25, 142, 146, 148n.25, 158, 165n.66, 168n.75, 171, 180, 212
serpent(s), 11, 35, 66–67, 133
Servant of the Lord (Suffering Servant), 6, 26, 59, 85, 88, 94, 94n.1, 95–99, 112, 154, 180, 219
Seth, 1, 5, 16, 17n.22, 55n.20
Seventh Day Adventists, 198n.
sexual imagery (including adultery), xvi, 45–46, 102, 122
Shadrach, 55
Shekinah, 39, 41n.22, 176, 176n.29, 177
Shem, 19–20
Shenuda III, 243
Sheol, 124–25

Shepherd, 52, 73–74, 74n.32, 107, 112, 164n.64, 166, 226
Shiloh, 38, 70–72
shofar, 210–12
Shoot (see Branch)
Simeon, 95, 112, 155–56
sin(s)/sinful (see also fall (into sin), 3–4, 6–7, 10n.7, 11–13, 13n.17, 14, 14n.22, 15–16, 16–17n.29, 17–18, 21, 22n.58, 23–24, 27, 29, 33, 37, 40, 43, 45–46, 53, 56, 59, 64, 66, 68–69, 82, 85–87, 90–91, 94, 105–7, 109, 112, 112n.44, 113–16, 118, 121, 124, 129–34, 136–37, 140, 144n.17, 147, 149, 152–53, 156, 158, 166, 168, 169n.1, 171–74, 176n.26, 178–82, 184, 187, 188n.11, 189, 192–94, 196, 201–6, 206n.27, 209, 211–14, 216, 218, 222–23, 227–28, 232, 234–36, 238, 251
Sittema, John, 200n.4, 206, 206n.27, 212
Smyth, Kevin, 71, 73
Solomon, xvi, 6, 24–25, 41n.22, 42, 85, 122, 139, 142n.10, 146, 175, 177
  as a type, 119–22, 142n.10, 146
son of David ("greater David"), 30, 79, 81, 84, 90, 120, 120n.58, 121, 143, 143n.12
Son of God (Son), xviii, 9, 33, 48, 49n.2, 51, 55–58, 62, 68, 72, 75–78, 80, 84, 87, 91, 101, 103, 104n.25, 109, 111, 120, 127, 137, 143–45, 152, 154, 154n.8, 160, 181, 205, 222–24, 230, 230n.40, 232, 237–44, 244n.21, 246, 248, 250–51
Son of Man, 26, 81, 86–88, 98, 115, 117, 120, 122–24, 127–29, 132–33, 135n.102, 154, 156, 168, 170, 194, 219
sons of God, 16–17n.32, 55, 98, 149
Stephen, 169
Stone (Rock) (incluoding cornerstone), 63, 73–75, 81, 132–33, 172, 226
Stoner, Peter, 91–93, 93n.90
Storms, Sam, xvii
Suh, Robert, 166
Sychar, 89–90

Syria/Syrians, 6, 29, 117–18

tabernacle, xvi, 22–23, 36, 38–40, 40n.15, 41, 41n.22, 42–44, 57, 70–71, 119–20, 130, 167,
  as fulfilled and replaced by Christ and the church, xi, xvii, 5, 130, 130n.94, 167, 169, 169n.1, 170–71, 171n.9, 172, 175, 175n.23, 176, 182,
"tabernacle of David," 158, 167
Tabernacles (Booths), feast of (see under feasts and festivals)
Tamar, 21
Targum Jerusalem, 67, 70
Targum Jonathan, 67
Targum Onkelos, 70
temple, xvi, xviin.4, 24, 26–30, 36–38, 40–41, 41n.22, 42, 42n.32, 43–44, 50, 56–57, 63, 69, 80, 84–85, 90, 95, 109, 112, 120, 134–35, 135n.102, 142n.10, 148n.35, 153, 155, 159, 163n.53, 173n.18, 176n.29, 191, 201–3, 210, 215, 219, 231
  as fulfilled and replaced by Christ and the church, xi, xvii, 5, 30, 47, 84–85, 90, 120, 126, 164, 147, 163–64, 169, 169n.1, 170–71, 171n.9, 172–77, 180–83, 212–15, 219
Ten Commandments, 17n.34, 22, 22–23n.58, 38–39, 69n.16, 113, 193–94, 227
throne of David, 31, 71–72, 83–84, 120, 142
Toledot, 16, 16n.31, 17, 20
Torah, 17n.34, 184, 191, 203, 208, 210
Tower of Babel (see Babel).
transfiguration (see Jesus Christ, transfiguration of)
Trinity, xviii, 8–9, 48, 48n.2, 51, 237–38, 240–42, 242n.18, 243, 252
  analogies of, 243–44, 244n.21, 245–47, 247n.29, 248, 248n.35, 249, 249n.39, 250
  doctrine of, 223–24, 238–39
  implications of, 250–52

Trumpets, feast of (see under feasts and festivals)
Twelve, the, 81, 87, 156, 167–68, 168n.75
Twiss, Paul, 71–72
typology (including type(s)/antitype; copy/copies; foreshadow; shadow(s); pattern; prefigure), xvi–xvii, 1, 3, 5, 10, 21n.45, 24, 36, 40, 42–44, 57, 57nn.23–24, 58, 82, 85, 89n.75, 100, 100n.1, 101, 101n.5, 102, 102n.11, 103–4, 104n.25, 105, 105n.31, 106, 106n.34, 107, 107n.35, 108–9, 109n.39, 110, 110n.42, 111–12, 112nn.43–44, 113–17, 117n.51, 118–35, 135nn102–3, 137, 141, 143, 147, 147n.31, 153, 164, 169–71, 171n.9, 176, 178, 186, 189, 192, 194, 194n.1, 195–96, 199, 199n.1, 206n.27, 212, 214, 221, 237

Unleavened Bread, feast of (see under feasts and festivals)

Van Til, Cornelius, 239
VanGemeren, Willem, xii, 17n.32

veil(s), 39–41, 41n.22, 42, 49, 69, 148, 171, 171n.9, 172, 212–13

Walker, P. W. L., 154, 169n.1, 177,
Walton, John, 9n.5, 40
Weeks (Pentecost), feast of (see under feasts and festivals)
Wells, Tom, 193, 193n.37
widow of Zarephath, 6, 117
wilderness, xvi, 23, 38, 52, 114–17, 132–33, 153, 169n.1, 195, 202, 213–14
Wright, N. T., 156

Yahweh (YHWH) (see also God), 52, 76, 125, 135n.102, 145, 176, 240.
Year of Jubilee. See Jubilee, year of.

Zacharias, 116, 140, 142
Zaspel, Fred, 193, 193n.37
Zealots, 29
Zebulon (Zebulun), 83, 145
Zechariah, 56, 64n.5, 84–85, 164n.64
Zerubbabel, 28, 41n.22, 85, 176n.29
Zion (see also Mount Zion), 5, 27, 58, 77, 155, 157, 163
Zuckerkandl, Victor, 245

Scripture Index

Genesis

1–3	18, 34n.101, 36
1–2	4, 8
1:1—2:3	9
1:1	8, 9n.5, 34, 168n.75, 199n.3, 226, 241
1:2	241
1:3	9n.5
1:4	9
1:5	34, 196
1:6–7	9n.5
1:8	196, 199n.3
1:9–10	18
1:10	9, 34
1:11	9n.5
1:12	9
1:13	197
1:14–18	18
1:14–16	9n.5
1:14–15	34
1:18	9
1:19	197, 199n.3
1:20–22	18
1:20–21	9n.5
1:21	9
1:23	197, 199n.3
1:24–25	18
1:24	9n.5
1:25	9
1:26–28	10, 37
1:26–27	9, 9n.5, 18, 37
1:26	10
1:27	9, 10
1:28–30	9
1:28	10, 15, 19
1:28a	18
1:28b	18
1:28c	18
1:29–30	18
1:29	10
1:31	8, 9, 199n.3
2–3	37n.3
2	38
2:1–3	195, 196
2:2–3	197, 200n.6
2:4–25	9
2:4	16n.31
2:7	7
2:8	44
2:10	18, 37
2:11–17	37
2:15–25	7
2:15	11, 15, 18, 37
2:16–17	9, 11n.8
2:17	11, 17, 34, 106, 130, 136n.3, 234n.66
2:18–25	10
2:19	9
2:23–24	16
2:23	106
2:24	xvi, 45, 46, 240
3–11	4, 11
3	66
3:1–13	66
3:1–4	11n.8
3:1	12
3:4–5	12

Genesis (*cont.*)

3:4	12, 66
3:5	11, 12
3:6	12n.12, 13n.16, 18, 106
3:7–19	13
3:7–10	13
3:7	107
3:8–9	9
3:8	7, 34, 37, 44
3:13	106
3:14–15	66
3:15	7, 34, 66, 67, 67n.8, 68, 68n.13, 89n.74, 138
3:16–19	13, 106
3:16	13n.17, 34
3:16b	13
3:17–19	107
3:17	34
3:19	17
3:21	7, 15
3:22–24	15
3:22	11, 37, 241n.16
3:23–24	6, 107
3:23	15
3:24	37, 39
4–11	15
4:1–24	16
4:2	107
4:3	16
4:4	107
4:5	16
4:7–8	16
4:8–10	108
4:8	18
4:9–15	6
4:9	16
4:10–11	188n.14
4:10	108
4:13–14	16
4:14	16
4:15	16
4:16–22	67n.10
4:16	16
4:18–19	16
4:23–24	16
4:24	16
4:25—6:8	16
4:25	5, 16
5:1–32	67n.10
5:1	16, 16n.31, 17
5:3	14n.22, 17
5:5	17n.33
5:8	17n.33
5:11	17n.33
5:14	17n.33
5:17	17n.33
5:20	17n.33
5:21–24	17
5:27	17n.33
5:31	17n.33
6:5—8:21	127
6:5–22	7
6:5–7	17, 18
6:5	234n.65
6:6	242
6:8	17
6:9—9:29	17
6:9	16n.31, 17
6:11–13	17
6:14	128
6:16	128
7:7	128
7:9–14	192
7:16	128
8:1–3	18
8:4	18, 128
8:17–19	18
8:20—9:17	5, 18
8:21—9:17	17
8:21	18
8:22	18
9	19
9:1	18, 19
9:1b	18
9:2	18
9:3–4	186
9:3	18
9:6	18
9:7	18
9:16	185n.4
9:20–27	17
9:20	18
9:21–27	17n.34
9:21	18

9:22	18	17:5–7	24
10:1–32	19, 67n.10	17:5	139
10:1	16n.31	17:7–10	53
11:1–9	19	17:7	140n.5, 185n.4
11:4	20	17:8	7n.12, 24, 139, 164n.61
11:7–8	19		
11:7	241n.16	17:9–15	165n.67
11:10–32	20	17:9–14	165
11:10	16n.31	17:9	140n.5
11:27—Revelation 20	4	17:18–21	139
11:27	16n.31	17:18–19	5
12—Revelation 20	20	17:19	108, 140n.5, 185n.4
12:1—50:26	20		
12:1–5	7	18:1–33	48
12:1–3	5, 20n.40, 138n.2, 159n.35	18:1–15	20
		18:10–21	49n.2
12:1	6, 139, 142	18:10–14	108
12:2–3	20	18:11–12	108
12:2	24, 139	18:25	136n.1, 226
12:3	24, 142	21:1–8	20
12:7	24	21:1–2	108
13:10	42n.33	21:9–19	52
13:14–17	5, 20n.40, 24, 138n.2, 159n.35	21:12	62
		21:17–18	52
13:14–15	139	22	211
13:15	24, 62, 140n.5, 142	22:1–14	108, 137n.5
		22:2	41, 108, 109, 154
14	57	22:4	109
14:18	58	22:6	109
15	69	22:8	109
15:1–21	5, 138n.2, 159n.35	22:9–18	52
15:1–18	68	22:9–10	109
15:3	140n.5	22:9	109
15:5–6	7	22:11–16	51n.6
15:5	52, 70, 140n.5	22:12	52, 108, 109
15:6	137n.6, 159n.36, 185	22:15–18	5, 20n.40, 138n.2, 159n.35
15:7	24	22:15–16	52
15:8	68	22:16	108, 109
15:13–14	21, 21n.50, 69n.16	22:17–18	62
15:17–18	137n.5	22:17	24, 139, 140n.5
15:17	65, 69	22:18	24, 67n.10, 139, 140n.5, 142
15:18–21	139		
15:18	24, 140n.5	25:12–16	67n.10
16	52	25:12	16n.31
16:7–13	51n.6, 52	25:19	16n.31, 67n.10
16:13	52	25:21–26	21
17:1–21	5, 20n.40, 138n.2	25:23	5

Genesis (*cont.*)

26:1–5	20n.41
26:24	20n.41
27:1–45	6
28	170
28:3–4	20n.42
28:12	170
28:13–15	20n.42
30:1–24	21n.46
31:11–13	51n.6
31:11	52
31:13	52
32:24–32	21, 21n.45, 52
32:28	52
32:30	52
34:1–31	21n.47
35:9–12	21
35:11–12	20n.42
35:16–18	21n.46
35:22–27	21n.46
35:22	21n.47
36:1	16n.31
36:9–43	67n.10
36:9	16n.31
37	21
37:2	16n.31
37:3	110
37:4–5	110
37:6–10	110
37:11	110
37:14	110
37:18–24	110
37:18	111
37:20	111
37:23	111
37:24	111
37:27–28	110
38:1–26	21n.47
38:12–19	21n.48
39–50	21
39:2	111
39:3	111
39:4	111
39:10–20	111
39:21	111
39:23	111
40:1–13	111
40:15	111
41:38–44	111
41:38	111, 161n.43
41:45	111
41:46	111
41:50–52	21n.46
41:55–57	111
42:8	111
42:17–18	126
45:1	111
45:3	111
45:5–8	110
45:9	111
45:26	112
46:30	112
47:25	111
48:8–21	5
48:15–20	71
48:15–16	51n.5, 52
48:15	74n.32
49	70, 71
49:1–28	21n.46
49:1–12	5
49:1	70
49:8–12	70
49:8–10	24
49:9	70
49:10	62, 70, 71, 72, 73
49:11–12	73
49:22–26	71, 73
49:24	74
50:20	110

Exodus

1:6–13	139
1:8–22	130
1:8–12	114
1:16	114
2:1—14:31	6
2:14	112
2:15	114
2:24	21
3–20	130
3:1	112
3:2–6	51n.6
3:2	53
3:4	53
3:5	53, 60
3:6–7	53

3:8	49n.2	14:19	49, 50, 53
3:11	53	14:22	241
3:13–22	22	14:23–31	131
3:13–15	53	16:1–21	114
3:13–14	225	16:4	132
3:14	21	16:22–30	195n.5
4:19–20	114	16:22–23	200n.6
4:19	113	16:31–36	39
4:22	152, 154, 164n.58	17:1–7	153
6:7	7n.12, 164n.61	17:1–6	215
7:20–21	112	17:3	132
8:19	113	17:6	132
11:8	113	17:11–12	104
12:1–51	112	18:13	112
12:1–27	22	19:1–11	208n.30
12:1–13	130, 201n.9	19:3–20	212
12:2	200n.4	19:5–6	164n.56
12:3	204	19–24	5, 22n.55, 159n.35
12:5	130n.93, 204	19:4–6	22n.52
12:6	165n.66	19:5–6	23
12:7	204	19:6	165n.70
12:13	204, 205	19:18	69n.16, 208
12:14–20	201n.11	19:20	114
12:14	199n.2, 205	20	130
12:15	206	20–23	22n.56
12:21–34	130	20:2	22n.52, 53
12:21–27	201n.9	20:3–5	60n.34
12:22	204	20:8–11	195
12:23	204	20:9–11	200n.6
12:24–27	205	20:10	87
12:27–28	205	20:11	9n.5, 195
12:29–32	114, 131	20:12	17n.34
12:43–45	205	20:18–21	112
12:46	204	20:19	115
12:47	204	21:1–6	200
12:48	205	21:2	216
13–15	159	23	22n.57
13–14	49	23:10–11	200
13	50	23:11	216
13:3–10	206	23:12	200n.6
13:4	200	23:14–17	201n.8
13:17–22	130	23:15	200
13:17–18	153	23:16–17	214n.51
13:21	49, 50, 53, 69n.16, 153	23:16	202n.14, 202n.17, 207
14	49, 50	23:20	51n.5, 53
14:10–12	131	23:21	53
14:15–22	131	24:7	147

Exodus (cont.)

24:8	113, 115
24:18—25:1	39
25–31	22n.57, 38n.7
25–30	38
25–27	130
25:10–22	171
25:10–15	39
25:16	39n.9
25:17–22	39, 171
25:17–18	40n.12
25:17	171, 180, 212
25:18–22	39
25:22	39nn.9–10
25:23–30	38
25:31–40	38
25:31–37	40
25:31	40n.12
25:33	39
25:40	39, 169
26:31–37	39
26:31–34	171
26:31	42n.32
26:33	38
27:1–8	38
27:9–19	38
27:21	39n.10
28:6–30	40
28:36–38	44
28:43	39n.10
29	40n.13
29:4	39n.10
29:45	7n.12, 164n.61
30:1–10	38
30:17–21	38
30:36	39
31:3	161n.43
31:12–17	195, 195n.5
31:13–17	200n.6
31:13	87n.65
31:15	87n.65
31:17	9n.5
32:1–6	23n.58, 45n.37, 153
32:10–14	112
32:11–14	23n.58
32:30–32	115
32:32	131
33:11	114n.45
33:20	43, 48, 50
34	23n.58, 49, 50
34:5	49, 50
34:6–7	22, 136n.1
34:11–16	45n.37
34:14	60n.34
34:18	201n.11
34:21–24	202n.14
34:21	200n.6
34:22–23	214n.51
34:22	202n.17, 207
34:23–24	201n.8
34:26	202n.12, 207
34:29–35	49
34:29	113
35–40	22n.57, 38n.7
35:2	87n.65
35:31	161n.43
38:13–19	40
38:24–28	40n.12
40:2	39n.10
40:34–38	39, 130, 170n.3
40:34–35	176
40:36–38	38

Leviticus

1–9	22n.57
1:1–17	179n.3
1:1	39n.10
2:1–16	179n.4
3:1–17	179n.6
3:2	39n.10
4:1—5:13	178n.1
5:14—6:7	178n.2
6:8–13	179n.3
6:24–30	178n.1
7:9–10	179n.4
7:11–34	179n.6
7:16–18	179nn.8–9
8:14–17	178n.1
8:18–21	179n.3
7:1–8	178n.2
9:7	181
9:24	175
11–15	22n.56
11:1–23	186
11:24–40	187

11:41–47	186, 192
11:44–45	188
11:44	136n.1
12:3	192
16–17	22n.57, 213
16	40
16:1–34	202n.16
16:2–3	212
16:2–19	213
16:3–22	178n.1
16:6	181
16:8–9	212
16:11	181
16:12–15	212
16:13	43
16:14–23	179n.4
16:14–15	212
16:15–16	181
16:15	212
16:19–22	181
16:20–21	212
16:20	212
16:21–22	213
16:23	212
16:24	179n.3, 181
16:32–33	212
16:33	212
17:3–7	45n.37
17:11	137n.5
7:12–15	179n.7
18–20	22n.56
19:2	23n.60, 188
19:3	87n.65
19:5–8	179n.6
19:19	188n.12
20:4–6	45n.37
20:11	189
20:26	188
21—25:22	22n.57
21:16–24	173n.18
22:18–30	179n.6
22:18–26	179n.9
22:18–25	179n.8
22:29–30	179n.7
23:3	87n.65
23:5–6	201n.10
23:5	201n.9
23:6–8	201n.11
23:10–14	202n.12, 207
23:11–12	207
23:14	199n.2
23:15–21	202n.14
23:15–16	207, 207n.29, 208
23:21	199n.2
23:23–25	202n.15, 209
23:24	209, 211
23:27–32	202n.16
23:31	199n.2
23:33–43	202n.17, 214n.51
23:37	179n.5
23:38	87n.65
23:41	199n.2
23:42–43	214
24:10–16	31n.89
25	60, 217
25:1–7	200
25:2	87n.65
25:8–55	201, 217
25:10	217
25:20–22	216
25:23–55	22n.56
25:23	218
25:24	218
26	23n.59, 184n.1
26:11–12	175
26:12	7n.12, 164n.61
26:34–35	201n.7
26:42–44	53
26:42	22
27	22n.56
27:30	60

Numbers

1:1	39n.10
1:47–54	38
2	38
2:2	39n.10
3–4	22n.57
3:5–10	40n.13
3:7–8	37
5	22n.56
5:5–10	178n.2
6–10	22n.57
8:1–26	40n.13
8:26	37
9:12	204

Numbers (cont.)

9:15–23	39, 170n.3
10:1–10	212n.45
10:10	200n.5
11:1–6	153
11:16–17	115
11:29	161n.43
12	50
12:1–14	50
12:3	113
12:6–8	114n.45
12:7	164n.63
12:8	50
14:5	165n.66
15	22n.57
15:1–10	179n.5
15:30–31	179
15:38–40	45n.37
17:8–11	39
18–19	22n.57
18:1–24	181
18:5–6	37, 40n.13
18:29–30	208
19:11–22	187
20:1–8	132
20:8–13	22
20:11	132
20:12	132
21	133
21:7	113
21:8–9	133
21:9	115, 133
22:22–35	51n.7, 53
22:23	60n.35
22:31	53
22:35	53
22:38	53
23:5	53
23:10	139
23:12	53
23:16	53
23:26	53
24:12–13	53
24:17	62
27:1–14	22n.56
28–30	22n.57
28:11	200n.5
28:16	201n.9
28:17–25	201n.11
28:26–31	202n.14
28:26	207
29:1–6	202n.15, 209
29:1	209
29:7–11	202n.16
29:12–38	202n.17, 214n.51
34–35	22n.57
35:1–34	188n.13
35:25–27	188
35:32–34	188
36	22n.56

Deuteronomy

1:10	139
4	23n.59, 184n.1
4:19	60n.34
4:20	164n.56
4:35	237n.1
4:39	237n.1
5	22n.56
5:5	115
5:6	22n.52
5:7–9	60n.34
5:12–15	195
5:14	87n.65
5:15	22n.52, 195
5:16	17n.34, 142
5:22–33	112
5:22	165n.66
6–9	23n.59, 184n.1
6:4	237n.1
6:13	153, 214
6:16	153, 214
7:6–8	159
7:6–7	164n.56
7:7–8	6
7:9	53
8:2	153
8:3	153, 214
8:5	153
8:19	60n.34
10:1–5	39n.9
10:8	183
10:16	159n.36, 165n.72
12–13	22n.56
12:9–10	195
14–19	22n.57

Scripture Index

14:1–21	186	34:9	116
14:1	164n.58	34:10–12	114n.45
14:2	164n.56	34:24–26	39
14:21	187, 192		
15:1–11	200	**Joshua**	
15:1–2	216	Joshua—1 Samuel 7	23
15:7–11	216	1:1—24:31	116
15:11	217	1–21	159
15:12–18	200	2:1–2	104n.25
16:1–8	201n.9	2:12–19	104
16:9–12	202n.14	5:2–9	133, 192
16:13–15	202n.17, 214n.51	5:10–11	38
16:16	201n.8	5:13	60, 60n.35
17:14–20	24	5:14–15	60
18:7	183	6:4–20	212n.45
18:15–19	75, 89	6:5	212n.46
18:15	62, 75, 112, 210n.40	7:1–26	168
		7:10–26	14n.21
18:18–19	210n.40	8:35	165n.66
18:18	62, 112	11:23	195
18:19	75	18:1	38
18:20–22	61n.2	21:43–45	139
19:1–10	188n.13	21:45	139
20–22	22n.56	23:14	139
22:9	188n.12	24:1–13	21n.49
22:10	188		
22:11	188n.12	**Judges**	
22:22	189	2:1–4	53
22:24	189	2:16–17	45n.37
23	22n.57	6:11–23	53
23:1–8	26	6:11	53
24–25	22n.56	6:12	53
25:4	105, 188	6:14–15	54
25:19	195	6:20	54
26	22n.57	6:21	53
27–29	23n.59, 184n.1	6:22	54
28:10	73	6:23	54
30:4–5	139	6:34	212nn.45–46
30:6	159n.36, 165n.67, 165n.72	7:16–22	212n.45
		7:16–20	212n.46
31:14–21	45n.37	8:22–35	45n.37
31:24–26	39	8:22–23	24
32:4	226	13:2–23	54
32:35	16	13:6–22	51n.6
32:39	226, 237n.1	13:3	54
32:43	83	13:6	54
33:4–5	112	13:8–9	51n.7
34:6	115		

Judges (cont.)

13:9	54
13:13	54
13:15	54
13:16	54
13:17	54
13:18	49n.2, 54
13:20	54
13:22	54

Ruth

4:11	144
4:18	21n.48
4:22	144

1 Samuel

1–7	23
2:2	242
2:3	241
2:6	226
2:35	89
4:10–11	70n.18
8—2 Samuel	24
8:1–18	24
8:7	24
8:20	24
13:3	212nn.45–46
15:22	179
16:1–13	6, 144
20:5	200n.5
21:1–6	38, 119
27:1–3	6
30:12–13	126

2 Samuel

2:1–4	6
4:17	11
6:15	212nn.45–46
6:20	212n.46
7	24
7:1–17	40n.19, 142
7:8–17	5, 24n.61, 159n.35
7:9	24
7:10	24
7:11	24
7:12–16	24, 62
7:12–14	120
7:12–13	110, 142, 143
7:12	24
7:14	91, 144, 144n.17, 146, 175
7:16	142, 146
14:17	54n.13
14:20	54n.13
15:10	212nn.45–46
15:13–16	6
17:23	121
19:8–15	6
19:27	54n.13
20:22	212n.45
22:32	226
22:50	83
23:5	24n.61, 185n.4
24:11–25	54n.14

1 Kings

1:5–40	6
1:34–39	212n.45
1:34	212n.46
1:39	212n.46
2:4	24
3:2	41n.22
3:4	38
3:9	11
3:12	24
4:20–21	139
5:17—6:36	177
6	40n.19
6:1	200
6:12–13	24
6:16–20	41n.23, 43, 171
6:18	42n.29
6:20–35	42n.27
6:20	41n.24, 42
6:23–28	41
6:29	42n.29
6:32	42n.29
6:35	42n.29
6:37	200
6:38	200
7:4	161n.43
7:15–22	42n.30
7:24–26	42n.29
7:42	42n.30

7:49–50	42n.29
8:1–11	40n.19
8:1–9	41
8:2	200
8:4	38
8:9	39n.9
8:10–11	41n.25, 170n.3
8:25	24
8:59–60	237n.1
9:4–9	24
9:6–7	60n.34
10:1–13	139
11	24
12—2 Kings 17	25
17	118
17:1	118
17:2–6	116
17:9	6
17:23	118
18:1	118
18:18	116
18:21	116
18:41–45	118
19:2–3	117
19:2	116, 118
19:4	116
19:7	54
19:8	118
19:10	117
19:11–18	7n.14
19:14	117
20:29	126
21:17–24	118
22:19	43n.34
22:28	61n.2

2 Kings

1:1–4	118
1:3	54
1:8	116
1:15	54
1:16	116
1:17	118
2:1–14	119
2:8	118
2:9–14	116
2:9	119
2:10	119
2:11	118
2:15	119
4–5	119
4:42–44	118
5:1–14	6
14:25	123
18–25	26
25:1–21	41n.22

1 Chronicles

1—2 Chronicles 9	24
3:1–5	6
5:2	70
6:31	176
16:17	185n.4
17:1–15	40n.19
17:3–15	24n.61, 159n.35
17:11–14	62
21:9–30	54
21:12–14	54n.14
21:12	54
21:13	54
21:14	54
21:15	54n.14
21:16	60n.35
21:18	54n.14
21:27	54n.14
21:30	60n.35
22:1–16	40n.19
28:1—29:22	41n.22
28:1—29:9	40n.19
28:1—29:2	41n.22
28:2	39, 176
28:9	226
29:1–9	177
29:1–8	42n.27

2 Chronicles

3—36:21	26
3–5	40n.19
3:1	41, 54n.14, 109
3:3–8	41n.23, 171
3:4–10	42n.27
3:8	41n.24, 42, 43
3:10–13	41
3:14	41, 42n.32, 171
3:15–16	42n.30

2 Chronicles (cont.)

5:1–10	41
5:10	39n.9
5:11–14	41n.25, 170n.3
5:13–14	176
5:13	212nn.45–46
6:16	24n.61
6:41	176
7:1–2	41n.25, 170n.3
7:1	175
7:6	212nn.45–46
9:1–12	139
10–31	25
10:5	126
10:12	126
13:5	185n.4
18:18	43n.34
29:27–28	212nn.45–46
36:11–21	41n.22
36:15–16	50
36:15	227
36:20–21	201n.7
36:22—Esther	28

Ezra

Ezra	28
2–5	28n.83
3–6	176n.29
2:64	165n.66
3–6	41n.22

Nehemiah

Nehemiah	28
1:1	200
2:1	200
4:20	212n.45
6:15	200
9:1–37	160
9:5–37	21n.49
9:13–14	195n.5
11:1	159n.33
11:18	159n.33

Esther

2:16	200
3:7	200
4:1—9:17	219
4:15–17	203
4:16	126
5:1	126
7:1—9:32	203
8:9	200

Job

Job	24
1:6	55
1:21	121
2:1	55
21:22	241
33:4	241
34:10–12	136n.1
38:7	55
42:7–9	121

Psalms

Psalms	24
Psalms—Song of Solomon	24
2	76, 144, 145n.23
2:1–2	63, 64, 76
2:2	76
2:6–12	89n.75
2:6–8	76, 77
2:6	62, 77n.39, 141
2:7	62, 65, 76, 77, 144, 145, 154
2:8	77
2:9	78
5:4	136n.1, 137
7:7–8	60
7:9	226
8	22n.51
8:3–5	9n.5
9:11	77n.39
15:4	170
16	78
16:8–11	78
16:10	65, 78, 146
18:49	83
19	22n.51
19:1	250, 252
22	79, 80, 155n.14
22:1	65, 79
22:6	92

22:7–8	64	51:1–5	136n.2
22:7	65, 79	51:5	14n.19, 234n.65
22:8	80	51:11	161n.43
22:14	65, 79	51:16–17	180
22:15	65, 79	55:12–14	64
22:16	64	58:4–5	133n.97
22:16b	79	62:12	226
22:17	65	63	22n.51
22:17a	79	65–68	22n.51
22:18	65, 79	66	22n.53
22:22	80	68:16	77n.39
23:1	226	68:18	65
24	22n.51	69	80
27:1	226	69:4	63, 80
28:7–8	242	69:8	63
29	22n.51	69:9	63, 80
31:5	65, 80	69:20	65
32	179	69:21	65, 80
32:1–2	137n.6	69:22–23	80
33	22n.51	69:25	80
33:6	9n.5	72:16	73
33:13–15	241	76	22n.51
34:7	54	76:1–2	77n.39
34:8	242	76:2	58
34:20	65	77	22n.53
35:5–6	57n.22	78	71
35:19	80	78:2	63
36:9	226	78:40	242
38:11	65	78:54–64	70n.18
40:6–8	180	78:60	71
41–43	155n.14	78:67	71
41:9	64, 121	78:68	42n.26, 71
43:3	77n.39	79	41n.22
45:6–7	50, 50n.4, 72, 225, 241	80	22n.53
		80:1	74, 226
45:6	73	80:9–16	154n.10
45:18	73	80:17	81
46–48	22n.51	81	22n.53
46:1–2	242	81:3	200n.5
47:2	73	82:1–2	60
47:10	73	84	22n.51
48:1–3	42n.26	84:1–7	42n.26
48:1–2	77	86:10	237n.1
48:12–14	42n.26	87	22n.51
50:4–6	226	89	120n.58
50:7–15	180	89:1–4	4, 24n.61
50:18	45n.37	89:3–4	120n.58
51	179	89:19–37	120n.58

Psalms (cont.)

89:26	226
89:28–29	24n.61
89:29	142
89:36–37	142
90:2	241
92	22n.51
93	22n.51
95:7–11	195
96–100	22n.51
96:13	226
98:6	212nn.45–46
99:5	39
99:6	112
101:26–27	50
102:25–27	226, 241
103	22n.51
103:19	43n.34
104	22n.51
104:30	241
105	22n.53
105:1–45	21n.49
105:6–7	164n.60
105:10	185n.4
105:26	112
106	22n.53
106:6–46	21n.49
106:7–12	195
107:3	162
109:8	81
110	81, 81n.50
110:1–7	89n.75
110:1–2	58, 89
110:1	50, 62, 65, 81, 110, 183n.26
110:1b	50, 81
110:3–4	89
110:4	59, 62, 89, 181
111	22n.51
113	22n.51
114	22n.53
115	22n.51
117	22n.51
117:1	83
118	81, 155n.14
118:22	63, 81, 172, 172n.15
118:26	63, 81
132:7–8	176
132:7	39
132:11	62, 146
132:13–14	42n.26
132:14	176
133:3	242
135	22n.51, 22n.53
136	22n.53
136:1	136n.1
139:7–10	241
139:23	226
140:3	133n.97
143:10	242
145–50	22n.51
145:17	136n.1
150:3	212n.45

Proverbs

Proverbs	24
6:26–32	45n.37
7:1–27	45n.37
15:3	241
30:20	45n.37

Ecclesiastes

Ecclesiastes	24
9:3	136n.4

Song of Solomon

Song of Solomon	24

Isaiah

Isaiah–Daniel	26
1:5–6	136n.4
1:21–23	45n.37
2	27n.70
2:2–5	77
2:2–4	26n.67
2:2–3	77, 77n.40
2:2	70
2:12–21	28n.80
4:2	84
5:1–7	154n.10, 163
5:7	163
6	50, 82
6:1–13	50

6:1–8	22n.51	32:3–4	63
6:1–6	39n.11	32:9–20	27n.75
6:1	43n.34, 50	33:22	62
6:8	50, 241n.16	34:8	28n.80
6:9–10	50, 82, 162	35:1–10	27n.70
6:10	50, 82	35:4	28n.80
6:11	82	35:5–6	63, 83, 155n.23
7:14	62, 67, 83	37:22	66n.6
8:12–13	51	37:36	57n.22
8:14	63, 74	40:1–5	26n.65
8:18	77n.39	40:1–2	26n.66, 156n.19
9:1–2	83, 145	40:1	155
9:1	63	40:3–5	117
9:2–7	26n.69	40:3	62, 117, 225, 241
9:2	95	40:9–11	28n.80
9:6–7	83, 143	40:11	226
9:6	49n.2, 70, 89n.75, 123, 145	40:28	226
		41:4	86, 225
9:7	83	41:8–9	94n.2
10:3	28n.80	42:1–9	26, 26n.68, 88, 94, 95
10:13	73		
10:20–23	26n.66	42:1–6	89n.74
11:1–5	26n.69, 89n.74	42:1–4	63, 94n.1, 95
11:1–2	84	42:1	62, 94, 95, 97, 98n.10, 154
11:1	62		
11:2	62, 84, 176	42:2	94
11:4	62	42:5–9	94n.1
11:6–9	27n.70	42:6–7	98
11:10	62, 73, 83, 84	42:6	63, 94, 95, 98
11:11–12	26n.66	42:8	60n.34
11:16	22n.54	42:14–17	27
12:6	27n.74, 27n.76	43:1–7	26n.65
13:6–13	28n.80	43:3	225
13:6	27n.78	43:5	162
14:1–4	26n.66	43:10–13	237n.1
14:6	73	43:10	241
16:5	26n.69	43:11	225
17:12	73	43:13	241
19:18–25	26n.67	43:15–21	26n.65
24:5	185n.4	43:15	226
25:6–7	77n.40	43:20–21	164n.56
25:6	73	43:25—44:3	156n.19
26:21	28n.80	44:1–2	94n.2
27:2	154n.10	44:6	86, 225, 237n.1
27:13	211	45:4	94n.2
28:16	51, 63, 74	45:14	237n.1
29:9–13	82	45:18	237n.1
29:13	83	45:21–22	237n.1

Isaiah (*cont.*)

45:21	158
45:23–24	225, 241
45:23	84
46:3–4	26n.66
46:6	170
46:9–11	241
46:9	237n.1
46:10	69
48:2	159n.33
48:5	61n.2
48:12	86, 225
48:17	242
48:20–21	26n.65
49:1–13	94, 95
49:1–6	26n.68, 88, 94, 94n.1, 95
49:1	95
49:2	95
49:3	98n.10, 154n.12
49:5–6	26n.67, 95, 96
49:6	63, 94, 95, 96, 98
49:7–13	94n.1
49:7	63
49:8	96, 98
49:13	155
49:24–26	26n.65
50:4–9	26n.68, 88, 94, 96
50:4	96
50:6	64, 94, 96, 99n.12
50:7	96
51:3	42n.33, 155
51:9–11	26n.65
51:11	26n.66
52:7–10	60
52:9	155
52:11	188n.11
52:13—53:12	26n.68, 88, 94, 97
52:13	97, 98n.10
52:14	94, 99n.12
52:15	98
53	180
53:1	82, 97, 98, 99n.12
53:2	84, 214
53:3	63, 94, 97, 108, 234, 242
53:4–12	128n.85, 180n.12
53:4–8	180n.13
53:4–7	97
53:4–6	94, 97
53:4–5	94, 99n.12, 137n.5, 212, 213
53:4	83, 97
53:5–6	64, 235n.67
53:5	64, 180
53:7–8	97
53:7	64, 92, 94, 97, 99n.12, 107
53:8–12	94, 97
53:8	64, 213
53:9	65, 97, 190n.19
53:10–12	64, 97
53:10–11	235n.67
53:10	94, 99n.12, 180n.13
53:12	64, 65, 97
54	27n.70
54:1	141
54:4–7	164n.62
54:5	226
55:3	78, 146, 148n.36, 185n.4
56:1–8	26n.67
56:3–8	26, 173
56:6–8	77n.40
56:7	83, 141, 173
57:1–13	45n.37
57:18	155
58:13	87n.65
59:1–2	136n.3
59:5	133n.97
59:20	89n.74
60–62	155n.15
60:3	63
60:19–20	219
60:20	226
61:1–3	26, 60
61:1–2	62, 63, 209, 217, 218, 242n.19
61:1	83, 95, 217
61:2	155
61:3—62:12	27n.70
61:4–7	26n.66
61:6	165n.70
61:8	148n.36, 185n.4
62:5	66n.6, 226

63:1–6	73	23:7–8	26n.65
63:1–4a	28n.80	23:7	22n.54
63:4b–5	28n.80	23:24	241
63:4	155	24:7	7n.12, 164n.61
63:7–14	55	25:11–12	201n.7
63:9	51n.6, 55	26:5	227
63:10	242	28:9	61n.2
64:6	136n.2	29:10–14	26n.66
65–66	27	29:10	201n.7
66:1–2	176	30–33	155n.15
66:1	43n.34	30:8–9	120
66:23	200n.5	30:10–11	26n.66
		30:15	152
		30:18–22	89n.74
		33:19–22	181

Jeremiah

		30:22	7n.12, 164n.61
2–3	45n.37	31:1	7n.12, 164n.61
2:6	22n.54	31:7–9	26n.66
2:21	154n.10	31:15	151
3:6–10	45n.36	31:16–17	152
3:18	168	31:31–34	5, 27n.72, 63,
4:4	165n.72		137n.5, 146, 147,
4:5	212nn.45–46		156n.19
5:17	162	31:31	27
7:1–11	173	31:32	27
7:11	173	31:33	7n.12, 27,
7:12–14	70n.18		164n.61, 209
7:22	22n.54	31:34	27, 147
7:23	7n.12, 164n.61	31:34a	27
7:25	22n.54	32:19	226
8:11–13	173	32:21	22n.54
8:13	162	32:28–44	41n.22
11:4	7n.12, 22n.54,	32:38–40	27n.72, 147n.31
	164n.61	32:38	7n.12, 164n.61
11:7	22n.54	32:40	5, 148n.36, 185n.4
11:16	165n.68	33:14–16	84
12:10	154n.10, 165n.65	33:23–26	142
12:11	148n.35	33:26	140
12:15	158	34:13	22n.54
16:14	22n.54	40:1	151
17:9	136n.4, 234n.65	46:10	28n.80
17:10	226	50:4–5	27n.72, 147n.31
18–19	64n.5	50:5	148n.36, 185n.4
19:8	148n.35	51:34	133n.97
23:1–8	26n.66		
23:1–6	26n.69		
23:3	139	## Lamentations	
23:5–6	58, 89, 89n.75	Lamentations	41n.22
23:5	62, 84	4:22	156n.19
23:6	62		

Ezekiel

6:14	148n.35
7:19	28n.80
9	177
9:3	41n.22, 170n.5, 176n.29
10:1–22	39n.11
10:1–19	41n.22, 170n.5, 176n.29
11:14–20	147n.31
11:16–20	27n.72
11:19–20	7n.12, 147n.31, 164n.61
11:22–23	41n.22, 170n.5, 176n.29
13:1–5	28n.80
14:4	82
14:7	82
14:10–11	7n.12, 164n.61
15:1–8	154n.10
16	45n.37
16:15–22	45n.36
16:60	148n.36, 185n.4
17:1–21	154n.10
17:22–23	77
18:4	136n.3, 234n.66
18:20	130, 234n.66
19:10–14	154n.10
21:27	71n.24
23	45n.37
28:13–16	37n.3
28:13	37
28:14	18, 37
28:16	18, 37
30:1–3	27n.78, 28n.80
33:1–9	212n.45
33:3	212n.46
33:7	212n.46
33:33	61n.2
34–37	155n.15
34	26, 74
34:1–6	26n.66
34:11–16	27n.70
34:11–12	74
34:12–16	164n.64
34:17	74
34:23–24	26n.69, 120
34:23	74
34:25–31	27n.70
36:10–11	139
36:22–28	5
36:22–24	26n.66
36:24–32	27n.72, 147n.31
36:25–28	27n.75
36:25–27	149
36:25	149
36:26–27	161, 209
36:26	27, 149
36:27	27
36:28	7n.12, 164n.61
36:29	27
36:33	27
36:35–38	27n.70
36:35	42n.33
37	26, 166
37:1–14	166
37:1–10	166
37:11–14	166
37:11	166
37:12	166
37:14	166
37:15–28	5, 27n.72, 147n.31, 166
37:15–23	166
37:15–22	26n.66
37:19–24	168
37:19	166
37:22	166
37:23	7n.12, 164n.61
37:24–28	166
37:24–25	26n.69
37:24	120, 166
37:26–28	167
37:26–27	166
37:26	148n.36, 166, 185n.4
37:27–28	27n.74, 27n.76
37:27	7n.12, 164n.61, 175
37:40–48	27n.74
40–48	27n.74, 27n.76
46:3	200n.5

Daniel

Daniel	134
2	74
2:34–35	74
2:44	74
3	55
3:23–27	241
3:25	55, 58
3:28	51n.5, 55, 58
3:29	55
4:2–3	55
6:22	55n.15
7	135n.102, 168
7:9–22	88
7:9	86
7:13–14	26, 86
7:13	86, 135n.102, 168
7:22	168
7:27	168
8:12	134n.100
8:13	134, 135n.102
9:24	134n.100, 159n.33
9:25–26	89
9:26	148n.35
9:27	134, 135n.102
11:30–35	134n.100
11:31	134, 135n.102
11:45	135n.102
12:1	135n.102
12:10	134n.100
12:11	134

Hosea

1–2	45n.37
1:10	164n.57
1:11	28n.80, 152n.4
2:1–3	46
2:2	45n.36
2:12	162
2:14–23	46
2:14–18	27n.71
2:15	22n.54
2:16	27n.77, 226
2:19–20	27n.77
2:23	7n.12, 164n.57, 164n.61, 167
3:5	27n.77, 70, 120, 152n.4, 158
4:1—10:15	46
4:12	45n.36
6:2	65
6:6	159n.36
9:10	162n.48
10:1–2	154n.10
10:1	165n.69
11:1–11	45n.37, 46, 152
11:1	22n.54, 152, 152n.4
12:1–6	21n.45
12:3–4	51n.5, 52
12:9	22n.54
12:13	22n.54
13:4	22n.54
14:1–9	45n.37, 46
14:6	165n.68

Joel

1:15	27n.78, 28n.80
2:1	27n.78, 28n.80
2:3	42n.33
2:11	28n.80
2:13	148n.35
2:16	165n.66
2:21–27	73
2:27	167
2:28–32	27n.75, 72n.30, 167
2:28	167
2:30–32	28n.80
2:32	51, 72n.30, 167, 225
3:1–2	167
3:4	28n.79
3:5	51
3:14	27n.78, 28n.80
3:16–17	27n.74, 27n.76
3:17	77n.39
3:18	27n.71

Amos

2:10	22n.54
3:1	22n.54
3:6	211, 212n.45
4:9	162

Amos (cont.)

5:18–20	28n.80
8:5	200n.5
8:9	65
9:7–10	167
9:7	22n.54
9:11–12	167
9:11	26n.69
9:11–12	158
9:13–15	27n.71, 167

Obadiah

15–16	28n.80
15	27n.78
17	28n.80
18–21	28n.79

Jonah

1–2	123
1:4	124
1:5–6	124
1:12	124
1:14	124
1:16	124
2:2	125
2:3	125
2:4	125
2:5	125
3:4	127
4:2	127

Micah

1:1–7	45n.37
2:12	26n.66
3:8	242n.18
4:1–5	77
4:1–4	26n.67
4:1–2	77n.40
4:1	70
4:3–4	27n.71
5:2–4	83
5:2	62, 89n.75, 91, 113, 144, 241
5:4	74, 83
5:5a	83
6:4	22n.54

7	162
7:1–6	162
7:1	162
7:8	226
7:13	148n.35
7:15	22n.54
7:17	133n.97

Nahum

Nahum–Zephaniah	26
1:3–6	241
3:12	162n.48

Habakkuk

1:13	136n.1, 137, 188
2:4	7n.13, 13n.14, 137n.6, 159n.36

Zephaniah

1:7—2:3	28n.80
1:7–11	28n.79
1:7	27n.78
1:14	27n.78
1:16	211
2:4–15	28n.79
3:8–20	145
3:9	26n.67
3:14–17	27n.74, 27n.76, 145
3:15	226

Haggai

Haggai–Malachi	26
1–2	28n.83, 41n.22, 176n.29
2:6–9	28n.84
2:10–14	187

Zechariah

1:7–17	56
1:7	200
1:12–13	56
2–4	41n.22, 176n.29
2:8–11	56
2:9	61n.2

2:10–13	28n.80	**Judith**	
2:11	61n.2	4:12	148n.35
3:1–7	56		
3:2	56	**1 Maccabees**	
3:4	56	1–2 Maccabees	134, 203
3:6–7	56	1:11–15	134n.100
3:8	85	1:43	134n.100
3:9	74	1:54	134
3:10	162n.48	4:36–59	203
4:9	61n.2		
6:12–13	59, 85, 89	**2 Maccabees**	
6:12	85	1:18–36	203
6:13	85	7:18	134n.100
6:15	61n.2	7:32	134n.100
7:12	149		
8:3	77n.39	**Matthew**	
8:8	7n.12, 164n.61	1:1–17	84, 231n.42
8:20–23	26n.67, 28n.84, 77, 77n.40	1:1	29, 62, 90n.80, 121, 143, 143n.12
9:8–17	145	1:2–3	181n.20
9:9	62, 63, 91, 120, 145	1:2	62
11	64n.5	1:3	21n.48
11:12	64, 91	1:4–5	104n.25
11:13	64, 64n.5, 92	1:6	62
12	56	1:13	28n.83
12:8	56	1:17	143n.12
12:10	64, 65, 79n.44	1:18—2:1	231n.43
13:6	64, 91	1:18–25	224
13:7	64, 164n.64	1:20–21	108
13:9	7n.12, 164n.61	1:21–23	95
14:1–21	28n.84	1:21	91n.85, 149n.39, 225, 228n.27
14:1–7	28n.80	1:22–23	83, 227n.21
14:8	215	1:23	62, 67, 170
14:9	89n.75	1:24	57n.22
14:16–21	215	2:1–23	118
14:16	216	2:1–6	144
		2:1–3	114
Malachi		2:1	62
2:13–16	45n.36	2:2	58, 144
3:1–5	177	2:4–11	90n.76, 120n.59
3:1	49n.2, 62, 63, 116, 117	2:4–8	62
4:1–6	28n.84	2:6	74, 83
4:5–6	26, 116, 156	2:13–15	114
4:5	28n.80	2:15	152
		2:16	114

Matthew (cont.)

2:17–18	151
2:19–21	114
2:20	113
2:22–23	123n.64
3:1–3	62
3:1–2	116
3:3	117
3:4b–6	116
3:7	66, 116, 133n.97
3:9	140
3:11–12	117
3:11	175, 227n.23
3:12	215n.57, 227n.20
3:13–17	116, 231n.54
3:15	153
3:16—4:1	232n.59
3:16–17	62, 123, 170n.4, 243
3:16	48n.2, 84, 95n.5
3:17	62, 76, 91, 95, 110, 144, 154, 242
4:1–11	153, 214
4:1–11	232n.60
4:1–2	153
4:1	153
4:2	118, 153, 231, 231n.45
4:3	91n.81, 144n.18, 153, 154n.8
4:4–10	232n.57
4:4	159n.33
4:5–6	153
4:6	91n.81, 144n.18, 153
4:8–9	153
4:10	60n.34
4:11	231n.46
4:12–16	83
4:12–13	63
4:14–16	145
4:17	63, 127, 156
5:1–48	115, 210
5:1–2	242
5:2–10	31n.93
5:2	31n.93
5:3	218
5:10	31n.93
5:14	98
5:17–18	189
5:17	xvii, 190, 232n.58
5:18	190, 192, 227
5:18b	190
5:18d	190
5:21–48	229n.34
5:21–22	115, 190n.24, 227n.22
5:27–28	115, 190n.24, 227n.22
5:31–34	115
5:31–32	190n.24, 227n.22
5:33–34	190n.24, 227n.22
5:34	43n.34
5:38–44	115
5:38–39	190n.24, 227n.22
5:43–44	190n.24, 227n.22
6:9	228n.30
7:13–14	171
7:21–23	227n.19
7:21	228n.29
7:22–23	211n.42
7:24–26	229n.34
7:28–29	190n.23, 227n.22
8:1–17	225n.3
8:1–4	187n.10
8:9	231n.41
8:10–12	162
8:10	231
8:12	69, 162n.44
8:14–17	97
8:16–17	83
8:17	63
8:23–27	118, 123, 155n.24, 225n.9
8:24	124, 231
8:25	124
8:26	124
8:27	231n.41
8:28–34	225n.4
8:29	144n.18
9:1–8	225n.3
9:2–8	90n.79, 191n.27, 228n.26
9:2–6	172n.11
9:2–3	31n.89
9:2	228

Scripture Index

9:3	228	12:28	157
9:4	225n.6	12:30	215n.57
9:6	86, 156	12:34	66, 118, 133n.97
9:12–13	90n.79, 228n.26	12:37	32
9:14–15	46n.39	12:38–41	122
9:15	226	12:38–39	46n.41
9:18	225n.7	12:39–40	126
9:20–22	225n.3	12:40	109, 118, 123, 124, 125, 153, 227n.24
9:23–25	225n.7		
9:27–31	225n.3	12:41	123
9:27	62, 84n.56, 90n.80, 121n.61, 143n.15	12:42	121
		12:50	228n.29
		13:10–17	162
9:32–35	63	13:12–14	162n.44
9:32–33	225n.4	13:13–15	82
9:36	215n.58, 231n.50	13:14	82
9:37–38	215	13:20	211n.43
10:1–2	156	13:24–30	32, 216
10:1	225n.5	13:30	215n.57
10:4	64	13:31–32	160n.41
10:17–23	227n.24	13:34	63
10:28	205	13:36–43	32, 211n.43, 216
10:32–33	228n.29	13:41–42	87
11:2–3	116	13:41	227n.19
11:4–6	63, 157	13:47–50	32, 211n.43
11:5	83	13:47–48	160n.41, 215n.57
11:10	62, 117, 232n.57	13:53–58	108
11:12–14	173	13:54	123n.64, 190n.23, 225n.10, 231n.41
11:13	189		
11:14	117	13:56	231n.41
11:20–24	173	14:3–4	116
11:27	226, 227n.17, 228n.29, 241	14:6–11	116
		14:13–21	118, 155n.26, 216n.60, 225n.8
11:28	96		
11:29	113	14:14	231n.50
12:1–8	119	14:22–33	118, 225
12:6	120, 172	14:22–31	155n.25
12:8	87, 120, 194, 227	14:28–31	225
12:9–15	225n.3	14:33	154n.8
12:9–14	191n.31	14:35–36	225n.3
12:17–21	62, 63, 95	15:1–3	191n.32
12:18	112	15:5–12	191n.30
12:22–29	225n.4	15:7–9	82, 83
12:22	225n.3	15:18–19	136n.4
12:23–24	231n.41	15:21–28	225n.4
12:23	84n.56, 121n.61, 143n.15	15:22	62, 84n.56, 90n.80, 121n.61, 143n.15
12:25	225n.6		

Matthew (cont.)

Reference	Pages
15:29–31	225n.3
15:32–38	155n.26, 216n.60, 225n.8
15:32	231n.50
16:1–4	46n.41, 122
16:4	123, 125
16:13	87
16:16–17	87
16:16	62, 90n.76, 120n.59
16:17	228n.29
16:18–19	31
16:18	33, 160n.341, 161
16:20	90n.76, 120n.59
16:21	227n.24
16:27–28	86
16:27	87, 211n.43, 226, 227n.19
17:2	113
17:5	75, 76, 95, 154
17:9	227n.24
17:10–13	117
17:11–13	156
17:12	88
17:14–18	225n.4
17:22–27	227n.24
17:24–27	232n.58
18:4	6
18:10	228n.29
18:15–20	189
18:19	228n.29
18:20	176n.27, 176n.29, 215n.57, 241
18:21–22	16
19:1–2	225n.3
19:3–6	16
19:4	9n.5
19:27–28	87, 168n.75
19:28	227n.17
20:17–19	227n.24, 231n.47
20:23	228n.29
20:25–28	6, 98
20:28	88, 94n.3, 128, 157, 168, 219
20:29–34	225n.3
20:30–31	62, 84n.56, 90n.80, 121n.61, 143n.15
20:34	231n.50
21:1–14	163
21:1–11	85n.61, 120, 145n.26
21:1–7	227n.24
21:5	62
21:6–11	63
21:9	30n.87, 62, 63, 82, 84n.56, 90n.80, 121n.61, 143n.15
21:11	62, 75, 123n.64
21:12–17	163n.50
21:12–13	173n.17, 231n.52
21:12	63
21:13	83
21:14	173, 225n.3
21:15	62, 90n.80
21:18–22	162n.47, 173
21:18–19	155n.27, 225n.9
21:18	231n.45
21:19	162
21:22–46	160n.37
21:28–33	163
21:28–32	163
21:33–46	163, 163n.51, 172
21:33–45	127n.82
21:38	111
21:39	111
21:42–43	63, 76n.36
21:42	63, 74, 81, 172, 232n.57
21:43	162n.44, 163
22:1–14	163
22:10	215n.57
22:13	69
22:15–21	232n.58
22:33	66
23:34–35	227
22:41–46	62, 81, 90, 121, 143
22:41–45	232n.57
22:42–45	90n.76, 120n.59
22:43–45	62
22:44	50, 81
23–24	163

Scripture Index

23:11	98n.11	26:20–25	227n.24
23:13–36	118	26:20–21	118
23:21	174	26:26–28	58n.25, 128n.85
23:22	43n.34	26:26	13n.16, 204
23:29–39	127n.82	26:27–29	204
23:29–33	82	26:28	113, 115, 115n.50,
23:33	133n.97		147, 204, 205
23:34–38	76n.36	26:29	206
23:34–36	227n.24	26:31–34	227n.24
23:34	50	26:31	64, 118
23:35	16	26:34	118
23:37–39	162n.44	26:36–44	231n.55
23:37	215n.57	26:37–38	231n.53
23:38	174	26:38	97, 231
23:39	82, 155n.14	26:39	109, 180n.14,
24–25	135		228n.29, 231n.49,
24:1–34	227n.24		241
24:1–2	76n.36, 127n.82,	26:40	111
	174n.21	26:42	228n.29
24:3	32	26:45	67
24:15–19	127n.82	26:47–56	118
24:15	135, 135n.102	26:47–50	64
24:22	143n.12	26:53	228n.29
24:27	86	26:56	97
24:30	86	26:57–68	190n.19
24:31	209n.35, 215n.57	26:60–61	170n.6
24:32–34	127n.82	26:60	111
24:35	227, 229n.34	26:61	174, 174nn.21–22,
24:37–39	129		231n.41
24:37	86	26:62–63	97
24:39	86	26:63–66	31n.89
24:42–44	87	26:63–65	87
24:44	86	26:63–64	90n.76, 91n.82,
25:30	69		120n.59, 144n.19
25:31–46	87, 211n.43,	26:63	76, 91n.81,
	227n.19		144n.18
25:31	86	26:64	81, 86, 227n.17
25:32	74	26:65	88
25:34	228n.29	26:67	64, 96n.7, 231n.47
25:40	6	26:69–75	97, 227n.24
25:45	6	26:69–74	64
26:1–2	227n.24	26:71–72	231n.41
26:11	217	26:71	123n.64
26:13	227n.24	26:74	231n.41
26:14–16	111	27:3–4	227n.21
26:15	64	27:3	64
26:17	201n.10	27:4	111, 124
26:20–29	112	27:5	64, 121

Matthew (cont.)

27:6–10	64
27:9	64n.5
27:11	58, 145n.27
27:12–14	97
27:12	64
27:18	110
27:26–31	96n.7, 231n.47
27:26	64
27:27–54	108
27:29	58
27:31	64
27:32	231n.46
27:34	65, 80
27:37	58, 62, 145n.28, 210n.39
27:38	64
27:39	65, 80
27:40	91n.81, 144n.18
27:42	145n.28
27:43	80, 91n.82, 144n.19
27:45	65, 69
27:46	65, 69, 79, 125, 213, 214
27:48	80, 231n.45
27:50	231n.48
27:51	43, 69, 171, 213
27:53	159n.33
27:54	91n.81, 144n.18
27:55–56	65
27:57–66	231n.48
27:57–62	206n.27
27:57–60	65, 97, 125
27:63–64	126
27:63	126
27:64	126
28:1–7	229n.36
28:1–6	109, 125, 207n.29
28:6	65, 115
28:8–10	229n.37
28:11–15	125
28:16–20	229n.37
28:18–20	10n.7, 31n.90, 77, 84
28:18	31n.92, 77, 210n.38, 218, 227n.17
28:19–20	33
28:19	77
28:20	176n.27, 176n.29, 241

Mark

1:1	91n.81, 144n.18
1:2–4	225, 241
1:2–3	117
1:4	156
1:6	116
1:8	227n.23
1:9	123n.64
1:9–11	231n.54
1:10–12	232n.59
1:10–11	62, 170n.4, 243
1:10	48n.2, 63, 84, 95n.5
1:11	76, 91, 95, 110, 144, 154
1:12–13	232n.60
1:15	33, 127, 156
1:21–22	190n.23
1:23–28	225n.4
1:24	123n.64, 187n.9, 227n.21
1:29–34	225n.3
1:34	225n.4
1:39	225n.4, 232n.56
1:40–44	187n.10
1:40–42	225n.3
1:41	231n.50
2:1–12	172n.11, 191n.27, 225n.3
2:3–12	90n.79, 228n.26
2:5–7	31n.89
2:5	228
2:7	228, 231n.41
2:8	225n.6
2:10	86, 156
2:18–20	46n.39
2:18–19	226
2:19–20	226
2:23–28	119
2:28	87, 120, 194, 227
3:1–5	225n.3

Scripture Index

3:5	231n.52, 231n.53, 242	8:1–10	216n.60
3:10	225n.3	8:1–9	155n.26, 225n.8
3:11	91n.81, 144n.18, 154n.8, 225n.4	8:2	231n.50
		8:22–25	225n.3
3:13–19	156	8:29	90n.76, 120n.59
3:14	168n.75	8:31	227n.24
3:22–27	225n.4	8:38	46n.41, 86
4	124	9:1	227n.24
4:12	82	9:7	62, 75, 76, 154
4:35–41	123, 155n.24, 225n.9	9:9	227n.24
		9:10	62
		9:12	231n.47
4:37	124	9:13	117
4:38	124, 231	9:17–27	225n.4
4:39	124	9:30–31	227n.24
4:41	124	9:35	6, 98n.11
5:1–13	225n.4	9:37	229
5:25–34	225n.3	10:21	231n.51
5:35–42	225n.7	10:30	32nn.94–95
6:1–6	108	10:32–34	227n.24, 231n.47
6:1	123n.64	10:33–34	64, 96
6:2	231n.41	10:42–45	98n.11
6:5	225n.3	10:45	97, 128
6:6	231	10:46–52	225n.3
6:7	225n.5	10:47–48	62, 84n.56, 90n.80, 121n.61, 143n.15
6:17–28	116		
6:30–44	216n.60		
6:32–44	155n.26	11:1–11	85n.61, 120, 145n.26
6:33–44	118, 225n.8		
6:34	231n.50	11:1–7	227n.24
6:45–52	241	11:9	63, 82
6:45–51	225	11:10	145
6:45–50	155n.25	11:12–14	155n.27, 162n.47, 225n.9
6:51	155n.24		
6:53–56	225n.3	11:12	231n.45
7:1–9	191n.32	11:15–18	163n.50, 173n.17
7:6–13	82	11:15–17	231n.52
7:6–7	83	11:20–24	162n.47
7:9–13	191n.30	11:20–21	155n.24, 225n.9
7:14–23	186, 191	12:1–12	127n.82, 163n.51
7:15	191	12:1–11	163
7:18–19	115	12:1–2	160n.37, 172
7:19	191	12:10–11	155n.14, 232n.57
7:20–23	136n.4	12:29	237n.1
7:24–30	225n.4	12:32	237n.1
7:31–35	225n.3	12:35–37	81, 84n.56, 90, 90n.76, 120n.59, 121, 143, 232n.57
7:33–35	63		
8:1–20	118		

Mark (cont.)

12:36	50, 81
13	135
13:1–27	227n.24
13:1–2	127n.82, 174n.21
13:14–19	127n.82
13:14	135, 135n.102
13:19	135n.102
13:26	86, 135n.102
13:27	215n.57
13:28–30	127n.82
13:32	231n.49
14:7	217
14:9	227n.24
14:12–25	112
14:12–21	227n.24
14:12	201n.10
14:18	155n.14
14:22–24	58n.25
14:22	204
14:23–25	204
14:24	95, 96, 113, 115, 115n.50, 204
14:25	206
14:27–30	227n.24
14:27	64, 164n.64
14:33–34	231n.53
14:34	155n.14
14:35–36	231n.55
14:35	67
14:36	180n.14
14:39	231n.55
14:41	67
14:50	64, 97
14:53–65	190n.19
14:57–58	170
14:57	111
14:58	174n.21
14:60–61	97
14:61–64	31n.89
14:61–63	87
14:61–62	90n.76, 91n.82, 120n.59, 144n.19
14:62	81, 86, 227n.17
14:65	231n.47
14:66–72	97, 227n.24
14:71	231n.41
15:1	110
15:2	145n.27
15:3–5	97
15:15–20	96n.7
15:16–20	231n.47
15:20	205
15:21	231n.46
15:23	80
15:24	79
15:26	145n.28, 210n.39
15:27–28	64
15:28	97
15:29	80, 170n.6
15:32	145n.28
15:34	79, 155n.14, 214
15:36	80, 231n.45
15:37	231n.48
15:38	171
15:39	91n.81, 144n.18, 231n.41, 231n.48
15:40	65
15:42–47	206n.27, 231n.48
15:42–46	125
16:1–13	109
16:1–7	229n.36
16:1–6	125, 207n.29
16:6–7	227n.24
16:6	65
16:9–14	229n.37
16:11	112
16:19	81, 146n.29, 183n.26, 229n.39

Luke

1:17	62, 116
1:26–38	108, 224
1:26–35	62
1:26	123n.64
1:27	67
1:31–33	143
1:31	95, 231n.43
1:32–33	72, 84, 110, 120, 227n.18
1:32	71, 83
1:33	62
1:35	91n.81, 144n.18, 154n.8, 227n.21, 241

Scripture Index

1:46–55	142	4:3	91n.81, 144n.18, 153
1:54–55	140		
1:67–79	140, 142	4:4–12	232n.57
1:68	128n.86, 155	4:5–7	153
2:1–22	112	4:8	60n.34
2:1–20	231n.43	4:9–11	153
2:4–7	62	4:9	91n.81, 144n.18
2:4	144	4:14–16	123n.64
2:11	62, 91n.85, 225, 227n.18, 228n.27	4:16–21	217
		4:16	232n.56, 232n.58
2:14	123	4:18–21	242n.19
2:21	231	4:17–21	83
2:25	155, 155n.17	4:18–21	63
2:29–32	218	4:18–19	60, 209, 217, 232n.57
2:29–30	112		
2:30–35	156	4:18	62, 90n.78, 95, 217
2:31–32	156		
2:32	95, 96, 219	4:21	62, 95, 209, 218
2:38	155, 155n.17, 156	4:23	117
2:40	231, 231n.49	4:24–27	117
2:41–49	232n.56	4:25–26	6
2:49	228n.29	4:27	6
2:52	231n.49	4:31–44	218n.64
3:3	116, 156	4:31–36	225n.4
3:4–6	117	4:31–32	190n.23
3:6	218	4:34	123n.64, 187n.9, 227n.21
3:7	66		
3:8	140	4:38–41	225n.3
3:16	175, 227n.23	4:41	90n.76, 91n.81, 120n.59, 144n.18, 225n.4
3:17	15n.57, 227n.20		
3:21–22	170n.4, 231n.54, 243		
		4:44	232n.56
3:22	48n.2, 76, 84, 91, 95, 95n.5, 110, 144, 154, 232n.59	5:4–11	157
		5:12–26	218n.64
		5:12–15	225n.3
3:23–38	84, 231n.42	5:12–14	187n.10
3:23	62, 111	5:17–26	90n.79, 225n.3, 228n.26
3:27	28n.83		
3:31	62	5:17–25	172n.11
3:32	62	5:18–26	191n.27
3:33–34	181n.20	5:21	231n.41
3:33	62	5:22	225n.6
3:34	62	5:24	86
3:38	91n.81, 144n.18	5:31–32	90n.79, 228n.26
4:1–13	153, 214	5:33–35	46n.39
4:1–12	232n.60	5:34–35	226
4:1	111, 153, 232n.59	6:1–5	119
4:2	231n.45	6:5	120, 194, 227

Luke (*cont.*)

6:6–10	218n.64, 225n.3	9:46–48	225n.6
6:8	225n.6	9:48	6
6:12–26	156	9:51	96, 96n.8
6:13	241	9:56	90n.79, 228n.26
6:17–26	218n.64	9:58	87, 88
6:17–19	225n.3	10:1–20	115
6:20	218	10:1	215n.58
7:1–15	218n.64	10:2	215
7:1–10	225n.3	10:17–24	218n.64
7:8	231n.41	10:17–19	225n.5
7:11–17	118	10:21	231, 231n.55
7:11–15	225n.7	10:22	227n.17, 228n.29, 241
7:13	231n.50	11:1	231n.55
7:15	118	11:2	228n.30
7:16	62, 75, 112	11:14–22	225n.4
7:21–22	225n.3	11:14–22	225n.4
7:27	232n.57	11:20	31, 113, 157
7:34	86	11:23	215n.57
7:36–50	218n.64	11:27	231n.43
7:39	231n.41	11:29–32	122
7:40–50	172n.11	11:30	123, 126
7:47–50	90n.79, 228n.26	11:31	121
7:49	231n.41	11:32	123, 127
8:1–2	218n.64	11:45–51	127n.82
8:10	82	11:49–51	227
8:22–56	218n.64	12:32	164n.64
8:22–25	123, 155n.24, 225n.9	12:40	86
8:23	124	13:10–17	191n.31, 218n.64
8:24	124, 231	13:10–13	225n.3
8:26–36	225n.4	13:33	75
8:43–48	225n.3	13:34–35	127n.82
8:49–56	227n.24	13:34	215n.57
8:49–55	225n.7	13:35	82
9:1	225n.5	14:1–6	218n.64
9:9	231n.41	14:1–4	225n.3
9:10–17	216n.60	14:16–24	30n.87
9:12–17	118, 155n.26, 218n.64, 225n.8	15:2	231n.41
		16:16	189
		16:19–31	162n.44
9:18	231n.55	17:11–19	218n.64
9:22	227n.24	17:20–21	31
9:26	86	17:22–36	227n.24
9:31	130	17:26–27	129
9:35	62, 75, 76, 95, 154, 242	18:8	7n.14, 86
		18:31–33	227n.24
9:37–42	225n.4	18:33–37	145
9:43–44	227n.24	18:35–43	218n.64, 225n.3

18:37	123n.64	22:20	5, 63, 97, 107, 108, 113, 115, 115n.50, 130, 147, 147n.32, 166, 193n.37, 204, 205
18:38–39	62, 84n.56, 90n.79, 121n.61, 143n.15		
19:9–10	87		
19:10	90n.79, 228n.26	22:25–27	88, 98n.11
19:11	155n.17	22:26	6
19:14	110	22:27	94n.3
19:28–40	85n.61, 120, 145n.26	22:28–30	157
		22:29–30	87, 168, 168n.75, 227n.17
19:29–35	227n.24		
19:35–37	63	22:29	228n.29
19:37–38	227n.18	22:31–34	227n.24
19:38	63, 82	22:37	64, 97, 232n.57
19:41–44	127n.82, 227n.24	22:41–45	231n.55
19:41	231	22:42	180n.14
19:45–48	163n.50	22:44	231n.44, 231n.53
10:45–46	173n.17, 231n.52	22:50–51	225n.3
20:9–19	127n.82, 160n.37, 172	22:54–62	227n.24
		22:54–61	97
20:9–18	163, 163n.51	22:63–65	64, 96n.7
20:17	63, 81	22:63–64	231n.47
20:20–25	232n.58	22:66–71	87, 190n.19
20:34	32n.94	22:67–70	90n.76, 120n.59
20:35	32	22:69	81, 146n.29, 183n.26, 227n.17
20:41–44	81, 90n.76, 120n.59, 232n.57		
		22:70–71	31n.89
20:42–43	50, 81	22:70	62, 91n.82, 144n.19
21	135		
21:5–6	127n.82	23:2–4	111
21:7–28	227n.24	23:2–3	90n.76, 120n.59
21:20–24	127n.82, 174n.21	23:2	231n.41
21:24	135n.102	23:3	145n.27
21:27	86	23:4	231n.41
21:44	163	23:6	231n.41
21:29–32	127n.82	23:9	97
22:1	201n.10, 203	23:11	96n.7, 231n.47
22:2	201n.10	23:14	231n.41
22:7–13	227n.24	23:18	231n.41
22:7–8	201n.10	23:22	227n.21, 231n.41
22:14–20	58n.25	23:26	231n.46
22:15–18	206	23:28–31	163n.53
22:15	204	23:28	210n.39
22:17–20	204	23:33	64
22:17–19	204	23:34	65, 79, 122
22:19–23	64	23:35	65
22:19	212	23:36	80
22:20–23	227n.24	23:37	145n.28

Luke (cont.)

23:38	145n.28
23:39–43	111
23:39	90n.76, 120n.59
23:40–41	190n.19, 227n.21
23:41	180n.12, 231n.41
23:42	227n.18
23:45	171
23:46	65, 170, 231n.48
23:47	108, 124, 180n.12, 227n.21, 231n.41
23:49	65
23:50–56	125, 206n.27, 231n.48
24:1–7	229n.36
24:1–6	109, 125, 207n.29
24:6–8	227n.24
24:11	112
24:13–49	229n.37
24:15–16	111
24:19–21	90
24:19	75
24:21	65, 109, 155n.17, 157
24:25–27	3
24:25–26	157
24:26	90, 90n.76, 120n.59
24:30–31	229n.38
24:31–35	111
24:36–43	229n.38
24:39–40	231n.44
24:39	79n.44, 111
24:41–43	231n.45
24:41	112
24:44–49	149n.40
24:44–47	3
24:46	65, 90, 90n.76, 120n.59, 153
24:49	227, 228n.29
24:50–51	229n.39

John

1:1–14	30n.86
1:1–2	62, 226n.11
1:1	114n.48, 225, 241
1:3	9n.5, 226, 226n.14
1:4–5	226
1:4	226, 242
1:9	96, 226
1:10	226, 226n.14, 241
1:11	63, 108, 110
1:14–15	226n.11
1:14	49, 108, 114n.48, 130, 130n.94, 170, 212, 214, 231n.44, 241
1:17	115, 184
1:18	48, 49n.2, 50, 108, 225, 226, 241
1:21	117n.51
1:23	62, 117
1:26–34	117
1:29–34	231n.54
1:29	91n.85, 97, 107, 109, 112, 130, 149, 156, 203, 214, 228n.27
1:30	62, 226n.11, 231n.41
1:32–34	123, 170n.4
1:32–33	49n.2
1:32	62, 84, 95n.5
1:33	227n.23
1:34	62, 91n.81, 144n.18, 154n.8
1:36	203
1:45–46	123n.64
1:45	75, 90, 210n.40
1:48	225n.10
1:49–51	87
1:49	62, 85n.61, 91n.81, 120, 144n.18, 145, 154n.8, 226
1:51	170
2:1–11	112, 157, 225
2:4	67, 173n.16
2:13–22	30n.88
2:13–16	173n.17, 231n.52
2:13–15	80
2:15–17	63
2:16	228n.29
2:17	63
2:18–22	212, 227n.24, 229n.36

2:18–19	126	5:2–9	225n.3
2:19–21	170	5:5–9	63
2:19	85, 241	5:6	231n.49
2:21–22	126	5:17–23	229n.33
2:21	85	5:17–20	180n.14
2:23	232n.56	5:17–18	31n.89, 194
2:24–25	225n.10	5:17	228n.29
3:2	111	5:19–29	87
3:3	15	5:19	114n.47, 229
3:5	15	5:21	242
3:8	242	5:22	112, 211n.42, 226, 227n.19
3:13	86, 226n.12		
3:14	115, 133	5:23–24	226n.12
3:16	108, 127, 226n.15, 241	5:23	229
		5:24	229n.34
3:17–19	211	5:25–29	226n.15
3:17	91n.85, 110, 228n.27	5:25	91n.82, 144n.19, 173n.16
3:18	91n.82, 108, 144n.19	5:26	227
		5:27–29	227n.19
3:19–21	215n.56	5:27	112
3:19	226	5:28–29	125
3:28–30	46n.39	5:28	173n.16
3:31	226n.13, 227n.18	5:30	62, 112, 114n.47, 180n.14, 227n.21
3:35	110, 111		
4:1	231n.49	5:33–34	90n.79, 228n.26
4:6	231nn.45–47	5:39–40	3
4:13–14	216n.61	5:40	226n.15
4:14	132, 226n.15	5:43	228n.29
4:16–19	225n.10	5:46	3
4:19	62, 75	6:54–58	180
4:20	172	6:1–14	155n.26, 216n.60
4:21–26	172	6:1–13	225n.8
4:21	172, 173, 173n.16, 227n.24	6:14	62, 75, 90 112, 210n.40
4:22	172	6:16–21	155n.25, 225
4:23	172, 173n.16	6:22	216
4:25–26	90, 90n.76, 120n.59, 211	6:27–29	7n.13
		6:27	87, 132, 226n.15
4:25	89	6:29	226n.12
4:28–29	225n.10	6:32–40	226n.15
4:29	231n.41	6:32–39	226n.12
4:34	180n.14	6:32	114, 228n.29
4:35	215	6:35	111, 114, 132, 216
4:42	90, 91n.85, 225, 228n.27	6:37	111
		6:38	49n.2, 114n.47, 180n.14, 231n.49
4:46–54	225n.3		
5:1–17	191n.31	6:39	111

John (*cont.*)

6:40	87, 228n.29
6:41–58	216n.61
6:41–42	226n.12
6:44	15, 226n.15
6:45	232n.57
6:46	48, 50, 114, 226, 226n.12, 229
6:47–58	226n.15
6:48–58	114
6:48	132, 216
6:50–51	226n.12
6:51–58	187
6:51	111, 132
6:52–57	204
6:52	231n.41
6:53–54	87
6:57–58	226n.12
6:57	110
6:62	86, 226n.12
6:64	225n.10, 241
6:65	15
6:68	226n.15
6:70–71	227n.24
7:1	231n.49
7:2	215
7:5	63, 108
7:10–14	232n.58
7:12	231n.41
7:15	231n.41
7:18	227n.21
7:25	231n.41
7:27	231n.41
7:28	241
7:30	173n.16
7:33	226n.12
7:35	231n.41
7:37–38	132, 215, 216n.61
7:37	30n.87, 215
7:40	62, 75
7:42	62, 121n.60, 144, 144n.20, 231n.42
7:46	190n.23, 231n.41
7:48	63
7:51	231n.41
7:52	123, 215n.55
7:53—8:11	215n.55
8:1–11	90n.79, 172n.11, 228n.26
8:12	95, 96, 215, 215n.55, 219, 226
8:19	228n.29
8:20	173n.16
8:23	226n.12
8:24	225
8:26–28	229n.34
8:28–29	180n.14
8:28	114n.47, 225
8:29	227n.21
8:30–31	114
8:31–58	140
8:31–36	205n.25
8:31–32	193, 216
8:33–44	141
8:34	130
8:38	228n.29
8:39–44	118
8:39–41	140
8:40	231
8:42	140, 226n.12
8:44–45	11
8:44	11n.10, 66, 140, 160
8:46	190n.19, 227n.21
8:49	228n.29
8:54	228n.29
8:56	100
8:58–59	31n.89
8:58	62, 225, 226, 226n.11
9:1–7	225n.3
9:5	95, 96, 226
9:6–11	63
9:11	231n.41
9:16	231n.41
9:17	75
9:29	231n.41
9:33	231n.41
10:7–9	90n.79, 228n.26
10:7	171, 171n.9
10:9	128
10:10	226n.15
10:11	74, 107, 112, 124, 226, 242
10:14	74, 112

10:15–16	164n.64	12:44	229
10:16	226	12:45	229
10:17–18	124	12:46	95, 96
10:18	180n.14, 228n.29	12:47	90n.79, 228n.26
10:23	229	12:48–50	229n.34, 242
10:25	228n.29	12:48	211n.43
10:27–28	226n.15	12:49–50	180n.14
10:28	226	12:49	114n.47
10:29	228n.29	13:1–3	112
10:30–33	31n.89	13:1	173n.16, 241
10:30	30n.86, 229n.33	13:3	226n.13, 227n.18
10:33	231n.41	13:5–17	98
10:34–38	229n.33	13:5–16	94n.3
10:36	91n.82, 144n.19	13:10–11	225n.6, 225n.10
10:37	228n.29	13:11	231
11:4	91n.82, 144n.19	13:15–16	98
11:5	231n.51	13:18–28	227n.24
11:11–44	225n.7	13:18	121
11:23	227n.24	13:21	231n.53
11:25–27	90n.76, 120n.59	13:23	231n.51
11:25–26	226n.15	13:29–30	226n.13
11:25	211, 226	13:36–38	227n.24
11:27	91n.81, 144n.18	14–16	32
11:33	231n.53	14:1	233
11:35	231	14:2	228n.29
11:36	231n.51, 241	14:6–11	30n.86, 227n.21, 229n.33
11:37	231n.41	14:6	128, 226n.15, 241
11:38	231n.53	14:7	228n.29
11:41–42	226n.12	14:9	229
11:43–47	63	14:10	114n.47, 180n.14
11:43–44	227n.24	14:12	119
11:47	231n.41	14:16–17	97n.9, 149, 209
11:50	231n.41	14:17	161, 176n.27, 242
11:52	215	14:19	226n.15
12:8	217	14:20	146n.30, 228n.29
12:12–16	85n.61, 120, 145n.26	14:21	228n.29
12:13	63, 82, 226	14:23	176n.27, 228n.29
12:23–28	67	14:24–26	193n.38
12:23	173n.16	14:24	180n.14
12:24	208	14:26	97n.9, 208, 242, 243
12:27–33	227n.24	14:27	58, 70, 123, 180n.15
12:27	173n.16, 231n.53	14:31	180n.14
12:32	215	15:1–5	165n.69
12:37–38	97	15:1	154, 228n.29
12:39–41	50	15:8	228n.29
12:40–41	82		
12:41	50		

John (*cont.*)

15:10	228n.29, 231n.51, 232n.58
15:12	231n.51
15:15	228n.29
15:18–25	80
15:20	99
15:23	228n.29, 229
15:24–25	110
15:24	228n.29
15:25	63, 80, 232n.57
15:26	97n.9, 227, 242n.18, 243
16:1	242
16:4	227n.24, 242
16:5	226n.12
16:7–14	97n.9
16:7	227
16:8	208
16:12–15	193n.38
16:13	208, 241, 242
16:14	48n.2, 251
16:16–20	227n.24
16:19–25	242
16:21	173n.16
16:27–28	226n.12
16:30	225n.10, 241
16:32	173n.16, 227n.24
16:33	180n.15
17:1–26	180n.14, 231n.55
17:1–3	226n.15
17:1	173n.16
17:2	227n.17
17:3	70, 226n.12, 237n.1
17:4–5	251
17:4	9n.6
17:5	62, 226, 226n.12
17:6	227n.21
17:8	193n.38, 226n.12
17:17	242
17:18–20	193n.38
17:18	226n.12
17:21–23	229n.33
17:23	146n.30, 226n.12
17:24	62, 226
17:25	226, 226n.12
18:4	225n.10, 227n.24
18:5–6	225
18:14	231n.41
18:15–18	97
18:17	231n.41
18:19–24	190n.19
18:22	96n.7, 231n.47
18:25–27	97, 227n.24
18:28–31	110
18:33–38	62
18:33–37	112, 145, 154
18:36–37	227n.17
18:36	31
18:40	231n.41
19:1–3	96n.7, 231n.47
19:5	9n.6, 231n.41
19:7	31n.89, 91n.82, 144n.19
19:12	231n.41
19:14–15	154
19:19–20	145n.28
19:9	97
19:14	203, 206n.27
19:17	109
19:19	112, 210n.39
19:21–22	145n.28
19:23–24	65, 111
19:23	110
19:24–25	79
19:26	67
19:27	67n.12
19:28–30	80, 231n.45
19:28–29	65
19:28	65, 79
19:30–42	206n.27, 231n.48
19:30	9n.6
19:31–36	204
19:31	9n.6, 125, 203
19:33	65
19:34–37	65
19:34	65, 231n.44
19:36	204
19:37	79n.44
19:38–42	125
20:1–28	109
20:1–2	207n.29
20:1	125
20:11–29	229n.37

20:17	228n.29	2:14–21	167
20:19–29	231n.44	2:14–18	149n.37
20:19–20	229n.38	2:16–21	137
20:21	33	2:16–17	210n.36
20:22	97, 176n.27, 227	2:17	32n.97
20:25–27	64, 109	2:22–36	72, 107, 143
20:25	79n.44	2:22–24	128
20:26–29	7n.13, 229n.38	2:22–23	231n.41
20:27	79n.44	2:22	137
20:28	225, 241	2:23	110, 133, 137
20:30–31	90n.76, 120n.59	2:24–36	84
20:30	241	2:24	137
20:31	91n.81, 144n.18	2:25–31	137
21:1–14	157, 229n.37	2:25–28	78
21:4–6	227n.24	2:27	146
21:17	225n.10, 241	2:29–36	31n.92, 91n.83, 146, 146n.29
21:18–19	227n.24	2:29–32	229n.36
21:20	231n.51	2:29	78
		2:30–36	90n.76, 120n.59, 227n.18

Acts

1–2	32	2:30–32	120
1:1–8	229n.37	2:30–31	78
1:1–2	229n.39	2:30	146
1:3	207	2:31	65, 146
1:4–8	30	2:32–36	137
1:4–5	207	2:32	137
1:5	118, 227n.24	2:33–35	229n.39
1:6–8	77, 157	2:33	81, 137
1:6	31, 96, 155n.17	2:34–36	83
1:7–8	98	2:34–35	50, 65, 81
1:8	10n.7, 19n.39, 31, 31n.90, 77, 98, 118, 176n.27, 209, 227n.23, 227n.24	2:36	111, 120, 137, 210n.38, 225
		2:37–41	208
1:9–11	30, 158, 229n.39	2:38–39	159, 176n.27
1:9	95	2:38–40	137
1:10	119	2:38	33, 137, 149n.40
1:11	118	3	75
1:20	81	3:2	42n.31
2	30, 72n.30, 137	3:10	42n.31
2:1–21	227n.23	3:11–26	95
2:1–11	19n.39, 176n.27	3:13	94n.4
2:1–4	98, 159, 208	3:14–15	180n.12
2:1	202n.13	3:14	187n.9, 227n.21, 242
2:2–4	175	3:15	229n.36
2:3	208	3:18–20	91n.83
2:4	176	3:18	3

Acts (cont.)

3:19–21	218
3:20–23	90, 210n.40
3:20–21	229n.39
3:22	62, 75
3:23	75
3:24	3
3:25–26	140
3:25	142
3:26	91n.85, 94n.4, 95, 228n.27
4:1–22	99n.13
4:5–12	91n.83
4:10–11	172n.15
4:10	229n.36
4:11	63, 81
4:12	91n.85, 228n.27, 236
4:25–28	64
4:25–26	63, 76
4:27–28	128, 133
4:27	90n.78, 94n.4, 187n.9, 227n.21
4:30	187n.9, 227n.21, 242
4:31	176n.27
4:37–38	110
5:1–11	168
5:3–4	241
5:17–32	99n.13
5:28	231n.41
5:29–32	91n.83
5:30–32	229n.37
5:30	229n.36
5:31	81, 91n.85, 149n.39, 227n.18, 228n.27
6:13–14	174n.21
6:13	231n.41
7:1–53	160
7:2–53	21n.49
7:9–18	110
7:9	111
7:25	113
7:27	112, 113
17:31	231n.41
7:35	112, 113
7:36	205n.24
7:37	62, 75
7:40	205n.24
7:44–50	169
7:49	43n.34
7:51–52	62
7:51	165n.67
7:54–60	30
7:55–56	81, 229
8:3	99n.13
8:14–17	176n.27
8:26–38	173
8:29	242
8:30–37	91n.83
8:32–35	64, 97
8:37	91n.81, 144n.18
9:1–7	229n.37
9:10–17	229n.37
9:20	91n.81, 144n.18, 154n.8
9:22	90n.76, 91n.83, 120n.59
10–11	31
10	104n.25, 158
10:9–16	191n.34
10:9–10	186
10:15	186
10:25–26	60n.34
10:28	186n.7
10:34–35	186n.7
10:36	227n.18
10:38	123n.64, 225n.3
10:39–40	109
10:40–41	229n.37
10:42	211n.42, 227n.20
10:43	149n.40
10:44–47	176n.27
10:45	161
11:1–18	186n.7
11:19	99n.13
12:1–5	99n.13
13	137
13:2	241, 242
13:7–23	143
13:10	66
13:16–23	137
13:17	205n.24

13:22–23	62, 121n.60, 144n.20	17:3	90n.76, 120n.59
		17:7	112
13:23–26	137	17:10–12	91n.83
13:23	91n.85, 228n.27	17:24–26	250
13:26–37	229n.36	17:28	8n.3
13:27–29	137	17:31	112, 211n.42, 227n.20, 229n.36
13:28	227n.21		
13:30–33	62	18:5	90n.76, 91n.83, 120n.59
13:30–31	137, 22n.37, 229n.37		
		18:24–28	91n.83
13:32–39	91n.83, 137	18:28	90n.76, 120n.59
13:32–34	158	20:7	197
13:32–33	76	20:16	202n.13
13:33	65, 76	20:27	2, 136
13:34–37	137	21:27–36	99n.13
13:34	78, 137, 146	22:17–21	229n.37
13:35	78, 227n.21	23:11	229n.37
13:38–39	91n.85, 137, 149n.40, 158, 228n.27	25:19	231n.41, 231n.48
		26:9	123n.64
		26:12–18	229n.37
13:39	7	26:15–18	149n.40
13:40–41	137	26:16–18	96, 98
13:46–48	96	26:22–23	3, 91n.83, 229n.36
13:47–48	63	26:23	63
13:47	98	28:20	91
14:11–18	60n.34	28:23–27	82
14:15	9n.5	28:23–24	91n.83
14:19–22	99n.13	28:28	63
15	134, 158, 191, 197		

Romans

15:1–2	191
15:1	134
15:5–6	191
1:1–4	137
1:3	30n.87, 121n.60, 144n.20, 231nn.42–44
15:5	134, 197
15:7–11	191
15:7–9	186n.7
1:4	91n.81, 144n.18, 229n.36
15:8	161
15:10–11	193
1:7	228n.30
15:10	185
1:16–17	159n.36
15:11	91n.85, 228n.27
1:17	7n.13
15:13–19	134, 167
1:18	136n.1
15:15–18	158
1:21	136n.4
15:17	158
2:1–16	211n.43
15:19–20	191
2:16	227n.20
15:28–29	191
2:28–29	134, 165n.67, 205
16:19–24	99n.13
2:29	166
16:31	91n.85, 228n.27, 233
3:9–18	234n.65, 236
17:2–3	91n.83
3:9	14n.19

321

Romans (*cont.*)

3:10–18	14n.20, 15, 136n.4
3:11	15
3:19–20	184
3:21–22	137n.6
3:21	184
3:23–25	115n.49
3:23	14n.20, 136n.2, 234n.65
3:24–26	91n.85, 228n.27
3:24	128n.86, 137n.6
3:25	58, 128n.85, 171, 180, 180n.16, 212
3:28	130n.92
3:29–30	237n.1
4	168
4:1–5	108
4:5	137n.6
4:9–25	108
4:11–18	141
4:11	108, 158
4:13–24	159n.36
4:13–16	164n.60
4:13	141
4:16	108
4:22–25	137n.6
4:24–25	229n.36
4:25	64, 91n.85, 97, 228n.27
5:1–11	180n.15
5:1	32, 91n.85, 228n.27
5:6–11	91n.85, 128n.85, 228n.27
5:6–8	115n.49
5:7–8	124
5:8	107, 231n.48
5:9	180n.16
5:12–21	106n.34
5:12–19	14n.18, 14n.21, 67, 106
5:12–14	136n.3
5:12	234n.66
5:14	105
5:15–21	91n.85, 228n.27
5:15	231n.41
5:15b–19	106
5:18–21	236
5:18–19	97
5:18	108
5:19	30n.87, 187n.9
6	176n.26
6:1–23	205n.25
6:2–7	180
6:3–23	112, 214
6:3–7	236
6:3–6	131
6:4–10	229n.36
6:4–6	130
6:4	129, 206
6:6–20	206
6:6	187n.9
6:14	192
6:16–17	15
6:17–20	216
6:20	130
6:22	216
6:23	136n.3, 226n.16, 236
7:1–6	192
7:1	192
7:4	192
7:5	185
7:6	192
7:7–12	184
7:8–21	136n.2
7:9–11	185
7:12	184
7:14–25	14n.19
7:14–24	234n.65
7:14	184
7:16	184
7:24–25	185
8:1–17	234
8:1–4	180n.13
8:1	128, 146n.30
8:2	91n.85, 228n.27
8:3–4	235
8:3	231n.44, 232
8:4	149
8:6–8	15
8:8–9	243
8:9	149n.37, 242
8:10	146n.30, 242

8:11	98, 207, 229n.36, 241	11:2–4	160
8:14–16	32	11:5	160
8:14	98, 149, 164n.58	11:8–10	80
8:15	228	11:17–24	160, 165n.68
8:16	164n.58	11:17–23	159n.36
8:18–25	15	11:17	161
8:18–21	44	11:26	113
8:20–21	106	11:36	9n.5, 226n.14
8:21	218	12:1–2	234
8:23	32, 208	12:1	46, 175
8:29	10n.7, 33, 193, 234	12:2	32n.94, 193
8:32	109	12:5	146n.30
8:33–39	176n.29	14:1–17	191n.34
8:34	81, 113, 122, 183n.26, 229n.36, 229n.39, 236	14:5	196, 196n.9
		14:9	227n.18, 229n.36
		14:10	211n.42, 227n.20
		15:3	80
8:38–39	128	15:8–12	83
9–11	160	15:12	84
9:4–5	160, 172	15:18–21	98
9:4	172	15:19	241
9:5	227n.18, 231n.42	15:30	241
9:6–8	141	16:6	146n.30
9:6	159	16:7	146n.30
9:10–13	5	16:9–10	146n.30
9:15–18	241	16:20	68n.13

1 Corinthians

9:22–26	164n.57
9:24–26	164n.57
9:25–26	167
9:25	164n.59
9:26	164n.58
9:27–33	159n.36
9:27	160
9:32–33	63, 74
9:32	160
10:3	82
10:4	58, 235n.67
10:9	91n.85, 130n.92, 228n.27
10:11	51
10:12–13	72n.30
10:13	51, 167, 225
10:16	97, 98
11:1–7	160
11:1–6	160
11:1–5	7n.14
11:1	160

1:2	146n.30
1:3	228n.30
1:20	32
1:24	225n.10
1:30	91n.85, 128n.86, 146n.30, 228n.27
2:6–8	32
2:10–11	241
2:14	15
2:16	234
3:9–17	177
3:9	165n.65, 174n.23
3:10–12	176
3:16–17	85, 174n.23
3:16	149n.37, 174n.22, 176n.27
3:17a	174n.22
3:17b	174n.22
4:4–5	227n.20

1 Corinthians (cont.)

4:5	211n.43
4:10	146n.30
4:15	146n.30
5:1–13	189
5:5	189
5:6–8	105, 206
5:7	130, 180, 204
5:11	188
5:12	159n.31
5:13	189
6:9–10	32n.96
6:11	91n.85, 228n.27
6:14	229n.36
6:15–20	46
6:15–18	45n.36
6:16	7n.12, 46
6:17	46
6:19	46, 149n.37, 175, 176n.27
6:20	46
7:10–13	187
7:14	187, 187n.11
7:39	187n.11, 188
8:1—9:4	191n.34
8:4	237n.1
8:6	9n.5, 226n.11, 226n.14
9:1	229n.37
9:9–10	105, 188
9:21	130
10:1–11	133
10:1–2	131
10:3	132
10:4	132, 226
10:6–10	133
10:6	133
10:9	133
10:11	133
10:16–17	205
10:18	168, 204
10:20–21	205
10:23–30	191n.34
11:23–26	58n.25
11:23	204
1:24–25	212
11:24	204
11:25–26	204, 205
11:25	5, 113, 115n.50, 147n.32, 148, 166, 180n.16, 193n.37
11:26	206
11:27–32	205
12:7–11	241
12:11	241
12:12–28	33
14:37	193n.38
15	105
15:3–4	231n.48
15:3	64, 97, 128n.85
15:4	229n.36
15:5–8	229n.37
15:12–23	125
15:17	91n.85, 228n.27
15:18	146n.30
15:20–58	207
15:20–28	32
15:20–23	79, 229n.36
15:20	125, 207
15:21–22	14n.18, 14n.21, 106, 187n.9
15:21	231n.41
15:22	30n.87, 67, 105, 146n.30, 211
15:23–28	227n.18
15:23	207
15:25	81
15:45	30n.87, 105
15:46	106
15:47	105, 106, 226n.13, 231n.41
15:48–49	106
15:50–58	125
15:50	32n.95
15:51–52	211
15:52	209n.35
16:2	197
16:8	202n.13

2 Corinthians

1:2	228n.30
1:19	91n.81, 144n.18
1:20	28
1:21	146n.30

1:22	208	6:16a	174n.22
2:7–9	49	6:16b	174n.22
2:12–13	49	6:18	146
2:18	49	11:1–3	46n.40
3	148	11:2	226
3:2–3	148	11:3	11n.10, 107
3:3	148, 149, 209	11:23–33	99n.13
3:5–6	148	12:2	146n.30
3:6–9	148	13:4	229n.36
3:6	5, 148, 193n.37	13:14	242
3:7–18	49		
3:7–11	148	**Galatians**	
3:7–9	185	1:1	229n.36, 241
3:7	148	1:3–4	91n.85, 228n.27
3:11	148	1:3	228n.30
3:12	148	1:4	32
3:13–16	148	1:11–12	193n.38
3:13	148	1:22	146n.30
3:14	5, 22n.55	2:11–14	33
3:17–18	241	2:14	193
3:17	14	2:16	7, 235
3:18	10n.7, 148, 180	2:20	91n.81, 144n.18, 146n.30, 206, 231n.41, 236
4:4	11, 227n.21		
4:6	49		
4:8–9	99n.13	2:22	154n.8
4:14	229n.36	3–4	141, 196
5:1–4	216	3–4:7	185
5:1	175	3:1–19	185
5:5	208	3:1–18	108
5:8	249n.39	3:6–11	196
5:10	211n.42, 226, 227n.20	3:6–9	141
		3:6	185
5:15	229n.36	3:7–8	165n.71
5:17	146n.30, 150, 210	3:8–9	142
5:18–21	91n.85, 180n.13, 228n.27	3:11–13	184
		3:11	7, 7n.13, 13n.14, 184
5:21	97, 108, 131, 133, 137n.5, 180n.12, 213, 227n.21, 232, 235n.67	3:13	192
		3:14	141, 142, 196
		3:15—4:31	185
6:2	98	3:16	30n.87, 62, 69, 70, 109, 140, 151, 196, 231n.42
6:14–17	193		
6:14	188		
6:15–17	187n.11	3:17	185
6:16—7:1	174n.23, 175	3:18	196
6:16–18	175	3:19–24	184
6:16	85, 164n.59, 164n.61, 175, 242	3:19	115, 184

Galatians (cont.)

3:19a	185
3:21–25	208
3:21–22	234n.65
3:21	184
3:22	196
3:23–25	196
3:23	186
3:24–25	185
3:24	186
3:25	186
3:26–29	165n.71
3:26	164n.58, 185
3:28	146n.30, 159n.31
3:29	108, 140, 158, 164n.60, 196
4:1–3	185
4:2	185
4:3	186, 186n.5
4:4–7	185
4:4–6	32
4:4–5	184
4:4	67, 190, 231n.43
4:6	228
4:8–11	196n.9
4:9–11	194, 199
4:9	186
4:17—5:21	193
4:21–31	105, 141, 159, 167, 168
4:24–25	148
4:24	105n.28, 148
4:25	148
4:26–31	165n.71, 167
4:26–27	148
4:26	148
4:28–29	109
4:31	148
5:1–6	191
5:1–3	192
5:2–12	165n.71
5:2	134
5:12	134
5:21	32n.96
6:2	130
6:11–18	165n.71
6:15	146n.30
6:16	159, 160, 165n.71

Ephesians

1:3	146n.30, 228n.30
1:4–5	164n.56
1:7	32, 128n.86, 180n.16, 236
1:9–10	2, 5
1:11	241
1:13–14	128, 149, 176, 208
1:17	241
1:18–23	31n.92, 218
1:20—2:6	229n.39
1:20–23	146n.29
1:20–22	81, 84, 111, 210n.38, 227n.18, 241
1:20–21	73, 183n.26
1:20	229n.36, 241
2	166
2:1–7	166
2:1–3	7, 15
2:1	14
2:2	32
2:4–5	236, 242
2:6	146n.30
2:8–10	166
2:8–9	7, 15, 130, 137n.6, 236
2:8	128
2:10	146n.30
2:11–22	31, 161
2:11–18	166
2:11	165n.67
2:12	159, 161
2:13–18	180n.15
2:13–16	91n.85, 228n.27
2:13	180n.16
2:14–19	159n.31
2:14–15	192
2:14	70
2:19–22	85, 166, 173n.19
2:19	161, 164n.63
2:20–22	172n.15
2:20	81, 193n.38
2:21–22	175
2:21	174n.23
3:9	226n.14
3:16	242
3:17	146n.30, 242

3:19	176n.27	3:3	165n.67, 166, 168, 205
4:3–6	237n.1		
4:4–6	243	3:9	58
4:8	65, 128	3:10	229n.36
4:10	229n.39, 241	3:20	91n.85, 228n.27
4:11–16	33	4:7	70
4:13	91n.81, 144n.18	4:13	242
4:22–24	10n.7, 206		
4:30	32, 128, 176	**Colossians**	
4:32	91n.85, 228n.27, 234	1:2	146n.30, 228n.30
		1:12–14	91n.85, 228n.27
5:2	91n.85, 108, 228n.27, 231n.41	1:13	33
		1:14	128n.86, 180n.16
5:5	32n.96, 208	1:15–17	226n.11, 226n.14
5:18	176n.27	1:15	30n.87, 49n.2, 227n.21, 233
5:25–32	164n.62		
5:25–26	91n.85, 228n.27	1:16–17	30n.86
5:25	106	1:16	9n.5, 226, 241
5:26–27	46	1:17	8n.3, 62
5:26	242	1:18–20	180n.15
5:29–32	46n.40	1:18	229n.36
5:29–30	106	1:19–20	235
5:30	46	1:19	227n.21
5:31–32	66n.6, 106, 107n.35	1:20	180n.16
		1:27	146n.30, 242
5:32	46	2:2–3	225n.10
6:2–3	142	2:9–10	210n.38
		2:9	30n.86, 227n.21, 231n.44, 233
Philippians			
1:1	146n.30	2:10	227n.18
1:2	228n.30	2:11–12	134
1:23	249n.39	2:11	165n.67, 166
2:5–11	233	2:12	229n.36
2:5–8	6	2:13–15	194
2:5–7	30n.86	2:13–14	192, 217
2:5–6	233	2:15–17	196n.9
2:6–8	45, 59	2:15	227n.18
2:6–7	226n.11	2:16–17	141, 191n.34, 194, 196, 199
2:7	94n.4, 231n.44, 233		
		2:16	200n.5
2:8	109, 231n.41, 231n.48, 233	2:17	227
		2:18	60n.34
2:9–11	210n.38, 227n.18, 233	3:1	81, 146n.29, 183n.26, 229n.39
2:9	97	3:9–10	10n.7
2:10–11	225, 241	3:11	159n.31
2:10	84, 110, 113	3:12	164n.56
3:2	165n.67	3:13	91n.85, 228n.27

1 Thessalonians

1:10	91n.85, 228n.27, 229n.36
2:13	193n.38
2:14	146n.30
3:6	193n.38
3:14	193n.38
4:12	159n.31
4:16	146n.30, 209n.35
5:9–10	91n.85, 228n.27

2 Thessalonians

1:1	228n.30
1:6–10	211n.43
2:4	174n.22

1 Timothy

1:15	91n.85, 228n.27
2:5	112, 115, 130, 181, 231n.41, 235, 237n.1
2:14	12, 12n.12, 106
3:13	146n.30
3:15	164n.63
3:16	227n.21, 229n.39, 231n.44
4:3–5	187, 191n.34
4:10	225
5:17–18	105, 188
5:20–25	189
6:10	48
6:15–16	227n.18
6:16	48, 50

2 Timothy

1:10	226n.16
2:8	121n.60, 144n.20, 229n.36, 231n.42
2:10	91n.85, 228n.27
3:12	99n.13, 146n.30
3:15	91n.85
4:1	62, 211n.42, 226, 227n.20
4:8	227n.18, 227n.20

Titus

1:4	91n.85, 228n.27
2:12–13	32
2:13–14	91n.85, 228n.27
2:13	30n.86, 225
2:14	164n.56
3:4–6	243

Philemon

3	228n.30
23	146n.30

Hebrews

1:1–3	172
1:1–2	226, 227n.22
1:2	32n.97, 70, 210n.36, 218, 226n.11, 226n.14
1:3	8n.3, 49n.2, 65, 81, 114, 146nn.29–30, 183n.26, 211, 218, 219, 227, 227n.21, 229n.39, 233, 241
1:5	76, 144
1:8–9	50, 72, 225, 241
1:8	30n.86
1:9	90n.79, 227n.21
1:10–12	226, 241
1:10–11	50
1:10	226n.14
1:13	50
2:3	193n.38
2:7–8	227n.18
2:11–12	80
2:14–18	106
2:14–15	205n.25
2:14	68, 231n.44, 231n.48
2:17–18	235n.67
2:17	85n.61, 90, 91n.85, 172n.13, 181n.19, 188n.15, 228n.27
2:18	232n.60, 235
3–4	196

3:1–6	112	7:3	58, 59, 91n.81, 144n.18
3:1	62, 181n.19		
3:2	227n.21	7:7	59
3:3	112	7:8	59
3:5–6	112	7:9–10	14n.18
3:7—4:11	141, 195	7:11–12	193
3:7–12	196	7:11	59, 181, 182n.23
3:7–11	195	7:12	181, 181n.19
3:15	195	7:14	62
3:16–19	195, 196	7:15–17	181n.19
4:1–11	131	7:15	59
4:2–3	196	7:17	59
4:2	196	7:23	182
4:3	195	7:24–25	182
4:4	116	7:24	112, 181n.19, 182, 182n.22
4:5–6	196		
4:7	195, 196	7:25	59, 91n.85, 113, 122, 228n.27, 236
4:8	116, 196		
4:10	196	7:26–28	227n.21
4:14—5:15	85n.61	7:26–27	213
4:14—5:10	90, 172n.13, 188n.15	7:26	180n.12, 181n.19, 182n.24, 229n.39, 242
4:14–15	181n.19, 182n.24, 212		
		7:27–28	59
4:14	91n.81, 144n.18, 213, 229n.39	7:27	182n.22, 212, 213
		7:28	181, 181n.19
4:15	180n.12, 190n.19, 227n.21, 232, 235	8–10	147
		8:1—10:22	141
4:16	182, 236	8:1—10:1	42
5:5–10	212	8	22n.55
5:5–6	62	8:1–6	212
5:5	76	8:1–5	40n.14
5:6	59, 181	8:1–2	181n.19, 182n.24, 212, 213
5:7	231n.55		
5:8–9	231n.49	8:1	43n.34, 81, 229n.39
5:8	231n.47		
5:9	91n.85, 228n.27	8:4–6	178
5:10	59	8:4	181n.20
6:6	91n.81, 144n.18	8:5	57, 169
6:18	188	8:6–13	5
6:19–20	213	8:6	5, 147
6:20	59	8:7–13	115n.50
7–10	213	8:8–13	193n.37
7:1—8:6	85n.61, 90, 172n.13, 181, 188n.15	8:8–12	147
		8:9	148, 205n.24
		8:10	7n.12, 164n.59, 164n.61
7:1–3	57, 58		
7:2	58		

Hebrews (*cont.*)

8:13	xvii, 5, 115, 148, 148n.35, 193
9:1–2	169
9:3–4	39
9:5	171n.8, 180
9:6	58
9:7	213
9:9–10	149, 182n.23
9:9	57, 147
9:11–28	180n.13
9:11–14	115n.50
9:11–12	169, 212
9:11	181n.19, 212
9:12–17	147 148
9:12–14	128n.85, 213
9:12	128n.86, 182n.22, 212, 213
9:14	149, 212, 214, 227n.21, 241
9:15	112, 128n.86, 147, 193n.37
9:20	113
9:22	107
9:23–24	40n.14, 147
9:23	57
9:24	57, 169, 212, 213, 229n.39
9:25–28	182n.22
9:25–26	213
9:25	182
9:26–28	115n.49
9:26	212
9:28	97, 212
10:1–4	213
10:1–2	182n.23, 186
10:1	57, 147, 182
10:3	182
10:4–10	213
10:5	231n.44
10:9	193
10:10–14	182n.22
10:10	133, 137n.5, 187, 242
10:11–22	90, 172n.13, 188n.15
10:11–18	147
10:11–12	115n.49, 178, 180n.13
10:11	182, 183
10:12–13	227n.18
10:12	107, 133, 183, 183n.26, 229n.39
10:14–16	182n.23
10:14	133, 149, 178, 183n.26
10:15–18	147
10:15–17	5
10:16–18	182
10:19–22	43, 182, 236
10:19–20	69, 171, 212
10:21	212
10:22	149
10:29	91n.81, 144n.18
10:38	7n.13, 13n.14
11:1—12:2	159n.36
11	131
11:3	9n.5
11:4	16, 16n.29, 107
11:6	15
11:7	128
11:8–10	108
11:10	141
11:16	141
11:17–19	108
11:19	57, 109
11:25–29	6
11:28	112
11:29	131
11:31	104n.25
11:40	160n.41
12:2	81, 229n.39
12:18	141, 159
12:22	141, 159, 167
12:24	108, 147
13:5	130
13:10–15	180n.13
13:10–14	182
13:10	182
13:11	182, 213
13:12	182
13:13	182
13:14	141, 183
13:20	74, 91n.85, 226, 228n.27, 229n.36

James

1:1	168
1:13	136n.1
1:18	216
2:1	168
2:19	237n.1
4:4	45n.36, 46n.41
4:7	68
4:12	62
5:1–3	210n.36
5:3	32n.97

1 Peter

1:2	242
1:3	229n.36
1:10–12	3, 100
1:18–19	91n.85, 107, 108, 228n.27
1:19	130n.93, 203, 204, 227n.21
1:20	32n.97, 128, 210n.36
1:21	229n.36
2:4–8	172n.15, 226
2:4	235n.67
2:5	85, 164n.56, 165n.70, 173n.19, 174n.23, 176, 181
2:7	63, 74
2:8	63, 74
2:9	164n.56, 165n.70, 173n.19, 181
2:10	164n.57, 167
2:20–21	233
2:21–24	97, 180n.12
2:22	227n.21
2:24	137n.5, 180, 212, 231n.44
2:25	226
3	129
3:14–15	51
3:18	91n.85, 187n.9, 228n.27, 235n.67
3:20–21	129
3:20	129
3:21–22	146nn.29–30, 183n.26
3:21	129, 130n.92, 229n.36
3:22	81, 210n.38, 227n.18, 229n.39
4:5	227n.20
4:12–16	177
4:14	176
4:17	177
5:2–3	164n.64
5:4	226
5:14	146n.30

2 Peter

1:1	225
1:11	91n.85, 228n.27
1:14	216
3:3–15	218

1 John

1:1–3	231n.44
1:3	242
1:5–7	215n.56
2:1	58, 236
2:2	115n.49, 128n.85
2:5–6	233
2:13–14	226n.11
2:18	32n.97, 210n.36
2:20	187n.9
2:22	90n.76, 120n.59
2:29	227n.21
3:1–2	164n.58
3:1	241
3:2	35
3:5	91n.85, 149n.39, 180n.12, 227n.21, 228n.27
3:8	66, 67, 91n.81, 144n.18
3:10	66
3:12	16n.29
3:16	124
3:23	7n.13
4:2	231n.44
4:7–21	234
4:8	250
4:9–10	91n.85, 226n.13, 228n.27

1 John (cont.)

4:9	108
4:14	91n.85, 226n.13, 228n.27
4:15	91n.81, 144n.18
5:1	90n.76, 120n.59
5:5	91n.81, 144n.18
5:6	241
5:10	91n.81, 144n.18
5:11–13	226n.16
5:12	91n.81, 144n.18
5:13	91n.81, 144n.18
5:20	91n.81, 144n.18, 226, 226n.16

2 John

7	231n.44

Jude

9	56
14–15	211n.42
18	32n.97
20–21	243

Revelation

1:5	146nn.29–30, 227n.18, 229n.36
1:6	164n.56, 165n.70, 173n.19, 181
1:7	79n.44
1:8	225
1:9—3:22	229n.37
1:10	197
1:11	193n.38
1:13–14	86
1:16	95
1:17	62, 86, 225
1:18	226n.15, 227, 229n.36
2:8	62, 225
2:12	95
2:18–22	45n.36
2:18	91n.82, 144n.19
2:23	225n.10, 226, 227n.19
2:26	78
2:27	78, 228n.29
3:5	228n.29
3:7	144n.20, 227n.21
3:12	43, 174nn.22–23
3:21	146nn.29–30, 228n.29
4–5	22n.51
4:1—5:10	229
4:2–10	43n.34
4:5–9	39n.11
4:11	9n.5
5:1–13	43n.34
5:1–8	227n.21
5:5	84, 144n.20
5:6	75, 97, 109, 130, 203
5:8	130, 203
5:9	31n.90, 73, 91n.85, 104n.25, 128n.85, 160n.41, 168n.75, 215n.58, 228n.27
5:10	164n.56, 165n.70, 173n.19, 181
5:12	225n.10, 227n.18
6:9	249n.39
6:16	43n.34
7:9–17	22n.51
7:9–15	43n.34
7:9	31n.90, 160n.41, 168n.75, 215n.58
7:15–17	167
7:15	174n.22
8:1—9:21	209n.35
8:3	43n.34
10—22:5	43n.34
11:1	174n.22
11:15–19	22n.51, 209n.35
11:15	227n.18
11:19	174n.22
12:1–6	66n.6
12:4	68n.13
12:5	43n.34, 78
12:9	11n.10, 66
12:10	227n.18
12:15–16	67
13:6	175n.23
14:3–5	43n.34

14:4	91n.85, 216, 228n.27	21:2–3	36, 43n.34
14:8	45n.36	21:2	43n.34, 47, 159, 226
14:11	197	21:3–6	167
14:13	197	21:3–4	43
14:14	227n.18	21:3	7n.12, 34, 44, 164n.61
14:19–20	73		
15:5	40n.14	21:4	34, 44
16:17	43n.34	21:5–6	225
17:1–5	45n.36	21:6	44
17:1	47	21:7–8	43
17:4	47	21:9–14	164n.62
17:5	46n.41	21:9–10	159
17:14	210n.38, 226, 227n.18	21:9	47, 66n.6
		21:10—22:5	43n.34
18:1–3	45n.36	21:10	44, 47
18:4	164n.59	21:16	43
18:16	47	21:18–22	44
19:1–6	22n.51	21:18	43
19:1–2	45n.36	21:22–23	43
19:4–5	43n.34	21:22	170
19:5–9	47	21:23	34, 219
19:7–8	47	21:25	34
19:8	47	21:27	43, 226n.16
19:10	60n.34	22:1–3	43n.34
19:11–16	227n.18	22:1	43, 44
19:11	211n.42	22:2	44
19:13	73, 114n.48	22:3–5	43
19:15	73, 78, 95	22:3	34, 44
19:16	62, 210n.38, 226	22:4	34, 35, 43
20–22	34n.101	22:5	34, 219
20:4–6	227n.18	22:8–9	60n.34
20:10	68	22:12–13	229n.37
20:11	43n.34	22:12	211n.43, 227n.19
21–22	4, 33, 43, 47, 141	22:13	62, 225
21:1—22:17	131	22:16	62, 84, 144n.20, 229n.37
21	43, 43n.34		
21:1–5	218	22:19	159
21:1	34, 36, 43n.34	22:20	229n.37

www.ingramcontent.com/pod-product-compliance
Lightning Source LLC
Chambersburg PA
CBHW050614300426
44112CB00012B/1503